Connected Mathematics 2

Variables and Patterns
Stretching and Shrinking
Comparing and Scaling
Accentuate the Negative
Moving Straight Ahead
Filling and Wrapping
What Do You Expect?
Data Distributions

Glenda Lappan
James T. Fey
William M. Fitzgerald
Susan N. Friel
Elizabeth Difanis Phillips

PEARSON

Prentice
Hall

Boston, Massachusetts
Upper Saddle River, New Jersey

Connected Mathematics™ was developed at Michigan State University with financial support from the Michigan State University Office of the Provost, Computing and Technology, and the College of Natural Science.

This material is based upon work supported by the National Science Foundation under Grant No. MDR 9150217 and Grant No. ESI 9986372. Opinions expressed are those of the authors and not necessarily those of the Foundation.

The Michigan State University authors and administration have agreed that all MSU royalties arising from this publication will be devoted to purposes supported by the MSU Mathematics Education Enrichment Fund.

All **Acknowledgments** pages constitute an extension of this copyright page.

Acknowledgments for *Variables and Patterns* appear on page 89 of *Variables and Patterns*.
Acknowledgments for *Stretching and Shrinking* appear on page 107 of *Stretching and Shrinking*.
Acknowledgments for *Comparing and Scaling* appear on page 72 of *Comparing and Scaling*.
Acknowledgments for *Accentuate the Negative* appear on page 85 of *Accentuate the Negative*.
Acknowledgments for *Moving Straight Ahead* appear on page 103 of *Moving Straight Ahead*.
Acknowledgments for *Filling and Wrapping* appear on page 87 of *Filling and Wrapping*.
Acknowledgments for *What Do You Expect?* appear on page 72 of *What Do You Expect?*.
Acknowledgments for *Data Distributions* appear on page 103 of *Data Distributions*.

ISBN 0-13-165622-8

5 6 7 8 9 10   09 08 07

Authors of Connected Mathematics

(from left to right) Glenda Lappan, Betty Phillips, Susan Friel, Bill Fitzgerald, Jim Fey

Glenda Lappan is a University Distinguished Professor in the Department of Mathematics at Michigan State University. Her research and development interests are in the connected areas of students' learning of mathematics and mathematics teachers' professional growth and change related to the development and enactment of K–12 curriculum materials.

James T. Fey is a Professor of Curriculum and Instruction and Mathematics at the University of Maryland. His consistent professional interest has been development and research focused on curriculum materials that engage middle and high school students in problem-based collaborative investigations of mathematical ideas and their applications.

William M. Fitzgerald *(Deceased)* was a Professor in the Department of Mathematics at Michigan State University. His early research was on the use of concrete materials in supporting student learning and led to the development of teaching materials for laboratory environments. Later he helped develop a teaching model to support student experimentation with mathematics.

Susan N. Friel is a Professor of Mathematics Education in the School of Education at the University of North Carolina at Chapel Hill. Her research interests focus on statistics education for middle-grade students and, more broadly, on teachers' professional development and growth in teaching mathematics K–8.

Elizabeth Difanis Phillips is a Senior Academic Specialist in the Mathematics Department of Michigan State University. She is interested in teaching and learning mathematics for both teachers and students. These interests have led to curriculum and professional development projects at the middle school and high school levels, as well as projects related to the teaching and learning of algebra across the grades.

Field Test Sites for CMP2

During the development of the revised edition of *Connected Mathematics* (CMP2), more than 100 classroom teachers have field-tested materials at 49 school sites in 12 states and the District of Columbia. This classroom testing occurred over three academic years (2001 through 2004), allowing careful study of the effectiveness of each of the 24 units that comprise the program. A special thanks to the students and teachers at these pilot schools.

Arkansas
Magnolia Public Schools
Kittena Bell*, Judith Trowell*; *Central Elementary School:* Maxine Broom, Betty Eddy, Tiffany Fallin, Bonnie Flurry, Carolyn Monk, Elizabeth Tye; *Magnolia Junior High School:* Monique Bryan, Ginger Cook, David Graham, Shelby Lamkin

Colorado
Boulder Public Schools
Nevin Platt Middle School: Judith Koenig

St. Vrain Valley School District, Longmont
Westview Middle School: Colleen Beyer, Kitty Canupp, Ellie Decker*, Peggy McCarthy, Tanya deNobrega, Cindy Payne, Ericka Pilon, Andrew Roberts

District of Columbia
Capitol Hill Day School: Ann Lawrence

Georgia
University of Georgia, Athens
Brad Findell

Madison Public Schools
Morgan County Middle School: Renee Burgdorf, Lynn Harris, Nancy Kurtz, Carolyn Stewart

Maine
Falmouth Public Schools
Falmouth Middle School: Donna Erikson, Joyce Hebert, Paula Hodgkins, Rick Hogan, David Legere, Cynthia Martin, Barbara Stiles, Shawn Towle*

---

* indicates a Field Test Site Coordinator

Michigan
Portland Public Schools
Portland Middle School: Mark Braun, Holly DeRosia, Kathy Dole*, Angie Foote, Teri Keusch, Tammi Wardwell

Traverse City Area Public Schools
Bertha Vos Elementary: Kristin Sak; *Central Grade School:* Michelle Clark; Jody Meyers; *Eastern Elementary:* Karrie Tufts; *Interlochen Elementary:* Mary McGee-Cullen; *Long Lake Elementary:* Julie Faulkner*, Charlie Maxbauer, Katherine Sleder; *Norris Elementary:* Hope Slanaker; *Oak Park Elementary:* Jessica Steed; *Traverse Heights Elementary:* Jennifer Wolfert; *Westwoods Elementary:* Nancy Conn; *Old Mission Peninsula School:* Deb Larimer; *Traverse City East Junior High:* Ivanka Berkshire, Ruthanne Kladder, Jan Palkowski, Jane Peterson, Mary Beth Schmitt; *Traverse City West Junior High:* Dan Fouch*, Ray Fouch

Sturgis Public Schools
Sturgis Middle School: Ellen Eisele

Minnesota
Burnsville School District 191
Hidden Valley Elementary: Stephanie Cin, Jane McDevitt

Hopkins School District 270
Alice Smith Elementary: Sandra Cowing, Kathleen Gustafson, Martha Mason, Scott Stillman; *Eisenhower Elementary:* Chad Bellig, Patrick Berger, Nancy Glades, Kye Johnson, Shane Wasserman, Victoria Wilson; *Gatewood Elementary:* Sarah Ham, Julie Kloos, Janine Pung, Larry Wade; *Glen Lake Elementary:* Jacqueline Cramer, Kathy Hering, Cecelia Morris,

Robb Trenda; *Katherine Curren Elementary:* Diane Bancroft, Sue DeWit, John Wilson; *L. H. Tanglen Elementary:* Kevin Athmann, Lisa Becker, Mary LaBelle, Kathy Rezac, Roberta Severson; *Meadowbrook Elementary:* Jan Gauger, Hildy Shank, Jessica Zimmerman; *North Junior High:* Laurel Hahn, Kristin Lee, Jodi Markuson, Bruce Mestemacher, Laurel Miller, Bonnie Rinker, Jeannine Salzer, Sarah Shafer, Cam Stottler; *West Junior High:* Alicia Beebe, Kristie Earl, Nobu Fujii, Pam Georgetti, Susan Gilbert, Regina Nelson Johnson, Debra Lindstrom, Michele Luke*, Jon Sorenson

Minneapolis School District 1
Ann Sullivan K-8 School: Bronwyn Collins; Anne Bartel* (Curriculum and Instruction Office)

Wayzata School District 284
Central Middle School: Sarajane Myers, Dan Nielsen, Tanya Ravenholdt

White Bear Lake School District 624
Central Middle School: Amy Jorgenson, Michelle Reich, Brenda Sammon

New York
New York City Public Schools
IS 89: Yelena Aynbinder, Chi-Man Ng, Nina Rapaport, Joel Spengler, Phyllis Tam*, Brent Wyso; *Wagner Middle School:* Jason Appel, Intissar Fernandez, Yee Gee Get, Richard Goldstein, Irving Marcus, Sue Norton, Bernadita Owens, Jennifer Rehn*, Kevin Yuhas

Ohio

Talawanda School District, Oxford
Talawanda Middle School: Teresa Abrams, Larry Brock, Heather Brosey, Julie Churchman, Monna Even, Karen Fitch, Bob George, Amanda Klee, Pat Meade, Sandy Montgomery, Barbara Sherman, Lauren Steidl

Miami University
Jeffrey Wanko*

Springfield Public Schools
Rockway School: Jim Mamer

Pennsylvania

Pittsburgh Public Schools
Kenneth Labuskes, Marianne O'Connor, Mary Lynn Raith*; *Arthur J. Rooney Middle School:* David Hairston, Stamatina Mousetis, Alfredo Zangaro; *Frick International Studies Academy:* Suzanne Berry, Janet Falkowski, Constance Finseth, Romika Hodge, Frank Machi; *Reizenstein Middle School:* Jeff Baldwin, James Brautigam, Lorena Burnett, Glen Cobbett, Michael Jordan, Margaret Lazur, Melissa Munnell, Holly Neely, Ingrid Reed, Dennis Reft

Texas

Austin Independent School District
Bedichek Middle School: Lisa Brown, Jennifer Glasscock, Vicki Massey

El Paso Independent School District
Cordova Middle School: Armando Aguirre, Anneliesa Durkes, Sylvia Guzman, Pat Holguin*, William Holguin, Nancy Nava, Laura Orozco, Michelle Peña, Roberta Rosen, Patsy Smith, Jeremy Wolf

Plano Independent School District
Patt Henry, James Wohlgehagen*; *Frankford Middle School:* Mandy Baker, Cheryl Butsch, Amy Dudley, Betsy Eshelman, Janet Greene, Cort Haynes, Kathy Letchworth, Kay Marshall, Kelly McCants, Amy Reck, Judy Scott, Syndy Snyder, Lisa Wang; *Wilson Middle School:* Darcie Bane, Amanda Bedenko, Whitney Evans, Tonelli Hatley, Sarah (Becky) Higgs, Kelly Johnston, Rebecca McElligott, Kay Neuse, Cheri Slocum, Kelli Straight

Washington

Evergreen School District
Shahala Middle School: Nicole Abrahamsen, Terry Coon*, Carey Doyle, Sheryl Drechsler, George Gemma, Gina Helland, Amy Hilario, Darla Lidyard, Sean McCarthy, Tilly Meyer, Willow Neuwelt, Todd Parsons, Brian Pederson, Stan Posey, Shawn Scott, Craig Sjoberg, Lynette Sundstrom, Charles Switzer, Luke Youngblood

Wisconsin

Beaver Dam Unified School District
Beaver Dam Middle School: Jim Braemer, Jeanne Frick, Jessica Greatens, Barbara Link, Dennis McCormick, Karen Michels, Nancy Nichols*, Nancy Palm, Shelly Stelsel, Susan Wiggins

---

* indicates a Field Test Site Coordinator

Reviews of CMP to Guide Development of CMP2

Before writing for CMP2 began or field tests were conducted, the first edition of *Connected Mathematics* was submitted to the mathematics faculties of school districts from many parts of the country and to 80 individual reviewers for extensive comments.

School District Survey Reviews of CMP

Arizona
Madison School District #38 (Phoenix)

Arkansas
Cabot School District, Little Rock School District, Magnolia School District

California
Los Angeles Unified School District

Colorado
St. Vrain Valley School District (Longmont)

Florida
Leon County Schools (Tallahassee)

Illinois
School District #21 (Wheeling)

Indiana
Joseph L. Block Junior High (East Chicago)

Kentucky
Fayette County Public Schools (Lexington)

Maine
Selection of Schools

Massachusetts
Selection of Schools

Michigan
Sparta Area Schools

Minnesota
Hopkins School District

Texas
Austin Independent School District, The El Paso Collaborative for Academic Excellence, Plano Independent School District

Wisconsin
Platteville Middle School

Individual Reviewers of CMP

Arkansas
Deborah Cramer; Robby Frizzell *(Taylor)*; Lowell Lynde *(University of Arkansas, Monticello)*; Leigh Manzer *(Norfork)*; Lynne Roberts *(Emerson High School, Emerson)*; Tony Timms *(Cabot Public Schools)*; Judith Trowell *(Arkansas Department of Higher Education)*

California
José Alcantar *(Gilroy)*; Eugenie Belcher *(Gilroy)*; Marian Pasternack *(Lowman M. S. T. Center, North Hollywood)*; Susana Pezoa *(San Jose)*; Todd Rabusin *(Hollister)*; Margaret Siegfried *(Ocala Middle School, San Jose)*; Polly Underwood *(Ocala Middle School, San Jose)*

Colorado
Janeane Golliher *(St. Vrain Valley School District, Longmont)*; Judith Koenig *(Nevin Platt Middle School, Boulder)*

Florida
Paige Loggins *(Swift Creek Middle School, Tallahassee)*

Illinois
Jan Robinson *(School District #21, Wheeling)*

Indiana
Frances Jackson *(Joseph L. Block Junior High, East Chicago)*

Kentucky
Natalee Feese *(Fayette County Public Schools, Lexington)*

Maine
Betsy Berry *(Maine Math & Science Alliance, Augusta)*

Maryland
Joseph Gagnon *(University of Maryland, College Park)*; Paula Maccini *(University of Maryland, College Park)*

Massachusetts
George Cobb *(Mt. Holyoke College, South Hadley)*; Cliff Kanold *(University of Massachusetts, Amherst)*

Michigan
Mary Bouck *(Farwell Area Schools)*; Carol Dorer *(Slauson Middle School, Ann Arbor)*; Carrie Heaney *(Forsythe Middle School, Ann Arbor)*; Ellen Hopkins *(Clague Middle School, Ann Arbor)*; Teri Keusch *(Portland Middle School, Portland)*; Valerie Mills *(Oakland Schools, Waterford)*; Mary Beth Schmitt *(Traverse City East Junior High, Traverse City)*; Jack Smith *(Michigan State University, East Lansing)*; Rebecca Spencer *(Sparta Middle School, Sparta)*; Ann Marie Nicoll Turner *(Tappan Middle School, Ann Arbor)*; Scott Turner *(Scarlett Middle School, Ann Arbor)*

Minnesota
Margarita Alvarez *(Olson Middle School, Minneapolis)*; Jane Amundson *(Nicollet Junior High, Burnsville)*; Anne Bartel *(Minneapolis Public Schools)*; Gwen Ranzau Campbell *(Sunrise Park Middle School, White Bear Lake)*; Stephanie Cin *(Hidden Valley Elementary, Burnsville)*; Joan Garfield *(University of Minnesota, Minneapolis)*; Gretchen Hall *(Richfield Middle School, Richfield)*; Jennifer Larson *(Olson Middle School, Minneapolis)*; Michele Luke *(West Junior High, Minnetonka)*; Jeni Meyer *(Richfield Junior High, Richfield)*; Judy Pfingsten *(Inver Grove Heights Middle School, Inver Grove Heights)*; Sarah Shafer *(North Junior High, Minnetonka)*; Genni Steele *(Central Middle School, White Bear Lake)*; Victoria Wilson *(Eisenhower Elementary, Hopkins)*; Paul Zorn *(St. Olaf College, Northfield)*

New York
Debra Altenau-Bartolino *(Greenwich Village Middle School, New York)*; Doug Clements *(University of Buffalo)*; Francis Curcio *(New York University, New York)*; Christine Dorosh *(Clinton School for Writers, Brooklyn)*; Jennifer Rehn *(East Side Middle School, New York)*; Phyllis Tam *(IS 89 Lab School, New York)*;

Marie Turini *(Louis Armstrong Middle School, New York)*; Lucy West *(Community School District 2, New York)*; Monica Witt *(Simon Baruch Intermediate School 104, New York)*

Pennsylvania
Robert Aglietti *(Pittsburgh)*; Sharon Mihalich *(Pittsburgh)*; Jennifer Plumb *(South Hills Middle School, Pittsburgh)*; Mary Lynn Raith *(Pittsburgh Public Schools)*

Texas
Michelle Bittick *(Austin Independent School District)*; Margaret Cregg *(Plano Independent School District)*; Sheila Cunningham *(Klein Independent School District)*; Judy Hill *(Austin Independent School District)*; Patricia Holguin *(El Paso Independent School District)*; Bonnie McNemar *(Arlington)*; Kay Neuse *(Plano Independent School District)*; Joyce Polanco *(Austin Independent School District)*; Marge Ramirez *(University of Texas at El Paso)*; Pat Rossman *(Baker Campus, Austin)*; Cindy Schimek *(Houston)*; Cynthia Schneider *(Charles A. Dana Center, University of Texas at Austin)*; Uri Treisman *(Charles A. Dana Center, University of Texas at Austin)*; Jacqueline Weilmuenster *(Grapevine-Colleyville Independent School District)*; LuAnn Weynand *(San Antonio)*; Carmen Whitman *(Austin Independent School District)*; James Wohlgehagen *(Plano Independent School District)*

Washington
Ramesh Gangolli *(University of Washington, Seattle)*

Wisconsin
Susan Lamon *(Marquette University, Hales Corner)*; Steve Reinhart *(retired, Chippewa Falls Middle School, Eau Claire)*

Table of Contents

Variables and Patterns
Introducing Algebra

Table of Contents

Stretching and Shrinking
Understanding Similarity

Table of Contents

Comparing and Scaling
Ratio, Proportion, and Percent

Comparing and Scaling

Table of Contents

Accentuate the Negative
Integers and Rational Numbers

Accentuate the Negative

Table of Contents

Moving Straight Ahead
Linear Relationships

Moving Straight Ahead

Table of Contents

Filling and Wrapping
Three-Dimensional Measurement

Filling and Wrapping

Table of Contents

What Do You Expect?
Probability and Expected Value

Table of Contents

Data Distributions
Describing Variability and Comparing Groups

Data Distributions

Connected Mathematics 2

Variables and Patterns

Introducing Algebra

Glenda Lappan

James T. Fey

William M. Fitzgerald

Susan N. Friel

Elizabeth Difanis Phillips

PEARSON

Prentice
Hall

Boston, Massachusetts
Upper Saddle River, New Jersey

Variables and Patterns

How does the number of daylight hours change with the passage of time in a year? Why does this happen?

Who offers the better deal for renting a truck? *East Coast Trucks: $4.25 for each mile driven* or *Philadelphia Truck Rental: $200 plus $2 per mile driven.*

The group admission price for Wild World Amusement park is $50, plus $10 per person. What equation relates the price to the number of people in the group?

Some things never seem to change. The sun always rises in the east and sets in the west. The United States holds a presidential election every four years. Labor Day always falls on the first Monday of September.

But many other things are always changing. Temperatures rise and fall within a day and from season to season. Store sales change in response to rising and falling prices and shopper demand. Audiences for television shows and movies change as viewers' interests change. The speeds of cars on streets and highways change in response to variations in traffic density and road conditions.

In mathematics, science, and business, quantities that change are called *variables.* Many problems require predicting how changes in the values of one variable are related to changes in the values of another. To help you solve such problems, you can represent the relationships between variables using word descriptions, tables, graphs, and equations. The mathematical ideas and skills used to solve such problems come from the branch of mathematics called *algebra.* This unit introduces some of the basic tools of algebra.

Mathematical Highlights

Introducing Algebra

In *Variables and Patterns,* you will study some basic ideas of algebra and learn some ways to use those ideas.

You will learn how to

- Identify variables in situations
- Recognize situations in which changes in variables are related in useful patterns
- Describe patterns of change shown in words, tables, and graphs
- Construct tables and graphs to display relationships between variables
- Observe how a change in the relationship between two variables affects the table, graph, and equation
- Use algebraic symbols to write equations relating variables
- Use tables, graphs, and equations to solve problems
- Use graphing calculators to construct tables and graphs of relationships between variables and to answer questions about these relationships

As you work on problems in this unit, ask yourself questions about problem situations that involve related quantitative variables:

What are the variables in the problem?

Which variables depend on, or change in relation to, others?

How can I use a table, graph, or equation to display and analyze a relationship between quantitative variables?

What does it mean when I see regular and predictable changes in a table of data or a graph?

How can I use these regular or predictable changes to make estimates or predictions about other data values?

Investigation 1

Variables, Tables, and Coordinate Graphs

The bicycle was invented in 1791. People of all ages use bicycles for transportation and sport. Many people spend their vacations taking organized bicycle tours.

Did You Know?

RAGBRAI, which stands for Register's Annual Great Bicycle Ride Across Iowa, is a weeklong cycling tour across the state of Iowa. The event has been held every summer since 1973. Although the tour follows a different route each year, it always begins with as many as 10,000 participants dipping their back bicycle wheels into the Missouri River along Iowa's western border and ends with the riders dipping their front wheels into the Mississippi River on Iowa's eastern border.

 **For:** Information about RAGBRAI
PHSchool.com **Web Code:** ane-9031

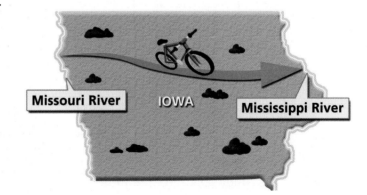

Preparing for a Bicycle Tour

Sidney, Celia, Liz, Malcolm, and Theo decide to operate bicycle tours as a summer business. The five college students choose a route from Atlantic City, New Jersey, to Norfolk, Virginia. The students name their business Ocean Bike Tours.

While planning their bike tour, the students need to determine how far the touring group can ride each day. To figure this out, they take test rides around their hometowns.

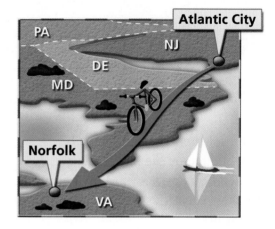

Getting Ready for Problem 1.1

- How far do you think you could ride in a day?
- How do you think the speed of your ride would change during the course of the day?
- What conditions would affect the speed and distance you could ride?

To accurately answer the questions above, you would need to take a test ride yourself. Instead you can perform an experiment involving jumping jacks. This experiment should give you some idea of the patterns commonly seen in tests of endurance.

Jumping Jack Experiment

You will need a group of at least four people:

- a jumper (to do jumping jacks)
- a timer (to keep track of the time)
- a counter (to count jumping jacks)
- a recorder (to write down the number of jumping jacks)

As a group, decide who will do each task.

When the timer says "go," the jumper begins doing jumping jacks. The jumper continues jumping for 2 minutes. The counter counts the jumping jacks out loud. Every 10 seconds, the timer says "time" and the recorder records the total number of jumping jacks the jumper has done.

A. Do the jumping jack experiment. For each jumper, prepare a table for recording the total number of jumping jacks after every 10 seconds, up to a total time of 2 minutes (120 seconds).

Jumping Jack Experiment

Time (seconds)	0	10	20	30	40	50	60	70	...
Total Number of Jumping Jacks									

Use the table of your jumping jack data to answer these questions:

B. How did the jumping jack rates (the number of jumping jacks per second) in your group change as time passed? How is this shown in your tables?

C. What might this pattern suggest about how bike-riding speed would change over a day's time on the bicycle tour?

ACE Homework starts on page 15.

1.2 Making Graphs

In the jumping jack experiment, the number of jumping jacks and the time are variables. A **variable** is a quantity that changes or varies. You recorded data for the experiment variables in a table. Another way to display your data is in a **coordinate graph.** Making a coordinate graph is a way to show the relationships between two variables.

There are four steps to follow when you make a coordinate graph.

Step 1 Identify two variables.

In Problem 1.1, the two variables are *time* and *number of jumping jacks*.

Step 2 Select an axis to represent each variable.

Often, you can assign each variable to an axis by thinking about how the variables are related. If one variable depends on the other, put the **dependent variable** on the **y-axis** (the vertical axis) and the **independent variable** on the **x-axis** (the horizontal axis). You may have encountered the terms *dependent variable* and *independent variable* in your science classes.

If time is a variable, you usually put it on the *x*-axis. This helps you see the "story" that occurs over time as you read the graph from left to right.

In Problem 1.1, the number of jumping jacks depends on time. So, put number of jumping jacks (the dependent variable) on the *y*-axis and time (the independent variable) on the *x*-axis.

Label your graph so that someone else can see what it represents. You can label the *x*-axis as "Time (seconds)" and the *y*-axis as "Number of Jumping Jacks." You can use these labels to help you choose a title for your graph. You might title this graph, "Jumping Jacks Over Time."

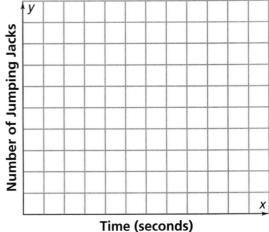

Jumping Jacks Over Time

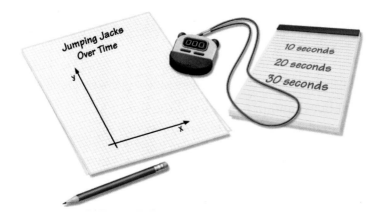

Step 3 Select a **scale** for each axis. For each axis, determine the least and greatest values to show. Then decide how to space the scale marks.

In Problem 1.1, the values for time are between 0 and 120 seconds. On the graph, label the *x*-axis (time) from 0 to 120. Because you collected data every 10 seconds, label by 10's.

The scale you use on the *y*-axis (number of jumping jacks) depends on the number of jumping jacks you did. For example, if you did 97 jumping jacks, you could label your scale from 0 to 100. Because it would take a lot of space to label the scale for every jumping jack, you could label by 10's.

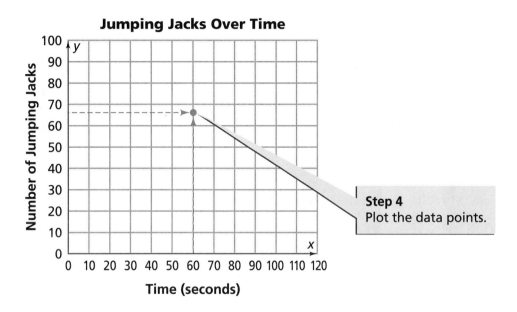

Jumping Jacks Over Time

Step 4
Plot the data points.

Step 4 Plot the data points.

Suppose that at 60 seconds, you had done 66 jumping jacks. To plot this information, start at 60 on the *x*-axis (time) and follow a line straight up. On the *y*-axis (number of jumping jacks), start at 66 and follow a line straight across. Make a point where the two lines intersect. You can describe this point with the **coordinate pair** (60, 66). The first number in a coordinate pair is the *x*-coordinate, and the second number is the *y*-coordinate.

Problem 1.2 Making Graphs

A. Make a graph of the jumping jack data for one of the jumpers in your group.

B. What does your graph show about the jumping jack rate as time passes? (Another way to say this is, what does your graph show about the **relationship** between the number of jumping jacks and time?)

C. Is the relationship you found between the number of jumping jacks and time easier to see in the table or in the graph? Explain.

ACE Homework starts on page 15.

Sidney, Liz, Celia, Malcolm, and Theo found they could comfortably ride from 60 to 90 miles in one day. They use these findings, as well as a map and campground information, to plan a three-day tour route. They wonder if steep hills and rough winds coming off the ocean might make the trip too difficult for some riders.

It is time to test the projected tour route. The students want the trip to attract middle school students, so Sidney asks her 13-year-old brother, Tony, and her 14-year-old sister, Sarah, to come along. The students will collect data during the trip and use the data to write detailed reports. Using the reports, they can improve their plans and explain the trip to potential customers.

They begin their bike tour in Atlantic City and ride five hours south to Cape May, New Jersey. Sidney and Sarah follow in a van with camping gear. Sarah records distances traveled until they reach Cape May. She makes the table at the right.

From Cape May, they take a ferry across the Delaware Bay to Lewes (LOO-is), Delaware. They camp that night in a state park along the ocean.

Atlantic City to Cape May

Time (hr)	Distance (mi)
0	0
0.5	8
1.0	15
1.5	19
2.0	25
2.5	27
3.0	34
3.5	40
4.0	40
4.5	40
5.0	45

Problem 1.3 Interpreting Graphs

A. Make a coordinate graph of the time and distance data in Sarah's table. Show time on the *x*-axis.

B. Analyze your graph by answering the following questions:

1. Give the coordinate pair for the third point on your graph. What information does this point give?

2. Connecting the points on a graph sometimes helps you see a pattern more clearly. You can connect the points to consider what is happening in the intervals between the points.

Connect the points on your graph with straight line segments. Use the line segments to estimate the distance traveled after $\frac{3}{4}$ of an hour (0.75 hours).

3. The straight-line segment you drew from (4.5, 40) to (5.0, 45) shows the progress if the riders travel at a steady rate for the entire half hour. The actual pace of the group, and of individual riders, may vary throughout the half hour. These paths show some possible ways the ride may have progressed:

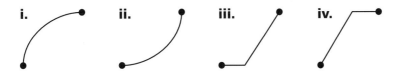

Match each of these connecting paths with the travel notes below.

   a. Celia rode slowly at first and gradually increased her speed.

   b. Tony and Liz rode quickly and reached the campsite early.

   c. Malcolm had to fix a flat tire, so he started late.

   d. Theo started off fast. He soon felt tired and slowed down.

C. Sidney wants to describe Day 1 of the tour. Using information from the table or the graph, what can she write about the day's travel? Consider the following questions:

   • How far did the group travel? How much time did it take them?

   • During which time interval(s) did they go the greatest distance? During which time interval(s) did they go the least distance?

   • Did the riders go farther in the first half or the second half of the day's ride?

D. Sidney wants to include either the table or the graph in her report. Which do you think she should include? Why?

ACE **Homework starts on page 15.**

On Day 2, the students leave Lewes, Delaware, and ride through Ocean City, Maryland. They stop for the day on Chincoteague (SHING kuh teeg) Island, which is famous for its annual pony auction.

Did You Know?

Assateague (A suh teeg) Island is home to herds of wild ponies. To survive in a harsh environment of beaches, sand dunes, and marshes, these sturdy ponies eat saltmarsh, seaweed, and even poison ivy!

To keep the population of ponies under control, an auction is held every summer. During the famous "Pony Swim," the ponies that will be sold swim across a quarter mile of water to Chincoteague Island.

Go Online
PHSchool.com **For:** Information about the "Pony Swim"
Web Code: ane-9031

Celia collects data along the way and uses it to make the graph below. Her graph shows the distance the riders are from Lewes as the day progresses. This graph is different from the graph made for Problem 1.3, which showed the total distance traveled as Day 1 progressed.

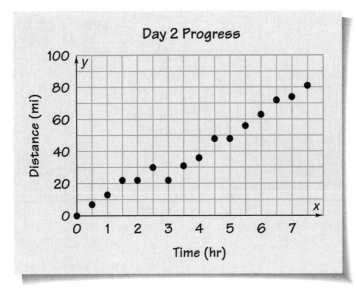

Day 2 Progress

A. Does it make sense to connect the points on this graph? Explain.

B. Make a table of (*time, distance*) data that matches the coordinate pairs of the graph. (You will need to estimate many of the distance values.)

C. What might have happened between hours 2 and 4? What do you think happened between hours 1.5 and 2?

D. During which interval(s) did the riders make the most progress? During which interval(s) did they make the least progress?

E. Which method of displaying the data helps you see the changes better, a table or a graph? Explain.

F. Use the graph to find the total distance the riders travel on Day 2. How did you find your answer?

 **ACE** **Homework starts on page 15.**

The Global Positioning System (GPS) is a satellite navigation system funded and operated by the U.S. Department of Defense. However, there are many thousands of civilian users of GPS worldwide. With the use of a portable computer, a Braille keyboard, and a GPS receiver, a blind person is able to get directions.

Go **Online**
PHSchool.com **For:** Information about GPS
Web Code: ane-9031

On Day 3, the group travels from Chincoteague Island to Norfolk, Virginia. Malcolm and Tony ride in the van. They forget to record the distance traveled each half hour, but they do write some notes about the trip.

- We started at 8:30 A.M. and rode into a strong wind until our midmorning break.

- About midmorning, the wind shifted to our backs.

- We stopped for lunch at a barbeque stand and rested for about an hour. By this time, we had traveled about halfway to Norfolk.

- Around 2:00 P.M., we stopped for a brief swim in the ocean.

- Around 3:30 P.M., we reached the north end of the Chesapeake Bay Bridge and Tunnel. We stopped for a few minutes to watch the ships passing. Because riding bikes on the bridge is not allowed, we put the bikes in the van and drove across.

- We took 7.5 hours to complete today's 80-mile trip.

Problem 1.5 Finding Average Speed

A. Make a table of (*time, distance*) data that reasonably fits the information in Malcolm and Tony's notes.

B. Sketch a coordinate graph that shows the same information.

C. Explain how you used each of the six notes to make your table and graph.

D. The riders traveled 80 miles in 7.5 hours. Suppose they had traveled at a constant speed for the entire trip. This constant speed would be the same as the *average speed* of the real trip. What was the average speed for this trip?

E. Suppose you made a (*time, distance*) graph for a rider who made the entire 7.5-hour trip traveling at the average speed you found in Question D. What would the graph look like? How would it compare with the graph you made in Question B?

ACE Homework starts on page 15.

Applications

1. A convenience store has been keeping track of its popcorn sales.

Popcorn Sales

Time	Total Bags Sold
6:00 A.M.	0
7:00 A.M.	3
8:00 A.M.	15
9:00 A.M.	20
10:00 A.M.	26
11:00 A.M.	30
noon	45
1:00 P.M.	58
2:00 P.M.	58
3:00 P.M.	62
4:00 P.M.	74
5:00 P.M.	83
6:00 P.M.	88
7:00 P.M.	92

a. Make a coordinate graph of the data in the table above. Which variable did you put on the *x*-axis? Why?

b. Describe how the number of bags of popcorn sold changed during the day.

c. During which hour did the store sell the most popcorn? During which hour did it sell the least popcorn?

active math
online

For: Climbing Monkeys Activity
Visit: PHSchool.com
Web Code: and-1101

2. At the right is a graph of jumping jack data. (On the *x*-axis, 20 means the interval from 0 seconds to 20 seconds, 40 means the interval 20 seconds to 40 seconds, and so on.)

a. What does the graph tell you about Mary's experiment?

b. How is this graph different from the graph you made in Problem 1.2?

c. What total number of jumping jacks did Mary do?

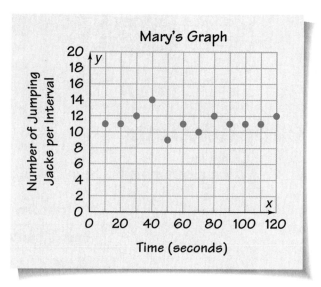

3. After doing the jumping jack experiment, Andrea and Ken compare their graphs. Because the points on his graph are higher, Ken said he did more jumping jacks in the 120 seconds than Andrea did. Do you agree? Explain.

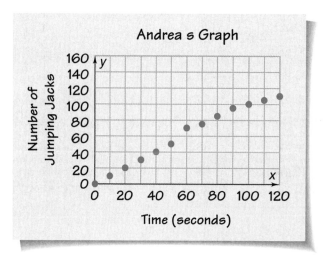

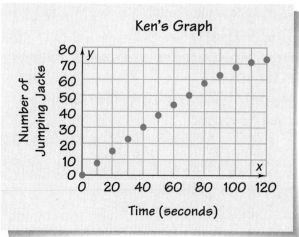

4. Katrina's parents kept this record of her growth from her birth until her 18th birthday.

Katrina's Height

Age (yr)	Height (in.)
birth	20
1	29
2	33.5
3	37
4	39.5
5	42
6	45.5
7	47
8	49
9	52
10	54
11	56.5
12	59
13	61
14	64
15	64
16	64
17	64.5
18	64.5

a. Make a coordinate graph of Katrina's height data.

b. During which time interval(s) did Katrina have her greatest "growth spurt"?

c. During which time interval(s) did Katrina's height change the least?

d. Would it make sense to connect the points on the graph? Why or why not?

e. Is it easier to use the table or the graph to answer parts (b) and (c)? Explain.

5. Below is a chart of the water depth in a harbor during a typical 24-hour day. The water level rises and falls with the tides.

Effect of the Tide on Water Depth

Hours Since Midnight	0	1	2	3	4	5	6	7	8
Depth (m)	10.1	10.6	11.5	13.2	14.5	15.5	16.2	15.4	14.6

Hours Since Midnight	9	10	11	12	13	14	15	16
Depth (m)	12.9	11.4	10.3	10.0	10.4	11.4	13.1	14.5

Hours Since Midnight	17	18	19	20	21	22	23	24
Depth (m)	15.4	16.0	15.6	14.3	13.0	11.6	10.7	10.2

a. At what time is the water the deepest? Find the depth at that time.

b. At what time is the water the shallowest? Find the depth at that time.

c. During what time interval does the depth change most rapidly?

d. Make a coordinate graph of the data. Describe the overall pattern you see.

e. How did you determine what scale to use for your graph? Do you think everyone in your class used the same scale?

6. Three students made graphs of the population of a town called Huntsville. The break in the *y*-axis in Graphs A and C indicates that there are values missing between 0 and 8.

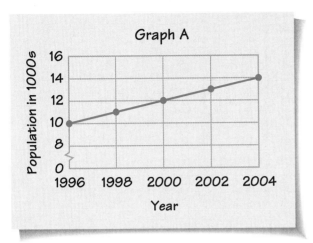

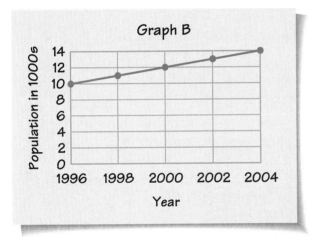

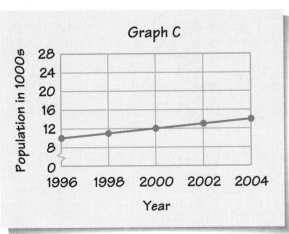

a. Describe the relationship between time and population as shown in each of the graphs.

b. Is it possible that all three graphs correctly represent the population growth in Huntsville? Explain.

7. On the *x*-axis of the graph below, 6 means the time from 5:00 to 6:00, 7 means the time from 6:00 to 7:00, and so on.

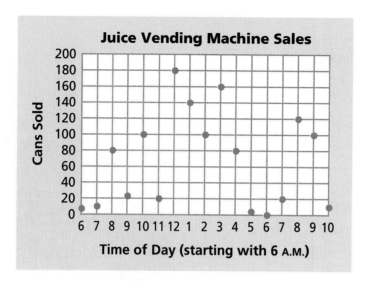

a. The graph shows the relationship between two variables. What are the variables?

b. Describe how the number of cans sold changed during the day. Explain why these changes might have occurred.

8. Here is a graph of temperature data collected on the students' trip from Atlantic City to Lewes.

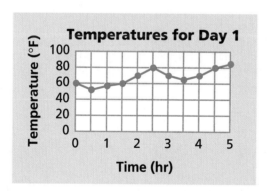

a. This graph shows the relationship between two variables. What are they?

b. Make a table of data from this graph.

c. What is the difference between the day's lowest and highest temperatures?

d. During which time interval(s) did the temperature rise the fastest? During which time interval did it fall the fastest?

e. Is it easier to use the table or the graph to answer part (c)? Why?

f. Is it easier to use the table or the graph to answer part (d)? Why?

g. What information can you get from the lines connecting the points? Do you think it is accurate information? Explain.

9. Here is a graph Celia drew on the bike trip.

Celia's Graph

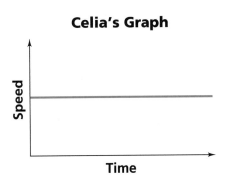

a. What does this graph show?

b. Is this a reasonable pattern for the speed of a cyclist? Is this a reasonable pattern for the speed of the van? Is this a reasonable pattern for the speed of the wind? Explain each of your conclusions.

10. Make a table and a graph of (*time, temperature*) data that fit the following information about a day on the road:

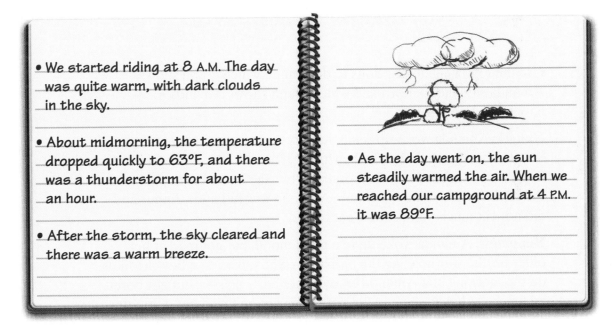

• We started riding at 8 A.M. The day was quite warm, with dark clouds in the sky.

• About midmorning, the temperature dropped quickly to 63°F, and there was a thunderstorm for about an hour.

• After the storm, the sky cleared and there was a warm breeze.

• As the day went on, the sun steadily warmed the air. When we reached our campground at 4 P.M. it was 89°F.

11. When Ben first started to play the electric guitar, his skill increased quite rapidly. Over time, Ben seemed to improve more slowly.

a. Sketch a graph to show how Ben's guitar-playing skill progressed over time since he began to play.

b. Your graph shows the relationship between two variables. What are those variables?

c. What other variables might affect the rate at which Ben's playing improves?

12. Amanda made the graphs below to show how her level of hunger and her feelings of happiness changed over the course of a day. She forgot to label the graphs.

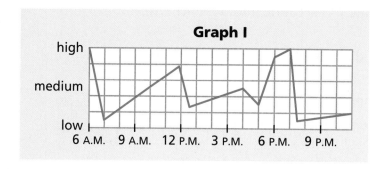

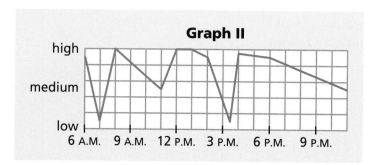

Use the following descriptions to determine which graph shows Amanda's hunger pattern and which graph shows Amanda's happiness. Explain.

Hunger: Amanda woke up really hungry and ate a large breakfast. She was hungry again by lunch, which began at 11:45. After school, she had a snack before basketball practice, but she had a big appetite by the time she got home for dinner. Amanda was full after dinner and did not eat much before she went to bed.

Happiness: Amanda woke up in a good mood, but got mad at her older brother for hogging the bathroom. She talked to a boy she likes on the morning bus. Amanda enjoyed her early classes, but got bored by lunch. At lunch, she had fun with friends. She loved her computer class, which was right after lunch, but she didn't enjoy her other afternoon classes. After school, Amanda had a good time at basketball practice. After dinner, she did homework and chores.

Connections

For Exercises 13–15, order the numbers from least to greatest. Then describe how each number in your ordered list can be obtained from the previous number.

For: Multiple-Choice Skills Practice
Web Code: ana-1154

13. 1.75, 0.25, 0.5, 1.5, 2.0, 0.75, 1.25, 1.00

14. $\frac{3}{8}$, 1, $\frac{1}{4}$, $\frac{7}{8}$, $\frac{3}{4}$, $\frac{1}{2}$, $\frac{1}{8}$, $\frac{5}{8}$

15. $\frac{4}{3}$, $\frac{1}{3}$, $\frac{1}{6}$, $\frac{4}{6}$, $\frac{8}{3}$, $\frac{32}{6}$

16. Draw the next shape in this pattern. Then, make a table of (*number of squares in bottom row, total number of squares*) data for the first five shapes in this pattern.

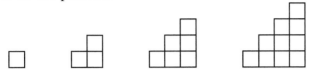

17. Make a table to show how the total number of cubes in these pyramids changes as the width of the base changes from 3 to 7.

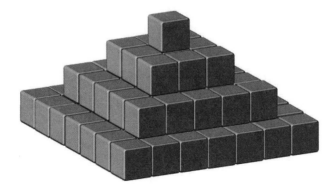

18. Multiple Choice Suppose you know that there are five blocks in a bag, and one of these is marked "winner."

You reach into the bag and choose one block at random. What is the probability you will choose the "winner"?

A. $\frac{1}{5}$ **B.** $\frac{1}{4}$ **C.** $\frac{1}{2}$ **D.** None of these

19. a. Suppose you replace the block you chose in Exercise 18 *and* add another "winner" block. Now there are six blocks in the bag. What is the probability of choosing a "winner" if you choose one block at random?

b. How does your probability of choosing a "winner" change for every extra "winner" block you add to the bag? Use a table or graph to explain your answer.

20. Suppose you toss a 6-sided die twice to make the coordinate pair (*roll 1, roll 2*). You will win a prize if the result is (2, 2), (4, 4), or (6, 6). What is the probability you will win a prize?

Homework Help Online
PHSchool.com

For: Help with Exercise 20
Web Code: ane-1120

21. The directors of Ocean Bike Tours want to compare their plans with other bicycle tour companies. The bike tour they are planning takes three days, and they wonder if this might be too short. Malcolm called 18 different companies and asked, "How many days is your most popular bike trip?" Here are the answers he received:

3, 6, 7, 5, 10, 7, 4, 2, 3, 3, 5, 14, 5, 7, 12, 4, 3, 6

Make a line plot of the data.

22. Multiple Choice What is the median of the data in Exercise 21?

F. 3 **G.** 5 **H.** 6 **J.** 14

23. On the basis of the information in Exercises 21 and 22, should Ocean Bike Tours change the length of the three-day trip? Explain.

24. The graph below shows the results of a survey of people over age 25 who had completed different levels of education.

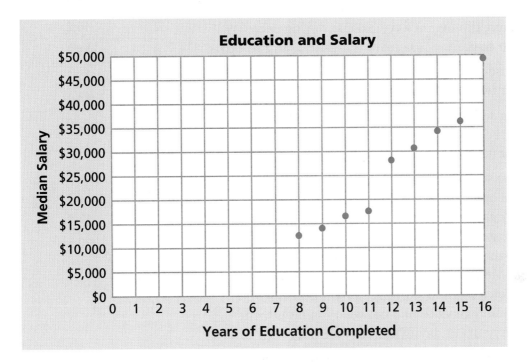

Education and Salary

a. Make a table that shows the information in the graph.

b. After how many years of education do salaries take a big jump? Why do you think this happens?

c. Do you find it easier to answer part (b) by looking at the graph or at your table? Explain.

25. Think of something in your life that varies with time, and make a graph to show how it might change as time passes. Some possibilities are the length of your hair, your height, your moods, or your feelings toward your friends.

Extensions

26. The number of hours of daylight in a day changes throughout the year. We say that the days are "shorter" in winter and "longer" in summer. The table shows the number of daylight hours in Chicago, Illinois, on a typical day during each month of the year (January is month 1, and so on).

a. Describe any relationships you see between the two variables.

b. On a grid, sketch a coordinate graph of the data. Put months on the *x*-axis and daylight hours on the *y*-axis. What patterns do you see?

c. The seasons in the southern hemisphere are the opposite of the seasons in the northern hemisphere. When it is summer in North America, it is winter in Australia. Chicago is about the same distance north of the equator as Melbourne, Australia, is south of the equator. Sketch a graph showing the relationship you would expect to find between the month and the hours of daylight in Melbourne.

Daylight Hours

Month	Daylight Hours
1	10.0
2	10.2
3	11.7
4	13.1
5	14.3
6	15.0
7	14.5
8	13.8
9	12.5
10	11.0
11	10.5
12	10.0

d. Put the (*month*, *daylight*) values from your graph in part (c) into a table.

27. Some students did a jumping jack experiment. They reported their data in the graph below.

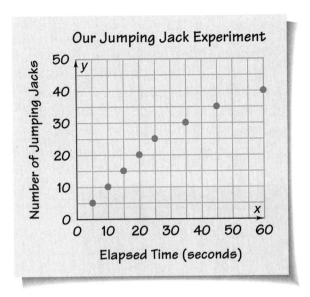

Our Jumping Jack Experiment

a. According to the graph, how many jumping jacks did the jumper make by the end of 10 seconds? By the end of 20 seconds? By the end of 60 seconds?

b. Give the elapsed time and number of jumping jacks for two other points on the graph.

c. What estimate would make sense for the number of jumping jacks in 30 seconds? The number in 40 seconds? In 50 seconds?

d. What does the overall pattern in the graph show about the rate at which the test jumper completed jumping jacks?

e. Suppose you connected the first and last data points with a straight line segment. Would this line show the overall pattern? Explain.

28. a. A school booster club sells sweatshirts. Which, if any, of the graphs describes the relationship you expect between the price charged for each sweatshirt and the profit? Explain your choice, or draw a new graph you think better describes this relationship.

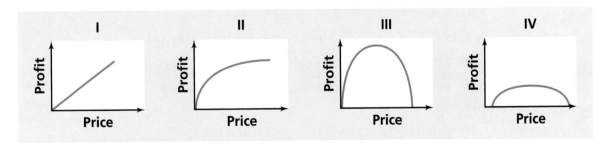

b. What variables might affect the club's profits?

29. Chelsea and Nicole can paddle a canoe at a steady rate of 5 miles per hour.

   a. On Saturday, they paddle for 3 hours on a calm river. Sketch a graph of their speed over the 3-hour period.

   b. On Sunday, they go canoeing again. They paddle with a 2-mile-per-hour current for 1 hour. Then, they turn into a tributary that feeds the river. They paddle against a 2-mile-per-hour current for 2 hours. On the same axes you used in part (a), sketch a graph of their speed over this 3-hour period.

   c. How does the speed of the current affect the speed of the canoe?

30. In parts (a)–(e) below, how does the value of one variable change as the value of the other changes? Estimate pairs of values that show the pattern of change you would expect. Record your estimates in a table with at least five data points.

   Sample *hours* of television you watch in a week and your school *grade-point average*

   As television time increases, I expect my grade-point average to decrease.

TV Time (hours per week)	0	5	10	15	20
Grade Point Average	3.5	3.25	3.0	2.75	2.5

   a. *distance* from school to your home and *time* it takes to walk home

   b. *price* of popcorn at a theater and *number of bags* sold

   c. *speed* of an airplane and *time* it takes the plane to complete a 500-mile trip

   d. *number of days* you keep a rented DVD and *rental charge*

   e. *length* of a long-distance telephone call in minutes and *cost* of the call

Mathematical Reflections 1

The problems in this investigation asked you to think about variables and the patterns relating the values of variables. You made tables and graphs to show how different variables are related. The following questions will help you summarize what you have learned.

Think about your answers to these questions. Discuss your ideas with other students and your teacher. Then write a summary of your findings in your notebook.

1. Describe the steps you would take in making a graph to show the relationship between two related variables.

2. How do you decide which variable should be on the *x*-axis and which should be on the *y*-axis?

3. **a.** What are the advantages and disadvantages of representing a relationship between variables in a table?

   b. What are the advantages and disadvantages of representing a relationship between variables in a graph?

   c. What are the advantages and disadvantages of describing a relationship between variables in a written report?

Investigation 2

Analyzing Graphs and Tables

In this investigation you will continue to use tables, graphs, and descriptions to compare information and make decisions. Using tables, graphs, and words to represent relationships is an important part of algebra.

Sidney, Celia, Liz, Malcolm, and Theo continue making plans for Ocean Bike Tours. Many of these plans involve questions about money.

> *How much will it cost to operate the tours?*
>
> *How much should customers pay?*
>
> *Will the company make a profit?*

The five tour operators decide to do some research.

Getting Ready for Problem 2.1

- With your classmates, make a list of things the tour operators must provide for their customers. Estimate the cost of each item per customer.

- Estimate how much customers would be willing to pay for the three-day tour.

- Based on your estimates, will the partners earn a profit?

2.1 Renting Bicycles

The tour operators decide to rent bicycles for their customers. They get information from two bike shops.

Rocky's Cycle Center sends a table of weekly rental fees for bikes.

Rocky's Weekly Rental Rates for Bikes

Number of Bikes	5	10	15	20	25	30	35	40	45	50
Rental Fee	$400	$535	$655	$770	$875	$975	$1,070	$1,140	$1,180	$1,200

Adrian's Bike Shop sends a graph of their weekly rental fees. Because the rental fee depends on the number of bikes, they put the number of bikes on the *x*-axis.

Adrian's Weekly Rental Rates for Bikes

Problem 2.1 Analyzing a Table and a Graph

A. Which bike shop should Ocean Bike Tours use? Explain.

B. Suppose you make a graph from the table for Rocky's Cycle Center. Would it make sense to connect the points? Explain.

C. How much do you think each company charges to rent 32 bikes?

D. 1. What patterns do you find in the table and in the graph?

   2. Based on the patterns you found in part (1), how can you predict values that are not included in the table or graph?

E. 1. Describe a way to find the costs for renting any number of bikes from Adrian's Bike Shop.

   2. Describe a way to find the costs for renting any number of bikes from Rocky's Cycle Center.

ACE Homework starts on page 35.

2.2 Finding Customers

The tour operators plan a route and choose a bike shop. Now they must figure out what price to charge so they can attract customers and make a profit.

To help set a price, they conduct a survey. They ask 100 people who have taken other bicycle tours which of the following amounts they would pay for the Ocean Bike Tour: $150, $200, $250, $300, $350, $400, $450, $500, $550, or $600. The results are shown in the table below.

Problem 2.2 Making and Analyzing a Graph

A. To make a graph of these data, which variable would you put on the *x*-axis? Which variable would you put on the *y*-axis? Explain.

B. Make a coordinate graph of the data on grid paper.

C. Based on your graph, what price do you think the tour operators should charge? Explain.

D. 1. The number of people who say they would take the tour depends on the price. How does the number of potential customers change as the price increases?

2. How is the change in the number of potential customers shown in the table? How is the change shown on the graph?

3. Describe a way to find the number of potential customers for a price between two prices in the table. For example, how can you predict the number of customers for a price of $425?

Price Customers Would Pay

Total Price	Number of Customers
$150	76
$200	74
$250	71
$300	65
$350	59
$400	49
$450	38
$500	26
$550	14
$600	0

ACE Homework starts on page 35.

2.3 What's the Story?

It's important to be good at reading the "story" in a graph. Remember that the *y*-axis, or vertical axis, of a graph usually represents the *dependent variable*, and the *x*-axis, or horizontal axis, represents the *independent variable*. Here are some questions to ask when you look at a graph.

> *What are the variables represented by the graph?*

> *Do the values of one variable seem to depend on the values of the other? In other words, do changes in one variable seem to be the result of changes in the other?*

> *What does the shape of the graph say about the relationship between the variables?*

Getting Ready for Problem 2.3

The number of cars in a school parking lot changes as time passes during a school day. These graphs show two possibilities for the way the number of cars might change over time.

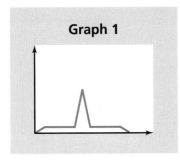
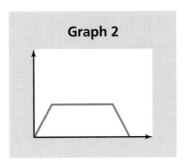

- Describe the "story" each graph tells about the school parking lot. Which graph shows the pattern you expect?

- How could you label the graph you chose so that someone else would know what it represents?

Questions A–G describe pairs of related variables. For each pair,

- Decide which variable is the dependent variable and which is the independent variable.
- Find a graph that tells a reasonable "story" about how the variables might be related. If no graph tells a reasonable story, sketch your own.
- Explain what the graph tells about the relationship of the variables.
- Give the graph a title.

A. The *number of students* who go on a school trip is related to the *price of the trip* for each student.

B. When a skateboard rider goes down one side of a half-pipe ramp and up the other side, her *speed* changes as *time* passes.

C. The *water level* changes over *time* when someone fills a tub, takes a bath, and empties the tub.

D. The *waiting time* for a popular ride at an amusement park is related to the *number of people in the park.*

E. The *number of hours of daylight* changes over *time* as the seasons change.

F. *Weekly attendance* at a popular movie changes as *time* passes from the date the movie first appears in theaters.

G. The *number of customers* at an amusement park with water slides is related to the *predicted high temperature* for the day.

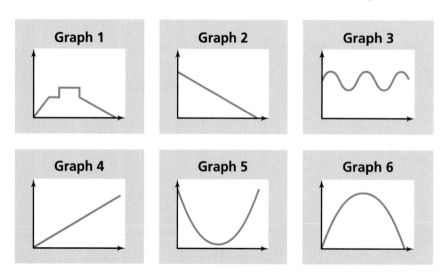

ACE Homework starts on page 35.

Applications

1. Use the table to answer parts (a)–(e).

| Typical Weights for Tiger Cubs ||
Age (weeks)	Expected Body Weight (kg)
birth	1.3
1	2.3
2	3.0
3	3.8
4	4.5
5	5.2
6	6.0
7	6.7
8	7.5
9	7.6
10	8.9
11	9.7

SOURCE: www.tigerlink.org

a. What weight is predicted for a 1-week-old tiger cub?

b. What weight is predicted for a 10-week-old tiger cub?

c. At what age do tiger cubs typically weigh 7 kilograms?

d. Describe the pattern relating age and weight. Do you expect this pattern to continue indefinitely?

e. Would it make sense to connect the points in a graph of these data?

2. Dezi researches DVD rental prices at local video stores. Source Video has a yearly membership package. The manager gives Dezi this table:

Source Video Membership/Rental Packages

Number of DVDs Rented	0	5	10	15	20	25	30
Total Cost	$30	$35	$40	$45	$50	$55	$60

Supreme Video does not have membership packages. Dezi makes the graph below to relate the cost at Supreme Video to the number of DVDs rented.

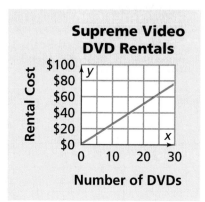

a. Both video stores have a good selection of movies. Dezi's family plans to watch about two movies a month. Which video store should they choose?

b. Write a paragraph explaining to Dezi how he can decide which video store to use.

c. For each store, describe the pattern of change relating the number of DVDs rented to the cost.

3. The table shows the fees charged at one of the campgrounds on the Ocean Bike Tour.

Campground Fees

Number of Campsites	1	2	3	4	5	6	7	8
Total Campground Fee	$12.50	$25.00	$37.50	$50.00	$62.50	$75.00	$87.50	$100.00

a. Make a coordinate graph of the data.

b. Does it make sense to connect the points on your graph? Explain.

c. Using the table, describe the pattern of change in the total campground fee as the number of campsites increases.

d. How is the pattern you described in part (c) shown in your graph?

4. Some class officers want to sell T-shirts to raise funds for a class trip. They ask the students in their class how much they would pay for a shirt and record the data in a table.

Projected Shirt Sales

Price per Shirt	$5	$10	$15	$20	$25
Number of Shirt Sales	50	40	30	20	10

a. Describe the relationship between the price per shirt and the expected number of shirt sales. Is this the sort of pattern you would expect?

b. Copy and complete this table to show the relationship between price per shirt and the expected total value of the shirt sales.

Projected Shirt Sales

Price per Shirt	$5	$10	$15	$20	$25
Number of Shirt Sales	50	40	30	20	10
Value of Shirt Sales	$250	$400	▓	▓	▓

c. How would you describe the relationship between price per shirt and expected total value of shirt sales? Is this the sort of pattern you would expect?

d. Use grid paper to make coordinate graphs of the data like the ones started below.

e. Explain how your answers to parts (a) and (c) are shown in the graphs.

5. A camping-supply store rents camping gear for $25 per person.

   a. Make a table of the total rental charges for 0, 5, 10, 15, 20, 25, 30, 35, 40, 45, and 50 campers.

   b. Make a coordinate graph using the data in your table.

   c. Compare the pattern of change in your table and graph with patterns you found in Exercise 3. Describe the similarities and differences between the two sets of data.

6. The tour operators need to rent a truck to transport camping gear, clothes, and bicycle repair equipment. They check prices at two truck-rental companies.

   a. East Coast Trucks charges $4.25 for each mile driven. Make a table of the charges for 0, 25, 50, 75, 100, 125, 150, 175, 200, 225, 250, 275, and 300 miles.

   b. Philadelphia Truck Rental charges $40 per day and an additional $2.00 for each mile driven. Make a table of the charges for renting a truck for five days and driving it 0, 25, 50, 75, 100, 125, 150, 175, 200, 225, 250, 275, and 300 miles.

   c. On one coordinate grid, plot the charge plans for both rental companies. Use a different color to mark each company's plan.

   d. Based on your work in parts (a)–(c), which company offers the better deal? Explain.

7. The table shows fees for using a campsite at a state park from 1 day up to the park limit of 10 days.

Campsite Fees

Days of Use	1	2	3	4	5	6	7	8	9	10
Campsite Fee	$20	$30	$40	$50	$60	$70	$75	$80	$85	$90

    a. Make a coordinate graph using the table.

    b. Does it make sense to connect the points on your graph? Why or why not?

    c. Describe the pattern relating the variables *days of use* and *campsite fee*.

8. Suppose a motion detector tracks the time and the distance traveled as you walk 40 feet in 8 seconds. Match the following (*time, distance*) graphs with the "stories" that describe each walk.

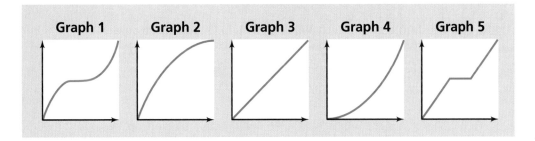

    a. You walk at a steady pace of 5 feet per second.

    b. You walk slowly at first and then steadily increase your walking speed.

    c. You walk rapidly at first, pause for several seconds, and then walk at an increasing rate for the rest of the trip.

    d. You walk at a steady rate for 3 seconds, pause for 2 seconds, and then walk at a steady rate for the rest of the trip.

    e. You walk rapidly at first, but gradually slow down as the end of the trip nears.

9. For each walk in Exercise 8, complete a (*time, distance*) table like the one below. Use numbers that will match the pattern of the walk and its graph.

Time (seconds)	1	2	3	4	5	6	7	8
Distance (feet)	■	■	■	■	■	■	■	40

10. The graphs below show five patterns of change in the price per gallon of gasoline. Match each (*time, price*) graph with the "story" it tells.

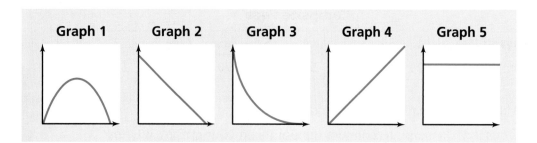

Graph 1   **Graph 2**   **Graph 3**   **Graph 4**   **Graph 5**

  a. The price declined at a steady rate.

  b. The price did not change.

  c. The price rose rapidly, then leveled off for a while, and then declined rapidly.

  d. The price rose at a steady rate.

  e. The price dropped rapidly at first and then at a slower rate.

11. Multiple Choice Jamie is going to Washington, D.C., to march in a parade with his school band. He plans to set aside $25 at the end of each month to use for the trip. Choose the graph that shows how Jamie's savings will build as time passes.

A.

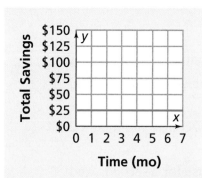

B.

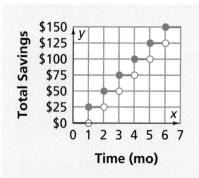

C.

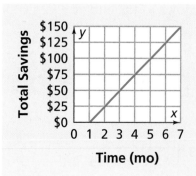

D. None of these is correct.

12. The graph shows how the temperature changed during an all-day hike by students.

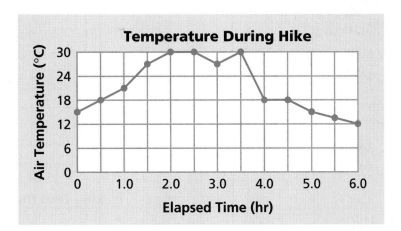

Temperature During Hike

a. What was the maximum temperature and when did it occur?

b. When was the temperature rising most rapidly?

c. When was the temperature falling most rapidly?

d. When was the temperature about 24°C?

e. The hikers encounter a thunderstorm with rain. When do you think this happened?

Jacy works at a department store. This graph shows parking costs at the parking garage Jacy uses.

13. **Multiple Choice** How much does Jacy spend to park for less than a half hour?

    F. $0.50   **G.** $0.75

    H. $1   **J.** $1.50

14. **Multiple Choice** How much does Jacy spend to park for 4 hours and 15 minutes?

    A. $6   **B.** $6.50

    C. $6.75   **D.** $7

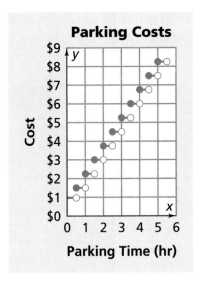

Parking Costs

Connections

15. The area of a rectangle is the product of its length and its width.

    a. Find all whole number pairs of length and width values that give an area of 24 square meters. Record the pairs in a table.

Rectangles with an Area of 24 m²

Length	■	■	■	…
Width	■	■	■	…

    b. Make a coordinate graph of the (*length, width*) data from part (a).

    c. Connect the points on your graph if it makes sense to do so. Explain your decision.

    d. Describe the relationship between length and width for rectangles of area 24 square meters.

16. The perimeter of any rectangle is the sum of its side lengths.

    a. Make a table of all possible whole-number pairs of length and width values for a rectangle with a perimeter of 18 meters.

    b. Make a coordinate graph of the (*length, width*) data from part (a).

    c. Connect the points on your graph if it makes sense to do so. Explain your decision.

    d. Describe the relationship between length and width for rectangles of perimeter 18 meters, and explain how that relationship is shown in the table and graph.

Homework Help Online
PHSchool.com

For: Help with Exercise 16
Web Code: ane-1216

17. The table below shows the winners and the winning times for the women's Olympic 400-meter dash since 1964.

Women's Olympic 400-meter Dash		
Year	Name	Time (seconds)
1964	Celia Cuthbert, AUS	52.0
1968	Colette Besson, FRA	52.0
1972	Monika Zehrt, E. GER	51.08
1976	Irena Szewinska, POL	49.29
1980	Martia Koch, E. GER	48.88
1984	Valerie Brisco-Hooks, USA	48.83
1988	Olga Bryzgina, USSR	48.65
1992	Marie-Jose Perec, FRA	48.83
1996	Marie-Jose Perec, FRA	48.25
2000	Cathy Freeman, AUS	49.11
2004	Tonique Williams-Darling, BAH	49.41

a. Make a coordinate graph of the (*year, time*) information. Choose a scale that allows you to see the differences between the winning times.

b. What patterns do you see in the table and graph? Do the winning times seem to be rising or falling? In which year was the best time earned?

18. The circumference of a circle is related to its radius by the formula $C = 2 \times \pi \times r$. The area of a circle is related to its radius by the formula $A = \pi \times r^2$.

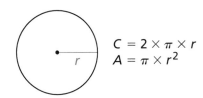

$C = 2 \times \pi \times r$
$A = \pi \times r^2$

a. Make a table showing how the circumference of a circle increases as the radius increases in 1-unit steps from 1 to 6. Make sure to express the circumferences in terms of π. Then describe the pattern relating those two variables.

b. Make a table showing how the area of a circle increases as the radius increases in 1-unit steps from 1 to 6. Make sure to express the areas in terms of π. Then describe the pattern relating those two variables.

19. Here are the box-office earnings for a movie during each of the first eight weeks following its release.

Box Office Earnings

Weeks in Theaters	1	2	3	4	5	6	7	8
Weekly Earnings (millions)	$16	$22	$18	$12	$7	$4	$3	$1

a. Make a coordinate graph showing the weekly earnings after each week. Because a film's weekly earnings depend on the number of weeks it is in theaters, put the weeks in theaters on the *x*-axis and the weekly earnings on the *y*-axis.

b. Explain how the weekly earnings changed as time passed. How is this pattern of change shown in the table and the graph? Why might this change have occurred?

c. What were the total earnings of the movie in the eight weeks?

d. Make a coordinate graph showing the total earnings after each week.

e. Explain how the movie's total earnings changed over time. How is this pattern of change shown in the table and the graph? Why might this change have occurred?

Extensions

20. Use what you know about decimals to find coordinates of five points that lie on the line segment between the labeled points on each graph:

a.

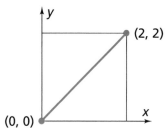

b.

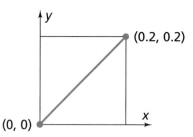

21. The graphs below each show relationships between independent (*x*-axis) and dependent (*y*-axis) variables. However, the scales on the coordinate axes are not the same for all the graphs.

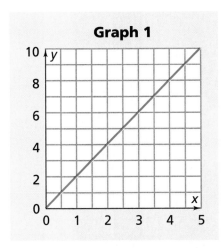

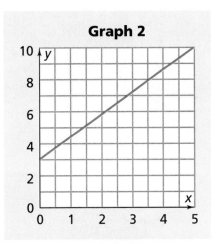

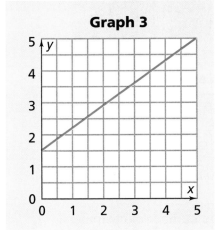

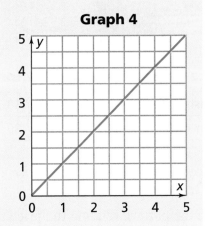

a. Which graph shows the dependent variable increasing most rapidly as the independent variable increases?

b. Which graph shows the dependent variable increasing most slowly as the independent variable increases?

22. To raise money, students plan to hold a car wash. They ask some adults how much they would pay for a car wash. The table below shows the results of their research.

Price Customers Would Pay for a Car Wash

Car Wash Price	$4	$6	$8	$10	$12	$14
Number of Customers	120	105	90	75	60	45

a. Make a coordinate graph of the (*price, customers*) data. Connect the points if it makes sense to do so.

b. Describe the pattern relating the price to the number of customers. Explain how the table and the graph show the pattern.

c. Based on the pattern, what number of customers would you predict if the price were $16? What number would you predict if the price were $20? What if the price were $2?

23. a. Copy and complete the table below, using the information from Exercise 22.

Projected Car Wash Income

Car Wash Price	$4	$6	$8	$10	$12	$14
Number of Customers	120	105	90	75	60	45
Projected Income	■	■	■	■	■	■

b. Make a graph of the (*price, projected income*) data. Connect the points if it makes sense to do so.

c. Describe the pattern relating the price and the projected income. Explain how the table and the graph show the pattern. Explain why the pattern does or does not make business sense to you.

d. Suppose the shopping center where the students plan to hold the car wash will charge the students $1.50 per car for water and cleaning supplies. How can you use this factor to find the profit from the car wash for various prices?

24. Adriana is at a skateboard park that has tracks shaped like regular polygons. Recall that a *regular polygon* is a polygon with congruent sides and congruent angles. Here are some examples:

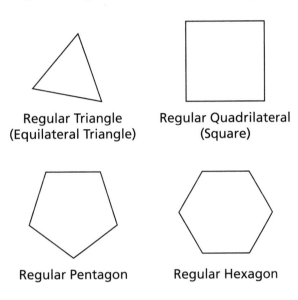

Regular Triangle
(Equilateral Triangle)

Regular Quadrilateral
(Square)

Regular Pentagon

Regular Hexagon

At each vertex of a track, Adriana must make a turn. The size of the turn relates to the number of sides in the polygon. For example, at each vertex of the triangle track, she must make a 120° turn.

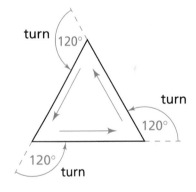

a. Copy and complete the table below to show how the size of the turn Adriana must make at each vertex is related to the number of sides of the polygon.

Track Turns

Number of Sides	3	4	5	6	7	8	9	10
Degrees in Turn	120	■	■	■	■	■	■	■

b. Make a coordinate graph of the (*sides, degrees*) data.

c. What pattern of change do you see in the degrees Adriana must turn as the number of sides increases? How does the table show that pattern? How does the graph show that pattern?

Mathematical Reflections 2

The problems in this investigation asked you to think about *patterns* relating the values of *variables*. These questions will help you to summarize what you have learned.

Think about your answers to these questions. Discuss your ideas with other students and your teacher. Then write a summary of your findings in your notebook.

1. Explain what the word *variable* means in mathematics.

2. What does it mean to say that two variables are related?

3. **a.** Suppose the *y*-values increase as the *x*-values increase. How is this indicated in a table? How is this indicated in a graph?

   b. Suppose the *y*-values decrease as the *x*-values increase. How is this indicated in a table? How is this indicated in a graph?

4. In a coordinate graph of two related variables, when does it make sense to connect the points?

Investigation 3

Rules and Equations

In the last investigation, you used tables and graphs of relationships to find values of one variable for given values of the other variable. In some cases, you could only estimate or predict a value.

For some relationships, you can write an equation, or formula, to show how the variables are related. Using an equation is often the most accurate way to find values of a variable.

In this investigation, you will use the patterns in tables to help you write equations for relationships. You will then use your equations to compute values of the dependent variable for specific values of the independent variable.

3.1 Writing Equations

On the last day of the Ocean Bike Tour, the riders will be near Wild World Amusement Park. Liz and Malcolm want to plan a stop there. They consider several variables that affect their costs and the time they can spend at Wild World.

Getting Ready for Problem 3.1

- What variables do you think are involved in planning for the amusement-park trip?

- How are those variables related to each other?

Malcolm finds out that it costs $21 per person to visit Wild World. Liz suggests they make a table or graph relating admission price to the number of people. However, Malcolm says there is a simple **rule** for calculating the cost:

The *cost* in dollars is equal to 21 times the *number of people*.

He writes the rule as an **equation**:

$cost = 21 \times number\ of\ people$

Liz shortens Malcolm's equation by using single letters to stand for the variables. She uses c to stand for the cost and n to stand for the number of people:

$c = 21 \times n$

When you multiply a number by a letter variable, you can leave out the multiplication sign. So, $21n$ means $21 \times n$. You can shorten the equation even more:

$c = 21n$

The equation $c = 21n$ involves one calculation. You multiply the number of customers n by the cost per customer $21. Many common equations involve one calculation.

Problem 3.1 Equations With One Operation

The riders visited Wild World and the tour is over. They put their bikes and gear into vans and head back to Atlantic City, 320 miles away. On their way back, they try to calculate how long the drive home will take. They use a table and a graph to estimate their travel time for different average speeds.

A. Copy and complete the table.

Distance Traveled at Different Average Speeds

Time (hr)	Distance for Speed of 50 mi/h	Distance for Speed of 55 mi/h	Distance for Speed of 60 mi/h
0	0	▦	▦
1	50	▦	▦
2	100	▦	▦
3	▦	▦	▦
4	▦	▦	▦
5	▦	▦	▦
6	▦	▦	▦

B. Copy and complete the graph for all three speeds below. Use a different color for each speed.

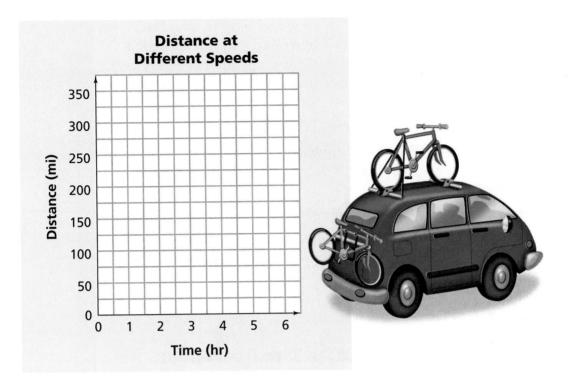

Distance at Different Speeds

C. Do the following for each of the three average speeds:

1. Look for patterns relating distance and time in the table and graph. Write a rule in words for calculating the distance traveled in any given time.

2. Write an equation for your rule, using letters to represent the variables.

3. Describe how the pattern of change shows up in the table, graph, and equation.

D. For each speed, (50, 55, and 60 mph) tell how far you would travel in the given time. Explain how you can find each answer by using the table, the graph, and the equation.

1. 3 hours　　　　**2.** $4\frac{1}{2}$ hours　　　　**3.** $5\frac{1}{4}$ hours

E. For each speed, find how much time it will take the students to reach these cities on their route:

1. Atlantic City, New Jersey, about 320 miles from Norfolk

2. Baltimore, Maryland, about $\frac{3}{4}$ of the way from Norfolk to Atlantic City

ACE Homework starts on page 55.

3.2 Writing More Equations

The equations you wrote in Problem 3.1 involved only multiplication. Some equations involve two or more arithmetic operations $(+, -, \times, \div)$. To write such equations, you can reason just as you do when you write one-operation equations:

Determine what the variables are.

Work out some specific numeric examples and examine them carefully. What patterns do you see? What is the role of each variable in the calculation?

Write a rule in words to describe the general pattern in the calculations.

Convert your rule to an equation with letter variables and symbols.

Think about whether your equation makes sense. Test it for a few values to see if it works.

Problem 3.2 Equations With Two Operations

When Liz tells Theo about the idea to visit Wild World, he suggests she check to see whether the park offers special prices for large groups. She finds this information on the park's Web site:

A. 1. Find the price of admission for a group of 20 people, a group of 35 people, and a group of 42 people.

    2. Describe in words how you can calculate the admission price for a group with any number of people.

3. Write an equation for the admission price p for a group of n people.

4. Sketch a graph to show the admission price for a group of any size.

5. How does the pattern of change show up in the equation and graph? How is this pattern similar to the pattern in Problem 3.1? How is it different?

B. Admission to Wild World includes a bonus card with 100 points that can be spent on rides. Rides cost 6 points each.

1. Copy and complete the table below to show a customer's bonus card balance after each ride. Pay close attention to the values in the Number of Rides row.

Bonus Card Balance

Number of Rides	0	1	2	3	5	7	10	13	16
Points on Card	100	▨	▨	▨	▨	▨	▨	▨	▨

2. Describe in words how you can calculate the number of points left after any number of rides.

3. Write an equation showing the relation between the number of rides and the points left on the bonus card. Use letters to represent the variables.

4. Sketch a graph of the data.

5. How does the pattern of change between the variables show up in the equation and graph? How is this pattern similar to the pattern in Question A? How is it different?

C. Liz wonders whether they should rent a golf cart to carry the riders' backpacks at the park. The equation $c = 20 + 5h$ shows the cost c in dollars of renting a cart for h hours:

1. Explain what information the numbers and variables in the equation represent.

2. Use the equation to make a table for the cost of renting a cart for 1, 2, 3, 4, 5, and 6 hours.

3. Make a graph of the data.

4. Describe how the pattern of change between the two variables shows up in the table, graph, and equation.

ACE Homework starts on page 55.

3.3 Paying Bills and Counting Profits

The students think that $350 is a fair price to charge for the tour. Sidney wants to be certain Ocean Bike Tours will make a profit if they charge $350. She starts making the table below.

Tour Revenue and Expenses

Number of Customers	Revenue	Bike Rental	Food and Camp Costs	Total Expenses	Profit
1	$350	$30	$ 125		
2	$700	$60	$250		
3	$1,050	$90	$375		

Problem 3.3 Equations for Revenue, Expenses, and Profit

A. Extend and complete Sidney's table for 1 to 6 customers.

B. Write a rule in words and an equation for calculating the

   1. revenue r for n customers

   2. total expenses e for n customers

   3. profit p for n customers

C. Use the equations you wrote in Question B to find the revenue, expenses, and profit for 20 customers and for 31 customers.

D. Sidney forgot that the tour operators need to rent a van to carry equipment. The rental cost for the van will be $700.

   1. How does this expense affect the equation for total expenses?

   2. How does this expense affect the equation for profit?

ACE Homework starts on page 55.

Applications

1. The El Paso Middle School girls' basketball team is going from El Paso to San Antonio for the Texas state championship game. The trip will be 560 miles. Their bus travels at an average speed of 60 miles per hour.

   a. Suppose the bus travels at an almost steady speed throughout the trip. Make a table and a graph of time and distance data for the bus.

   b. Estimate the distance the bus travels in 2 hours, $2\frac{3}{4}$ hours, $3\frac{1}{2}$ hours, and 7.25 hours.

   c. How are 2 hours and the distance traveled in 2 hours represented in the table? How are they shown on the graph?

   d. How are $2\frac{3}{4}$ hours and the distance traveled in $2\frac{3}{4}$ hours represented in the table? How are they shown on the graph?

   e. Describe in words a rule you can use to calculate the distance traveled for any given time on this trip.

   f. The bus route passes through Sierra Blanca, which is 90 miles from El Paso. About how long does it take the bus to get to Sierra Blanca?

   g. The bus route also passes through Balmorhea, which is $\frac{1}{3}$ of the way from El Paso to San Antonio. About how long does it take the bus to get to Balmorhea?

   h. How long does it take the bus to complete its 560-mile trip to San Antonio?

2. Celia writes the equation $d = 8t$ to represent the distance in miles d that bikers could travel in t hours at a speed of 8 miles per hour.

   a. Make a table that shows the distance traveled every half hour, up to 5 hours, if bikers ride at this constant speed.

   b. How far would bikers travel in 1 hour, 6 hours, 8.5 hours, and 10 hours?

3. The equation $d = 70t$ represents the distance in miles covered after traveling at 70 miles per hour for t hours.

   a. Make a table that shows the distance traveled every half hour from 0 hours to 4 hours.

   b. Sketch a coordinate graph that shows the distance traveled between 0 and 4 hours.

   c. What is d when $t = 2.5$ hours?

   d. What is t when $d = 210$ miles?

   e. You probably made your graph by plotting points. In this situation, would it make sense to connect these points?

4. a. Use the table to write an equation that relates lunch cost L and number of riders n.

Bike Tour Box Lunch Costs

Riders	1	2	3	4	5	6	7	8	9
Lunch Cost	$4.25	$8.50	$12.75	$17.00	$21.25	$25.50	$29.75	$34.00	$38.25

   b. Use your equation to find the lunch cost for 25 riders.

   c. How many riders could eat lunch for $89.25?

For Exercises 5–7, use the equation to complete the table.

5. $y = 4x + 3$

x	1	2	5	10	20
y	▪	▪	▪	▪	▪

6. $m = 100 - k$

k	1	2	5	10	20
m	▪	▪	▪	▪	▪

7. $d = 3.5t$

t	1	2	5	10	20
d	▪	▪	▪	▪	▪

8. Sean is buying a new DVD player and speakers for $315. The store offers him an interest-free payment plan that allows him to pay in monthly installments of $25.

   a. How much will Sean still owe after one payment? After two payments? After three payments?

   b. Use *n* to stand for the number of payments and *a* for the amount still owed. Write an equation for calculating *a* for any value of *n*.

   c. Use your equation to make a table and a graph showing the relationship between *n* and *a*.

   d. As *n* increases by 1, how does *a* change? How is this change shown in the table? How is it shown on the graph?

   e. How many payments will Sean have to make in all? How is this shown in the table? How is this shown on the graph?

For Exercises 9–12, express each rule as an equation. Use single letters to stand for the variables. Identify what each letter represents.

9. The area of a rectangle is its length multiplied by its width.

10. The number of hot dogs needed for the picnic is two for each student.

11. The amount of material needed to make the curtains is 4 square yards per window.

12. Taxi fare is $2.00 plus $1.10 per mile.

13. The sales tax in a state is 8%. Write an equation for the amount of tax *t* on an item that costs *p* dollars.

14. An airplane is traveling at 550 miles per hour. Write an equation for the distance *d* the plane travels in *h* hours.

15. Potatoes sell for $0.25 per pound at the produce market. Write an equation for the cost *c* of *p* pounds of potatoes.

16. A cellular family phone plan costs $49 per month plus $0.05 per minute of long-distance service. Write an equation for the monthly bill *b* when *m* minutes of long-distance service are used.

For Exercises 17–19, describe the relationship between the variables in words and with an equation.

17.

x	1	2	5	10	20
y	4	8	20	40	80

Homework Help Online
PHSchool.com
For: Help with Exercise 17
Web Code: ane-1317

18.

s	1	2	3	6	12
t	49	48	47	44	38

19.

n	1	2	3	4	5
z	6	11	16	21	26

20. Multiple Choice Which equation describes the relationship in the table?

n	0	1	2	3	4	5	6
C	10	20	30	40	50	60	70

A. $C = 10n$ **B.** $C = 10 + n$ **C.** $C = 10$ **D.** $C = 10 + 10n$

Connections

21. The perimeter P of a square is related to the side length s by the formula $P = 4s$. The area, A, is related to the side length by the formula $A = s \times s$, or $A = s^2$.

a. Make a table showing how the perimeter of a square increases as the side length increases from 1 to 6 in 1-unit steps. Describe the pattern of change.

b. Make a table showing how the area of a square increases as the side length increases from 1 to 6. Describe the pattern of change.

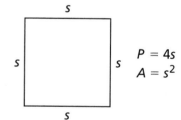

$P = 4s$
$A = s^2$

For Exercises 22–27, find the indicated value or values.

22. the mean, or average, of 4.5 and 7.3

23. the area of a circle with radius 6 centimeters

24. the sum of the angle measures in a triangle, in a parallelogram, in a pentagon, and in a hexagon

Go Online
PHSchool.com
For: Multiple-Choice Skills Practice
Web Code: ana-1354

25. the 10th odd number (1 is the first odd number, 3 is the second odd number, and so on.)

26. the area of a triangle with a base of 10 centimeters and a height of 15 centimeters

27. $3^3 \times 5^2 \times 7$

28. The wheels on Kai's bike are 27 inches in diameter. His little sister, Masako, has a bike with wheels that are 20 inches in diameter. Kai and Masako are on a bike ride.

   a. How far does Kai go in one complete turn of his wheels?

   b. How far does Masako go in one complete turn of her wheels?

   c. How far does Kai go in 500 turns of his wheels?

   d. How far does Masako go in 500 turns of her wheels?

   e. How many times do Kai's wheels have to turn to cover 100 feet?

   f. How many times do Masako's wheels have to turn to cover 100 feet? To cover 1 mile?

29. Bicycles that were popular in the 1890s were called "penny farthing" bicycles. These bikes had front wheels with diameters as great as 5 feet! Suppose the front wheel of these bicycles have a diameter of 5 feet.

   a. What is the radius of the front wheel?

   b. How far will one bike travel in 100 turns of the front wheel?

   c. How many times will the front wheel turn in a 3-mile trip?

   d. Compare the number of times the wheels of Masako's bike turn in a 1-mile trip [see part (f) of Exercise 28] with the number of times the front wheel of this penny-farthing bike turns in a 3-mile trip. Why are the numbers related this way?

Write a formula for the given quantity.

30. the area A of a rectangle with length ℓ and width w

31. the area A of a parallelogram with base b and height h

32. the perimeter P of a rectangle with base b and height h

33. the mean m of two numbers p and q

34. the area A of a circle with radius r

35. the sum S of the measures of angles in a polygon of n sides

36. the nth odd number, O (1 is the first odd number, 3 is the second odd number, and so on.)

37. the area A of a triangle with base b and height h

Complete the table of values for the given equation.

38. $y = x + \frac{1}{2}$

x	$\frac{1}{5}$	$\frac{1}{4}$	$\frac{1}{3}$	$\frac{2}{5}$	$\frac{1}{2}$	$\frac{2}{3}$	$\frac{3}{4}$	5
y	■	■	■	■	■	■	■	■

39. $y = \left(\frac{1}{2}\right)x$

x	$\frac{1}{5}$	$\frac{1}{4}$	$\frac{1}{3}$	$\frac{2}{5}$	$\frac{1}{2}$	$\frac{2}{3}$	$\frac{3}{4}$	5
y	■	■	■	■	■	■	■	■

Describe the relationship between x and y in words.

40.

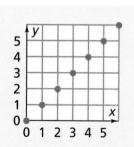

41.

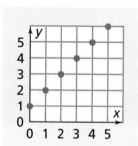

42.

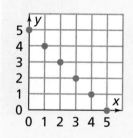

Extensions

43. a. You can calculate the average speed of a car trip if you know the distance and time traveled. Copy and complete the table below.

Car Trips

Distance (mi)	Time (hr)	Average Speed (mi/h)
145	2	■
110	2	■
165	2.5	■
300	5.25	■
446	6.75	■
528	8	■
862	9.5	■
723	10	■

   b. Write a formula for calculating the average speed s for any given distance d and time t.

For Exercises 44–47, solve each problem by estimating and checking.

44. The equation $p = 50 + 10n$ gives the admission price p to Wild World for a group of n people. A club's budget has $500 set aside for a visit to the park. How many club members can go?

45. The equation $b = 100 - 6r$ gives the number of bonus points b left on a Wild World bonus card after r rides.

   a. Rosi has 34 points left. How many rides has she been on?

   b. Dwight has 16 points left. How many rides has he been on?

46. The equation $d = 2.5t$ describes the distance in meters d covered by a canoe-racing team in t seconds. How long does it take the team to go 125 meters? How long does it take them to go 400 meters?

47. The equation $d = 400 - 2.5t$ describes the distance in meters d of a canoe-racing team from the finish line t seconds after a race starts. When is the team 175 meters from the finish line? When is it 100 meters from the finish line?

48. Armen builds models from rods. When he builds bridges, he makes the sides using patterns of triangles like the ones below. The total number of rods depends on the number of rods along the bottom.

Rods along bottom = 3
Total number of rods = 11

Rods along bottom = 4
Total number of rods = 15

a. Copy and complete the table.

Rod Bridges

Rods Along the Bottom	1	2	3	4	5	6	7	8	9	10
Total Number of Rods	3	7	11	▪	▪	▪	▪	▪	▪	▪

b. Write an equation relating the total number of rods t to the number of rods along the bottom b. Explain how the formula you write relates to the way Armen puts the rods together.

c. What do you know about the properties of triangles and rectangles that makes the design above better than the one below?

49. The students in Problem 3.3 decide to visit Wild World Amusement Park on the tour. They include the cost of this and the van in their revenue and expenses. How does this affect the equation for profit?

Mathematical Reflections 3

In this investigation, you wrote equations to express relationships between variables. The following questions will help you summarize what you have learned.

Think about your answers to these questions. Discuss your ideas with other students and your teacher. Then write a summary of your findings in your notebook.

1. What decisions do you need to make when you write an equation to represent a relationship between variables?

2. In what ways are equations useful?

3. In this unit, you have represented relationships with tables, graphs, and equations. List some advantages and disadvantages of each of these representations.

Calculator Tables and Graphs

In the last investigation, you wrote equations to describe patterns and to show how variables are related. Such equations are used in mathematics, science, economics, and many other subject areas. Tables, graphs, and equations are all useful ways of representing relationships between variables. When you have an equation relating variables, you can use a *graphing calculator* to make a graph or table of the relationship quickly.

4.1 Making and Using Calculator Tables

Suppose you want to use your calculator to make a table of values for the formulas for the circumference C and area A of a circle with radius r:

$$C = 2\pi r \text{ and } A = \pi r^2.$$

To enter the equations into your calculator, press $\boxed{Y=}$ to get a screen like the one below.

```
Plot1 Plot2 Plot3
\Y1 =▮
\Y2 =
\Y3 =
\Y4 =
\Y5 =
\Y6 =
\Y7 =
```

On most calculators, you enter the independent variable as X; the dependent variable is Y. Enter the equation for circumference as Y1 and the equation for area as Y2 as shown below.

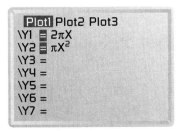

Next, press **2nd** **TblSet** and enter the table settings shown below. The settings indicate that the *x*-values (radius values) in the table should start at 0 and increase in steps of 1.

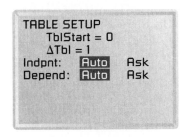

Press **2nd** **TABLE**, and you will see the table.

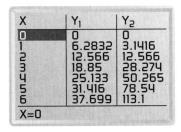

You can use the scroll keys to see more values for radius, circumference, and area.

Getting Ready for Problem

- What does the number 28.274 in the third column mean?
- What does 25.133 in the second column mean?
- What does 5 in the first column mean?

In the following problem, you will use calculator tables to explore relationships between variables. You will scan the tables to solve problems or look for interesting patterns in the entries.

Problem 4.1 Making and Using Calculator Tables

A. The equation $p = 50 + 10n$ represents the Wild World admission price in dollars p for a group of n people. To study this relationship, enter the equation Y1 = 50 + 10X into your calculator.

1. Make a calculator table showing (n, p) values for $n = 1, 2, 3$, and so on.

2. Scan the table to find the admission price for a group of 26 people.

3. Find the value of n for which $p = 480$. Explain what this entry tells you about the admission price and the number of people.

4. Use the table to find the value of n for which $950 = 50 + 10n$. Explain what this table entry tells you about the admission price and the number of people.

B. The equation $d = 2.5t$ represents the distance a canoe team paddles in meters d in t seconds.

1. Make a calculator table showing (t, d) values for $t = 4, 8, 12$, and so on.

2. Use the table to find the distance the team paddles in 40 seconds.

3. Use the table to find the value of t for which $2.5t = 437.5$. Explain what this entry tells you about the time and distance traveled.

C. The equation $b = 100 - 6r$ gives the number of bonus points b left on a Wild World bonus card after r rides.

1. Make a calculator table showing (r, b) values for $r = 0, 2, 4$, and so on.

2. How does the number of bonus points change as the number of rides increases in steps of 2? Why does that pattern occur?

3. Use your table to find a value of r for which $100 - 6r = 10$. (Adjust the table settings if you need to.) Explain what this entry tells you about the number of rides and the bonus points left on the card.

ACE Homework starts on page 72.

Graphing calculators can help you make and study graphs. Just as when you make a graph with pencil and paper, the key step is choosing ranges and scales for the axes.

Suppose you want to graph $y = 1.5x + 2$. Press **Y=** and enter the equation, just as you do when you make a table. Next, set the boundaries of the graphing window. Press **WINDOW** to see the screen below. The settings shown here are the *standard* window settings.

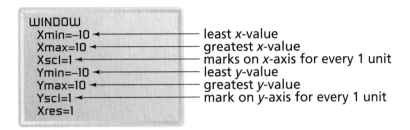

Press **GRAPH** to see what the graph looks like in this window.

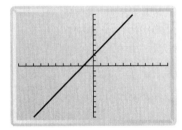

Suppose you want to focus on the part of the graph that shows positive *x*- and *y*-values. Press **WINDOW** again and change the settings. Use the settings shown below at the left. Then press **GRAPH** to see the screen on the right.

 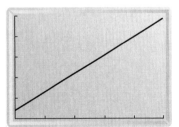

To find coordinates of particular points on the graph, press TRACE . Use the arrow keys to move the cursor along the graph and see coordinates of highlighted points.

When the cusor is on the line, the coordinates appear at the bottom of the screen and the equation appears in the upper left.

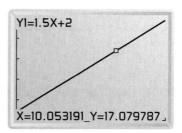

Y1=1.5X+2

X=10.053191_Y=17.079787

Getting Ready for Problem 4.2

Experiment with your graphing calculator and the following equations. Graph one set of equations at a time. Use the standard window.

Set 1
$y = 3x - 4$
$y = x^2$
$y = 3x + 2$

Set 2
$y = 5$
$y = 3x$
$y = 1x$

Set 3
$y = 2x + 3$
$y = 2x - 5$
$y = (0.5)x + 2$

Set 4
$y = 2x$
$y = 2 \div x$
$y = 2^x$

Answer the following questions for each set of equations.

- Which, if any, of the graphs show similar patterns of change? How are the graphs similar? How are the equations for the graphs similar?

- How are the graphs different? How are the equations for the graphs different?

Problem 4.2 Making and Using Calculator Graphs

A. One popular attraction at Wild World is the climbing wall. Supports for the wall are frames of squares made from steel rods. The number of rods depends on the number of square sections in the frame.

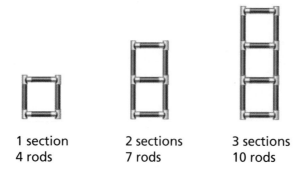

1 section
4 rods

2 sections
7 rods

3 sections
10 rods

1. An engineer at Wild World wrote the equation $r = 3s + 1$ to relate the number of sections and the number of rods. Do you think this formula is correct? Explain. What does each variable in the equation represent?

2. Use your calculator to graph the engineer's equation. Use the window settings Xmin = 0, Xmax = 15, Ymin = 0, and Ymax = 50. Sketch your graph on axes like these. Give your graph a title.

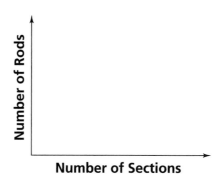

3. Press **TRACE** and use the arrow keys to move along the graph. Locate a point with a *y*-value of about 19. Mark this point on your sketch and label it with its coordinates. Then, find a point with a *y*-value of about 43. Mark and label this point on your sketch.

4. Explain what the coordinates of each point in part (3) tell you about the number of sections and the number of rods.

5. Use your calculator graph to find a value of *s* for which $3s + 1 = 28$. Give the coordinates of that point, and explain what they tell you about sections and rods.

B. Make a calculator graph of $b = 100 - 6r$, which gives the bonus card balance *b* after *r* rides. Experiment with the window settings until you have a good view of the graph. (You might find it helpful to look at the table you made in Problem 4.1.)

1. Make a sketch of the graph. Label the axes with variable names and scales. Add a descriptive title to your graph.

2. Find a point on the calculator graph for which $b \approx 58$. (The symbol $\approx$ means "is approximately equal to.") Mark this point on your sketch and label it with its coordinates. Explain what the coordinates tell you about the number of rides taken and the balance on the card.

3. Use your calculator graph to find a value of *r* for which $100 - 6r \approx 22$. Give the coordinates of that point and explain what they tell you about the rides taken and the card balance.

ACE Homework starts on page 72.

The bike tour was a success! So many people signed up for the tour that the students decide to offer an additional two-day bike tour. Two bike rental companies submit bids to the students. Their price quotes are shown here.

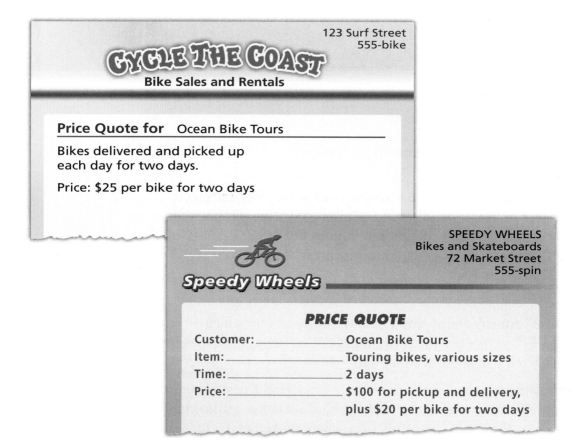

In the next problem, you will use your graphing calculator to analyze the price quotes and advise Ocean Bike Tours about which company to use.

Study the price quotes from the two companies. The following questions will help you analyze the information.

A. Make a table showing the costs for renting bikes from each company. Include costs for 5, 10, 15, 20, 25, 30, 35, and 40 bikes in your table.

B. Plot the (*number of bikes, rental cost*) data for both companies on a graph like the one below. Use a different color or plotting symbol for each company.

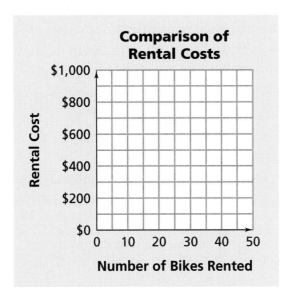

C. For each company, write an equation relating the number of bikes rented to the total cost. Tell what the letter variables in your equation represent.

D. Enter your equations into your calculator as Y1 and Y2. Graph both equations in the same window. Compare the calculator graph with the graph you made by hand.

E. Is there a number of bikes for which both companies charge the same rental fee? How can the graph help you find the answer?

F. How does the graph show the number of bikes for which Cycle the Coast is the most economical? How does it show the number of bikes for which Speedy Wheels offers the better deal?

G. What advice would you give Ocean Bike Tours about which company to rent bikes from? Use your analysis of the two plans to justify your advice.

ACE Homework starts on page 72.

Applications

1. Sean bought a DVD player and a receiver. The store offered him an interest-free payment plan with weekly installments. Sean figured out that after n weeks of payments, he would still owe $175 - 7.5n$ dollars.

   a. Make a calculator table showing what Sean owes after payments 1, 2, 3, and so on. Study the table to figure out the amount of his weekly payment. How is this amount shown in the table pattern?

   b. Scan the table to find out how much Sean will owe after 20 weeks. Record the (x, y) table entry that shows the answer.

   c. When will the amount Sean owes fall below $100? Which (x, y) table entry shows the answer to this question?

   d. When will Sean have paid for his items in full? How is this shown in the table?

2. Trevor entered an equation into his graphing calculator, and the calculator displayed this graph and table. The graph is shown in the standard window.

   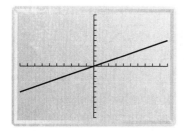

X	Y₁
0	0
1	.5
2	1
3	1.5
4	2
5	2.5
6	3
X=0	

   a. What is the value of y when $x = 6$? How is this shown in the table? How is it shown in the graph?

   b. What equation did Trevor enter into his calculator?

3. Ziamara used her calculator to make a graph of $y = 3x$. She noticed that the point $(0, 0)$ was on the graph. Name three other points on the graph. Explain how you found these points.

   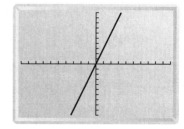

4. The operators of Ocean Bike Tours consider leasing a small bus. They compare two companies. Superior Buses charges $5 for each mile driven. East Coast Transport charges $1,000, plus $2.50 per mile driven.

   a. For each company, write an equation to show how the lease cost c depends on number of miles driven m.

   b. Enter both equations into your calculator. Choose window settings that make sense for this situation and that show a good view of both graphs. Sketch the graphs, and tell what axes limits (Xmin, Xmax, Ymin, Ymax) you used.

   c. Press TRACE. Trace your graph to estimate the coordinates of the point at which the lease cost is the same for both companies. Explain what the coordinates of the point tell you about the bus-rental situation.

   d. For what driving mileage would the East Coast lease be a better deal? For what mileage would the Superior Buses lease be better? Explain how your answers are shown on the graph from part (b).

5. The Mudville Manatees won the league baseball championship. The manager of the souvenir shop wants to order special shirts and caps to sell to fans. She does market research and predicts these relationships between price in dollars p and number sold n:

   Shirts: $n = 5{,}000 - 150p$

   Caps: $n = 3{,}000 - 100p$

   Use these equations to answer the questions below. Making calculator tables and graphs might help.

   a. What are the projected shirt sales if the price is $20 per shirt?

   b. Suppose the manager wants to sell 3,500 shirts. How much should she charge for each shirt?

   c. What are the projected cap sales if the price is $17 per cap?

   d. Suppose the manager wants to sell 1,800 caps. How much should she charge for each cap?

6. The principal of Lincoln Middle School wants to send her top science students on a field trip to the state science center. The trip costs $250 for a bus and driver, plus $17.50 per student for food and admission.

   a. What equation relates the trip cost *c* to the number of students who go on the trip *n*?

   b. What is the cost of sending 30 students? What is the cost for 60 students?

   c. How many students can go if the budget allows a maximum cost of $1,000?

Connections

For Exercises 7–10, use the pattern to find the missing entries. Then, write an equation relating the two variables.

7.

a	0	1	2	3	▦	8	20	100
b	0	7	14	21	28	▦	▦	▦

8.

x	0	1	2	3	4	8	20	100
y	6	7	8	9	▦	▦	▦	▦

9.

m	0	1	2	3	4	8	20	100
n	1	3	5	7	▦	▦	▦	▦

10.

r	0	1	2	3	4	6	10	20
s	0	1	4	9	16	▦	▦	▦

11. José used his graphing calculator to find the whole-number factors of 960. Here are the steps he followed:

   Step 1: Enter the equation $y = 960 \div x$.
   Step 2: Set TblStart = 1 and ΔTbl = 1.
   Step 3: Scan the table, looking for whole numbers in the *y* column.

   a. Use José's strategy. Make a list of the factor pairs for 960.

   b. Explain why José's strategy works for 960. How could you modify his strategy to find factors of a different whole number?

   c. What is the greatest *x*-value you need to check to guarantee you have found all the factors of 960? Explain.

12. Most states add sales tax to the cost of non-food items. Let p stand for the list price of an item, t for the additional amount you must pay due to the sales tax, and c for the total cost of buying the item.

   a. What equation relates c, p, and t?

   b. Suppose a state has a sales tax of 8%. What equation relates t and p? What equation relates c and p?

   c. Enter the equations from part (b) in your calculator. Make a calculator table showing list price, tax, and total cost for items priced from $0 to $100 in steps of $5.

   d. What is the total cost of a non-food item that is priced $65?

13. You have seen that many of the costs for the Ocean Bike Tour depend on the number of customers. This table shows a new relationship between the number of customers and the cost of a ferry ride.

Costs for Ferry Ride

Customers	1	2	3	4	5	6	7	8	9
Ferry Cost	$2.50	$5.00	$7.50	$10.00	$12.50	$15.00	$17.50	$20.00	$22.50

   a. Write an equation for the rule relating ferry cost f and number of customers n.

   b. Use your equation to find the cost if 35 people are on the tour.

   c. How many people can go on the ferry if the tour leader has $75?

14. Look back at Exercise 12 in Investigation 1. The first graph shown is the relationship between Amanda's hunger and the time of day. Could you represent this relationship in a table? Could you represent this relationship with an equation? Explain.

15. You know from your work with polygons that one way to find the sum of the interior angles of a polygon is to divide the shape into triangles by drawing diagonals from one of the vertices, as shown below.

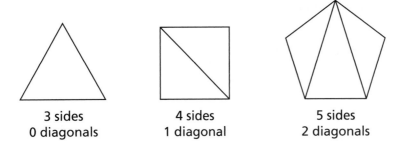

3 sides
0 diagonals

4 sides
1 diagonal

5 sides
2 diagonals

a. Copy and complete the table below. The last row should contain formulas for *D*, *S*, and *A* for a regular polygon with *n* sides. (Remember that a *regular polygon* is a polygon in which all sides are the same length and all angles are the same size.)

Regular Polygons

Number of Sides, *n*	Number of Diagonals, *D* (from a single vertex)	Sum of Interior Angles, *S*	Size of Each Angle if Polygon is Regular, *A*
3	0	180°	60°
4	▨	▨	▨
5	▨	▨	▨
6	▨	▨	▨
⋮	⋮	⋮	⋮
n	*D* = ▨	*S* = ▨	*A* = ▨

b. Enter your formula for *D* into your calculator. Use a table or graph to find the number of sides a polygon must have if you can draw exactly 10 diagonals from a single vertex.

c. Enter your formula for *S* into your calculator. Use a table or graph to find the sum of the angles for a polygon with 10 sides.

d. Enter your formula for *A* into your calculator. Using a table or graph, look at the *A* values for polygons with up to 20 sides. Identify (by giving the number of sides) all regular polygons that have whole number interior angle measures.

16. The area, A, of a circle is related to the radius, r, by the equation $A = \pi r^2$. Enter this formula into your calculator. Use a calculator graph or table to estimate the answers to the questions below. Make your estimates correct to the nearest tenth.

a. What is the radius of a circle that has area 144 square inches (1 square foot)?

b. What is the radius of a circle that has area 9 square feet (1 square yard)?

Extensions

17. In this unit, you have studied a variety of relationships between variables. The equations below are simple cases of three important types of patterns of change.

$$y_1 = 2x \qquad\qquad y_2 = x^2 \qquad\qquad y_3 = \frac{3}{x}$$

a. For each equation, make a table of (x, y) values for $x = 0, 1, 2, 3$, and so on. Describe the pattern of change in each table by completing this sentence:

As the value of x *increases, the value of* y _____.

Be as precise as you can in describing the patterns. Then, compare each individual pattern of change with the others.

b. Graph the three equations in the same viewing window, with Xmin = 0, Xmax = 5, Ymin = 0, and Ymax = 15. Describe the patterns of change shown by the graphs. Explain how each pattern can be predicted by thinking about the calculations required to find y from x.

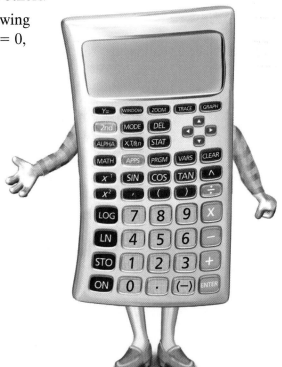

18. You can use your graphing calculator to simulate probability experiments that involve rolling dice or flipping coins.

a. Press [Y=].

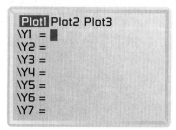

Then, press [MATH], highlight PRB on the top of the screen, and press 5 to select "randInt(."

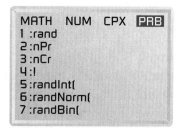

You will be back to the Y= screen. Complete the equation by typing 0 [,] 1 [)].

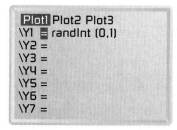

The equation $y = \text{randInt}(0, 1)$ randomly gives a y-value of either 0 or 1, no matter what the x-value is. Consider 0 to mean "heads" and 1 to mean "tails."

Press [2nd] [TblSet] and specify TblStart = 1 and $\triangle$Tb = 1. Then press [2nd] [TABLE]. The X column counts the coin tosses, and the Y1 column tells you whether the result is heads (0) or tails (1).

Copy and complete the table below.

Graphing Calculator Coin Tossing

Number of Tosses	5	10	20	30	40	50
Number of Heads	▨	▨	▨	▨	▨	▨
Fraction of Heads	▨	▨	▨	▨	▨	▨
Fraction of Tails	▨	▨	▨	▨	▨	▨

Describe patterns in the results. Are the results what you would expect? Explain.

b. Revise the procedures of part (a) to simulate rolling a fair die 50 times. Calculate the number of times and fraction of times the outcome 1 occurs in the 50 rolls. Are the results what you would expect? Explain. (**Hint:** The equation $y = \text{randInt}(3, 5)$ randomly gives a y-value of 3, 4, or 5. The equation $y = \text{randInt}(13, 17)$ randomly gives a y-value of 13, 14, 15, 16, or 17. What equation would give random dice rolls?)

19. The bike tour holds a 30-mile race on the last day. They give the two youngest riders, Tony and Sarah, a half-hour head start. For this first half hour, Tony and Sarah ride at a steady pace of 12 miles per hour. Then, they keep up a steady pace of about 10 miles per hour. When the others start riding, they go at a steady pace of about 15 miles per hour.

a. Write an equation for the distance d in miles Tony and Sarah travel in t hours.

b. Write an equation for the distance d in miles the other riders travel in t hours.

c. Use the equations from parts (a) and (b) to make a table and a graph showing the relationship between distance and time for the two groups of riders.

d. Will the older riders catch up with Tony and Sarah before the end of the 30-mile race? Explain using both the table and the graph.

Mathematical Reflections 4

In this investigation, you used a graphing calculator to help you understand relationships between variables. These questions will help you summarize what you have learned.

Think about your answers to these questions. Discuss your ideas with other students and your teacher. Then write a summary of your findings in your notebook.

1. a. Describe the steps required to make a calculator table that shows how two variables are related.

   b. How can you scan a calculator table to answer questions about a relationship?

2. a. Describe the steps required to make a calculator graph that shows how two variables are related.

   b. How can you trace a calculator graph to answer questions about a relationship?

3. What are the advantages and disadvantages of using tables and graphs to solve problems and search for patterns? In what ways is using a calculator more useful than using paper-and-pencil methods? In what ways is it less useful?

Looking Back and Looking Ahead

In this unit, you studied some basic ideas of algebra. You learned ways to use those ideas to solve problems about variables and the patterns relating variables. In particular, you studied how to

Go Online
PHSchool.com

For: Vocabulary Review Puzzle
Web Code: anj-1051

- recognize situations in which changes in variables are related in useful patterns
- describe patterns of change shown in tables and graphs of data
- construct tables and graphs to display relationships between variables
- use algebraic symbols to write equations relating variables
- use tables, graphs, and equations to solve problems
- use a graphing calculator to construct tables and graphs of relationships and to solve equations

Use Your Understanding: Algebraic Reasoning

To test your understanding of algebraic ideas and your skill in using algebraic techniques, consider how algebra is involved in a business we all depend on—the shipping of packages from town to town, across the country, and around the world.

1. A shipping company offers two-day shipping of any package weighing up to 2 pounds for $5 plus $0.01 per mile.

   a. Copy and complete the table.

   Two-Day Shipping Costs

Distance (mi)	100	200	300	400	500	1,000	1,500	2,000
Shipping Cost	■	■	■	■	■	■	■	■

   b. Describe the pattern by which the shipping cost increases as the shipping distance increases.

   c. Make a graph showing shipping charges for distances from 0 to 2,000 miles. Use appropriate labels and scales on the axes.

   d. Write an equation for the relationship between distance d in miles and shipping cost c in dollars.

   e. Use a graphing calculator and the equation in part (d) to check the graph you made in part (c).

   f. Use the table, graph, or equation to find the cost to ship a 1-pound package 450 miles.

   g. Use the table, graph, or equation to figure out how far you can ship a 2-pound package for $35.

Explain Your Reasoning

Answer the following questions in your own words to summarize what you know about variables and patterns.

2. What does the word *variable* mean in algebra?

3. What are *dependent* and *independent variables* and how are they usually related to each other in a problem situation?

4. Give examples that show at least two common patterns that occur in the values of related variables.

5. What are the main decisions and procedures involved in making a table to illustrate the relationship between two variables? How does a table help you describe and study a relationship?

6. What are the main decisions and procedures involved in making a graph to illustrate the relationship between two variables? How does a graph help you describe and study a relationship?

7. What are the main decisions and procedures involved in writing an equation to illustrate the relationship between two variables? How does an equation help you describe and study a relationship?

8. How can you use a graphing calculator to study relationships between variables? What do you need to know about a situation in order to use a calculator? How can the calculator be used to solve problems about variables and relationships?

Look Ahead

Your understanding of algebraic ideas and skills will grow as you work on future *Connected Mathematics* units. You will use variables and symbolic expressions in the geometry unit *Stretching and Shrinking,* the proportional-reasoning unit *Comparing and Scaling,* the algebra unit *Moving Straight Ahead,* and all units in the next *Connected Mathematics* course.

English / Spanish Glossary

C

change To become different. For example, temperatures rise and fall, prices increase and decrease, and so on. In mathematics, quantities that change are called *variables*.

cambiar Variar, volverse diferente. Por ejemplo, las temperaturas suben y bajan, los precios aumentan y se reducen, y así sucesivamente. En matemática, las cantidades que cambian se llaman *variables*.

coordinate graph A graphical representation of pairs of related numerical values that shows the relationship between two variables. It relates the independent variable (shown on the *x*-axis) and the dependent variable (shown on the *y*-axis).

gráfica de coordenadas Una representación gráfica de pares de valores numéricos asociados que muestra la relación existente entre dos variables. Dicha representación relaciona la variable independiente (mostrada en el eje de las *x*) y la variable dependiente (mostrada en el eje de las *y*).

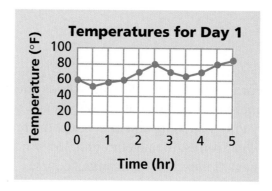

coordinate pair An ordered pair of numbers used to locate a point on a coordinate grid. The first number in a coordinate pair is the value for the *x*-coordinate, and the second number is the value for the *y*-coordinate. A coordinate pair for the graph shown above is (0, 60).

par de coordenadas Un par ordenado de números utilizado para localizar un punto en una cuadrícula de coordenadas. El primer número del par de coordenadas es el valor de la coordenada *x* y el segundo número es el valor de la coordenada *y*. Un par de coordenades para la gráfica que aparece abajo es (0, 60).

D

dependent variable One of the two variables in a relationship. Its value depends upon or is determined by the other variable called the *independent variable*. For example, the cost of a long-distance phone call (dependent variable) depends on how long you talk (independent variable).

variable dependiente Una de las dos variables en una relación. Su valor depende del valor de la otra variable llamada variable independiente, o está determinado por dicho valor. Por ejemplo, el costo de una llamada telefónica de larga distancia (variable dependiente) depende de la duración de la conversación (variable independiente).

E

equation, formula A rule containing variables that represents a mathematical relationship. An example is the formula for finding the area of a circle: $A = \pi r^2$.

ecuación, fórmula Una regla que contiene variables que representa una relación matemática. Un ejemplo de ello es la fórmula para hallar el área de un círculo: $A = \pi r^2$.

I

independent variable One of the two variables in a relationship. Its value determines the value of the other variable called the *dependent variable.* If you organize a bike tour, for example, the number of people who register to go (independent variable) determines the cost for renting bikes (dependent variable).

variable independiente Una de las dos variables relacionadas. Su valor determina el de la otra variable, llamada variable dependiente. Por ejemplo, si organizas un recorrido en bicicleta, el número de personas inscritas (variable independiente) determina el costo del alquiler de las bicicletas (variable dependiente).

P

pattern A change that occurs in a predictable way. For example, the squares on a checkerboard form a pattern in which the colors of the squares alternate between red and black. The sequence of square numbers: 1, 4, 9, 16, . . . forms a pattern in which the numbers increase by the next odd number. That is, 4 is 3 more than 1, 9 is 5 more than 4, 16 is 7 more than 9, and so on.

patrón Una variación que ocurre de manera predecible. Por ejemplo, los cuadrados del tablero de damas forman un patrón en el que los colores de los cuadrados se alternan. La secuencia de números cuadrados: 1, 4, 9, 16, . . . forma un patrón en el que los números aumentan según la cifra del siguiente número impar. Es decir, 4 es 3 más que 1, 9 es 5 más que 4, 16 es 7 más que 9, y así sucesivamente.

R

relationship An association between two or more variables. If one of the variables changes, the other variable may also change, and the change may be predictable.

relación Una asociación entre dos o más variables. Si una de las variables cambia, la otra variable también puede cambiar, y dicho cambio puede ser predecible.

rule A summary of a predictable relationship that tells how to find the value of a variable. A rule may be given in words or as an equation. For example, this rule relates time, rate, and distance: distance is equal to rate times time, or $d = rt$.

regla Un resumen de una relación predecible que indica cómo hallar el valor de una variable. Se trata de un patrón que, debido a su coherencia, puede escribirse, convertirse en una ecuación, representarse gráficamente o utilizarse para hacer una tabla. Por ejemplo, la siguiente regla relaciona tiempo, velocidad y distancia: la distancia es igual al producto de la velocidad y el tiempo, o sea $d = rt$.

S

scale A labeling scheme used on each of the axes on a coordinate grid.

escala Un esquema de rotulación empleado en los ejes de una cuadrícula de coordenadas.

T

table A list of values for two or more variables that shows the relationship between them. Tables often represent data made from observations, from experiments, or from a series of arithmetic operations. A table may show a pattern of change between two variables that can be used to predict values not in the table.

tabla Una lista de valores para dos o más variables que muestra la relación existente entre ellas. Frecuentemente, las tablas contienen datos provenientes de observaciones, experimentos o de una serie de operaciones aritméticas. Una tabla puede mostrar un patrón de variación existente entre dos variables, el cual puede utilizarse para predecir los valores de otras entradas de la tabla.

V

variable A quantity that can change. Letters are often used as symbols to represent variables in rules or equations that describe patterns.

variable Una cantidad que puede cambiar. Suelen usarse letras como símbolos para representar las variables de las reglas o ecuaciones que describen patrones.

x-axis The number line that is horizontal on a coordinate grid.

eje de las x La línea numérica horizontal en una cuadrícula de coordenadas.

y-axis The number line that is vertical on a coordinate grid.

eje de las y La línea numérica vertical en una cuadrícula de coordenadas.

Index

Acknowledgments

Team Credits

The people who made up the **Connected Mathematics 2** team—representing editorial, editorial services, design services, and production services—are listed below. Bold type denotes core team members.

Leora Adler, Judith Buice, Kerry Cashman, Patrick Culleton, Sheila DeFazio, Katie Hallahan, Richard Heater, **Barbara Hollingdale, Jayne Holman,** Karen Holtzman, **Etta Jacobs,** Christine Lee, Carolyn Lock, Catherine Maglio, **Dotti Marshall,** Rich McMahon, Eve Melnechuk, Kristin Mingrone, Terri Mitchell, **Marsha Novak,** Irene Rubin, Donna Russo, Robin Samper, Siri Schwartzman, **Nancy Smith,** Emily Soltanoff, **Mark Tricca,** Paula Vergith, Roberta Warshaw, Helen Young

Additional Credits

Diana Bonfilio, Mairead Reddin, Michael Torocsik, nSight, Inc.

Technical Illustration

WestWords, Inc.

Cover Design

tom white.images

Photo

2 t, David Maenza/SuperStock; **2 b,** SuperStock/PictureQuest; **3,** Peter Griffith/Masterfile; **5,** Michael Kevin Daly/Corbis; **7,** RubberBall Productions/Index Stock Imagery, Inc.; **12,** Medford Taylor/SuperStock; **13,** Marcio Jose/AP/Wide World Photos; **17,** Michael Newman/PhotoEdit; **18,** Roy Ooms/Masterfile; **25,** Big Cheese Photo/SuperStock; **26 l,** David Maenza/SuperStock; **26 r,** Free Agents Limited/Corbis; **28,** Tom Stewart/Corbis; **30,** Brian Bailey/Getty Images, Inc.; **32,** Kindra Clineff/Index Stock Imagery, Inc.; **34,** Chris Trotman/Corbis; **35,** Michael Kooren/Corbis; **41,** Wilson Goodrich/Index Stock Imagery, Inc.; **43,** Chris Cole/Corbis; **46,** Paul Barton/Corbis; **49,** Jeff Greenberg/AGE Fotostock; **55,** BERNSTEIN KEITH-FSP/GAMMA; **59,** Rob Walls/Alamy; 64, Michael Newman/PhotoEdit; **66,** SuperStock/PictureQuest; **75,** Kevin Fleming/Corbis; **79,** Bill Bachman/Photo Researchers, Inc.

Acknowledgments

Connected Mathematics 2™

Stretching and Shrinking

Understanding Similarity

$$\frac{10}{8} = \frac{5}{4}$$

Glenda Lappan
James T. Fey
William M. Fitzgerald
Susan N. Friel
Elizabeth Difanis Phillips

PEARSON

Prentice
Hall

Boston, Massachusetts
Upper Saddle River, New Jersey

Stretching and Shrinking

Understanding Similarity

A teacher in disguise will appear for a few minutes at school each day for a week. The student who guesses the identity of the mystery teacher wins a prize. How might a photograph help in identifying the teacher?

A good map is similar to the place it represents. You can use a map to find actual distances of any place in the world. How can you estimate the distance from Cape Town, South Africa to Port Elizabeth, South Africa?

Here is a picture of Duke, a real dog. If you know the scale factor from Duke to the picture, how can you determine how long Duke is from his nose to the tip of his tail?

You probably use the word *similar* quite a bit in everyday conversation. For example, you might say that one song sounds similar to another song or that your friend's bike is similar to yours.

In many cases, you might use the word similar to describe objects and images that are the same shape but not the same size. A floor plan of a house is the same shape as the actual floor, but it is much smaller. The images on a movie screen are the same shape as the real people and objects they depict, but they are much larger.

You can order your school portrait in a variety of sizes, but your face will have the same shape in each photo.

In this unit, you will learn what it means for two shapes to be mathematically similar. The ideas you learn can help you answer questions like those on the previous page.

Mathematical Highlights

Understanding Similarity

In *Stretching and Shrinking*, you will learn the mathematical meaning of similarity and explore the properties of similar figures.

You will learn how to

- Identify similar figures by comparing corresponding parts
- Use scale factors and ratios to describe relationships among the side lengths of similar figures
- Construct similar polygons
- Draw shapes on coordinate grids and then use coordinate rules to stretch and shrink those shapes
- Predict the ways that stretching or shrinking a figure affects lengths, angle measures, perimeters, and areas
- Use the properties of similarity to find distances and heights that you can't measure

As you work on the problems in this unit, make it a habit to ask yourself questions about situations that involve similar figures:

What is the same and what is different about two similar figures?

What determines whether two shapes are similar?

When figures are similar, how are the lengths, areas, and scale factor related?

How can I use information about similar figures to solve a problem?

Investigation 1

Enlarging and Reducing Shapes

In this investigation, you will explore how some properties of a shape change when the shape is enlarged or reduced.

1.1 Solving a Mystery

The Mystery Club at P.I. Middle School meets monthly. Members watch videos, discuss novels, play "whodunit" games, and talk about real-life mysteries. One day, a member announces that the school is having a contest. A teacher in disguise will appear a few minutes at school each day for a week. Any student can pay $1 for a guess at the identity of the mystery teacher. The student with the first correct guess wins a prize.

The club decides to enter the contest together. Each member brings a camera to school in hopes of getting a picture of the mystery teacher.

How might a photograph help in identifying the mystery teacher?

One of Daphne's photos looks like the picture below. Daphne has a copy of the *P.I. Monthly* magazine shown in the picture. The *P.I. Monthly* magazine is 10 inches high. She thinks she can use the magazine and the picture to estimate the teacher's height.

A. What do you think Daphne has in mind? Use this information and the picture to estimate the teacher's height. Explain your reasoning.

The adviser of the Mystery Club says that the picture is similar to the actual scene.

B. What do you suppose the adviser means by *similar*? Is it different from saying that two students in your class are similar?

ACE **Homework starts on page 12.**

Michelle, Daphne, and Mukesh are the officers of the Mystery Club.
Mukesh designs this flier to attract new members.

Daphne wants to make a large poster to publicize the next meeting. She
wants to redraw the club's logo, "Super Sleuth," in a larger size. Michelle
shows her a clever way to enlarge the figure by using rubber bands.

Instructions for Stretching a Figure

1. Make a "two-band stretcher" by tying the ends of two identical rubber bands together. The rubber bands should be the same width and length. Bands about 3 inches long work well.

2. Take the sheet with the figure you want to enlarge and tape it to your desk. Next to it, tape a blank sheet of paper. If you are right-handed, put the blank sheet on the right. If you are left-handed, put it on the left (see the diagram below).

3. With your finger, hold down one end of the rubber-band stretcher on point *P*. Point *P* is called the anchor point. It must stay in the same spot.

4. Put a pencil in the other end of the stretcher. Stretch the rubber bands with your pencil until the knot is on the outline of your picture.

5. Guide the knot around the original picture while your pencil traces out a new picture. (Don't allow any slack in the rubber bands.) The new drawing is called the **image** of the original.

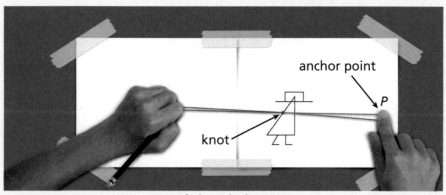

Left-handed setup

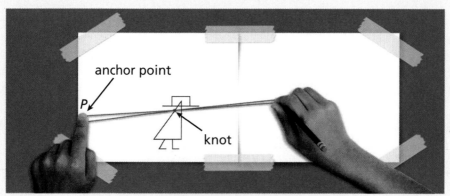

Right-handed setup

Problem 1.2 Comparing Similar Figures

Use the rubber-band method to enlarge the figure on the Mystery Club flier. Draw as carefully as you can, so you will be able to compare the size and shape of the image to the size and shape of the original figure.

A. Tell how the original figure and the image are alike and how they are different. Compare these features:

- the general shapes of the two figures
- the lengths of the line segments in the hats and bodies
- the areas and perimeters of the hats and bodies
- the angles in the hats and bodies

Explain each comparison you make. For example, rather than simply saying that two lengths are different, tell which lengths you are comparing and explain how they differ.

B. Use your rubber-band stretcher to enlarge another simple figure, such as a circle or a square. Compare the general shapes, lengths, areas, perimeters, and angles of the original figure and the image.

ACE | Homework starts on page 12.

Did You Know?

Measurement is used in police work all the time. For example, some stores with cameras place a spot on the wall 6 feet from the floor. When a person standing near the wall is filmed, it is easier to estimate the person's height. Investigators take measurements of tire marks at the scene of auto accidents to help them estimate the speed of the vehicles involved. Photographs and molds of footprints help the police determine the shoe size, type of shoe, and the weight of the person who made the prints.

Go Online
PHSchool.com **For:** Information about police work.
Web Code: ane-9031

In studying similar figures, we need to compare their sides and angles. In order to compare the right parts, we use the terms **corresponding sides** and **corresponding angles.** Each side in one figure has a corresponding side in the other figure. Also, each angle has a corresponding angle. The corresponding angles and sides of the triangles are given.

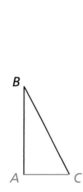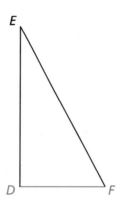

Corresponding sides

AC and DF

AB and DE

BC and EF

Corresponding angles

A and D

B and E

C and F

Daphne thinks the rubber-band method is clever, but she believes the school copier can make more accurate copies in a greater variety of sizes. She makes a copy with the size factor set at 75%. Then, she makes a copy with a setting of 150%. The results are shown on the next page.

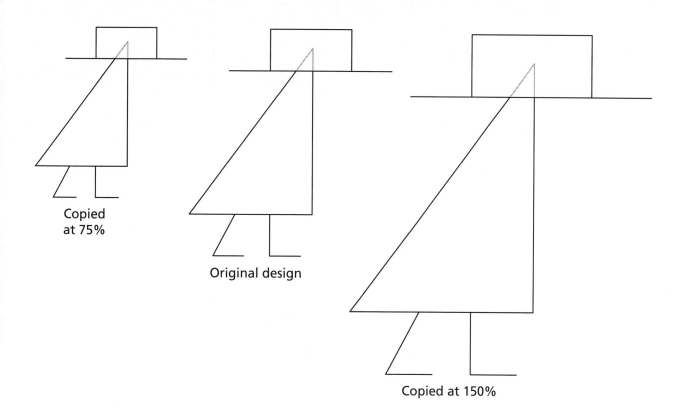

Copied
at 75%

Original design

Copied at 150%

Problem 1.3 Corresponding Sides and Angles

A. For each copy, tell how the side lengths compare to the corresponding side lengths in the original design.

B. For each copy, tell how the angle measures compare to the corresponding angle measures in the original design.

C. Describe how the perimeter of the triangle in each copy compares to the perimeter of the triangle in the original design.

D. Describe how the area of the triangle in each copy compares to the area of the triangle in the original design.

E. How do the relationships in the size comparisons you made in Questions A–D relate to the copier size factors used?

ACE Homework starts on page 12.

Applications

For Exercises 1 and 2, use the drawing at the right, which shows a person standing next to a construction scaffold.

1. Find the approximate height of the scaffold if the person is

   a. 6 feet tall

   b. 5 feet 6 inches tall

2. Find the approximate height of the person if the scaffold is

   a. 28 feet tall

   b. 36 feet tall

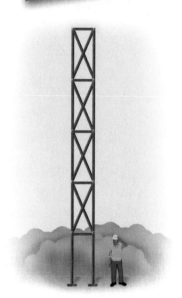

3. Copy square *ABCD* and anchor point *P* onto a sheet of paper. Use the rubber-band method to enlarge the figure. Then answer parts (a)–(d) below.

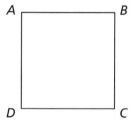

   a. How do the side lengths of the original figure compare to the side lengths of the image?

   b. How does the perimeter of the original figure compare to the perimeter of the image?

   c. How do the angle measures of the original figure compare to the angle measures of the image?

   d. How does the area of the original figure compare to the area of the image? How many copies of the original figure would it take to cover the image?

4. Copy parallelogram *ABCD* and anchor point *P* onto a sheet of paper. Use the rubber-band method to enlarge the figure. Then, answer parts (a)–(d) from Exercise 3 for your diagram.

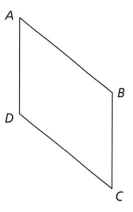

•
P

5. The diagram below is the original floor plan for a dollhouse. The diagram on the right is the image of the floor plan after you reduce it with a copier.

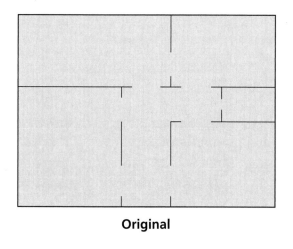

Original

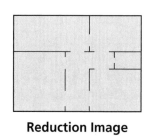

Reduction Image

a. Estimate the copier size factor used. Give your answer as a percent.

b. How do the segment lengths in the original plan compare to the corresponding segment lengths in the image?

c. Compare the area of the entire original floor plan to the area of the entire image. Then, do the same with one room in both plans. Is the relationship between the areas of the rooms the same as the relationship between the areas of the whole plans?

d. The scale on the original plan is 1 inch = 1 foot. This means that 1 inch on the floor plan represents 1 foot on the actual dollhouse. What is the scale on the smaller copy?

6. Multiple Choice Suppose you reduce the design below with a copy machine. Which of the following can be the image?

A.

B.

C.

D.

7. Suppose you copy a drawing of a polygon with the given size factor. How will the side lengths, angle measures, and perimeter of the image compare to those of the original?

a. 200%   **b.** 150%   **c.** 50%   **d.** 75%

Homework Help Online
PHSchool.com

For: Help with Exercise 7
Web Code: ane-2107

Connections

For Exercises 8–12, find the perimeter (or circumference) and the area of each figure.

8.

17.5 km

7.5 km

Rectangle

9.

15 m

6 m

5 m

Parallelogram

10.

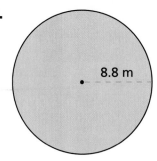

8.8 m

11.

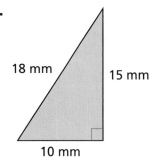

18 mm 15 mm

10 mm

12.

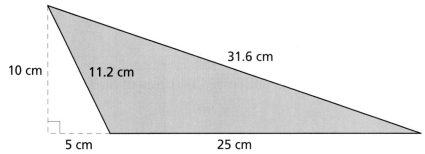

10 cm 11.2 cm 31.6 cm

5 cm 25 cm

13. Copy the circle and anchor point *P* onto a sheet of paper. Make an enlargement of the circle using your two-band stretcher.

•
P

C

a. How do the diameters of the circles compare?

b. How do the areas of the circles compare?

c. How do the circumferences of the circles compare?

14. Find the given percent of each number. Show your work.

a. 25% of 120

b. 80% of 120

c. 120% of 80

d. 70% of 150

e. 150% of 200

f. 200% of 150

15. Multiple Choice What is the 5% sales tax on a $14.00 compact disc?

A. $0.07 **B.** $0.70 **C.** $7.00 **D.** $70.00

16. Multiple Choice What is the 15% service tip on a $25.50 dinner in a restaurant?

F. $1.70 **G.** $3.83 **H.** $5.10 **J.** $38.25

17. Multiple Choice What is the 28% tax on a $600,000 cash prize?

A. $16,800 **B.** $21,429 **C.** $168,000 **D.** $214,290

18. Multiple Choice What is the 7.65% Social Security/Medicare tax on a paycheck of $430?

F. $3.29 **G.** $5.62 **H.** $32.90 **J.** $60.13

19. A circle has a radius of 4 centimeters.

a. What are the circumference and the area of the circle?

b. Suppose you copy the circle using a size factor of 150%. What will be the radius, diameter, circumference, and area of the image?

c. Suppose you copy the original circle using a size factor of 50%. What will be the radius, diameter, circumference, and area of the image?

20. While shopping for sneakers, Juan finds two pairs he likes. One pair costs $55 and the other costs $165. He makes the following statements about the prices.

"The expensive sneakers cost $110 more than the cheaper sneakers."

"The expensive sneakers cost three times as much as the cheaper sneakers."

a. Are both of his statements accurate?

b. How are the comparison methods Juan uses similar to the methods you use to compare the sizes and shapes of similar figures?

c. Which method is more appropriate for comparing the size and shape of an enlarged or reduced figure to the original? Explain.

Extensions

21. A movie projector that is 6 feet away from a large screen shows a rectangular picture that is 3 feet wide and 2 feet high.

    a. Suppose the projector is moved to a point 12 feet from the screen. What size will the picture be (width, height, and area)?

    b. Suppose the projector is moved to a point 9 feet from the screen. What size will the picture be (width, height, and area)?

22. Circle B is an enlargement of a smaller circle A, made with a two-band stretcher. Circle A is not shown.

Circle B

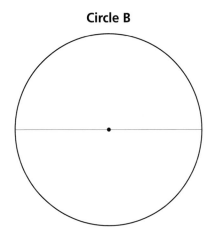

    a. How does the diameter of circle B compare to the diameter of circle A?

    b. How does the area of circle B compare to the area of circle A?

    c. How does the circumference of circle B compare to the circumference of circle A?

23. Make a three-band stretcher by tying three rubber bands together. Use this stretcher to enlarge the "Super Sleuth" drawing from Problem 1.2.

    a. How does the shape of the image compare to the shape of the original figure?

    b. How do the lengths of the segments in the two figures compare?

    c. How do the areas of the two figures compare?

24. Two copies of a small circle are shown side by side inside a large circle. The diameter of the large circle is 2 inches.

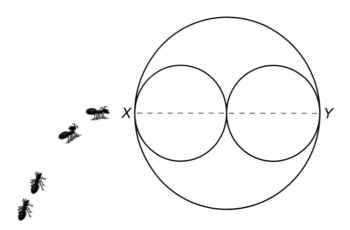

    a. What is the combined area of the two small circles?

    b. What is the area of the region inside the large circle that is *not* covered by the two small circles?

    c. Suppose an ant walks from X to Y. It travels only along the perimeter of the circles. Describe possible paths that the ant can travel. Which path is the shortest? Explain.

25. Suppose you enlarge some triangles, squares, and circles with a two-band stretcher. You use an anchor point inside the original figure, as shown in the sketches below.

a. In each case, how does the shape and position of the image compare to the shape and position of the original?

b. What relationships do you expect to find between the side lengths, angle measures, perimeters, and areas of the figures?

c. Test your ideas with larger copies of the given shapes. Make sure the shortest distance from the anchor point to any side of a shape is at least one band length.

26. Suppose you make a stretcher with two different sizes of rubber band. The band attached to the anchor point is twice as long as the band attached to the pencil.

a. If you use the stretcher to enlarge polygons, what relationships do you expect to find between the side lengths, angle measures, perimeters, and areas of the figures?

b. Test your ideas with copies of some basic geometric shapes.

Mathematical Reflections 1

In this investigation, you solved problems that involved enlarging (stretching) and reducing (shrinking) figures. You used rubber-band stretchers and copy machines. These questions will help you summarize what you learned.

Think about your answers to these questions. Discuss your ideas with other students and your teacher. Then write a summary of your findings in your notebook.

1. When you enlarge or reduce a figure, what features stay the same?

2. When you enlarge or reduce a figure, what features change?

3. Rubber-band stretchers, copy machines, overhead projectors, and movie projectors all make images that are similar to the original shapes. What does it mean for two shapes to be similar? That is, how can you complete the sentence below?

   "Two geometric shapes are similar if . . ."

Similar Figures

Zack and Marta want to design a computer game that involves several animated characters. Marta asks her uncle Carlos, a programmer for a video game company, about computer animation.

Carlos explains that the computer screen can be thought of as a grid made up of thousands of tiny points, called pixels. To animate a figure, you need to enter the coordinates of key points on the figure. The computer uses these key points to draw the figure in different positions.

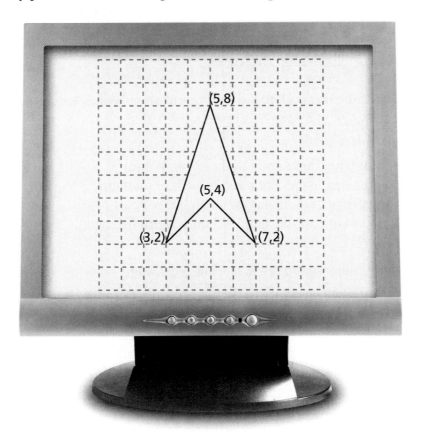

Sometimes the figures in a computer game need to change size. A computer can make a figure larger or smaller if you give it a rule for finding key points on the new figure, using key points from the original figure.

Zack and Marta's computer game involves a family called the Wumps. The members of the Wump family are various sizes, but they all have the same shape. That is, they are similar. Mug Wump is the game's main character. By enlarging or reducing Mug, a player can transform him into other Wump family members.

Zack and Marta experiment with enlarging and reducing figures on a coordinate grid. First, Zack draws Mug Wump on graph paper. Then, he labels the key points from A to X and lists the coordinates for each point. Marta writes the rules that will transform Mug into different sizes.

Problem 2.1 Making Similar Figures

Marta tries several rules for transforming Mug into different sizes. At first glance, all the new characters look like Mug. However, some of the characters are quite different from Mug.

A. To draw Mug on a coordinate graph, refer to the "Mug Wump" column in the table on the next page. For parts (1)–(3) of the figure, plot the points in order. Connect them as you go along. For part (4), plot the two points, but do not connect them. When you are finished, describe Mug's shape.

B. In the table, look at the columns for Zug, Lug, Bug, and Glug.

  1. For each character, use the given rule to find the coordinates of the points. For example, the rule for Zug is $(2x, 2y)$. This means that you multiply each of Mug's coordinates by 2. Point A on Mug is $(0, 1)$, so the corresponding point on Zug is $(0, 2)$. Point B on Mug is $(2, 1)$, so the corresponding point B on Zug is $(4, 2)$.

  2. Draw Zug, Lug, Bug, and Glug on separate coordinate graphs. Plot and connect the points for each figure, just as you did to draw Mug.

C. 1. Compare the characters to Mug. Which are the impostors?

  2. What things are the same about Mug and the others?

  3. What things are different about the five characters?

active math online

For: Mug Wumps, Reptiles, and Sierpinski Triangles Activity
Visit: PHSchool.com
Web Code: and-2201

ACE Homework starts on page 28.

Coordinates of Game Characters

Rule	Mug Wump (x, y)	Zug (2x, 2y)	Lug (3x, y)	Bug (3x, 3y)	Glug (x, 3y)
Point	Part 1				
A	(0, 1)	(0, 2)			
B	(2, 1)	(4, 2)			
C	(2, 0)				
D	(3, 0)				
E	(3, 1)				
F	(5, 1)				
G	(5, 0)				
H	(6, 0)				
I	(6, 1)				
J	(8, 1)				
K	(6, 7)				
L	(2, 7)				
M	(0, 1)				
	Part 2 (Start Over)				
N	(2, 2)				
O	(6, 2)				
P	(6, 3)				
Q	(2, 3)				
R	(2, 2)				
	Part 3 (Start Over)				
S	(3, 4)				
T	(4, 5)				
U	(5, 4)				
V	(3, 4)				
	Part 4 (Start Over)				
W	(2, 5) (make a dot)				
X	(6, 5) (make a dot)				

2.2 Hats Off to the Wumps

Zack experiments with multiplying Mug's coordinates by different whole numbers to make other characters. Marta asks her uncle how multiplying the coordinates by a decimal or adding numbers to or subtracting numbers from each coordinate will affect Mug's shape. He gives her a sketch for a new shape (a hat for Mug) and some rules to try.

Mug's Hat

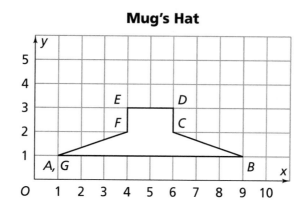

Problem 2.2 Changing a Figure's Size and Location

A. Look at the rules for Hats 1–5 in the table. Before you find any coordinates, predict how each rule will change Mug's hat.

B. Copy and complete the table. Give the coordinates of Mug's hat and the five other hats. Plot each new hat on a separate coordinate grid and connect each point as you go.

Rules for Mug's Hat

Point	Mug's Hat (x, y)	Hat 1 (x + 2, y + 3)	Hat 2 (x − 1, y + 4)	Hat 3 (x + 2, 3y)	Hat 4 (0.5x, 0.5y)	Hat 5 (2x, 3y)
A	(1, 1)					
B	(9, 1)					
C						
D						
E						
F						
G						

C. 1. Compare the angles and side lengths of the hats.

    2. Which hats are similar to Mug's hat? Explain why.

D. Write rules that will make hats similar to Mug's in each of the following ways.

    1. The side lengths are one third as long as Mug's.

    2. The side lengths are 1.5 times as long as Mug's.

    3. The hat is the same size as Mug's, but has moved right 1 unit and up 5 units.

E. Write a rule that makes a hat that is *not* similar to Mug's.

ACE | Homework starts on page 28.

2.3 Mouthing Off and Nosing Around

How did you decide which of the computer game characters were members of the Wump family and which were imposters?

In general, how can you decide whether or not two shapes are similar?

Your experiments with rubber-band stretchers, copiers, and coordinate plots suggest that for two figures to be **similar,** there must be the following correspondence between the figures.

> How can I decide whether or not two shapes are similar?

- The side lengths of one figure are multiplied by the same number to get the corresponding side lengths in the second figure.

- The corresponding angles are the same size.

The number that the side lengths of one figure can be multiplied by to give the corresponding side lengths of the other figure is called the **scale factor.**

The rectangles below are similar. The scale factor from the smaller rectangle to the larger rectangle is 3.

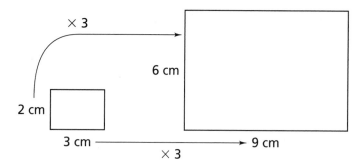

- What is the scale factor from the larger rectangle to the smaller rectangle?

The diagram shows a collection of mouths (rectangles) and noses (triangles) from the Wump family and from some impostors.

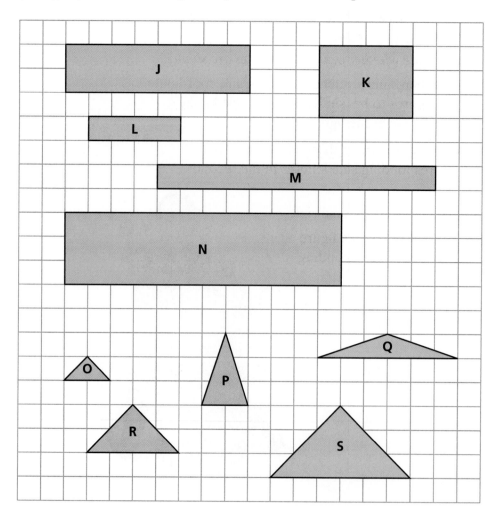

A. After studying the noses and mouths in the diagram, Marta and Zack agree that rectangles J and L are similar. However, Marta says the scale factor is 2, while Zack says it is 0.5. Is either of them correct? How would you describe the scale factor so there is no confusion?

B. Decide which pairs of rectangles are similar and find the scale factor.

C. Decide which pairs of triangles are similar and find the scale factor.

D. 1. Can you use the scale factors you found in Question B to predict the relationship between the perimeters for each pair of similar rectangles? Explain.

    2. Can you use the scale factors in Question B to predict the relationship between the areas for each pair of similar rectangles? Explain.

E. For parts (1)–(3), draw the figures on graph paper.

    1. Draw a rectangle that is similar to rectangle J, but is larger than any rectangle shown in the diagram. What is the scale factor from rectangle J to your rectangle?

    2. Draw a triangle that is *not* similar to any triangle shown in the diagram.

    3. Draw a rectangle that is *not* similar to any rectangle shown in the diagram.

F. Explain how to find the scale factor from a figure to a similar figure.

ACE Homework starts on page 28.

Did You Know?

You can make figures and then rotate, slide, flip, stretch, and copy them using a computer graphics program. There are two basic kinds of graphics programs. Paint programs make images out of pixels (which is a short way of saying "picture elements"). Draw programs make images out of lines that are drawn from mathematical equations.

The images you make in a graphics program are displayed on the computer screen. A beam of electrons activates a chemical in the screen, called phosphor, to make the images appear on your screen. If you have a laptop computer with a liquid crystal screen, an electric current makes the images appear on the screen.

Go Online
PHSchool.com
For: Information about computer images
Web Code: ane-9031

Applications

1. This table gives key coordinates for drawing the mouth and nose of Mug Wump. It also gives rules for finding the corresponding points for four other characters—some members of the Wump family and some impostors.

Coordinates of Characters

Point	Mug Wump (x, y)	Glum (1.5x, 1.5y)	Sum (3x, 2y)	Tum (4x, 4y)	Crum (2x, y)
Rule	*(x, y)*	*(1.5x, 1.5y)*	*(3x, 2y)*	*(4x, 4y)*	*(2x, y)*
Point	Mouth				
M	(2, 2)				
N	(6, 2)				
O	(6, 3)				
P	(2, 3)				
Q	(2, 2) (connect *Q* to *M*)				
	Nose (Start Over)				
R	(3, 4)				
S	(4, 5)				
T	(5, 4)				
U	(3, 4) (connect *U* to *R*)				

a. Before you find coordinates or plot points, predict which characters are the impostors.

b. Copy and complete the table. Then plot the figures on grid paper. Label each figure.

c. Which of the new characters (Glum, Sum, Tum, and Crum) are members of the Wump family, and which are impostors?

d. Choose one of the new Wumps. How do the mouth and nose measurements (side lengths, perimeter, area, angle measures) compare with those of Mug Wump?

e. Choose one of the impostors. How do the mouth and nose measurements compare with those of Mug Wump? What are the dimensions?

f. Do your findings in parts (b)–(e) support your prediction from part (a)? Explain.

2. a. Design a Mug-like character of your own on grid paper. Give him/her eyes, a nose, and a mouth.

   b. Give coordinates so that someone else could draw your character.

   c. Write a rule for finding coordinates of a member of your character's family. Check your rule by plotting the figure.

   d. Write a rule for finding the coordinates of an impostor. Check your rule by plotting the figure.

3. a. On grid paper, draw triangle *ABC* with vertex coordinates $A(0, 2)$, $B(6, 2)$ and $C(4, 4)$.

Go Online
PHSchool.com

For: Multiple-Choice Skills Practice
Web Code: ana-2254

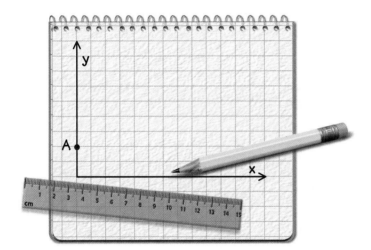

b. Apply the rule $(1.5x, 1.5y)$ to the vertices of triangle *ABC* to get triangle *PQR*. Compare the corresponding measurements (side lengths, perimeter, area, angle measures) of the two triangles.

c. Apply the rule $(2x, 0.5y)$ to the vertices of triangle *ABC* to get triangle *FGH*. Compare the corresponding measurements (side lengths, perimeter, area, angle measures) of the two triangles.

d. Which triangle, *PQR* or *FGH*, seems similar to triangle *ABC*? Why?

4. a. On grid paper, draw parallelogram *ABCD* with vertex coordinates $A(0, 2)$, $B(6, 2)$, $C(8, 6)$, and $D(2, 6)$.

   b. Write a rule to find the vertex coordinates of a parallelogram *PQRS* that is larger than, but similar to, *ABCD*. Test your rule to see if it works.

   c. Write a rule to find the vertex coordinates of a parallelogram *TUVW* that is smaller than, but similar to, *ABCD*. Test your rule.

For Exercises 5–6, study the size and shape of the polygons shown on the grid below.

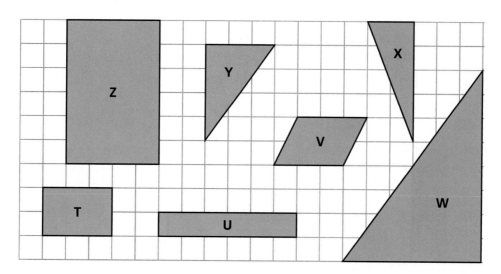

5. Multiple Choice Choose the pair of similar figures.

   A. Z and U   **B.** U and T   **C.** X and Y   **D.** Y and W

6. Find another pair of similar figures. How do you know they are similar?

For: Help with Exercise 6
Web Code: ane-2206

7. Copy the figures below accurately onto your own grid paper.

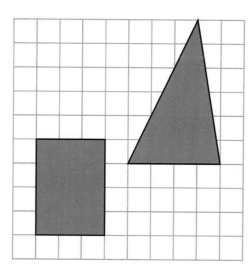

   a. Draw a rectangle that is similar, but not identical, to the given rectangle.

   b. Draw a triangle that is similar, but not identical, to the given triangle.

   c. How do you know the figures you drew are similar to the original figures?

8. Use the diagram of two similar polygons.

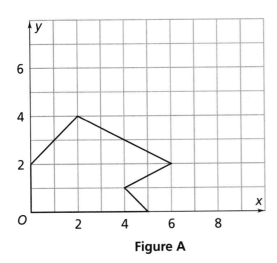

Figure A

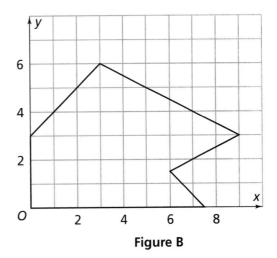

Figure B

  a. Write a rule for finding the coordinates of a point on Figure B from the corresponding point on Figure A.

  b. Write a rule for finding the coordinates of a point on Figure A from the corresponding point on Figure B.

  c. i. What is the scale factor from Figure A to Figure B?

    ii. Use the scale factor to describe how the perimeter and area of Figure B are related to the perimeter and area of Figure A.

  d. i. What is the scale factor from Figure B to Figure A?

    ii. Use the scale factor to describe how the perimeter and area of Figure A are related to the perimeter and area of Figure B.

9. a. Suppose you make Figure C by applying the rule $(2x, 2y)$ to the points on Figure A in Exercise 8. Find the coordinates of the vertices of Figure C.

  b. i. What is the scale factor from Figure A to Figure C?

    ii. Use the scale factor to describe how the perimeter and area of Figure C are related to the perimeter and area of Figure A.

  c. i. What is the scale factor from Figure C to Figure A?

    ii. Use the scale factor to describe how the perimeter and area of Figure A are related to the perimeter and area of Figure C.

    iii. Write a coordinate rule in the form (mx, my) that can be used to find the coordinates of any point in Figure A from the corresponding points of Figure C.

10. What is the scale factor from an original figure to its image if the image is made using the given method?

   a. a two-rubber-band stretcher

   b. a copy machine with size factor 150%

   c. a copy machine with size factor 250%

   d. the coordinate rule $(0.75x, 0.75y)$

11. a. Study the polygons below. Which pairs seem to be similar figures?

   b. For each pair of similar figures, list the corresponding sides and angles.

   c. For each pair of similar figures, estimate the scale factor that relates side lengths in the larger figure to the corresponding side lengths in the smaller figure.

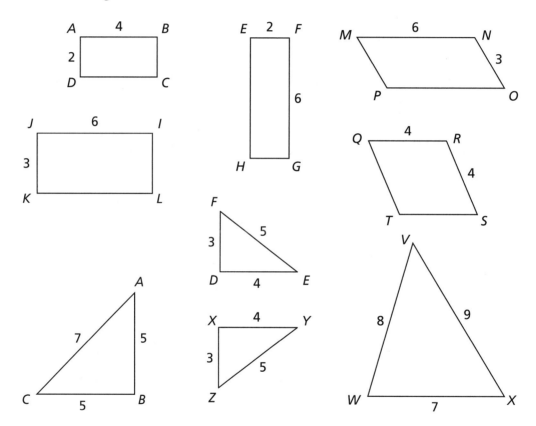

12. On grid paper, draw a rectangle with an area of 14 square centimeters. Label it *ABCD*.

   a. Write and use a coordinate rule that will make a rectangle similar to rectangle *ABCD* that is three times as long and three times as wide. Label it *EFGH*.

b. How does the perimeter of rectangle *EFGH* compare to the perimeter of rectangle *ABCD*?

c. How does the area of rectangle *EFGH* compare to the area of rectangle *ABCD*?

d. How do your answers to parts (b) and (c) relate to the scale factor from rectangle *ABCD* to rectangle *EFGH*?

13. Suppose a student draws the figures below. The student says the two shapes are similar because there is a common scale factor for all of the sides. The sides of the larger figure are twice as long as those of the smaller figure. What do you say to the student to explain why they are *not* similar?

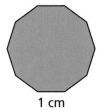

1 cm   2 cm

Connections

For Exercises 14–15, the rule $\left(x, \frac{3}{4}y\right)$ is applied to a polygon.

14. Is the image similar to the original polygon? Explain.

15. The given point is on the original polygon. Find the image of the point.

    a. $(6, 8)$ **b.** $(9, 8)$ **c.** $\left(\frac{3}{2}, \frac{4}{3}\right)$

Multiple Choice For Exercises 16–17, what is the scale factor as a percent that will result if the rule is applied to a point (x, y) on a coordinate grid?

16. $(1.5x, 1.5y)$

    A. 150%   **B.** 15%   **C.** 1.5%   **D.** None of these

17. $(0.7x, 0.7y)$

    F. 700%   **G.** 7%   **H.** 0.7%   **J.** None of these

18. The rule $\left(x + \frac{2}{3}, y - \frac{3}{4}\right)$ is applied to a polygon. Find the coordinates of the point on the image that corresponds to each of these points on the original polygon.

   a. $(5, 3)$ **b.** $\left(\frac{1}{6}, \frac{11}{12}\right)$ **c.** $\left(\frac{9}{12}, \frac{4}{5}\right)$

19. A good map is similar to the place it represents. Below is a map of South Africa.

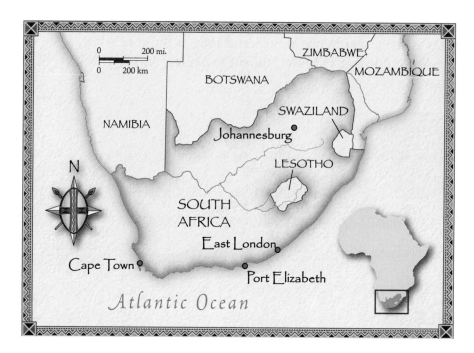

   a. Use the scale to estimate the distance from Cape Town to Port Elizabeth.

   b. Use the scale to estimate the distance from Johannesburg to East London.

   c. What is the relationship between the scale for the map and a "scale factor"?

Find each quotient.

20. $\frac{1}{2} \div \frac{1}{4}$ **21.** $\frac{1}{4} \div \frac{1}{2}$ **22.** $\frac{3}{7} \div \frac{4}{7}$

23. $\frac{4}{7} \div \frac{3}{7}$ **24.** $\frac{3}{2} \div \frac{3}{5}$ **25.** $1\frac{1}{2} \div \frac{3}{8}$

26. At a bake sale, 0.72 of a pan of corn bread has not been sold. A serving is 0.04 of a pan.

   a. How many servings are left?

   b. Use a hundredths grid to show your reasoning.

27. Each pizza takes 0.3 of a large block of cheese. Charlie has 0.8 of a block of cheese left.

    a. How many pizzas can he make?

    b. Use a diagram to show your reasoning.

28. Use the grid for parts (a)–(c).

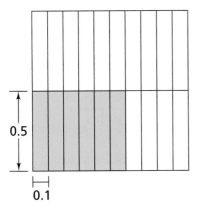

    a. What part of the grid is shaded?

    b. If the grid shows the part of a pan of spinach appetizers left, how many servings are left if a serving is 0.04?

    c. Use the grid picture to confirm your answer.

Extensions

29. Select a drawing of a comic strip character from a newspaper or magazine. Draw a grid over the figure or tape a transparent grid on top of the figure. Identify key points on the figure and then enlarge the figure by using each of these rules. Which figures are similar? Explain.

    a. $(2x, 2y)$ **b.** $(x, 2y)$ **c.** $(2x, y)$

30. Suppose you use the rule $(3x + 1, 3y - 4)$ to transform Mug Wump into a new figure.

    a. How will the angle measures in the new figure compare to corresponding angle measures in Mug?

    b. How will the side lengths of the new figure compare to corresponding side lengths of Mug?

    c. How will the area and perimeter of this new figure compare to the area and perimeter of Mug?

31. The vertices of three similar triangles are given.

- triangle ABC: $A(1,2)$, $B(4,3)$, $C(2,5)$
- triangle DEF: $D(3,6)$, $E(12,9)$, $F(6,15)$
- triangle GHI: $G(5,9)$, $H(14,12)$, $I(8,18)$

   a. Find a rule that changes the vertices of triangle ABC to the vertices of triangle DEF.

   b. Find a rule that changes the vertices of triangle DEF to the vertices of triangle GHI.

   c. Find a rule that changes the vertices of triangle ABC to the vertices of triangle GHI.

32. If you drew Mug and his hat on the same grid, his hat would be at his feet instead of on his head.

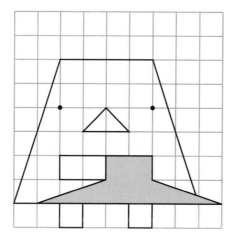

   a. Write a rule that puts Mug's hat centered on his head.

   b. Write a rule that changes Mug's hat to fit Zug and puts the hat on Zug's head.

   c. Write a rule that changes Mug's hat to fit Lug and puts the hat on Lug's head.

33. Films are sometimes modified to fit a TV screen. Find out what that means. What exactly is modified? If Mug is in a movie that has been modified, is he still a Wump when you see him on the TV screen?

Mathematical Reflections 2

In this investigation, you drew a character named Mug Wump on a coordinate grid. Then you used rules to transform Mug into other characters. Some of the characters you made were similar to Mug Wump and some were not. These questions will help you summarize what you learned.

Think about your answers to these questions. Discuss your ideas with other students and your teacher. Then write a summary of your findings in your notebook.

1. How did you decide which characters were similar to Mug Wump and which were *not* similar?

2. What types of rules produced figures similar to Mug Wump? Explain.

3. What types of rules produced figures that were *not* similar to Mug Wump? Explain.

4. When a figure is transformed to make a similar figure, some features change and some stay the same. What does the scale factor tell you about how the figure changes?

Similar Polygons

In *Shapes and Designs*, you learned that some polygons can fit together to cover, or tile, a flat surface. For example, the surface of a honeycomb is covered with a pattern of regular hexagons. Many bathroom and kitchen floors are covered with a pattern of square tiles.

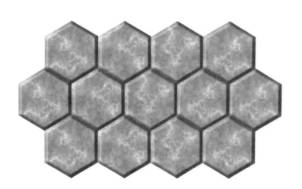
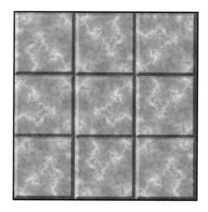

If you look closely at the pattern of squares on the right above, you can see that the large square, which consists of nine small squares, is similar to each of the nine small squares. The nine-tile square has sides made of three small squares, so the scale factor from the small square to the nine-tile square is 3. You can also take four small squares and put them together to make a four-tile square that is similar to the nine-tile square. The scale factor in this case is 2.

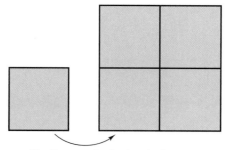

Similar; scale factor is 2.

However, no matter how closely you look at the hexagon pattern, you cannot find a large hexagon made up of similar smaller hexagons.

If congruent copies of a shape can be put together to make a larger, similar shape, the original shape is called a **rep-tile.** A square is a rep-tile, but a regular hexagon is not.

3.1 Rep-Tile Quadrilaterals

In the next problem, you will see if rectangles and non-rectangular quadrilaterals are also rep-tiles.

Problem 3.1 Forming Rep-Tiles With Similar Quadrilaterals

Sketch and make several copies of each of the following shapes:

- a non-square rectangle
- a non-rectangular parallelogram
- a trapezoid

A. Which of these shapes can fit together to make a larger shape that is similar to the original? Make a sketch to show how the copies fit together.

B. Look at your sketches from Question A.

   1. What is the scale factor from the original figure to the larger figure? Explain.

   2. How does the perimeter of the new figure relate to the perimeter of the original?

   3. How does the area of the new figure relate to the area of the original?

C. 1. Extend the rep-tile patterns you made in Question A. Do this by adding copies of the original figure to make larger figures that are similar to the original.

   2. Make sketches showing how the figures fit together.

   3. Find the scale factor from each original figure to each new figure. Explain.

   4. Explain what the scale factor indicates about the corresponding side lengths, perimeters, and areas.

ACE **Homework starts on page 44.**

3.2 Rep-Tile Triangles

While rep-tiles must tessellate, not every shape that tessellates is a rep-tile. *Are the birds in the tessellation below rep-tiles?*

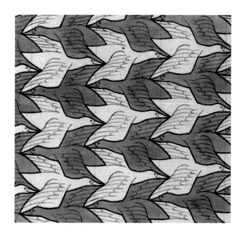

All triangles tessellate. Are all triangles rep-tiles?

Problem 3.2 Forming Rep-Tiles With Similar Triangles

Sketch and make several copies of each of the following shapes:

- a right triangle
- an isosceles triangle
- a scalene triangle

A. Which of these triangles fit together to make a larger triangle that is similar to the original? Make a sketch to show how the copies fit together.

B. Look at your sketches from Question A.

1. What is the scale factor from each original triangle to each larger triangle? Explain.

2. How is the perimeter of the new triangle related to the perimeter of the original?

3. How is the area of the new triangle related to the area of the original?

C. 1. Extend the rep-tile patterns you made in Question A. Do this by adding copies of the original triangle to make larger triangles that are similar to the original.

2. Make sketches to show how the triangles fit together.

3. Find the scale factor from each original triangle to each new triangle. Explain.

4. Explain what the scale factor indicates about the corresponding side lengths, perimeters, and areas.

D. Study the rep-tile patterns. See if you can find a strategy for dividing each of the triangles below into four or more similar triangles. Make sketches to show your ideas.

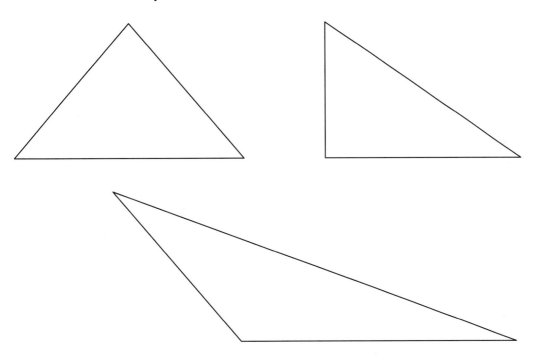

ACE Homework starts on page 44.

You know that the scale factor from one figure to a similar figure gives you information about how the side lengths, perimeters, and areas of the figures are related. You will use what you learned in the next problem.

Problem 3.3 Scale Factors and Similar Shapes

For Questions A and B, use the two figures on the grid.

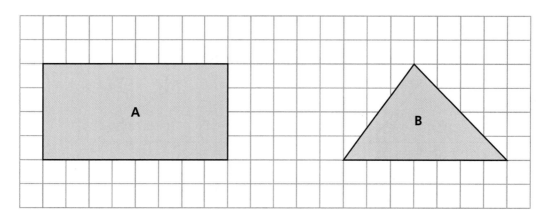

A. For parts (1)–(3), draw a rectangle similar to rectangle A that fits the given description. Find the base and height of each new rectangle.

1. The scale factor from rectangle A to the new rectangle is 2.5.

2. The area of the new rectangle is $\frac{1}{4}$ the area of rectangle A.

3. The perimeter of the new rectangle is three times the perimeter of rectangle A.

B. For parts (1)–(2), draw a triangle similar to triangle B that fits the given description. Find the base and height of each new triangle.

1. The area of the new triangle is nine times the area of triangle B.

2. The scale factor from triangle B to the new triangle is $\frac{1}{2}$.

C. 1. Rectangles *ABCD* and *EFGH* are similar. Find the length of side *AD*. Explain.

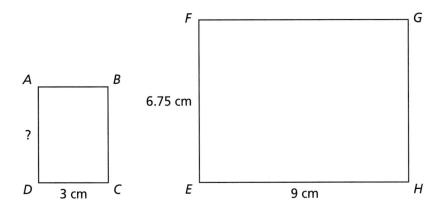

2. Triangles *ABC* and *DEF* are similar.

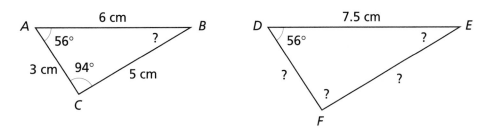

    a. By what number do you multiply the length of side *AB* to get the length of side *DE*?

    b. Find the missing side lengths and angle measures. Explain.

ACE Homework starts on page 44.

Applications

1. Look for rep-tile patterns in the designs below. For each design, tell whether the small quadrilaterals are similar to the large quadrilateral. Explain. If the quadrilaterals are similar, give the scale factor from each small quadrilateral to the large quadrilateral.

a.

b.

c.

d.

2. Suppose you put together nine copies of a rectangle to make a larger, similar rectangle.

   a. What is the scale factor from the smaller rectangle to the larger rectangle?

   b. How is the area of the larger rectangle related to the area of the smaller rectangle?

3. Suppose you divide a rectangle into 25 smaller rectangles. Each rectangle is similar to the original rectangle.

   a. What is the scale factor from the original rectangle to each of the smaller rectangles?

   b. How is the area of each of the smaller rectangles related to the area of the original rectangle?

4. Look for rep-tile patterns in the designs below. For each design, tell whether the small triangles seem to be similar to the large triangle. Explain. When the triangles are similar, give the scale factor from each small triangle to the large triangle.

a.

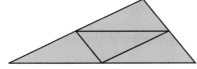

b.

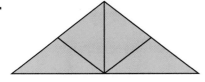

c.

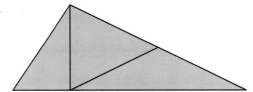

d.

5. Copy polygons A–D onto grid paper. Draw line segments that divide each of the polygons into four congruent polygons that are similar to the original polygon.

Homework Help Online
PHSchool.com
For: Help with Exercise 5
Web Code: ane-2305

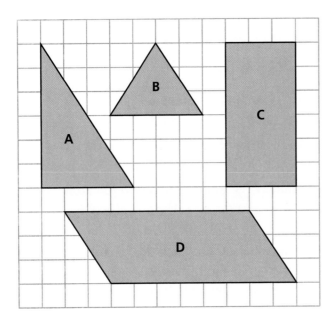

6. a. For rectangles E–G, give the length and width of a different similar rectangle. Explain how you know the new rectangles are similar.

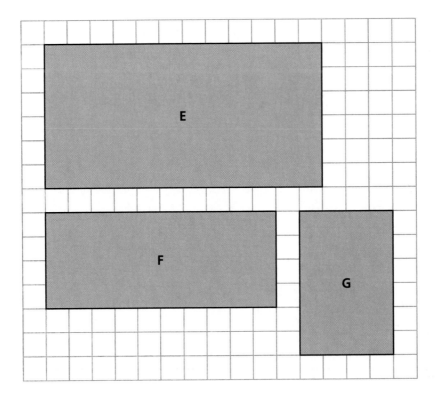

b. Give the scale factor from each original rectangle in part (a) to the similar rectangles you described. Explain what the scale factor tells you about the corresponding lengths, perimeters, and areas.

7. Use the polygons below.

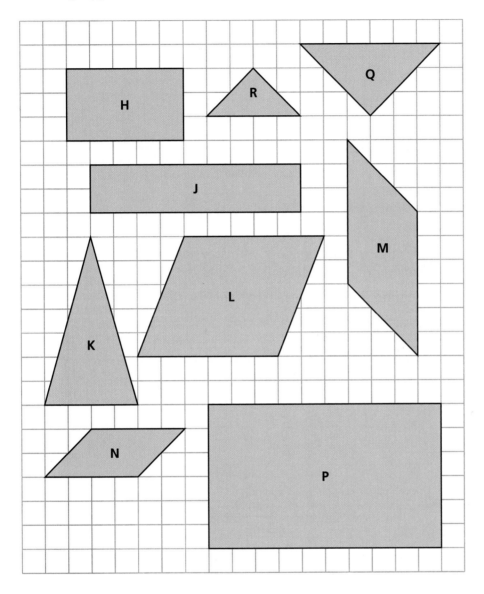

a. List the pairs of similar shapes.

b. For each pair of similar shapes, find the scale factor from the smaller shape to the larger shape.

8. For parts (a)–(c), use grid paper.

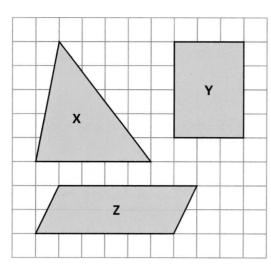

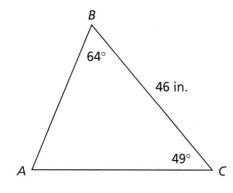

a. Sketch a triangle similar to triangle X with an area that is $\frac{1}{4}$ the area of triangle X.

b. Sketch a rectangle similar to rectangle Y with a perimeter that is 0.5 times the perimeter of rectangle Y.

c. Sketch a parallelogram similar to parallelogram Z with side lengths that are 1.5 times the side lengths of parallelogram Z.

Triangle *ABC* is similar to triangle *PQR*. For Exercises 9–14, use the given side and angle measurements to find the indicated angle measure or side length.

Go Online
PHSchool.com

For: Multiple-Choice
Skills Practice
Web Code: ana-2354

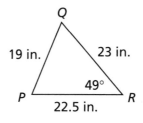

9. angle *A*

10. angle *Q*

11. angle *P*

12. length of side *AB*

13. length of side *AC*

14. perimeter of triangle *ABC*

Multiple Choice For Exercises 15–18, use the similar parallelograms below.

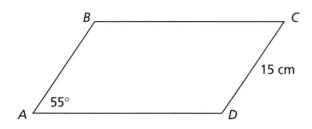 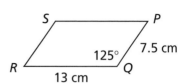

15. What is the measure of angle *D*?

    A. 55°   **B.** 97.5°   **C.** 125°   **D.** 135°

16. What is the measure of angle *R*?

    F. 55°   **G.** 97.5°   **H.** 125°   **J.** 135°

17. What is the measure of angle *S*?

    A. 55°   **B.** 97.5°   **C.** 125°   **D.** 135°

18. What is the length of side *AB* in centimeters?

    F. 3.75   **G.** 13   **H.** 15   **J.** 26

19. Suppose a rectangle B is similar to rectangle A below. If the scale factor from rectangle A to rectangle B is 4, what is the area of rectangle B?

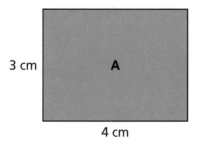

20. Suppose rectangle E has an area of 9 square centimeters and rectangle F has an area of 900 square centimeters. The two rectangles are similar. What is the scale factor from rectangle E to rectangle F?

21. Suppose rectangles X and Y are similar. The dimensions of rectangle X are 5 centimeters by 7 centimeters. The area of rectangle Y is 140 square centimeters. What are the dimensions of rectangle Y?

Connections

22. In the figure below, lines L_1 and L_2 are parallel.

  a. Use what you know about parallel lines to find the measures of angles *a* through *g*.

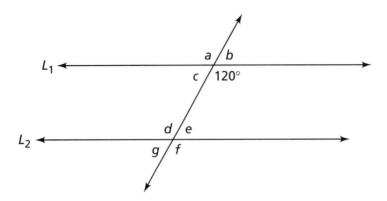

  b. When the sum of the measures of two angles is 180°, the angles are **supplementary angles.** For example, angles *a* and *b* above are supplementary angles because they fit together to form a straight line (180°). List all pairs of supplementary angles in the diagram.

23. Suppose you have two supplementary angles (explained above). The measure of one angle is given. Find the measure of the other angle.

  a. 160°   **b.** 90°   **c.** $x°$

24. The two right triangles are similar.

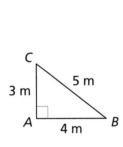
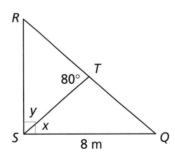

  a. Find the length of side *RS*.
  b. Find the length of side *RQ*.
  c. Suppose the measure of angle *x* is 40°. Find the measure of angle *y*.

d. Find the measure of angle R. Explain how you can find the measure of angle C.

Angle x and angle y are called **complementary angles.** Complementary angles are a pair of angles whose measures add to 90°.

e. Find two more pairs of complementary angles in triangles ABC and QRS besides angles x and y.

25. For parts (a)–(f), find the number that makes the fractions equivalent.

a. $\frac{1}{2} = \frac{3}{\blacksquare}$
 b. $\frac{5}{6} = \frac{\blacksquare}{24}$

c. $\frac{3}{4} = \frac{6}{\blacksquare}$
 d. $\frac{8}{12} = \frac{2}{\blacksquare}$

e. $\frac{3}{5} = \frac{\blacksquare}{100}$
 f. $\frac{6}{4} = \frac{\blacksquare}{10}$

26. For parts (a)–(f), suppose you copy a figure on a copier using the given size factor. Find the scale factor from the original figure to the copy in decimal form.

a. 200%
 b. 50%

c. 150%
 d. 125%

e. 75%
 f. 25%

27. Write each fraction as a decimal and as a percent.

a. $\frac{2}{5}$
 b. $\frac{3}{4}$

c. $\frac{3}{10}$
 d. $\frac{1}{4}$

e. $\frac{7}{10}$
 f. $\frac{7}{20}$

g. $\frac{4}{5}$
 h. $\frac{7}{8}$

i. $\frac{3}{5}$
 j. $\frac{15}{20}$

28. For parts (a)–(d), tell whether the figures are mathematically similar. Explain. If the figures are similar, give the scale factor from the left figure to the right figure.

a.

b.

c.

d.

For Exercises 29–31, decide if the statement is true or false. Justify your answer.

29. All squares are similar.

30. All rectangles are similar.

31. If the scale factor between two similar shapes is 1, then the two shapes are the same size. (Note: If two similar figures have a scale factor of 1, they are *congruent*.)

32. a. Suppose the following rectangle is reduced by a scale factor of 50%. What are the dimensions of the reduced rectangle?

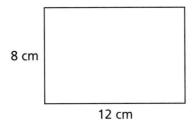

8 cm

12 cm

b. Suppose the reduced rectangle in part (a) is reduced again by a scale factor of 50%. Now, what are the dimensions of the rectangle?

c. How does the reduced rectangle from part (b) compare to the original rectangle from part (a)?

Extensions

33. Trace each shape. Divide each shape into four smaller pieces that are similar to the original shape.

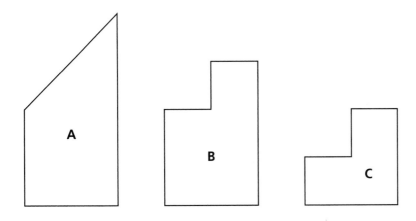

A

B

C

34. The **midpoint** is a point that divides a line segment into two segments of equal length. Draw a figure on grid paper by following these steps:

Step 1 Draw a square.

Step 2 Mark the midpoint of each side.

Step 3 Connect the midpoints in order with four line segments to form a new figure. (The line segments should not intersect inside the square.)

Step 4 Repeat Steps 2 and 3 three more times. Work with the newest figure each time.

   a. What kind of figure is formed when the midpoints of the sides of a square are connected?

   b. Find the area of the original square.

   c. Find the area of the new figure that is formed at each step.

   d. How do the areas change between successive figures?

   e. Are there any similar figures in your final drawing? Explain.

35. Repeat Exercise 34 using an equilateral triangle.

36. Suppose rectangle A is similar to rectangle B and to rectangle C. Can you conclude that rectangle B is similar to rectangle C? Explain. Use drawings and examples to illustrate your answer.

37. The mathematician Benoit Mandelbrot called attention to the fact that you can subdivide figures to get smaller figures that are mathematically similar to the original. He called these figures *fractals*. A famous example is the Sierpinski triangle.

You can follow these steps to make the Sierpinski triangle.

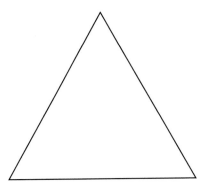

Step 1 Draw a large triangle.

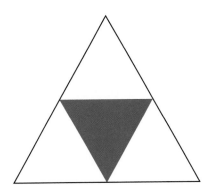

Step 2 Mark the midpoint of each side. Connect the midpoints to form four identical triangles that are similar to the original. Shade the center triangle.

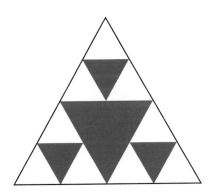

Step 3 For each unshaded triangle, mark the midpoints. Connect them in order to form four identical triangles. Shade the center triangle in each case.

Step 4 Repeat Steps 2 and 3 over and over. To make a real Sierpinski triangle, you need to repeat the process an infinite number of times! This triangle shows five subdivisions.

a. Follow the steps for making the Sierpinski triangle until you subdivide the original triangle three times.

b. Describe any patterns you observe in your figure.

c. Mandelbrot used the term *self-similar* to describe fractals like the Sierpinski triangle. What do you think this term means?

For Exercises 38–42, read the paragraph below and answer the questions that follow.

When you find the area of a square, you multiply the length of the side by itself. For a square with a side length of 3 units, you multiply 3×3 (or 3^2) to get 9 square units. For this reason, you call 9 the *square* of 3.

Three is called the *square root* of 9. The symbol, "$\sqrt{\ }$" is used for the square root. This gives the fact family below.

$$3^2 = 9$$
$$\sqrt{9} = 3$$

38. The square has an area of 10 square units. Write the side length of this square using the square root symbol.

39. Multiple Choice What is the square root of 144?

    A. 7   **B.** 12   **C.** 72   **D.** 20,736

40. What is the length of the side of a square with an area of 144 square units?

41. You have learned that if a figure grows by a scale factor of s, the area of the figure grows by a factor of s^2. If the area of a figure grows by a factor of f, what is the scale factor?

42. Find three examples of squares and square roots in the work you have done so far in this unit.

Mathematical Reflections 3

This investigation explored similar polygons and scale factors. These questions will help you summarize what you learned.

Think about your answers to these questions. Discuss your ideas with other students and your teacher. Then write a summary of your findings in your notebook.

1. How can you tell if two polygons are similar?

2. If two polygons are similar, how can you find the scale factor from one polygon to the other? Show specific examples. Describe how you find the scale factor from the smaller figure to the enlarged figure. Then, describe how you find the scale factor from the larger figure to the smaller figure.

3. For parts (a)–(c), what does the scale factor between two similar figures tell you about the given measurements?

   a. side lengths

   b. perimeters

   c. areas

Similarity and Ratios

You can enhance a report or story by adding photographs, drawings, or diagrams. Once you place a graphic in an electronic document, you can enlarge, reduce, or move it. In most programs, clicking on a graphic causes it to appear inside a frame with buttons along the sides, like the figure below.

You can change the size and shape of the image by grabbing and dragging the buttons.

Here are examples of the image after it has been resized.

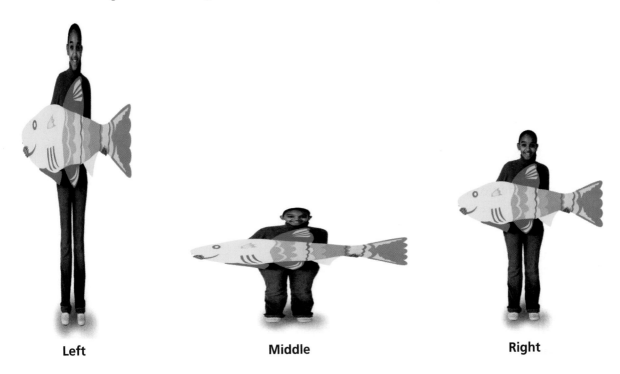

| Left | Middle | Right |

Getting Ready for Problem 4.1

- How do you think this technique produced these variations of the original shape?
- Which of these images appears to be similar to the original? Why?

One way to describe and compare shapes is by using **ratios.** A ratio is a comparison of two quantities such as two lengths. The original figure is about 10 centimeters tall and 8 centimeters wide. You say, "the *ratio* of height to width is 10 to 8."

This table gives the ratio of height to width for the images.

Image Information

Figure	Height (cm)	Width (cm)	Height to Width Ratio
Original	10	8	10 to 8
Left	8	3	8 to 3
Middle	3	6	3 to 6
Right	5	4	5 to 4

- What do you observe about the ratios of height to width in the similar figures?

The comparisons "10 to 8" and "5 to 4" are **equivalent ratios.** Equivalent ratios name the same number. In both cases, if you write the ratio of height to width as a decimal, you get the same number.

$$10 \div 8 = 1.25 \qquad 5 \div 4 = 1.25$$

The same is true if you write the ratio of width to height as a decimal.

"8 to 10" "4 to 5"

$$8 \div 10 = 0.8 \qquad 4 \div 5 = 0.8$$

Equivalence of ratios is a lot like equivalence of fractions. In fact, ratios are often written in the form of fractions. You can express equivalent ratios with equations like these:

$$\frac{10}{8} = \frac{5}{4}$$
$$\frac{8}{10} = \frac{4}{5}$$

Ratios Within Similar Parallelograms

When two figures are similar, you know there is a scale factor that relates each length in one figure to the corresponding length in the other. You can also find a ratio between any two lengths in a figure. This ratio will describe the relationship between the corresponding lengths in a similar figure. You will explore this relationship in the next problem.

When you work with the diagrams in this investigation, assume that all measurements are in centimeters. Many of the drawings are not shown at actual size.

Problem 4.1 Ratios Within Similar Parallelograms

A. The lengths of two sides are given for each rectangle.

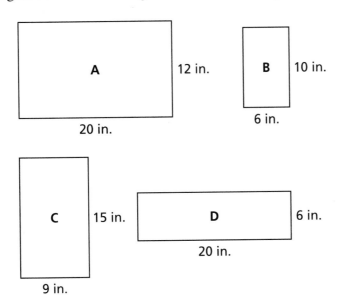

1. For each rectangle, find the ratio of the length of a short side to the length of a long side.

2. What do you notice about the ratios in part (1) for similar rectangles? About the ratios for non-similar rectangles?

3. For two similar rectangles, find the scale factor from the smaller rectangle to the larger rectangle. What information does the scale factor give about two similar figures?

4. Compare the information given by the scale factor to the information given by the ratios of side lengths.

B. 1. For each parallelogram, find the ratio of the length of a longer side to the length of a shorter side. How do the ratios compare?

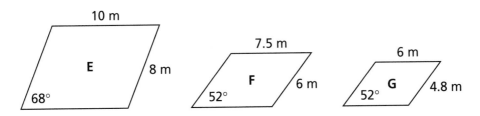

2. Which of the parallelograms are similar? Explain.

C. If the ratio of adjacent side lengths in one parallelogram is equal to the ratio of the corresponding side lengths in another, can you say that the parallelograms are similar? Explain.

ACE Homework starts on page 66.

4.2 Ratios Within Similar Triangles

Since all rectangles contain four 90° angles, you can show that rectangles are similar just by comparing side lengths. You now know two ways to show that rectangles are similar.

(1) Show that the scale factors between corresponding side lengths are equal. (compare length to length and width to width)

(2) Show that the ratios of corresponding sides within each shape are equal. (compare length to width in one rectangle and length to width in the other)

However, comparing only side lengths of a non-rectangular parallelogram or a triangle is not enough to understand its shape. In this problem, you will use angle measures and side-length ratios to find similar triangles.

For Questions A and B, use the triangles below. Side lengths are approximate.

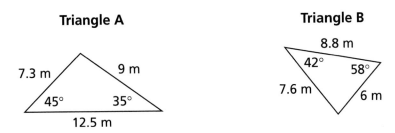

Triangle A

7.3 m   9 m

45°   35°

12.5 m

Triangle B

8.8 m

42°   58°

7.6 m   6 m

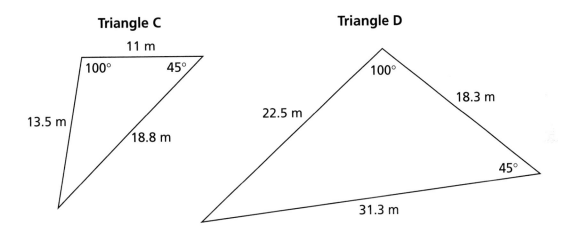

Triangle C

11 m

100°   45°

13.5 m

18.8 m

Triangle D

100°

18.3 m

22.5 m

45°

31.3 m

A. Identify the triangles that are similar to each other. Explain how you use the angles and sides to identify the similar triangles.

B. **1.** Within each triangle, find the ratio of shortest side to longest side. Find the ratio of shortest side to "middle" side.

2. How do the ratios of side lengths compare for similar triangles?

3. How do the ratios of side lengths compare for triangles that are *not* similar?

ACE Homework starts on page 66.

4.3 Finding Missing Parts

When you know that two figures are similar, you can find missing lengths in two ways.

    (1) Use the scale factor from one figure to the other.

    (2) Use the ratios of the side lengths within each figure.

Problem 4.3 Using Similarity to Find Measurements

For Questions A–C, each pair of figures is similar. Find the missing side lengths. Explain.

A.

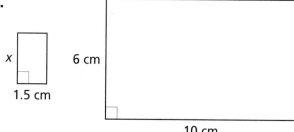

B.

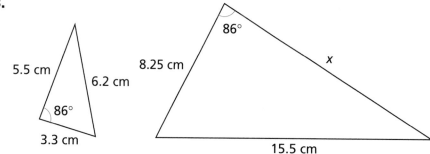

C.

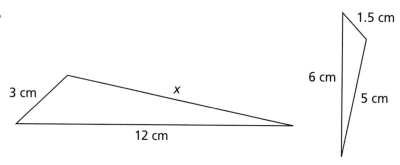

D. The figures are similar. Find the missing measurements. Explain.

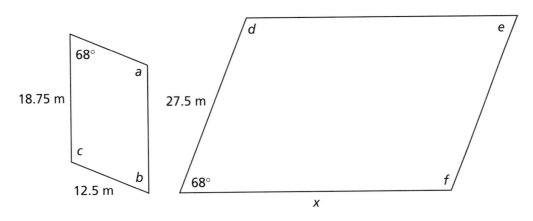

E. The figures below are similar. The measurements shown are in inches.

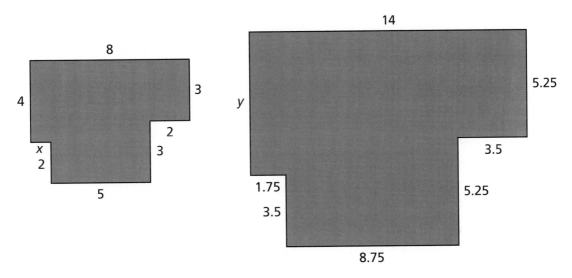

1. Find the value of *x* using ratios.
2. Find the value of *y* using scale factors.
3. Find the area of one of the figures.
4. Use your answer to part (3) and the scale factor. Find the area of the other figure. Explain.

ACE **Homework starts on page 66.**

Applications

1. Figures A–F are parallelograms.

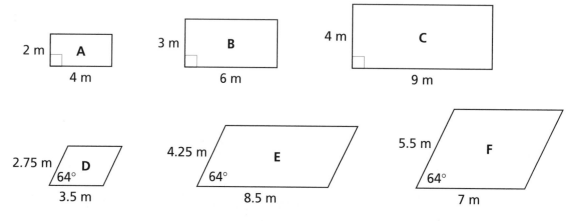

a. List all the pairs of similar parallelograms.

b. For each pair of similar parallelograms, find the ratio of two adjacent side lengths in one parallelogram and compare it to the ratio of the corresponding side lengths in the other parallelogram.

c. For each pair of similar parallelograms, find the scale factor from one shape to the other. Explain how the information given by the scale factors is different from the information given by the ratios of side lengths.

2. For parts (a)–(c), use the triangles below and on the next page.

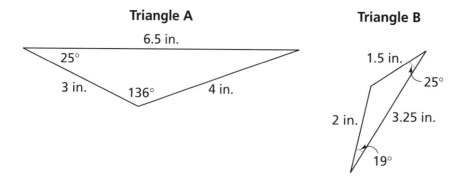

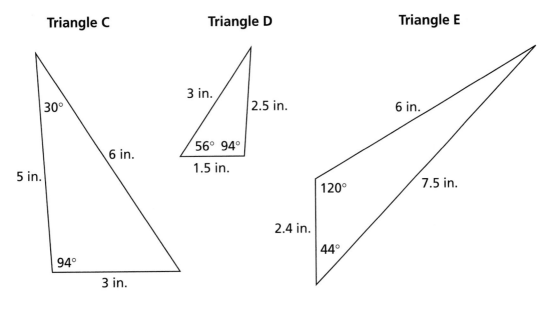

Triangle C

30°

5 in.

6 in.

94°

3 in.

Triangle D

3 in.

2.5 in.

56° 94°

1.5 in.

Triangle E

6 in.

120°

7.5 in.

2.4 in.

44°

a. List all the pairs of similar triangles.

b. For each pair of similar triangles, find the ratio of two side lengths in one triangle and the ratio of the corresponding pair of side lengths in the other. How do these ratios compare?

c. For each pair of similar triangles, find the scale factor from one shape to the other. Explain how the information given by the scale factors is different than the information given by the ratios of side lengths.

3. a. On grid paper, draw two similar rectangles so that the scale factor from one rectangle to the other is 2.5. Label the length and width of each rectangle.

b. Find the ratio of the length to the width for each rectangle.

4. a. Draw a third rectangle that is similar to one of the rectangles in Exercise 3. Find the scale factor from one rectangle to the other.

b. Find the ratio of the length to the width for the new rectangle.

c. What can you say about the ratios of the length to the width for the three rectangles? Is this true for another rectangle that is similar to one of the three rectangles? Explain.

Applications

For Exercises 5–8, each pair of figures is similar. Find the missing measurement. (Note: Although each pair of figures is drawn to scale, the scales for Exercises 5–8 are not the same.)

5.

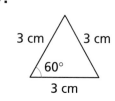

6.

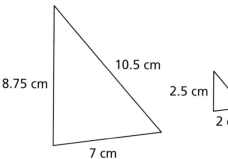

Go Online
PHSchool.com

For: Multiple-Choice Skills Practice
Web Code: ana-2454

7.

8.

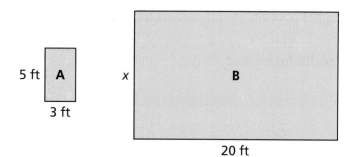

For Exercises 9–11, rectangles A and B are similar.

9. Multiple Choice What is the value of x?

    A. 4   **B.** 12   **C.** 15   **D.** $33\frac{1}{3}$

10. What is the scale factor from rectangle B to rectangle A?

11. Find the area of each rectangle. How are the areas related?

12. Rectangles C and D are similar.

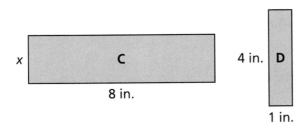

For: Help with Exercise 12
Web Code: ane-2412

   a. What is the value of *x*?

   b. What is the scale factor from rectangle C to rectangle D?

   c. Find the area of each rectangle. How are the areas related?

13. Suppose you want to buy new carpeting for your bedroom. The bedroom floor is a 9-foot-by-12-foot rectangle. Carpeting is sold by the square yard.

   a. How much carpeting do you need to buy?

   b. The carpeting costs $22 per square yard. How much will the carpet for the bedroom cost?

14. Suppose you want to buy the same carpet described in Exercise 13 for a library. The library floor is similar to the floor of the 9-foot-by-12-foot bedroom. The scale factor from the bedroom to the library is 2.5.

   a. What are the dimensions of the library? Explain.

   b. How much carpeting do you need for the library?

   c. How much will the carpet for the library cost?

Connections

For Exercises 15–20, tell whether each pair of ratios is equivalent.

15. 3 to 2 *and* 5 to 4

16. 8 to 4 *and* 12 to 8

17. 7 to 5 *and* 21 to 15

18. 1.5 to 0.5 *and* 6 to 2

19. 1 to 2 *and* 3.5 to 6

20. 2 to 3 *and* 4 to 6

21. Choose a pair of equivalent ratios from Exercises 15–20. Write a similarity problem that uses the ratios. Explain how to solve your problem.

For Exercises 22–25, write two other ratios equivalent to the given ratio.

22. 5 to 3 **23.** 4 to 1 **24.** 3 to 7 **25.** 1.5 to 1

26. Here is a picture of Duke, a real dog. The scale factor from Duke to the picture is 12.5%. Use an inch ruler to make any measurements.

a. How long is Duke from his nose to the tip of his tail?

b. To build a doghouse for Duke, you need to know his height so you can make a doorway to accommodate him. How tall is Duke?

c. The local copy center has a machine that prints on poster-size paper. You can enlarge or reduce a document with a setting between 50% and 200%. How can you use the machine to make a life-size picture of Duke?

27. Samantha draws triangle ABC on a grid. She applies a rule to make the triangle on the right.

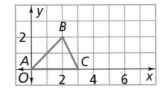 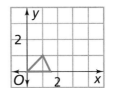

a. What rule did Samantha apply to make the new triangle?

b. Is the new triangle similar to triangle ABC? Explain. If the triangles are similar, give the scale factor from triangle ABC to the new triangle.

28. a. Find the ratio of the circumference to the diameter for each circle.

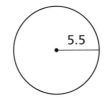

b. How do the ratios you found in part (a) compare? Explain.

For Exercises 29–30, read the paragraph below.

The Rosavilla School District wants to build a new middle school building. They ask architects to make scale drawings of possible layouts for the building. The district narrows the possibilities to the layouts shown.

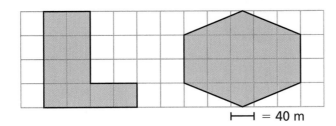

$\vdash\!\dashv$ = 40 m

29. a. Suppose the layouts above are on centimeter grid paper. What is the area of each scale drawing?

b. What will be the area of each building?

30. Multiple Choice The board likes the L-shaped layout but wants a building with more space. They increase the L-shaped layout by a scale factor of 2. For the new layout, choose the correct statement.

A. The area is two times the original.

B. The area is four times the original.

C. The area is eight times the original.

D. None of the statements above is correct.

31. Use the table for parts (a)–(c).

Student Heights and Arm Spans

Height (in.)	60	65	63	50	58	66	60	63	67	65
Arm Span (in.)	55	60	60	48	60	65	60	67	62	70

    a. Find the ratio of arm span to height for each student. Write the ratio as a fraction. Then write the ratio as an equivalent decimal. How do the ratios compare?

    b. Find the mean of the ratios.

    c. Use your answer from part (b). Predict the arm span of a person who is 62 inches tall. Explain.

32. Suppose you enlarge this spinner by a factor of 3. Does this change the probabilities of the pointer landing in any of the areas? Explain.

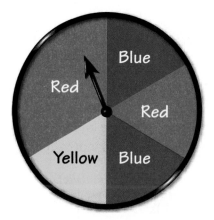

33. Suppose you enlarge the square dartboard below by a scale factor of 3. Will the probabilities that the dart will land in each region change? Explain.

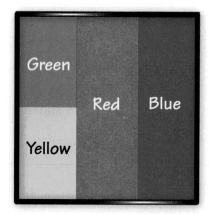

34. For each angle measure, find the measure of its complement and the measure of its supplement.

      Sample 30°
                complement: 60°
                supplement: 150°

    a. 20°   **b.** 70°   **c.** 45°

Extensions

35. For parts (a)–(e), use the similar triangles below.

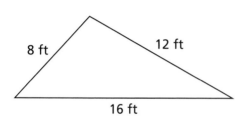 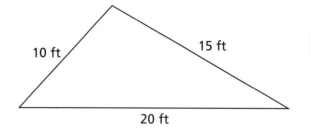

    a. What is the scale factor from the smaller triangle to the larger triangle? Give your answer as a fraction and a decimal.

    b. Choose any side of the larger triangle. What is the ratio of the length of this side to the corresponding side length in the smaller triangle? Write your answer as a fraction and as a decimal. How does the ratio compare to the scale factor in part (a)?

    c. What is the scale factor from the larger triangle to the smaller triangle? Write your answer as a fraction and a decimal.

    d. Choose any side of the smaller triangle. What is the ratio of the length of this side to the corresponding side length in the larger triangle? Write your answer as a fraction and as a decimal. How does the ratio compare to the scale factor in part (c)?

    e. Is the pattern for scale factors and ratios in this exercise the same for any pair of similar figures? Explain.

36. For parts (a) and (b), use a straightedge and an angle ruler or protractor.

    a. Draw two different triangles that each have angle measures of 30°, 60°, and 90°. Do the triangles appear to be similar?

    b. Draw two different triangles that each have angle measures of 40°, 80°, and 60°. Do the triangles appear to be similar?

    c. Based on your findings for parts (a) and (b), make a conjecture about triangles with congruent angle measures.

37. Which rectangle below do you think is "most pleasing to the eye?"

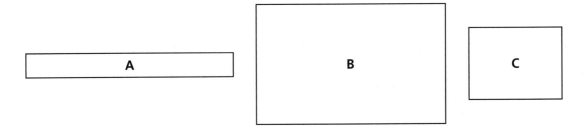

The question of what shapes are attractive has interested builders, artists, and craftspeople for thousands of years. The ancient Greeks were particularly attracted to rectangular shapes similar to rectangle B above. They referred to such shapes as "golden rectangles." They used golden rectangles frequently in buildings and monuments.

The photograph of the Parthenon (a temple in Athens, Greece) below shows several examples of golden rectangles.

The ratio of the length to the width in a golden rectangle is called the "golden ratio."

a. Measure the length and width of rectangles A, B, and C in inches. In each case, estimate the ratio of the length to the width as accurately as possible. The ratio for rectangle B is an approximation of the golden ratio.

b. Measure the dimensions of the three golden rectangles in the photograph in centimeters. Write the ratio of length to width in each case. Write each ratio as a fraction and then as a decimal. Compare the ratios to each other and to the ratio for rectangle B.

c. You can divide a golden rectangle into a square and a smaller rectangle similar to the original rectangle.

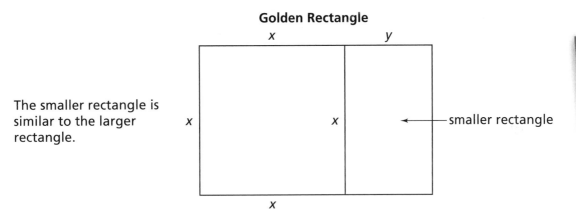

Golden Rectangle

The smaller rectangle is similar to the larger rectangle.

smaller rectangle

Copy rectangle B from the previous page. Divide this golden rectangle into a square and a rectangle. Is the smaller rectangle a golden rectangle? Explain.

Extensions

38. For parts (a) and (b), use the triangles below.

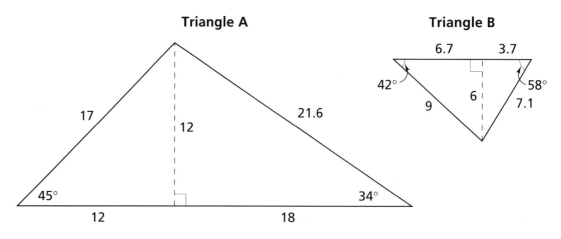

Triangle A

Triangle B

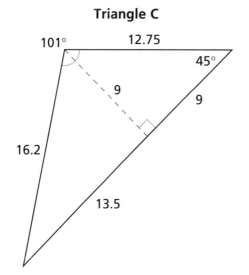

Triangle C

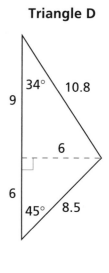

Triangle D

a. Identify the triangles that are similar to each other. Explain.

b. For each triangle, find the ratio of the base to the height. How do these ratios compare for the similar triangles? How do these ratios compare for the non-similar triangles?

39. The following sequence of numbers is called the *Fibonacci sequence*. It is named after an Italian mathematician in the 14th century who contributed to the early development of algebra.

   1, 1, 2, 3, 5, 8, 13, 21, 34, 55, 89, 144, 233, 377 . . .

a. Look for patterns in this sequence. Figure out how the numbers are found. Use your idea to find the next four terms.

b. Find the ratio of each term to the term before. For example, 1 to 1, 2 to 1, 3 to 2, and so on. Write each of the ratios as a fraction and then as an equivalent decimal. Compare the results to the golden ratios you found in Exercise 37. Describe similarities and differences.

Mathematical Reflections 4

In this investigation, you used the idea of ratios to describe and compare the size and shape of rectangles, triangles, and other figures. These questions will help you summarize what you learned.

Think about your answers to these questions. Discuss your ideas with other students and your teacher. Then write a summary of your findings in your notebook.

1. If two parallelograms are similar, what do you know about the ratios of the two side lengths within one parallelogram and the ratios of the corresponding side lengths in the other parallelogram?

2. If two triangles are similar, what can you say about the ratios of the two side lengths within one triangle and the ratios of the corresponding side lengths in the other triangle?

3. Describe at least two ways of finding a missing side length in a pair of similar figures.

Investigation 5

Using Similar Triangles and Rectangles

You can find the height of a school building by climbing a ladder and using a long tape measure. You can also use easier and less dangerous ways to find the height. In this investigation, you can use similar triangles to estimate heights and distances that are difficult to measure directly.

5.1 Using Shadows to Find Heights

If an object is outdoors, you can use shadows to estimate its height. The diagram below shows how the method works. On a sunny day, any upright object casts a shadow. The diagram below shows two triangles.

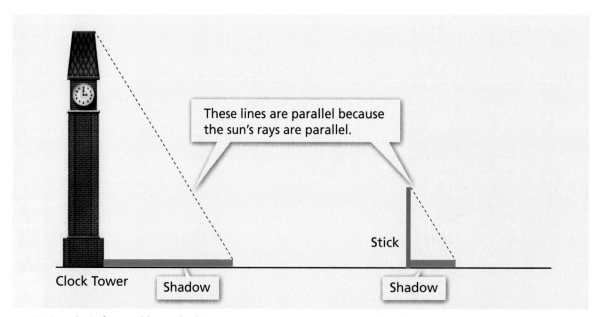

These lines are parallel because the sun's rays are parallel.

Stick

Clock Tower | Shadow | Shadow

A triangle is formed by a clock tower, its shadow, and an imaginary line from the top of the tower to the end of the shadow.

A triangle is formed by a stick, its shadow, and an imaginary line from the top of the stick to the end of its shadow.

Examine the diagram of the shadow method. Why does each angle of the large triangle have the same measure as the corresponding angle of the small triangle? What does this suggest about the similarity of the triangles?

To find the height of the building, you can measure the lengths of the stick and the two shadows and use similar triangles.

Problem 5.1 Using Shadows to Find Heights

Suppose you want to use the shadow method to estimate the height of a building. You make the following measurements:

- length of the stick: 3 m

- length of the stick's shadow: 1.5 m

- length of the building's shadow: 8 m

A. Make a sketch of the building, the stick, and the shadows. Label each given measurement. What evidence suggests that the two triangles formed are similar?

B. Use similar triangles to find the building's height from the given measurements.

C. A tree casts a 25-foot shadow. At the same time, a 6-foot stick casts a shadow 4.5 feet long. How tall is the tree?

D. A radio tower casts a 120-foot shadow. At the same time, a 12-foot-high basketball backboard (with pole) casts a shadow 18 feet long. How high is the radio tower?

ACE Homework starts on page 84.

5.2 Using Mirrors to Find Heights

The shadow method only works outdoors on sunny days. As an alternative, you can also use a mirror to estimate heights. The mirror method works both indoors and outdoors.

The mirror method is shown below. Place a mirror on a level spot at a convenient distance from the object. Back up from the mirror until you can see the top of the object in the center of the mirror.

The two triangles in the diagram are similar. To find the object's height, you need to measure three distances and use similar triangles.

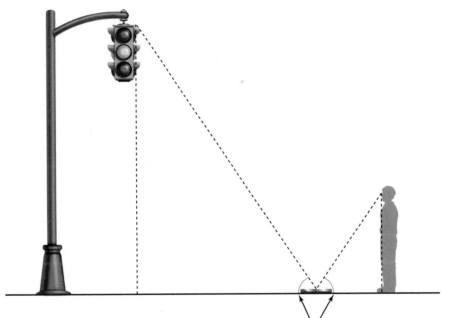

These angles are congruent because light reflects off a mirror at the same angle it arrives.

Getting Ready for Problem 5.2

Examine the diagram above. Explain why each angle of the large triangle has the same measure as the corresponding angle of the small triangle. What does this suggest about the similarity of the triangles?

A. Jim and Su use the mirror method to estimate the height of a traffic signal near their school. They make the following measurements:

> • height from the ground to Jim's eyes: 150 cm
>
> • distance from the middle of the mirror to Jim's feet: 100 cm
>
> • distance from the middle of the mirror to a point directly under
>
> the traffic signal: 450 cm

1. Make a sketch. Show the similar triangles formed and label the given measurements.

2. Use similar triangles to find the height of the traffic signal.

B. Jim and Su also use the mirror method to estimate the height of the gymnasium in their school. They make the following measurements:

> • height from the ground to Su's eyes: 130 cm
>
> • distance from the middle of the mirror to Su's feet: 100 cm
>
> • distance from the middle of the mirror to the gym wall: 9.5 m

1. Make a sketch. Show the similar triangles formed and label the given measurements.

2. Use similar triangles to find the height of the gymnasium.

C. Use the mirror method to find the height of your classroom. Make a sketch showing the distances you measured. Explain how you used the measurements to find the height of the room.

D. Compare the two methods (shadow or mirror) for finding missing measurements. What types of problems may arise when using these methods?

ACE   **Homework starts on page 84.**

On the Ground . . . but Still Out of Reach

Darnell, Angie, and Trevor are at a park along the Red Cedar River with their class. They decide to use similar triangles to find the distance across the river. After making several measurements, they sketch the diagram below.

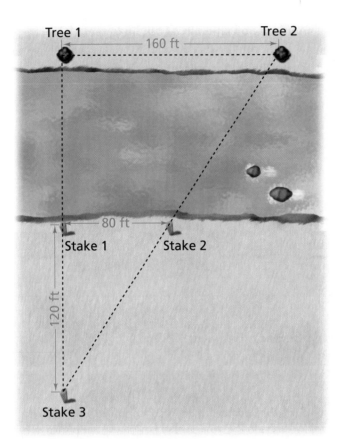

Getting Ready for Problem

In the two previous problems, you used the fact that if two triangles have corresponding angles with the same measure, then the triangles are similar. This is not true for other polygons in general.

- What do you know about parallelograms and rectangles that explains this?

- Which triangles in the river diagram are similar? Why?

A. Use the river diagram. Which triangles appear to be similar? Explain.

B. What is the distance across the river from Stake 1 to Tree 1? Explain.

C. The diagram shows three stakes and two trees. In what order do you think Darnell, Angie, and Trevor located the key points and measured the segments?

D. Another group of students repeats the measurement. They put their stakes in different places. The distance from Stake 1 to Stake 2 is 32 feet. The distance from Stake 1 to Stake 3 is 30 feet. Does this second group get the same measurement for the width of the river? Explain.

ACE **Homework starts on page 84.**

Applications

1. The Washington Monument is the tallest structure in Washington, D.C. At the same time the monument casts a shadow that is about 500 feet long, a 40-foot flagpole nearby casts a shadow that is about 36 feet long. Make a sketch. Find the approximate height of the monument.

2. Darius uses the shadow method to estimate the height of a flagpole. He finds that a 5-foot stick casts a 4-foot shadow. At the same time, he finds that the flagpole casts a 20-foot shadow. Make a sketch. Use Darius's measurements to estimate the height of the flagpole.

3. The school principal visits Ashton's class one day. The principal asks Ashton to show her what they are learning. Ashton uses the mirror method to estimate the principal's height. This sketch shows the measurements he records.

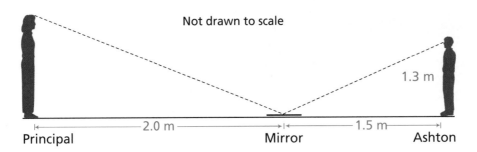

Not drawn to scale

Principal — 2.0 m — Mirror — 1.5 m — Ashton

1.3 m

a. What estimate should Ashton give for the principal's height?

b. Is your answer to part (a) a reasonable height for an adult?

4. Stacia stands 8 feet from a mirror on the ground. She can see the top of a 100-foot radio tower in the center of the mirror. Her eyes are 5 feet from the ground. How far is the mirror from the base of the tower?

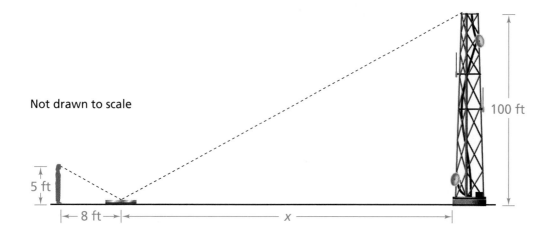

Not drawn to scale

5 ft

|← 8 ft →|← ———————— x ———————— →|

100 ft

5. Judy lies on the ground 45 feet from her tent. Both the top of the tent and the top of a tall cliff are in her line of sight. Her tent is 10 feet tall. About how high is the cliff?

Not drawn to scale

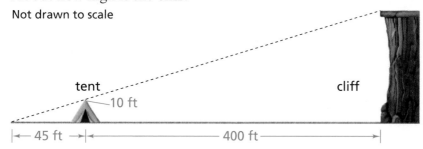

tent
10 ft

cliff

|← 45 ft →|← ————— 400 ft ————— →|

Connections

Find the value of x that makes the fractions equivalent.

6. $\frac{5}{2} = \frac{x}{8}$ **7.** $\frac{2}{5} = \frac{7}{x}$ **8.** $\frac{7}{5} = \frac{28}{x}$ **9.** $\frac{7.5}{10} = \frac{3}{x}$

10. $\frac{1}{7} = \frac{x}{35}$ **11.** $\frac{x}{5} = \frac{60}{100}$ **12.** $\frac{4}{10} = \frac{x}{5}$ **13.** $\frac{3}{3.6} = \frac{x}{6}$

Find the given percent or fraction of the number.

14. 30% of 256 **15.** 25% of 2,048

16. $\frac{2}{3}$ of 24 **17.** $\frac{5}{6}$ of 90

Write each comparison as a percent.

18. 55 out of 100

19. 13 out of 39

20. 2.5 out of 10

21. 5 out of 100

22. The rectangles below are similar. The figures are not shown at actual size.

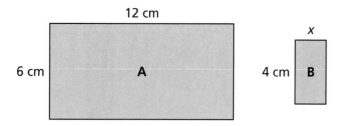

12 cm

6 cm — A

4 cm — B — x

a. What is the scale factor from rectangle A to rectangle B?

b. Complete the following sentence in two different ways. Use the side lengths of rectangles A and B.

The ratio of ■ to ■ is equivalent to the ratio of ■ to ■.

c. What is the value of *x*?

d. What is the ratio of the area of rectangle A to the area of rectangle B?

For Exercises 23 and 24 on page 87, use the rectangles below. The rectangles are not shown at actual size.

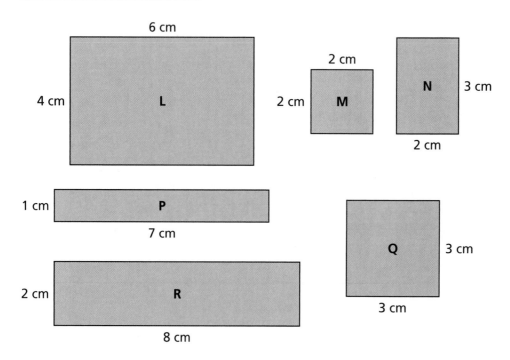

6 cm

4 cm — L

2 cm

2 cm — M

N — 3 cm

2 cm

1 cm — P

7 cm

Q — 3 cm

3 cm

2 cm — R

8 cm

23. Multiple Choice Which pair of rectangles is similar?

A. L and M **B.** L and Q **C.** L and N **D.** P and R

24. a. Find at least one more pair of similar rectangles.

b. For each similar pair, find both the scale factor relating the larger rectangle to the smaller rectangle and the scale factor relating the smaller rectangle to the larger rectangle.

c. For each similar pair, find the ratio of the area of the larger rectangle to the area of the smaller rectangle.

25. The two triangles are similar.

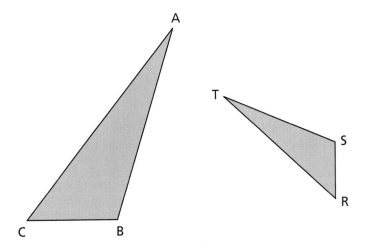

a. Find the corresponding vertices.

b. Estimate the scale factor that relates triangle *ABC* to triangle *TSR*.

c. Estimate the scale factor that relates triangle *TSR* to triangle *ABC*.

d. Use your result from part (b). Estimate the ratio of the area of triangle *ABC* to the area of triangle *TSR*.

e. Use the result from part (c). Estimate the ratio of the area of triangle *TSR* to the area of triangle *ABC*.

26. Parallel lines *BD* and *EG* are intersected by line *AH*. Eight angles are formed by the lines, four around point *C* and four around point *F*.

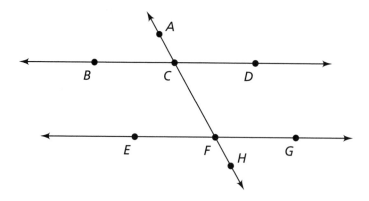

  a. Name every angle that is congruent to (has the same measure as) angle *ACD*.

  b. Name every angle that is congruent to angle *EFC*.

For Exercises 27–31, suppose a photographer for a school newspaper takes this picture for a story. The editors want to resize the photo to fit in a specific space of the paper.

Homework Help Online
PHSchool.com

For: Help with Exercise 27
Web Code: ane-2527

27. The original photo is a rectangle that is 4 inches wide and 6 inches high. Can it be changed to a similar rectangle with the given measurements (in inches)?

  a. 8 by 12   **b.** 9 by 11   **c.** 6 by 9   **d.** 3 by 4.5

28. Suppose that the school copier only has three paper sizes (in inches): $8\frac{1}{2}$ by 11, 11 by 14, and 11 by 17. You can enlarge or reduce documents by specifying a percent from 50% to 200%. Can you make copies of the photo that fit exactly on any of the three paper sizes?

29. How can you use the copy machine to reduce the photo to a copy whose length and width are 25% of the original dimensions? How does the area of the new copy relate to the area of the original photo? (**Hint:** The machine accepts only factors from 50% to 200%.)

30. How can you use the copy machine to reduce the photo to a copy whose length and width are 12.5% of the original dimensions? 36% of the original dimensions? How does the area of the reduced figure compare to the area of the original in each case?

31. What is the greatest enlargement of the photo that will fit on paper that is 11 inches by 17 inches?

32. Multiple Choice What is the correct value for *x*? The figure is not shown at actual size.

A. 3 cm   **B.** 10 cm

C. 12 cm   **D.** 90 cm

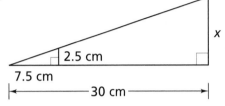

For Exercises 33–34, find each missing measure. The figures are not shown at actual size.

33.

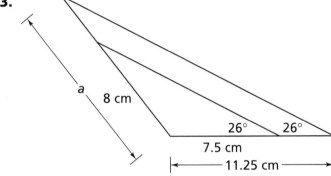

34.

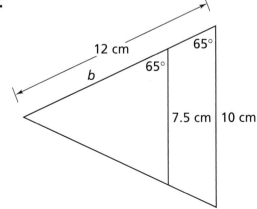

Extensions

35. Use the mirror method, the shadow method, or another method involving similar triangles to find the height of a telephone pole, a light pole, a tall tree, or a tall building in your town. Explain your method.

36. Tang thinks he has found a way to use similar triangles to find the height of the building. He stands 15 meters from a building and holds a 30-centimeter ruler in front of his eyes. The ruler is 45 centimeters from his eyes. He can see the top and bottom of the building as he looks above and below the ruler.

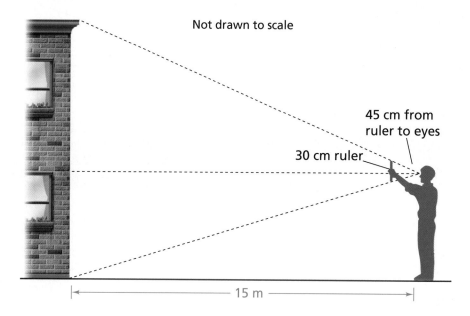

Not drawn to scale

45 cm from ruler to eyes

30 cm ruler

15 m

a. Do you see any similar triangles in the diagram that can help Tang find the height of the building?

b. How tall is the building?

37. In an annular eclipse (a kind of solar eclipse), the moon moves between Earth and the sun, blocking part of the sun's light for a few minutes. Around 240 B.C., a scientist used eclipses to estimate the distances between Earth, the moon, and the sun.

Not drawn to scale

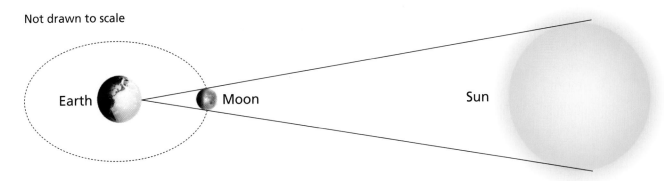

In 1994, there was an annular eclipse. A class constructed a viewing box like the one shown.

Not drawn to scale

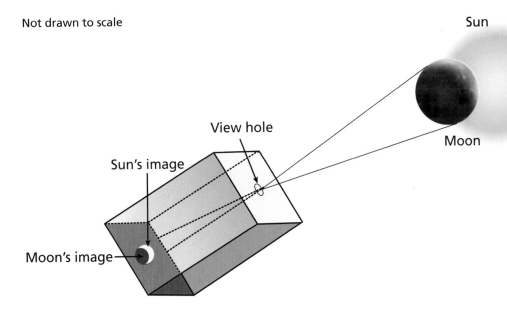

During the eclipse, the image of the moon almost completely covered the sun. The moon's shadow and the ring of light surrounding it appeared on the bottom of the viewing box. The moon's image was 1 meter from the view hole, and its diameter was 0.9 centimeter. The actual diameter of the moon is about 3,500 kilometers. Estimate the distance to the moon at the time of the eclipse.

38. Some evening when you see a full moon, go outside with a friend and use a coin to exactly block the image of the moon.

    a. How far from your eyes do you have to hold the coin? Can you hold it yourself or does your friend have to hold it for you?

    b. The diameter of the moon is about 2,160 miles. The distance from the Earth to the moon is about 238,000 miles. Use these numbers, the diameter of your coin, and similar triangles to find the distance you have to hold the coin from your eye to just block the moon. How does the distance you find compare to the distance you measured in part (a)?

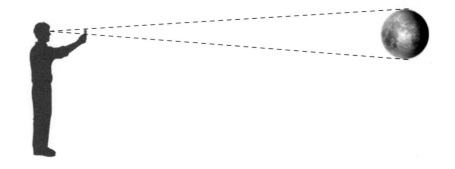

Mathematical Reflections 5

In this investigation, you used what you know about similar triangles to find heights of buildings and to estimate other inaccessible distances. These questions will help you summarize what you learned.

Think about your answers to these questions. Discuss your ideas with other students and your teacher. Then write a summary of your findings in your notebook.

1. How can you estimate heights and distances you can't easily measure with rulers or tape measures by using the following methods?

   a. shadows and similar triangles

   b. mirrors and similar triangles

   c. small triangles nested within larger triangles

2. How can you decide whether a photo or drawing can be enlarged or reduced to fit a space without distorting the shapes?

Unit Project

1. Shrinking or Enlarging Pictures

Your final project for this unit involves two parts.

(1) the drawing of a similar image of a picture

(2) a written report on making similar figures

Part 1: Drawing

You will enlarge or shrink a picture or cartoon of your choice. You may use the technique of coordinate graphing rules to produce a similar image.

If you enlarge the picture, the image must have a scale factor of at least 4. If you shrink the picture, the image must have a scale factor of at most $\frac{1}{4}$.

Your final project must be presented in a display for others. Both the original picture and the image need to be in the display, and you must do the following:

- identify the scale factor and show how the lengths compare between the picture and the image
- identify two pairs of corresponding angles and show how the angles compare between the picture and the image
- compare some area of the picture with the corresponding area of the image

Part 2: Write a Report

Write a report describing how you made your similar figure. Your report should include the following:

- a description of the technique or method you used to make the image
- a description of changes in the lengths, angles, and area between the original picture and the image
- A paragraph (or more) on other details you think are interesting or which help readers understand what they see (for example, a description of any problems or challenges you had and decisions you made as a result).

Unit Project

2. All-Similar Shapes

Throughout this unit, you worked with problems that helped you understand the similarity of two shapes. You learned that not all rectangles are similar. For example, an $8\frac{1}{2}$-by-11-inch sheet of paper is rectangular and so is a business-size envelope. However, the envelope is not the same shape as the paper.

A group of students decided to look at rectangles that are square. They find that no matter what size square they drew, every square was similar to shape B in the Shapes Set and to all other squares. They found that *all squares are similar!* They decided to call a square an All-Similar shape.

The students wanted to know whether there were any other All-Similar shapes like the square. That is, are there any other groups of shapes called by the same name that are similar to all other shapes called by that name? Use your Shapes Set to investigate.

Investigate Four Questions

1. Make a list of the names of all the different types of shapes in the Shapes Set (squares, rectangles, triangles, equilateral triangles, circles, and regular hexagons).

2. For each type of shape, list the shapes (using their letter names) that belong in that group.

3. Sort the different types of shapes into two groups: All-Similar shapes (such as squares) and shapes that are not All-Similar (such as rectangles).

4. Describe ways in which All-Similar shapes are alike.

Looking Back and Looking Ahead

Go Online
PHSchool.com

For: Vocabulary Review Puzzle
Web Code: anj-2051

The problems in this unit helped you understand the concept of similarity as it applies to geometric shapes. You learned how

- to make similar shapes
- to determine whether two shapes are similar
- side lengths, perimeters, angle measures, and areas of similar shapes relate to each other
- to investigate the use of similarity to solve problems

Use Your Understanding: Similarity

Test your understanding of similarity by solving the following problems.

1. The square below is subdivided into six triangles and four parallelograms. Some of the shapes are similar.

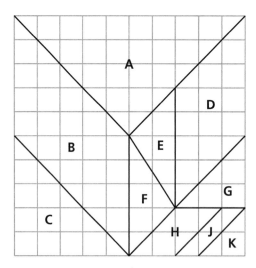

a. List all the pairs of similar triangles in the figure. For each pair, give the scale factor from one figure to the other.

b. Pick a pair of similar triangles. Explain how their perimeters are related and how their areas are related.

c. List several pairs of triangles in the figure that are *not* similar.

d. List all pairs of similar parallelograms in the figure. For each pair, give the scale factor from one figure to the other.

e. Pick a pair of similar parallelograms. Explain how their perimeters are related and how their areas are related.

f. List several pairs of parallelograms in the figure that are *not* similar.

2. a. Suppose a triangle is on a coordinate grid. Which of the following rules will change the triangle into a similar triangle?

    i. $(3x, 3y)$ **ii.** $(x + 3, y + 2)$

    iii. $(2x, 4y)$ **iv.** $(2x, 2y + 1)$

    v. $(1.5x, 1.5y)$ **vi.** $(x - 3, 2y - 3)$

b. For each of the rules in part (a) that will produce a similar triangle, give the scale factor from the original triangle to its image.

3. A school photograph measures 12 centimeters by 20 centimeters. The class officers want to enlarge the photo to fit on a large poster.

a. Can the original photo be enlarged to 60 centimeters by 90 centimeters?

b. Can the original photo be enlarged to 42 centimeters by 70 centimeters?

Explain Your Reasoning

Answer the following questions to summarize what you know.

4. What questions do you ask yourself when deciding whether two shapes are similar?

5. Suppose shape A is similar to shape B. The scale factor from shape A to shape B is k.

   a. How are the perimeters of the two figures related?

   b. How are the areas of the two figures related?

6. If two triangles are similar, what do you know about the following measurements?

   a. the side lengths of the two figures

   b. the angle measures of the two figures

7. Tell whether each statement is true or false. Explain.

   a. Any two equilateral triangles are similar.

   b. Any two rectangles are similar.

   c. Any two squares are similar.

   d. Any two isosceles triangles are similar.

Look Ahead

You will study and use ideas of similarity in several future *Connected Mathematics* units, especially where it is important to compare sizes and shapes of geometric figures. Basic principles of similarity are also used in a variety of practical and scientific problems where figures are enlarged or reduced.

C

complementary angles Complementary angles are a pair of angles whose measures add to 90°.

ángulos complementarios Los ángulos complementarios son un par de ángulos cuyas medidas suman 90°.

corresponding Corresponding sides or angles have the same relative position in similar figures. In this pair of similar shapes, side AB corresponds to side HJ, and angle BCD corresponds to angle JKF.

correspondientes Se dice que los lados o ángulos son correspondientes cuando tienen la misma posición relativa en figuras semejantes. En el siguiente par de figuras semejantes, el lado AB es correspondiente con el lado HJ y el ángulo BCD es correspondiente con el ángulo JKF.

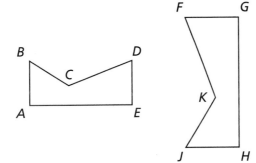

E

equivalent ratios Ratios whose fraction representations are equivalent are called equivalent ratios. For instance, the ratios 3 to 4 and 6 to 8 are equivalent because $\frac{3}{4} = \frac{6}{8}$.

razones equivalentes Las razones, cuyas representaciones de fracciones son equivalentes, se llaman razones equivalentes. Por ejemplo, las razones 3 a 4 y 6 a 8 son equivalentes porque $\frac{3}{4} + \frac{6}{8}$.

I

image The figure that results from some transformation of a figure. It is often of interest to consider what is the same and what is different about a figure and its image.

imagen La figura que resulta de alguna transformación de una figura. A menudo es interesante tener en cuenta en qué se parecen y en qué se diferencian una figura y su imagen.

M

midpoint A point that divides a line segment into two segments of equal length. In the figure below M is the midpoint of segment LN.

punto medio Punto que divide un segmento de recta en dos segmentos de igual longitud. En la figura de abajo, M es el punto medio del segmento de recta LN.

nested triangles Triangles that share a common angle are sometimes called nested. In the figure below, triangle *ABC* is nested in triangle *ADE*.

triángulos semejantes Los triángulos que comparten un ángulo común a veces se llaman semejantes. En la siguiente figura, el triángulo *ABC* es semejante al triángulo *ADE*.

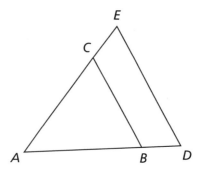

ratio A ratio is a comparison of two quantities. It is sometimes expressed as a fraction. For example, suppose the length of side *AB* is 2 inches and the length of side *CD* is 3 inches. The ratio of the length of side *AB* to the length of side *CD* is 2 to 3, or $\frac{2}{3}$. The ratio of the length of side *CD* to the length of side *AB* is 3 to 2, or $\frac{3}{2}$.

razón La razón es una comparación de dos cantidades. A veces se expresa como una fracción. Por ejemplo, supón que la longitud de *AB* es 2 pulgadas y la longitud de *CD* es 3 pulgadas. La razón de la longitud *AB* a la longitud *CD* es de 2 a 3, es decir, $\frac{2}{3}$. La razón de la longitud *CD* a la longitud *AB* es de 3 a 2, es decir, $\frac{3}{2}$.

rep-tile A figure you can use to make a larger, similar version of the original is called a rep-tile. The smaller figure below is a rep-tile because you can use four copies of it to make a larger similar figure.

baldosa repetida Una figura que puedes usar para hacer una versión más grande y semejante a la original, se llama baldosa repetida. La figura más pequeña de abajo es una baldosa repetida porque se pueden usar cuatro copias de ella para hacer una figura semejante más grande.

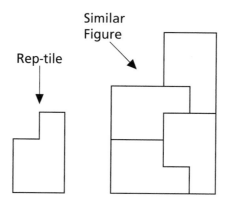

Similar
Figure

Rep-tile

scale factor The number used to multiply the lengths of a figure to stretch or shrink it to a similar image. If we use a scale factor of 3, all lengths in the image are 3 times as long as the corresponding lengths in the original. When you are given two similar figures, the scale factor is the ratio of the image side length to the corresponding original side length.

factor de escala El número utilizado para multiplicar las longitudes de una figura para ampliarla o reducirla a una imagen semejante. Si el factor de escala es 3, todas las longitudes de la imagen son 3 veces más largas que las longitudes correspondientes de la figura original. Cuando se dan dos figuras semejantes, el factor de escala es la razón de la longitud del lado de la imagen a la longitud del lado original correspondiente.

similar Similar figures have corresponding angles of equal measure and the ratios of each pair of corresponding sides are equivalent.

semejante Las figuras semejantes tienen ángulos correspondientes de igual medida y las razones de cada par de lados correspondientes son equivalentes.

supplementary angles Supplementary angles are two angles that form a straight line. The sum of the angles is 180°.

ángulos suplementarios Los ángulos suplementarios son dos ángulos que forman una recta. La suma de los ángulos es de 180°.

Index

Acknowledgments

Team Credits

The people who made up the **Connected Mathematics 2** team—representing editorial, editorial services, design services, and production services—are listed below. Bold type denotes core team members.

Leora Adler, Judith Buice, Kerry Cashman, Patrick Culleton, Sheila DeFazio, Katie Hallahan, Richard Heater, **Barbara Hollingdale, Jayne Holman,** Karen Holtzman, **Etta Jacobs,** Christine Lee, Carolyn Lock, Catherine Maglio, **Dotti Marshall,** Rich McMahon, Eve Melnechuk, Kristin Mingrone, Terri Mitchell, **Marsha Novak,** Irene Rubin, Donna Russo, Robin Samper, Siri Schwartzman, **Nancy Smith,** Emily Soltanoff, **Mark Tricca,** Paula Vergith, Roberta Warshaw, Helen Young

Additional Credits

Diana Bonfilio, Mairead Reddin, Michael Torocsik, nSight, Inc.

Illustration

Michelle Barbera: 2, 6, 52

Technical Illustration

WestWords, Inc.

Cover Design

tom white.images

Photos

2, Raoul Minsart/Masterfile; **3,** Lee Snider/The Image Works; **5,** Raoul Minsart/Masterfile; **8 both,** Richard Haynes; **16,** SW Productions/Getty Images, Inc.; **21,** Ryan McVay/PhotoDisc/Getty Images, Inc.; **22,** Richard Haynes; **25,** Richard Haynes; **40,** M.C. Escher's "Symmetry Drawing E18" © 2004 The M.C. Escher Company-Baarn-Holland. All rights reserved.; **51,** Richard Haynes; **54,** Geoffrey Clifford/IPN Stock; **58,** Richard Haynes; **59 all,** Richard Haynes; **62,** J. Neubauer/Robertstock; **69,** F64/Getty Images, Inc.; **74,** Izzet Keribar/Lonely Planet Images; **83,** Raymond Gehman/Corbis; **84,** Alan Schein Photography/Corbis; **88,** Arthur Tilley/PictureQuest; **94,** Russ Lappa; **96,** Richard Haynes; **99,** Gabe Palmer/Corbis

Connected Mathematics 2™

Comparing and Scaling

Ratio, Proportion, and Percent

Glenda Lappan

James T. Fey

William M. Fitzgerald

Susan N. Friel

Elizabeth Difanis Phillips

PEARSON

Prentice Hall

Boston, Massachusetts
Upper Saddle River, New Jersey

Comparing and Scaling

Ratio, Proportion, and Percent

At camp, Miriam uses a pottery wheel to make 3 bowls in 2 hours. Duane makes 5 bowls in 3 hours. Who is the faster potter? Suppose they continue to work at the same pace. How long will it take each of them to make a set of 12 bowls?

It takes 100 maple trees to make 25 gallons of maple syrup. How many maple trees does it take for one gallon of syrup?

Two summers ago, a biologist captured, tagged, and released 20 puffins on an island. When she returned this past summer, she captured 50 puffins. Two of them were tagged. About how many puffins are on the island?

Many everyday problems and decisions call for comparisons. Which car is safer? Which horse is the fastest? Which Internet service is cheaper? In some cases, the comparisons involve only counting, measuring, or rating, then ordering the results from least to greatest. In other cases, more complex reasoning is required.

How would you answer the comparison questions on the previous page?

In this unit, you will explore many ways to compare numbers. You'll learn how to both choose and use the best comparison strategies to solve problems and make decisions.

Mathematical Highlights

In *Comparing and Scaling*, you will develop several methods for comparing quantities. You will use these methods to solve problems.

You will learn how to

- Use informal language to ask comparison questions

    Examples:

    "What is the ratio of boys to girls in our class?"

    "What fraction of the class is going to the spring picnic?"

    "What percent of the girls play basketball?"

    "Which model of car has the best fuel economy?"

- Choose an appropriate method to make comparisons among quantities using ratios, percents, fractions, rates, or differences

- Find equivalent forms of given ratios and rates to scale comparisons up and down

- Find and interpret unit rates, and use them to make comparisons

- Use unit rates to write an equation to represent a pattern in a table of data

- Set up and solve proportions

- Use proportional reasoning to solve problems

As you work on the problems in this unit, ask yourself questions about problem situations that involve comparisons:

What quantities should be compared?

What type of comparison will give the most useful information?

How can the comparison be expressed in different but useful ways?

How can given comparison data be used to make predictions about unknown quantities?

Investigation 1

Making Comparisons

Surveys may report people's preferences in food, cars, or political candidates. Often, the favorites are easy to recognize. Explaining how much more popular one choice is than another can be more difficult. In this investigation, you will explore strategies for comparing numbers in accurate and useful ways. As you work on the problems, notice how the different ways of making comparisons send different messages about the numbers being compared.

1.1 Ads That Sell

An ad for the soft drink Bolda Cola starts like this:

Which Soft Drink Do You Like Better?

Bolda Cola

OR

COLA·NOLA

Take the Cola Taste Test Yourself!

To complete the ad, the Bolda Cola company plans to report the results of taste tests. A copywriter for the ad department has proposed four possible conclusions.

1. In a taste test, people who preferred Bolda Cola outnumbered those who preferred Cola Nola by a ratio of 17,139 to 11,426.

2. In a taste test, 5,713 more people preferred Bolda Cola.

3. In a taste test, 60% of the people preferred Bolda Cola.

4. In a taste test, people who preferred Bolda Cola outnumbered those who preferred Cola Nola by a ratio of 3 to 2.

Problem 1.1 Exploring Ratios and Rates

A. Describe what you think each statement above means.

B. Which of the proposed statements do you think would be most effective in advertising Bolda Cola? Why?

C. Is it possible that all four statements are based on the same survey data? Explain your reasoning.

D. In what other ways can you express the claims in the four proposed advertising statements? Explain.

E. If you were to survey 1,000 cola drinkers, what numbers of Bolda Cola and Cola Nola drinkers would you expect? Explain.

ACE Homework starts on page 10.

1.2 Targeting an Audience

Some middle and high school students earn money by delivering papers, mowing lawns, or baby-sitting. Students with money to spend are a target audience for some radio and television ads. Companies gather information about how much students watch television or listen to the radio. This information influences how they spend their advertising dollars.

As you work on this problem and the rest of the unit, you will see statements about ratio comparisons. In mathematics, it is acceptable to write ratios in different ways. Each way is useful.

Ways to Write a Ratio

3 to 2   3 : 2 $\dfrac{3}{2}$

It can be confusing to see a fraction representing a ratio. A ratio is usually, but not always, a *part-to-part* comparison. A fraction usually means a *part-to-whole* comparison. The context can help you decide whether a fraction represents a ratio.

Problem 1.2 Analyzing Comparison Statements

Students at Neilson Middle School are asked if they prefer watching television or listening to the radio. Of 150 students, 100 prefer television and 50 prefer radio.

A. How would you compare student preferences for radio or television?

B. Decide if each statement accurately reports results of the Neilson Middle School survey.

  1. At Neilson Middle School, $\frac{1}{3}$ of the students prefer radio to television.

  2. Students prefer television to radio by a ratio of 2 to 1.

  3. The ratio of students who prefer radio to television is 1 to 2.

  4. The number of students who prefer television is 50 more than the number of students who prefer radio.

  5. The number of students who prefer television is two times the number who prefer radio.

  6. 50% of the students prefer radio to television.

C. Compare statements in parts (4) and (5) above. Which is more informative? Explain.

D. Consider only the accurate statements in Question B.

  1. Which statement would best convince merchants to place ads on radio? Why?

  2. Which statement would best convince merchants to place ads on television? Why?

ACE **Homework starts on page 10.**

People are amazed and amused by records like the highest mountain, the longest fingernails, or the most spoons balanced on a face. What you have learned so far can help you make comparisons. In Problem 1.3, you will compare the largest living trees of different species.

Did You Know?

The champion white "Wye" oak tree near Wye Mills, Maryland, was about 460 years old when it fell during a thunderstorm in 2002. When the tree fell, thousands came by to gawk, shed tears, and pick up a leaf or a twig. Maryland officials carefully gathered and stored as much of the tree as they could until a suitable use could be found.

The challenge to find a white oak bigger than the Wye Mills tree launched the National Register of Big Trees. The search led to the discovery of a new national champion white oak in Virginia.

 **Go Online**
PHSchool.com   **For:** Information about big trees
Web Code: ane-9031

You can describe the size of a tree by comparing it to other trees or familiar things.

Selected Champion Trees

Tree Type	Circumference (ft)	Height (ft)	Spread/Diameter (ft)
Giant Sequoia (Calif.)	83.2	275	107
Coast Redwood (Calif.)	79.2	321	80
Swamp Chestnut Oak (Tenn.)	23.0	105	216
Florida Crossopetalum (Fla.)	0.4	11	3
White Oak (Md.)	31.8	96	119

SOURCE: *Washington Post*

A. Use the table on the previous page.

    1. How many coast redwood spreads does it take to equal the spread of the white oak?

    2. Kenning says that the spread of the white oak is greater than that of the coast redwood by a ratio of about 3 to 2. Is he correct? Explain.

    3. Mary says the difference between the heights of the coast redwood and the giant sequoia is 46 feet. Is she correct? Explain.

    4. How many giant sequoia spreads does it take to equal the spread of the swamp chestnut oak?

    5. Jaime says the spread of the giant sequoia is less than 50% of the spread of the swamp chestnut oak. Is he correct?

    6. Len says the circumference of the swamp chestnut oak is about three fourths the circumference of the white oak. Is he correct?

B. The tallest person in history, according to the *Guinness Book of World Records*, was Robert Wadlow. He was nearly 9 feet tall. Write two statements comparing Wadlow to the trees in the table. Use fractions, ratios, percents, or differences.

C. Average waist, height, and arm-span measurements for a small group of adult men are given.

Waist = 32 inches   Height = 72 inches   Arm Span = 73 inches

Write two statements comparing the data on these men to the trees in the table. Use fractions, ratios, percents, or differences.

D. When a problem requires comparison of counts or measurements, how do you decide whether to use differences, ratios, fractions, or percents?

ACE **Homework starts on page 10.**

Applications

1. In a comparison taste test of two drinks, 780 students preferred Berry Blast. Only 220 students preferred Melon Splash. Complete each statement.

   a. There were ▦ more people who preferred Berry Blast.

   b. In the taste test, ▦% of the people preferred Berry Blast.

   c. People who preferred Berry Blast outnumbered those who preferred Melon Splash by a ratio of ▦ to ▦.

2. In a comparison taste test of new ice creams invented at Moo University, 750 freshmen preferred Cranberry Bog ice cream while 1,250 freshmen preferred Coconut Orange ice cream.

   Complete each statement.

   a. The fraction of freshmen who preferred Cranberry Bog is ▦.

   b. The percent of freshmen who preferred Coconut Orange is ▦%.

   c. Freshmen who preferred Coconut Orange outnumbered those who preferred Cranberry Bog by a ratio of ▦ to ▦.

3. A town considers whether to put in curbs along the streets. The ratio of people who support putting in curbs to those who oppose it is 2 to 5.

   a. What fraction of the people *oppose* putting in curbs?

   b. If 210 people in the town are surveyed, how many do you expect to *favor* putting in curbs?

   c. What percent of the people oppose putting in curbs?

Students at a middle school are asked to record how they spend their time from midnight on Friday to midnight on Sunday. Carlos records his data in the table below. Use the table for Exercises 4–7.

Weekend Activities	
Activity	**Number of Hours**
Sleeping	18
Eating	2.5
Recreation	8
Talking on the Phone	2
Watching Television	6
Doing Chores or Homework	2
Other	9.5

4. How would you compare how Carlos spent his time on various activities over the weekend? Explain.

5. Decide if each statement is an accurate description of how Carlos spent his time that weekend.

   a. He spent one sixth of his time watching television.

   b. The ratio of hours spent watching television to hours spent doing chores or homework is 3 to 1.

   c. Recreation, talking on the phone, and watching television took about 33% of his time.

   d. Time spent doing chores or homework was only 20% of the time spent watching television.

   e. Sleeping, eating, and "other" activities took up 12 hours more than all other activities combined.

6. Estimate what the numbers of hours would be in *your* weekend activity table. Then write a ratio statement like statement (b) to fit your data.

7. Write other accurate statements comparing Carlos's use of weekend time for various activities. Use each concept at least once.

   a. ratio

   b. difference

   c. fraction

   d. percent

8. A class at Middlebury Middle School collected data on the kinds of movies students prefer. Complete each statement using the table.

Types of Movies Preferred by Middlebury Students

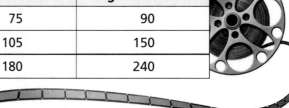

Type of Movie	Seventh-Graders	Eighth-Graders
Action	75	90
Comedy	105	150
Total	180	240

a. The ratio of seventh-graders who prefer comedies to eighth-graders who prefer comedies is ■ to ■.

b. The fraction of total students (both seventh- and eighth-graders) who prefer action movies is ■.

c. The fraction of seventh-graders who prefer action movies is ■.

d. The percent of total students who prefer comedies is ■.

e. The percent of eighth-graders who prefer action movies is ■.

f. Grade ■ has the greater percent of students who prefer action movies.

Homework
Help  nline
PHSchool.com

For: Help with Exercise 8
Web Code: ane-3108

9. Use the table.

Selected Champion Trees

Tree Type	Height (ft)	Spread (ft)
Florida Crossopetalum	11	3
White Oak	96	119

a. The height of the crossopetalum (kroh soh PET uh lum) is what fraction of the height of the white oak?

b. The height of the crossopetalum is what percent of the height of the white oak?

c. The spread of the crossopetalum is what fraction of the spread of the white oak?

d. The spread of the crossopetalum is what percent of the spread of the white oak?

10. In a survey, 100 students were asked if they prefer watching television or listening to the radio. The results show that 60 students prefer watching television while 40 prefer listening to the radio. Use each concept at least once to express student preferences.

a. ratio
b. percent
c. fraction
d. difference

Connections

11. A fruit bar is 5 inches long. The bar will be split into two pieces. For each situation, find the lengths of the two pieces.

   a. One piece is $\frac{3}{10}$ of the whole bar.

   b. One piece is 60% of the bar.

   c. One piece is 1 inch longer than the other.

12. Exercise 11 includes several numbers or quantities: 5 inches, 3, 10, 60%, and 1 inch. Determine whether each number or quantity refers to the whole, a part, or the difference between two parts.

The sketches below show two members of the Grump family. The figures are geometrically similar. Use the figures for Exercises 13–16.

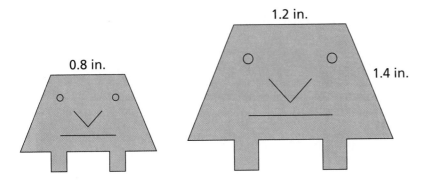

13. Write statements comparing the lengths of corresponding segments in the two Grump drawings. Use each concept at least once.

   a. ratio   **b.** fraction

   c. percent   **d.** scale factor

14. Write statements comparing the areas of the two Grump drawings. Use each concept at least once.

   a. ratio   **b.** fraction

   c. percent   **d.** scale factor

15. How long is the segment in the smaller Grump that corresponds to the 1.4-inch segment in the larger Grump?

16. **Multiple Choice** The mouth of the smaller Grump is 0.6 inches wide. How wide is the mouth of the larger Grump?

   A. 0.4 in.   **B.** 0.9 in.   **C.** 1 in.   **D.** 1.2 in.

The drawing below shows the Big Wheel spinner used in a game at the Waverly School Fun Night. It costs 20 cents to spin the wheel, and winners receive $1.00. The chart shows the data from 236 spins of the Big Wheel. Use the spinner and the chart for Exercises 17–21.

Win	Lose
46	190

17. The sectors of the spinner are identical in size. What is the measure in degrees of each central angle?

18. You play the game once. What is the theoretical probability that you win?

19. Do the results in the table agree with the probability statement you made in Exercise 18? Why or why not?

20. Write statements comparing the number of wins to the number of losses. Use each concept at least once.

    a. ratio   **b.** percent   **c.** difference

21. Which comparison from Exercise 20 is the best way to convey probability information about this game? Explain.

22. Copy the number line below. Add labels for 0.25, $\frac{6}{8}$, $1\frac{3}{4}$, and 1.3.

23. Write two unequal fractions with different denominators. Which fraction is greater? Explain.

24. Write a fraction and a decimal so that the fraction is greater than the decimal. Explain.

Copy each pair of numbers in Exercises 25–33. Insert <, >, or = to make a true statement.

25. $\frac{4}{5}$ ■ $\frac{11}{12}$

26. $\frac{14}{21}$ ■ $\frac{10}{15}$

27. $\frac{7}{9}$ ■ $\frac{3}{4}$

28. 2.5 ■ 0.259

29. 30.17 ■ 30.018

30. 0.006 ■ 0.0060

31. 0.45 ■ $\frac{9}{20}$

32. $1\frac{3}{4}$ ■ 1.5

33. $\frac{1}{4}$ ■ 1.3

Extensions

34. Rewrite this ad so that it will be more effective.

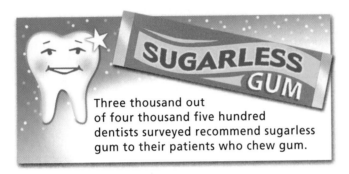

Three thousand out of four thousand five hundred dentists surveyed recommend sugarless gum to their patients who chew gum.

35. Use the table below.

Money Spent for Food

Where Food Is Eaten	1990	1998
Home	$303,900,000,000	$401,800,000,000
Away From Home	$168,800,000,000	$354,400,000,000

SOURCE: U.S. Census Bureau. Go to PHSchool.com for a data update. Web Code: ang-9041

a. Compare money spent on food eaten at home and food eaten away from home to the total money spent for food. Write statements for each year.

b. Explain how the statements you wrote in part (a) show the money spent for food away from home increasing or decreasing in relation to the total spent for food.

Use the table for Exercises 36–41.

Advertising Spending in the United States (millions)		
Placement	1990	2000
Newspapers	$32,281	$46,582
Magazines	$6,803	$11,096
Television	$29,073	$50,843
Radio	$8,726	$16,930
Yellow Pages	$8,926	$12,666
Internet	$0	$1,840
Direct Mail	$23,370	$41,601
Other	$20,411	$33,671
Total	$129,590	$215,229

Source: U.S. Census Bureau. Go to **PHSchool.com** for a data update. Web code: ang–9041

36. Which placement has the greatest difference in advertising dollars between 1990 and 2000?

37. Find the percent of all advertising dollars spent on each placement in 1990.

38. Find the percent of all advertising dollars spent on each placement in 2000.

39. Use your results from Exercises 36–38. Write several sentences describing how advertising spending changed from 1990 to 2000.

40. Suppose you were thinking about investing in either a television station or a radio station. Which method of comparing advertising costs (differences or percents) makes television seem like the better investment? Which makes radio seem like the better investment?

41. Suppose you are a reporter writing an article about trends in advertising over time. Which method of comparison would you choose?

Mathematical Reflections 1

In this investigation, you explored several ways of comparing numbers. The problems were designed to help you understand and use different comparison strategies and recognize when each is most useful. The following questions will help you summarize what you have learned.

Think about your answers to these questions. Discuss your ideas with other students and your teacher. Then write a summary of your findings in your notebook.

1. Explain what you think each word means when it is used to make a comparison.

   a. ratio

   b. percent

   c. fraction

   d. difference

2. Give an example of a situation using each concept to compare two quantities.

   a. ratio

   b. percent

   c. fraction

   d. difference

Comparing Ratios, Percents, and Fractions

You used ratios, fractions, percents, and differences to compare quantities in Investigation 1. Now, you will develop strategies for choosing and using an appropriate comparison strategy. As you work through the problems, you will make sense of the statements in the *Did You Know?*

Did You Know?

- In 2001, 20.8% of all radio stations in the United States had country music as their primary format, while only 4.5% had a Top-40 format.

- For the first 60 miles of depth, the temperature of Earth increases 1°F for every 100 to 200 feet.

- In 2000, cancer accounted for about $\frac{1}{5}$ of all deaths in the United States.

- In 2001, silver compact cars and silver sports cars outsold black cars by a ratio of 5 to 3.

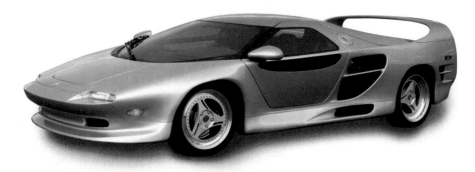

Go Online
PHSchool.com
For: Information about any of these topics
Web Code: ane-9031

2.1 Mixing Juice

Julia and Mariah attend summer camp. Everyone at the camp helps with the cooking and cleanup at meal times.

One morning, Julia and Mariah make orange juice for all the campers. They plan to make the juice by mixing water and frozen orange-juice concentrate. To find the mix that tastes best, they decide to test some mixes.

Mix A
2 cups concentrate | 3 cups cold water

Mix B
5 cups concentrate | 9 cups cold water

Mix C
1 cup concentrate | 2 cups cold water

Mix D
3 cups concentrate | 5 cups cold water

Problem 2.1 Developing Comparison Strategies

A. Which mix will make juice that is the most "orangey"? Explain.

B. Which mix will make juice that is the least "orangey"? Explain.

C. Which comparison statement is correct? Explain.

$\frac{5}{9}$ of Mix B is concentrate. $\frac{5}{14}$ of Mix B is concentrate.

D. Assume that each camper will get $\frac{1}{2}$ cup of juice.

  1. For each mix, how many batches are needed to make juice for 240 campers?

  2. For each mix, how much concentrate and how much water are needed to make juice for 240 campers?

E. For each mix, how much concentrate and how much water are needed to make 1 cup of juice?

ACE Homework starts on page 24.

2.2 Sharing Pizza

The camp dining room has two kinds of tables. A large table seats ten people. A small table seats eight people. On pizza night, the students serving dinner put four pizzas on each large table and three pizzas on each small table.

Problem 2.2 More Comparison Strategies

A. Suppose the pizzas are shared equally by everyone at the table. Does a person sitting at a small table get the same amount as a person sitting at a large table? Explain your reasoning.

B. Which table relates to $\frac{3}{8}$? What do the 3 and the 8 mean? Is $\frac{3}{8}$ a part-to-whole comparison or a part-to-part comparison?

C. Selena thinks she can decide at which table a person gets the most pizza. She uses the following reasoning:

$10 - 4 = 6$ and $8 - 3 = 5$ so the large table is better.

1. What does the 6 mean and what does the 5 mean in Selena's method of reasoning?

2. Do you agree or disagree with Selena's method?

3. Suppose you put nine pizzas on the large table. What answer does Selena's method give? Does this answer make sense?

4. What can you now say about Selena's method?

D. 1. The ratio of large tables to small tables in the dining room is 8 to 5. There are exactly enough seats for the 240 campers. How many tables of each kind are there?

2. What fraction of the campers sit at small tables?

3. What percent of the campers sit at large tables?

ACE Homework starts on page 24.

2.3 Finding Equivalent Ratios

It is often helpful, when forming ratios, to replace the actual numbers being compared with simpler numbers that have the same relationship to each other.

- People prefer Bolda Cola over Cola Nola by a ratio of 17,139 to 11,426, or 3 to 2.
- Students prefer television to radio by a ratio of 100 to 50, or 2 to 1.
- Monthly sales of *Reader's Digest* magazine exceed those of *National Geographic* by 11,044,694 to 6,602,650, or about 3 to 2.

Getting Ready for Problem

Suppose all classes at your grade level took the cola taste test. The result was 100 to 80 in favor of Bolda Cola.

- How do you scale down this ratio to make it easier to understand?
- What are some other ratios equivalent to this ratio in which the numbers are greater? Finding greater numbers is scaling *up* the ratio.
- How is scaling ratios like finding equivalent fractions for $\frac{100}{80}$? How is it different?

Problem 2.3 Scaling Ratios

One of Ming's tasks at the county zoo's primate house is to mix food for the chimpanzees. The combination of high-fiber nuggets and high-protein nuggets changes as the chimps grow from babies to adults.

Ming has formulas for mixing high-fiber and high-protein nuggets for the chimps.

- Baby chimps: 2 cups high-fiber nuggets and 3 cups high-protein nuggets per serving
- Young adult chimps: 6 cups high-fiber nuggets and 4 cups high-protein nuggets per serving
- Older chimps: 4 cups high-fiber nuggets and 2 cups high-protein nuggets per serving

A. 1. What amounts of high-fiber and high-protein nuggets will Ming need when she has to feed 2 baby chimps? 3 baby chimps? 4 baby chimps?

Copy and complete the table below.

Dietary Needs of Baby Chimps

Number of Baby Chimps	1	2	3	4	5	10
Cups of High-Fiber Nuggets	■	■	■	■	■	■
Cups of High-Protein Nuggets	■	■	■	■	■	■

2. What patterns do you see in your table?

3. Ming puts 48 cups of high-protein nuggets into the baby chimp mix. How many cups of high-fiber nuggets does she put into the mix? Explain.

4. Ming has a total of 125 cups of mix for baby chimps. How many cups of high-fiber nuggets are in the mix? Explain.

B. 1. What is the ratio of high-fiber to high-protein nuggets for young adult chimps?

2. Scale this ratio up to show the ratio of high-fiber to high-protein nuggets that will feed 21 young adult chimps.

3. To feed 18 young adults, you need 108 cups of high-fiber nuggets and 72 cups of high-protein nuggets. Show how to scale down this ratio to feed 3 young adult chimps.

C. 1. Darla wants to compare the amount of high-fiber nuggets to the total amount of food mix for young adult chimps. She makes this claim:

"High-fiber nuggets are $\frac{3}{2}$ of the total."

Lamar says Darla is wrong. He makes this claim:

"High-fiber nuggets are $\frac{3}{5}$ of the total."

Who is correct? Explain.

2. What fraction of the total amount of food mix for older chimps is high-fiber nuggets?

3. Suppose the ratio of male chimps to female chimps in a zoo is 5 to 4. What fraction of the chimps are male?

4. Suppose $\frac{2}{3}$ of the chimps in a zoo are female. Find the ratio of female chimps to male chimps in that zoo.

ACE Homework starts on page 24.

Applications

As you work on the ACE exercises, try a variety of reasoning methods.
Then think about conditions when each method seems most helpful.

1. Compare these four mixes for apple juice.

Mix W	
5 cups concentrate	8 cups cold water

Mix X	
3 cups concentrate	6 cups cold water

Mix Y	
6 cups concentrate	9 cups cold water

Mix Z	
3 cups concentrate	5 cups cold water

   a. Which mix would make the most "appley" juice?

   b. Suppose you make a single batch of each mix. What fraction of each batch is concentrate?

   c. Rewrite your answers to part (b) as percents.

   d. Suppose you make only 1 cup of Mix W. How much water and how much concentrate do you need?

2. Examine these statements about the apple juice mixes in Exercise 1. Decide whether each is accurate. Give reasons for your answers.

   a. Mix Y has the most water, so it will taste least "appley."

   b. Mix Z is the most "appley" because the difference between the concentrate and water is 2 cups. It is 3 cups for each of the others.

   c. Mix Y is the most "appley" because it has only $1\frac{1}{2}$ cups of water for each cup of concentrate. The others have more water per cup.

   d. Mix X and Mix Y taste the same because you just add 3 cups of concentrate and 3 cups of water to turn Mix X into Mix Y.

3. If possible, change each comparison of concentrate to water into a ratio. If not possible, explain why.

   a. The mix is 60% concentrate.

   b. The fraction of the mix that is water is $\frac{3}{5}$.

   c. The difference between the amount of concentrate and water is 4 cups.

4. At camp, Miriam uses a pottery wheel to make three bowls in 2 hours. Duane makes five bowls in 3 hours.

   a. Who makes bowls faster, Miriam or Duane?

   b. At the same pace, how long will it take Miriam to make a set of 12 bowls?

   c. At the same pace, how long will it take Duane to make a set of 12 bowls?

5. Guests at a pizza party are seated at 3 tables. The small table has 5 seats and 2 pizzas. The medium table has 7 seats and 3 pizzas. The large table has 12 seats and 5 pizzas. The pizzas at each table are shared equally. At which table does a guest get the most pizza?

6. For each business day, news reports tell the number of stocks that gained (went up in price) and the number that declined (went down in price). In each of the following pairs of reports, determine which is better news for investors.

For: Help with Exercise 6
Web Code: ane-3206

   a. $\begin{bmatrix} \text{Gains outnumber declines} \\ \text{by a ratio of 5 to 3.} \end{bmatrix}$ OR $\begin{bmatrix} \text{Gains outnumber declines} \\ \text{by a ratio of 7 to 5.} \end{bmatrix}$

   b. $\begin{bmatrix} \text{Gains outnumber declines} \\ \text{by a ratio of 9 to 5.} \end{bmatrix}$ OR $\begin{bmatrix} \text{Gains outnumber declines} \\ \text{by a ratio of 6 to 3.} \end{bmatrix}$

   c. $\begin{bmatrix} \text{Declines outnumber gains} \\ \text{by a ratio of 10 to 7.} \end{bmatrix}$ OR $\begin{bmatrix} \text{Declines outnumber gains} \\ \text{by a ratio of 6 to 4.} \end{bmatrix}$

7. Suppose a news story about the Super Bowl claims "Men outnumbered women in the stadium by a ratio of 9 to 5." Does this mean that there were 14 people in the stadium—9 men and 5 women? If not, what does the statement mean?

8. Multiple Choice Which of the following is a correct interpretation of the statement "Men outnumbered women by a ratio of 9 to 5?"

A. There were four more men than women.

B. The number of men was 1.8 times the number of women.

C. The number of men divided by the number of women was equal to the quotient of $5 \div 9$.

D. In the stadium, five out of nine fans were women.

Connections

9. If possible, change each comparison of red paint to white paint to a percent comparison. If it is not possible, explain why.

a. The fraction of a mix that is red paint is $\frac{1}{4}$.

b. The ratio of red to white paint in a different mix is 2 to 5.

10. If possible, change each comparison to a fraction comparison. If it is not possible, explain why.

a. The nut mix has 30% peanuts.

b. The ratio of almonds to other nuts in the mix is 1 to 7.

11. Find a value that makes each sentence correct.

a. $\frac{3}{15} = \frac{\blacksquare}{30}$

b. $\frac{1}{2} < \frac{\blacksquare}{20}$

c. $\frac{\blacksquare}{20} > \frac{3}{5}$

d. $\frac{9}{30} \leq \frac{\blacksquare}{15}$

e. $\frac{\blacksquare}{12} \geq \frac{3}{4}$

f. $\frac{9}{21} = \frac{12}{\blacksquare}$

12. Use the table to answer parts (a)–(e).

Participation in Walking for Exercise

	Ages 12–17	Ages 55–64
People Who Walk	3,781,000	8,694,000
Total in Group	23,241,000	22,662,000

Source: U.S. Census Bureau. Go to **PHSchool.com** for a data update. Web Code: ang-9041

a. What percent of the 55–64 age group walk for exercise?

b. What percent of the 12–17 age group walk for exercise?

c. Write a ratio statement to compare the number of 12- to 17-year-olds who walk to the number of 55- to 64-year-olds who walk. Use approximate numbers to simplify the ratio.

d. Write a ratio statement to compare the percent of 12- to 17-year-olds who walk for exercise to the percent of 55- to 64-year-olds who walk for exercise.

e. Which data—actual numbers of walkers or percents—would you use in comparing the popularity of exercise walking among various groups? Explain.

13. The probability of getting a sum of 5 when you roll two number cubes is $\frac{4}{36}$. How many times should you expect to get a sum of 5 if you roll the cubes each number of times?

a. 9   **b.** 18   **c.** 27   **d.** 100   **e.** 450

14. For each diagram, write three statements comparing the areas of the shaded and unshaded regions. In one statement, use fraction ideas to express the comparison. In the second, use percent ideas. In the third, use ratio ideas.

a.   **b.**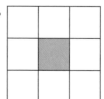

15. Multiple Choice Choose the value that makes $\frac{18}{30} = \frac{\blacksquare}{15}$ correct.

F. 7   **G.** 8   **H.** 9   **J.** 10

16. Multiple Choice Choose the value that makes $\frac{\blacksquare}{15} \leq \frac{3}{5}$ correct.

A. 9   **B.** 10   **C.** 11   **D.** 12

17. Find a value that makes each sentence correct. Explain your reasoning in each case.

For: Multiple-Choice Skills Practice
Web Code: ana-3254

a. $\dfrac{3}{4} = \dfrac{\blacksquare}{12}$ **b.** $\dfrac{3}{4} < \dfrac{\blacksquare}{12}$ **c.** $\dfrac{3}{4} > \dfrac{\blacksquare}{12}$ **d.** $\dfrac{9}{12} = \dfrac{12}{\blacksquare}$

18. The sketches show floor plans for dorm rooms for two students and for one student.

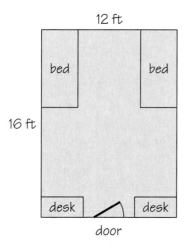
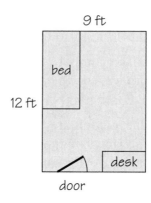

a. Are the floor plans similar rectangles? If so, what is the scale factor? If not, why not?

b. What is the ratio of floor areas of the two rooms (including space under the beds and desks)?

c. Which type of room gives more space per student?

19. Find values that make each sentence correct.

a. $\dfrac{6}{14} = \dfrac{\blacksquare}{21} = \dfrac{\blacksquare}{28}$ **b.** $\dfrac{\blacksquare}{27} = \dfrac{8}{36} = \dfrac{\blacksquare}{63}$

c. $\dfrac{\blacksquare}{20} = \dfrac{\blacksquare}{25} = \dfrac{6}{30}$ **d.** $\dfrac{\blacksquare}{8} = \dfrac{15}{\blacksquare} = \dfrac{24}{32}$

20. Suppose a news story reports, "90% of the people in the Super Bowl stadium were between the ages of 25 and 55." Alicia thinks this means only 100 people were in the stadium, and 90 of them were between 25 and 55 years of age. Do you agree with her? If not, what does the statement mean?

21. Suppose a news story reports, "A survey found that $\frac{4}{7}$ of all Americans watched the Super Bowl on television." Bishnu thinks this means the survey reached seven people and four of them watched the Super Bowl on television. Do you agree with him? If not, what does the statement mean?

Extensions

22. Mammals vary in the length of their pregnancies, or gestations. *Gestation* is the time from conception to birth. Use the table to answer the questions that follow.

Gestation Times and Life Spans of Selected Mammals

Animal	Gestation (days)	Life Span (years)
Chipmunk	31	6
Cat	63	12
Fox	52	7
Lion	100	15
Black Bear	219	18
Gorilla	258	20
Moose	240	12
Giraffe	425	10
Elephant (African)	660	35

SOURCE: *The World Almanac and Book of Facts*

Connections Extensions

a. Plan a way to compare life span and gestation time for animals and use it with the data.

b. Which animal has the greatest ratio of life span to gestation time? Which has the least ratio?

c. Plot the data on a coordinate graph using (*gestation, life span*) as data points. Describe any interesting patterns that you see. Decide whether there is any relation between the two variables. Explain how you reached your conclusion.

d. What pattern would you expect to see in a graph if each statement were true?

   i. Longer gestation time implies longer life span.

   ii. Longer gestation time implies shorter life span.

23. The city of Spartanville runs two summer camps—the Green Center and the Blue Center. The table below shows recent attendance at the two camps.

	Green	Blue
Boys	125	70
Girls	75	30

In this exercise, you will show how several approaches can be used to answer the following question.

Which center seems to offer a camping program that appeals best to girls?

a. What conclusion would you draw if you focused on the differences between the numbers of boy and girl campers from each center?

b. How could you use fractions to compare the appeal of the two centers' camping programs for boys and girls? What conclusion would you draw?

c. How could you use percents to compare the appeal of the two centers' camping programs for boys and girls? What conclusion would you draw?

d. How could you use ratios to compare the appeal of the two centers' camping programs for boys and girls? What conclusion would you draw?

24. Use the table below.

**Participation in Team Sports
at Springbrook Middle School**

Sport	Girls	Boys
Basketball	30	80
Football	10	60
Soccer	120	85
Total Surveyed	160	225

a. In which sport do boys most outnumber girls?

b. In which sport do girls most outnumber boys?

c. The participation in these team sports is about the same for students at Key Middle School.

   i. Suppose 250 boys at Key play sports. How many would you expect to play each of the three sports?

   ii. Suppose 240 girls at Key play sports. How many would you expect to play each of the three sports?

Mathematical Reflections 2

In this investigation, you solved problems by comparing ratios, percents, and fractions. You also used ratio, percent, and fraction data to solve problems of larger or smaller scale. The following questions will help you summarize what you have learned.

Think about your answers to these questions. Discuss your ideas with other students and your teacher. Then write a summary of your findings in your notebook.

1. The director of a recreation center wants to compare the 10 boys to the 20 girls who attend its camping program.

   a. How would you make a comparison using fractions?

   b. How would you make a comparison using percents?

   c. How would you make a comparison using ratios?

   d. How is your percent comparison related to your ratio comparison?

   e. How is your fraction comparison related to your percent comparison?

2. **a.** Explain how you would scale up the ratio 10 boys to 14 girls to find equivalent ratios.

   b. Explain how you would scale down the ratio 10 boys to 14 girls to find equivalent ratios.

Comparing and Scaling Rates

The following examples illustrate situations involving another strategy to compare numbers.

- My mom's car gets 45 miles per gallon on the expressway.
- We need two sandwiches for each person at the picnic.
- I earn $3.50 per hour baby-sitting for my neighbor.
- The mystery meat label says 355 Calories per 6-ounce serving.
- My brother's top running rate is 8.5 kilometers per hour.

Each of these statements compares two different quantities. For example, one compares miles to gallons of gas. A comparison of two quantities measured in different units is a **rate.** You have used rates in earlier problems. For example, you used rates in finding pizza per person.

Getting Ready for Problem

- What two quantities are being compared in the rate statements above?
- Which of the rate statements is different from the others?

3.1 Technology on Sale

Stores, catalogs, and Web sites often use rates in their ads. The ads sometimes give the costs for several items. You might see an offer like the one shown at the right.

Calculators for School

Fraction:	$120 for 20
Scientific:	$240 for 15
Graphing:	$800 for 10

The listed prices are for orders of 10, 15, or 20 calculators But it's possible to figure the price for any number you want to purchase. One way to figure those prices is to build a *rate table*. A rate table is started below.

Price of Calculators for Schools

Number Purchased	1	2	3	4	5	10	15	20
Fraction	▥	▥	▥	▥	▥	▥	▥	$120
Scientific	▥	▥	▥	▥	▥	▥	$240	▥
Graphing	▥	▥	▥	▥	▥	$800	▥	▥

Problem 3.1 Making and Using a Rate Table

Suppose you take orders over the phone for the calculator company. You should be quick with price quotes for orders of different sizes.

A. Build a rate table like the one above. Fill in prices for each type of calculator for orders of the sizes shown.

Use your rate table to answer Questions B–F.

B. How much does it cost to buy 53 fraction calculators? How much to buy 27 scientific calculators? How much to buy 9 graphing calculators?

C. How many fraction calculators can a school buy if it can spend $390? What if the school can spend only $84?

D. How many graphing calculators can a school buy if it can spend $2,500? What if the school can spend only $560?

E. What *arithmetic operation* (addition, subtraction, multiplication or division) do you use to find the cost per calculator?

F. Write an equation for each kind of calculator to show how to find the price for any number ordered.

ACE Homework starts on page 40.

Sascha cycled on a route with different kinds of conditions. Sometimes he went uphill, sometimes he went mostly downhill. Sometimes he was on flat ground. He stopped three times to record his time and distance:

- Stop 1: 5 miles in 20 minutes
- Stop 2: 8 miles in 24 minutes
- Stop 3: 15 miles in 40 minutes

Problem 3.2 Finding Rates

Show your work. Label any rate that you find with appropriate units.

A. Find Sascha's rate in miles per hour for each part of the route.

B. 1. On which part was Sascha cycling fastest? On which part was he cycling slowest?

2. How do your calculations in Question A support your answers?

C. Suppose you can maintain a steady rate of 13 miles per hour on a bike. How long will it take you to travel the same distance Sascha traveled in 1 hour and 24 minutes?

D. Suppose you were racing Sascha. What steady rate would you have to maintain to tie him?

ACE Homework starts on page 40.

Did You Know?

The highest rate ever recorded on a pedal-powered bicycle was 166.944 miles per hour. Fred Rompelberg performed this amazing feat on October 3, 1995, at the Bonneville Salt Flats in Utah. He was able to reach this rate by following a vehicle. The vehicle acted as a windshield for him and his bicycle.

Go Online

For: Information about speed records
PHSchool.com **Web Code:** ane-9031

The ads below use rates to describe sale prices. To compare prices in sales such as these, it's often useful to find a unit rate. A **unit rate** is a rate in which one of the numbers being compared is 1 unit. The comparisons "45 miles per gallon," "$3.50 per hour," "8.5 kilometers per hour," and "two sandwiches for each person" are all unit rates. "Per gallon" means "for one gallon" and "per hour" means "for one hour."

Problem 3.3 Unit Rates and Equations

Use unit rates to compare the ad prices and to find the costs of various numbers of CDs at each store.

A. Which store has the lower price per CD?

B. For each store, write an equation (a rule) that you can use to calculate the cost c for any purchase of n compact discs.

C. Use the equations you just wrote for Question B. Write new equations to include 5% sales tax on any purchase.

D. Suppose a Web site sells CDs for $8.99 per disc. There is no tax, but there is a shipping charge of $5 for any order. Write an equation to give the cost c of any order for n discs from the Web site.

E. Use your equations from Question C or make a rate table to answer each question.

    1. How many discs do you have to order from the Web site to get a better deal than buying from Music City?

    2. How many discs do you have to order from the Web site to get a better deal than buying from CD World?

ACE Homework starts on page 40.

3.4 What Does Dividing Tell You?

In this problem, the questions will help you decide which way to divide when you are finding a unit rate. The questions will also help you with the meaning of the quotient after you divide.

Getting Ready for Problem

Dario has two options for buying boxes of pasta. At CornerMarket he can buy seven boxes of pasta for $6. At SuperFoodz he can buy six boxes of pasta for $5.

At CornerMarket, he divided 7 by 6 and got 1.16666667. He then divided 6 by 7 and got 0.85714286. He was confused. What do these numbers tell about the price of boxes of pasta at CornerMarket?

Decide which makes more sense to you. Use that division strategy to compare the two store prices. Which store offers the better deal?

Use division to find unit rates to solve the following questions. Label each unit rate.

A. SuperFoodz has oranges on sale at 10 for $2.

   1. What is the cost per orange?

   2. How many oranges can you buy for $1?

   3. What division did you perform in each case? How did you decide what each division means?

   4. Complete this rate table to show what you know.

Cost of Oranges at SuperFoodz

Oranges	10	▪	1	20	11	▪
Cost	$2.00	$1.00	▪	▪	▪	$2.60

B. Noralie used 22 gallons of gas to go 682 miles.

   1. What are the two unit rates that she might compute?

   2. Compute each unit rate and tell what it means.

   3. Which seems more useful to you? Why?

C. It takes 100 maple trees to make 25 gallons of maple syrup.

   1. How many maple trees does it take for 1 gallon of syrup?

   2. How much syrup can you get from one maple tree?

D. A 5-minute shower requires about 18 gallons of water.

   1. How much water per minute does a shower take?

   2. How long does a shower last if you use only 1 gallon of water?

E. 1. At the CornerMarket grocery store, you can buy eight cans of tomatoes for $9. The cans are the same size as those at CannedStuff, which sells six cans for $5. Are the tomatoes at CornerMarket a better buy than the tomatoes at CannedStuff?

   2. What comparison strategies did you use to choose between CornerMarket and CannedStuff tomatoes? Why?

ACE **Homework starts on page 40.**

Applications

The problems that follow will give you practice in using rates (especially unit rates) in different situations. Be careful to use measurement units that match correctly in the rates you compute.

1. Maralah can drive her car 580 miles at a steady speed using 20 gallons of gasoline. Make a rate table showing the number of miles her car can be driven at this speed. Show 1, 2, 3, . . . , and 10 gallons of gas.

2. Joel can drive his car 450 miles at a steady speed using 15 gallons of gasoline. Make a rate table showing the number of miles his car can be driven at this speed. Show 1, 2, 3, . . . , and 10 gallons of gas.

3. Franky's Trail Mix Factory gives customers the following information. Use the pattern in the table to answer the questions.

**Caloric Content of
Franky's Trail Mix**

Grams of Trail Mix	Calories
50	150
150	450
300	900
500	1,500

a. Fiona eats 75 grams of trail mix. How many Calories does she eat?

b. Rico eats trail mix containing 1,000 Calories. How many grams of trail mix does he eat?

c. Write an equation that you can use to find the number of Calories in any number of grams of trail mix.

d. Write an equation that you can use to find the number of grams of trail mix that will provide any given number of Calories.

For Exercises 4–8, you will explore relationships among time, rate, and distance.

4. When she drives to work, Louise travels 10 miles in about 15 minutes. Kareem travels 23 miles in about 30 minutes. Who has the faster average speed?

5. Rolanda and Mali ride bikes at a steady pace. Rolanda rides 8 miles in 32 minutes. Mali rides 2 miles in 10 minutes. Who rides faster?

6. Fasiz and Dale drive at the same speed along a road. Fasiz drives 8 kilometers in 24 minutes. How far does Dale drive in 6 minutes?

7. On a long dirt road leading to camp, buses travel only 6 miles in 10 minutes.

   a. At this speed, how long does it take the buses to travel 18 miles?

   b. At this speed, how far do the buses go in 15 minutes?

8. **Multiple Choice** Choose the fastest walker.

   A. Montel walks 3 miles in 1 hour.

   B. Jerry walks 6 miles in 2 hours.

   C. Phil walks 6 miles in 1.5 hours.

   D. Rosie walks 9 miles in 2 hours.

9. The dairy store says it takes 50 pounds of milk to make 5 pounds of cheddar cheese.

   a. Make a rate table showing the amount of milk needed to make 5, 10, 15, 20, . . . , and 50 pounds of cheddar cheese.

   b. Make a coordinate graph showing the relationship between pounds of milk and pounds of cheddar cheese. First, decide which variable should go on each axis.

   c. Write an equation relating pounds of milk m to pounds of cheddar cheese c.

   d. Explain one advantage of each method (the graph, the table, and the equation) to express the relationship between milk and cheddar cheese production.

10. A dairy manager says it takes 70 pounds of milk to make 10 pounds of cottage cheese.

   a. Make a rate table for the amount of milk needed to make 10, 20, . . . , and 100 pounds of cottage cheese.

   b. Make a graph showing the relationship between pounds of milk and pounds of cottage cheese. First, decide which variable should go on each axis.

   c. Write an equation relating pounds of milk m to pounds of cottage cheese c.

   d. Compare the graph in part (b) to the graph in Exercise 9. Explain how they are alike and how they are different. What is the cause of the differences between the two graphs?

11. A store sells videotapes at $3.00 for a set of two tapes. You have $20. You can split a set and buy just one tape for the same price per tape as the set.

   a. How many tapes can you buy?

   b. Suppose there is a 7% sales tax on the tapes. How many can you buy? Justify your solution.

Homework Help Online
PHSchool.com
For: Help with Exercise 11
Web Code: ane-3311

12. Study the data in these rate situations. Then write the key relationship in three ways:

   • in fraction form with a label for each part

   • as two different unit rates with a label for each rate

   a. Latanya's 15-mile commute to work each day takes an average of 40 minutes.

   b. In a 5-minute test, one computer printer produced 90 pages of output.

   c. An advertisement for a Caribbean cruise trip promises 168 hours of fun for only $1,344.

   d. A long-distance telephone call lasts 20 minutes and costs $4.50.

Connections

Rewrite each equation, replacing the variable with a number that makes a true statement.

13. $\frac{4}{9} \times n = 1\frac{1}{3}$

14. $n \times 2.25 = 90$

15. $n \div 15 = 120$

16. $180 \div n = 15$

17. Write two fractions with a product between 10 and 11.

18. Write two decimals with a product between 1 and 2.

A recent world-champion milk producer was a 4-year-old cow from Marathon, Wisconsin. The cow, Muranda Oscar Lucinda, produced a record 67,914 pounds of milk in one year! Use this information for Exercises 19–22.

19. Look back at your answers to Exercise 10. How much cottage cheese could be made from the amount of milk that Muranda Oscar Lucinda produced during her record year?

20. The average weight of a dairy cow is 1,500 pounds. How many dairy cows would be needed to equal the weight of the cottage cheese you found in Exercise 19?

21. One gallon of milk weighs about 8.7 pounds. Suppose a typical milk bucket holds about 3 gallons. About how many milk buckets would Muranda Oscar Lucinda's average daily production of milk fill?

22. One pound of milk fills about two glasses. About how many glasses of milk could you fill with Muranda Oscar Lucinda's average daily production of milk?

23. Some campers bike 10 miles for a nature study. Use this setting to write questions that can be answered by solving each equation. Find the answers, and explain what they tell about the bike ride.

a. $10 \div 8 = \blacksquare$

b. $1.2 \times \blacksquare = 10$

c. $\blacksquare \div 2 = 5$

The table shows the mean times that students in one seventh-grade class spend on several activities during a weekend. The data are also displayed in the stacked bar graph below the table. Use both the table and the graph for Exercises 24 and 25.

Weekend Activities (hours)

Category	Boys	Girls	All Students
Sleeping	18.8	18.2	18.4
Eating	4.0	2.7	3.1
Recreation	7.8	6.9	7.2
Talking on the Phone	0.5	0.7	0.6
Watching TV	4.2	3.0	3.4
Doing Chores and Homework	3.6	5.8	5.1
Other	9.1	10.7	10.2

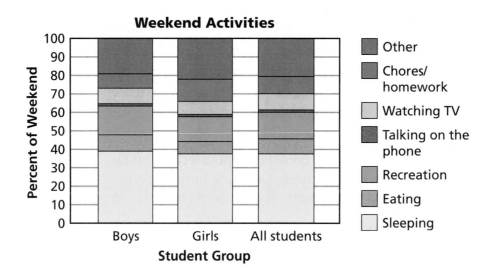

24. The stacked bar graph was made using the data from the table. Explain how it was constructed.

25. Suppose you are writing a report summarizing the class's data. You have space for either the table or the graph, but not both. What is one advantage of including the table? What is one advantage of including the stacked bar graph?

26. This table shows how to convert liters to quarts.

Liters	Quarts
1	1.06
4	4.24
5	5.30
9	9.54

   a. About how many liters are in 5.5 quarts?

   b. About how many quarts are in 5.5 liters?

   c. Write an equation for a rule that relates liters L to quarts Q.

Express each of the relationships in Exercises 27–31 as a unit rate. Label each unit rate with measurement units.

27. 12 cents for 20 beads

28. 8 cents for 10 nails

29. 405 miles on 15 gallons of gasoline

30. 3 cups of water for 2 cups of orange concentrate

31. $4 for 5 cans of soup

Go Online
PHSchool.com
For: Multiple-Choice Skills Practice
Web Code: ana-3354

32. The two clocks shown below are geometrically similar. One is a reduction of the other. Each outside edge of the larger clock is 2 centimeters long. Each outside edge of the smaller clock is 1.6 centimeters long.

   a. Write an equation relating the length L of any part of the large clock to the length S of the corresponding part of the small clock.

   b. Write an equation relating the area R of any part of the large clock to the area M of the corresponding part of the small clock.

   c. Write a decimal scale factor relating lengths in the large clock to lengths in the small clock. Explain how that scale factor is like a unit rate.

Extensions

33. Chemistry students analyzed the contents of rust. They found that it is made up of iron and oxygen. Tests on samples of rust gave these data.

Contents of Rust

Amount of Rust (g)	Amount of Iron (g)	Amount of Oxygen (g)
50	35.0	15.0
100	70.0	30.0
135	94.5	40.5
150	105.0	45.0

a. Suppose the students analyze 400 grams of rust. How much iron and how much oxygen should they find?

b. Is the ratio of iron to oxygen the same in each sample? If so, what is it? If not, explain.

c. Is the ratio of iron to total rust the same in each sample? If so, what is it? If not, explain.

34. A cider mill owner has pressed 240 liters of apple juice. He has many sizes of containers in which to pack the juice.

a. The owner wants to package all the juice in containers of the same size. Copy and complete this table to show the number of containers of each size needed to hold the juice.

Containers Needed by Volume

Volume of Container (liters)	10	4	2	1	$\frac{1}{2}$	$\frac{1}{4}$	$\frac{1}{10}$
Number of Containers Needed	■	■	■	■	■	■	■

b. Write an equation that relates the volume v of a container and the number n of containers needed to hold 240 liters of juice.

Mathematical Reflections 3

In this investigation, you learned to compare rates, to find unit rates, and to use rates to make tables and graphs and to write equations. The following questions will help you summarize what you have learned.

Think about your answers to these questions. Discuss your ideas with other students and your teacher. Then write a summary of your findings in your notebook.

The Picked Today fruit stand sells three green peppers for $1.50.

1. a. Describe the process for finding a unit rate for the peppers.

   b. Find two different unit rates to express the relationship between peppers and price. Explain what each unit rate tells.

   c. Fresh Veggie sells green peppers at five for $2.25. Compare Picked Today pepper prices with Fresh Veggie prices using two different kinds of unit rates.

   d. How do you decide whether the larger unit rate or the smaller unit rate is the better buy?

2. How would you construct a rate table for green pepper prices at the two vegetable stands? Explain what the entries in the table tell.

3. a. How would you write an equation to show the price for *n* peppers bought at Picked Today?

   b. Explain how the unit rate is used in writing the equation.

Making Sense of Proportions

In the following comparison problems, you have information about the relationship between quantities, but one or more specific values are unknown.

- **Calculators** Calculators are on sale at a price of $1,000 for 20. How many can be purchased for $1,250?

- **Similar Figures** The scale factor relating two similar figures is 2. One side of the larger figure is 10 centimeters long. How long is the corresponding side of the smaller figure?

- **Country Music** Country music is the primary format of 20% of American radio stations. There are about 10,600 radio stations in the United States. About how many stations focus on country music?

- **Doctors** Among American doctors, males outnumber females by a ratio of 15 to 4. If about 450,000 doctors are males, about how many are females?

Each of these problems can be solved in several ways. You will learn specific ways to set up ratios for problems like this and find missing values.

There are many ways to solve problems such as the ones on the previous page. One standard way is to create two ratios to represent the information in the problem. Then set these two ratios equal to each other to form a proportion. A **proportion** is an equation that states two ratios are equal.

For example, in the problem about doctors, you have enough information to write one ratio. Then write a proportion to find the missing quantity. There are four different ways to write a proportion representing the data in the problem.

Write the known ratio of male to female doctors. Complete the proportion with the ratio of actual numbers of doctors.

$$\frac{15 \text{ (male)}}{4 \text{ (female)}} = \frac{450{,}000 \text{ males}}{x \text{ females}}$$

Write a ratio of male to male data. Complete the proportion with female to female data.

$$\frac{15 \text{ (male)}}{450{,}000 \text{ males}} = \frac{4 \text{ (female)}}{x \text{ females}}$$

Write the known ratio of female to male doctors. Complete the proportion with the ratio of actual numbers of doctors.

$$\frac{4 \text{ (female)}}{15 \text{ (male)}} = \frac{x \text{ females}}{450{,}000 \text{ males}}$$

Write a different ratio of male to male data. Complete the proportion with female to female data.

$$\frac{450{,}000 \text{ males}}{15 \text{ (male)}} = \frac{x \text{ females}}{4 \text{ (female)}}$$

Using your knowledge of equivalent ratios, you can now find the number of female doctors from any one of these proportions.

Does any arrangement seem easier than the others?

Analyze the "Similar Figures" problem in the introduction.

The scale factor relating two similar figures is 2. One side of the larger figure is 10 centimeters long. How long is the corresponding side of the smaller figure?

• The scale factor means that the lengths of the sides of the larger figure are 2 times the lengths of the sides of the smaller. What is the ratio of the side lengths of the smaller figure to those of the larger figure?

• Write a proportion to represent the information in the problem.

• Solve your proportion to find the length of the corresponding side of the smaller figure.

Problem 4.1 Setting Up and Solving Proportions

A. Figure out whether each student's thinking about each line in the following problem is correct. Explain.

Dogs outnumber cats in an area by a ratio of 9 to 8. There are 180 dogs in the area. How many cats are there?

Adrianna's Work:

$$\frac{9 \text{ dogs}}{8 \text{ cats}} = \frac{180 \text{ dogs}}{x \text{ cats}}$$

$$\frac{9}{8} \times \frac{20}{20} = \frac{180}{160}$$

$$\frac{180}{160} = \frac{180}{x}$$

$$x = 160$$

1. Why did Adrianna multiply by $\frac{20}{20}$? How did she find what to multiply by?

2. What does this proportion tell you about the denominators? Why?

3. Is the answer correct? Explain.

Joey's Work:

$$\frac{8 \text{ cats}}{9 \text{ dogs}} = \frac{x \text{ cats}}{180 \text{ dogs}}$$

$$\frac{8}{9} = \frac{80}{90} = \frac{160}{180}$$

There are 160 cats.

4. What strategy did Joey use?

5. Why can he make this claim?

B. 1. Calculators are on sale at a price of $1,000 for 20. How many can be purchased for $1,250? Write and solve a proportion that represents the problem. Explain.

2. Country music is the primary format of 20% of American radio stations. There are about 10,600 radio stations in the United States. About how many stations focus on country music?

C. Use the reasoning you applied in Question B to solve these proportions for the variable x. Explain.

1. $\frac{8}{5} = \frac{32}{x}$ **2.** $\frac{7}{12} = \frac{x}{9}$ **3.** $\frac{25}{x} = \frac{5}{7}$ **4.** $\frac{x}{3} = \frac{8}{9}$

D. Use proportions to find the missing lengths in the following similar shapes.

1.

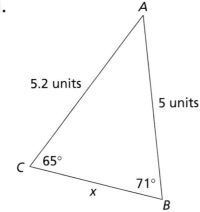

2. Find the height of the tree.

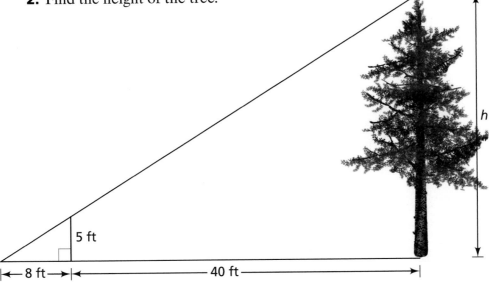

ACE Homework starts on page 55.

4.2 Everyday Use of Proportions

In our everyday lives, we often need to solve proportion problems. So do bakers, tailors, designers, and people in many other occupations.

You may have heard someone say, "A pint is a pound the world around." This saying suggests how to compare liquid measures with weight. It tells us that a pint of liquid weighs about a pound. If you drink a quart of milk a day, you might ask,

"About how much does a quart of liquid weigh?"

Problem 4.2 Applications of Proportions

A. Jogging 5 miles burns about 500 Calories. How many miles will Tanisha need to jog to burn off the 1,200-Calorie lunch she ate?

B. Tanisha jogs about 8 miles in 2 hours. How long will it take her to jog 12 miles?

C. Sam's grandmother says that "a stitch in time saves nine."

   1. What do you think Sam's grandmother means?

   2. Sam's grandmother takes 25 stitches in time. How many does she save?

D. Imani gives vitamins to her adult dogs. The recommended dosage is 2 teaspoons per day for adult dogs weighing 20 pounds. She needs to give vitamins to Bruiser, who weighs 75 pounds, and to Dust Ball, who weighs 7 pounds. What is the correct dosage for each dog?

E. The scale factor relating two similar figures is 1.8. One side of the larger figure is 12 centimeters. How long is the corresponding side of the smaller figure?

`ACE` **Homework starts on page 55.**

4.3 Developing Strategies for Solving Proportions

When mathematicians find the same kind of problem occurring often, they look for a systematic method, or algorithm, that can be applied in each case.

So far in this investigation, you have found ways to solve proportions in specific cases with nice numbers. Now you will develop general strategies that will guide you in solving proportions when the numbers are not so nicely related.

Problem 4.3 Developing Strategies for Solving Proportions

A. A jet takes 10 miles to descend 4,000 feet. How many miles does it take for the jet to descend 5,280 feet?

  1. Set up two different proportions that can be solved to answer the question.

  2. Solve one of your proportions by whatever method you choose. Check to see that your answer makes sense.

B. Jack works at a restaurant and eats one enchilada for lunch every day that he works. He figures that he ate 240 enchiladas last year. Three enchiladas have a total of 705 Calories. How many Calories did he take in last year from eating enchiladas?

  1. Set up a proportion that can be solved to answer the question.

  2. Solve your proportion. Check to see that your answer makes sense.

  3. Describe each step in your solution strategy.

  4. Can your strategy be used to solve any proportion? Explain.

  5. How many Calories did he eat for lunch each working day?

C. In Pinecrest Middle School, there are 58 sixth-graders, 76 seventh-graders, and 38 eighth-graders. The school council is made up of 35 students who are chosen to represent all three grades fairly.

   1. Write fractions to represent the part of the school population that is in each grade.

   2. Use these fractions to write and solve proportions that will help you determine a fair number of students to represent each grade on the school council. Explain.

   3. How would the number of students from each grade change if the number of members of the school council were increased to 37? Explain your reasoning.

D. Ms. Spencer needs 150 graphing calculators for her math students. Her budget allows $5,000 for calculators. She needs to know if she can buy what she needs at the discount store where calculators are on sale at 8 for $284.

   She writes the following statement:

   $$\frac{8}{284} = \frac{150}{x} \quad \text{or} \quad \frac{8}{284} = 150 \div x$$

   1. Use fact-family relationships to rewrite the proportion so that it is easier to find x.

   2. Solve the proportion, recording and explaining each of your steps.

   3. Is your method a general method that can be used to solve any proportion? Explain.

ACE   **Homework starts on page 55.**

Applications

1. Jared and Pedro walk 1 mile in about 15 minutes. They can keep up this pace for several hours.

   a. About how far do they walk in 90 minutes?

   b. About how far do they walk in 65 minutes?

2. Swimming $\frac{1}{4}$ of a mile uses about the same number of Calories as running 1 mile.

   a. Gilda ran a 26-mile marathon. About how far would her sister have to swim to use the same number of Calories Gilda used during the marathon?

   b. Juan swims 5 miles a day. About how many miles would he have to run to use the same number of Calories used during his swim?

3. After testing many samples, an electric company determined that approximately 2 of every 1,000 light bulbs on the market are defective. Americans buy more than 1 billion light bulbs every year. Estimate how many of these bulbs are defective.

4. The organizers of an environmental conference order buttons for the participants. They pay $18 for 12 dozen buttons. Write and solve proportions to answer each question. Assume that price is proportional to the size of the order.

   a. How much do 4 dozen buttons cost?

   b. How much do 50 dozen buttons cost?

   c. How many dozens can the organizers buy for $27?

   d. How many dozens can the organizers buy for $63?

Homework Help Online
PHSchool.com

For: Help with Exercise 4
Web Code: ane-3404

5. Denzel makes 10 of his first 15 shots in a basketball free-throw contest. His success rate stays about the same for his next 100 free throws. Write and solve a proportion to answer each part. Round to the nearest whole number. Start each part with the original 10 of 15 free throws.

    a. About how many free throws does Denzel make in his next 60 attempts?

    b. About how many free throws does he make in his next 80 attempts?

    c. About how many attempts does Denzel take to make 30 free throws?

    d. About how many attempts does he take to make 45 free throws?

For Exercises 6–13, solve each equation.

6. $12.5 = 0.8x$ **7.** $\frac{x}{15} = \frac{20}{50}$ **8.** $\frac{x}{18} = 4.5$ **9.** $\frac{15.8}{x} = 0.7$

10. $\frac{5}{9} = \frac{12}{x}$ **11.** $245 = 0.25x$ **12.** $\frac{18}{x} = \frac{4.5}{1}$ **13.** $\frac{0.1}{48} = \frac{x}{960}$

Go Online
PHSchool.com
For: Multiple-Choice Skills Practice
Web Code: ana-3454

14. Multiple Choice Middletown sponsors a two-day conference for selected middle-school students to study government. There are three middle schools in Middletown.

Suppose 20 student delegates will attend the conference. Each school should be represented fairly in relation to its population. How many should be selected from each school?

North Middle School
618 students
    Central Middle School
378 students
    South Middle School
204 students

    A. North: 10 delegates, Central: 8 delegates, South: 2 delegates

    B. North: 11 delegates, Central: 7 delegates, South: 2 delegates

    C. North: 6 delegates, Central: 3 delegates, South: 2 delegates

    D. North: 10 delegates, Central: 6 delegates, South: 4 delegates

Connections

For Exercises 15–17, use ratios, percents, fractions, or rates.

15. **Multiple Choice** Which cereal is the best buy?

    F. a 14-ounce box for $1.98   **G.** a 36-ounce box for $2.59

    H. a 1-ounce box for $0.15   **J.** a 72-ounce box for $5.25

16. Which is the better average: 10 of 15 free throws, or 8 of 10 free throws?

17. Which is the better home-run rate: two home runs per 60 times at bat, or five home runs per 120 times at bat?

18. A jar contains 150 marked beans. Scott takes several samples from the jar and gets the results shown.

Bean Samples

Number of Beans	25	50	75	100	150	200	250
Number of Marked Beans	3	12	13	17	27	38	52
Percent of Marked Beans	12%	▧	▧	▧	▧	▧	▧

    a. Copy and complete the table.

    b. Graph the data using (*number of beans, marked beans*) as data points. Describe the pattern of data points in your graph. What does the pattern tell you about the relationship between the number of beans in a sample and the number of marked beans you can expect to find?

19. **Multiple Choice** Ayanna is making a circular spinner to be used at the school carnival. She wants the spinner to be divided so that 30% of the area is blue, 20% is red, 15% is green, and 35% is yellow. Choose the spinner that fits the description.

A.

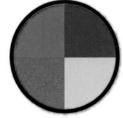

B.

C.

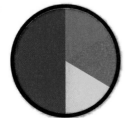

D.

20. Hannah is making her own circular spinner. She makes the ratio of green to yellow 2:1, the ratio of red to yellow 3:1, and the ratio of blue to green 2:1. Make a sketch of her spinner.

21. a. Plot the points $(8, 6)$, $(8, 22)$, and $(24, 14)$ on grid paper. Connect them to form a triangle.

b. Draw the triangle you get when you apply the rule $(0.5x, 0.5y)$ to the three points from part (a).

c. How are lengths of corresponding sides in the triangles from parts (a) and (b) related?

d. The area of the smaller triangle is what percent of the area of the larger triangle?

e. The area of the larger triangle is what percent of the area of the smaller triangle?

22. The sketch shows two similar polygons.

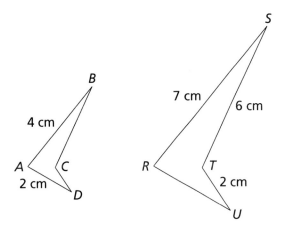

a. What is the length of side BC?

b. What is the length of side RU?

c. What is the length of side CD?

23. To earn an Explorer Scout merit badge, Yoshi and Kai have the task of measuring the width of a river. Their report includes a diagram that shows their work.

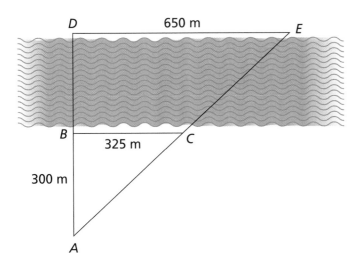

a. How do you think they came up with the lengths of the segments *AB*, *BC*, and *DE*?

b. How can they find the width of the river from segments *AB*, *BC*, and *DE*?

Extensions

24. Angela, a biologist, spends summers on an island in Alaska. For several summers she studied puffins. Two summers ago, Angela captured, tagged, and released 20 puffins. This past summer, she captured 50 puffins and found that 2 of them were tagged. Using Angela's findings, estimate the number of puffins on the island. Explain.

25. Rita wants to estimate the number of beans in a large jar. She takes out 100 beans and marks them. Then she returns them to the jar and mixes them with the unmarked beans. She then gathers some data by taking a sample of beans from the jar. Use her data to predict the number of beans in the jar.

> **Sample**
>
> Number of marked beans: 2
> Beans in sample: 30

26. The two histograms below display information about gallons of water used per person in 24 households in a week.

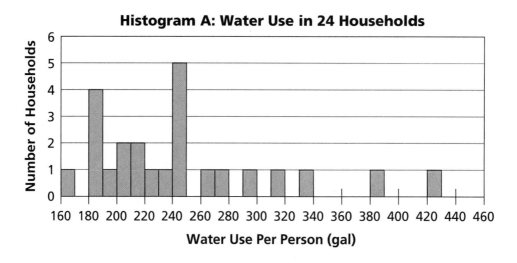

a. Compare the two histograms and explain how they differ.

b. Where do the data seem to clump in Histograms A and B?

27. The picture at the right is drawn on a centimeter grid.

   a. On a grid made of larger squares than those shown here, draw a figure similar to this figure. What is the scale factor between the original figure and your drawing?

   b. Draw another figure similar to this one, but use a grid made of smaller squares than those shown here. What is the scale factor between the original and your drawing?

   c. Compare the perimeters and areas of the original figure and its copies in each case (enlargement and reduction of the figure). Explain how these values relate to the scale factor in each case.

28. The people of the United States are represented in Congress, which is made up of the House of Representatives and the Senate.

   a. In the House of Representatives, the number of representatives from each state varies. From what you know about Congress, how is the number of representatives from each state determined?

   b. How is the number of senators from each state determined?

   c. Compare the two methods of determining representation in Congress. What are the advantages and disadvantages of these two forms of representation for states with large populations? How about for states with small populations?

Mathematical Reflections 4

In this investigation, you used ratios and proportions to solve a variety of problems. You found that most of those problems can be expressed in proportions such as $\frac{a}{b} = \frac{c}{x}$ or $\frac{a}{b} = \frac{x}{c}$. The next questions will help you summarize what you have learned.

Think about your answers to these questions. Discuss your ideas with other students and your teacher. Then write a summary of your findings in your notebook.

1. For each situation, write a problem that can be solved using a proportion. Then solve your problem.

   a. The fraction of girls in grade seven is $\frac{3}{5}$.

   b. Bolda Cola sells at 5 for $3.

   c. Sora rides her bike at a speed of 12 miles per hour.

   d. A triangle is similar to another one with a scale factor of 1.5.

2. Write four different proportions for the problem you created in part (c). Show that the answer to the problem is the same no matter which proportion you use.

3. What procedures do you use to solve proportions such as those you wrote in Question 2?

Unit Project

Paper Pool

The unit project is a mathematical investigation of a game called Paper Pool. For a pool table, use grid paper rectangles like the one shown at the right. Each outside corner is a pocket where a "ball" could "fall."

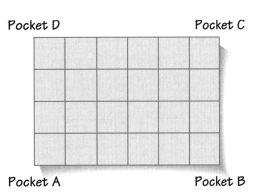

Pocket D   Pocket C

Pocket A   Pocket B

How to Play Paper Pool

- The ball always starts at Pocket A.
- To move the ball, "hit" it as if you were playing pool.
- The ball always moves on a 45° diagonal across the grid.
- When the ball hits a side of the table, it bounces off at a 45° angle and continues to move.
- If the ball moves to a corner, it falls into the pocket at that corner.

The dotted lines on the table at the right show the ball's path.

- The ball falls in Pocket D.
- There are five "hits," including the starting hit and the final hit.
- The dimensions of the table are 6 by 4 (always mention the horizontal length first).

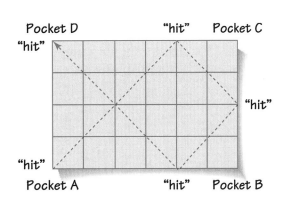

Pocket D   "hit"   Pocket C
"hit"

"hit"

"hit"

"hit"
Pocket A   "hit"   Pocket B

Part 1: Investigate Two Questions

Use the three Paper Pool labsheets to play the game. Try to find rules that tell you (1) the pocket where the ball will fall and (2) the number of hits along the way. Keep track of the dimensions because they may give you clues to a pattern.

Part 2: Write a Report

When you find some patterns and reach some conclusions, write a report that includes

- A list of the rules you found and an explanation of why you think they are correct

- Drawings of other grid paper tables that follow your rule

- Any tables, charts, or other tools that helped you find patterns

- Other patterns or ideas about Paper Pool

Extension Question

Can you predict the length of the ball's path on any size Paper Pool table? Each time the ball crosses a square, the length is 1 diagonal unit. Find the length of the ball's path in diagonal units for any set of dimensions.

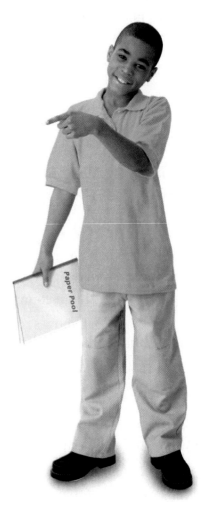

For: Paper Pool Activity
Visit: PHSchool.com
Web Code: and-3000

Looking Back and Looking Ahead

The problems in this unit required you to compare measured quantities. You learned when it seems best to use subtraction, division, percents, rates, ratios, and proportions to make those comparisons. You developed a variety of strategies for writing and solving proportions. These strategies include writing equivalent ratios to scale a ratio up or down. You also learned to compute and reason with unit rates.

For: Vocabulary Review Puzzle
Web Code: anj-3051

Use Your Understanding: Proportional Reasoning

Test your understanding of percents, rates, ratios, and proportions by solving the following problems.

1. There are 300 students in East Middle School. To plan transportation services for the new West Middle School, the school system surveyed East students. The survey asked whether students ride a bus to school or walk.

   - In Mr. Archer's homeroom, 20 students ride the bus and 15 students walk.

   - In Ms. Brown's homeroom, 14 students ride the bus and 9 students walk.

   - In Mr. Chavez's homeroom, 20 students ride the bus and the ratio of bus riders to walkers is 5 to 3.

   a. In what ways can you compare the number of students in Mr. Archer's homeroom who are bus riders to the number who are walkers? Which seems to be the best comparison statement?

   b. In what ways can you compare the numbers of bus riders and walkers in Ms. Brown's homeroom to those in Mr. Archer's homeroom? Again, which seems the best way to make the comparison?

   c. How many students in Mr. Chavez's homeroom walk to school?

d. Use the information from these three homerooms. About how many East Middle School students would you expect to walk to school? How many would you expect to ride a bus?

e. Suppose the new West Middle School will have 450 students and a ratio of bus riders to walkers that is about the same as that in East Middle School. About how many West students can be expected in each category?

2. The Purr & Woof Kennel buys food for animals that are boarded. The amounts of food eaten and the cost for food are shown below.

a. Is cat food or dog food cheaper per pound?

b. Is it cheapest to feed a cat, a small dog, or a large dog?

c. On an average day, the kennel has 20 cats, 30 small dogs, and 20 large dogs. Which will last longer: a bag of cat food or a bag of dog food?

d. How many bags of dog food will be used in the month of January? How many bags of cat food will be used?

e. The owner finds a new store that sells Bow-Chow in 15 pound bags for $6.75 per bag. How much does that store charge for 50 pounds of Bow-Chow?

f. Which is a better buy on Bow-Chow: the original source or the new store?

Explain Your Reasoning

Answering comparison questions often requires knowledge of rates, ratios, percents, and proportional reasoning. Answer the following questions about your reasoning strategies. Use the preceding problems and other examples from this unit to illustrate your ideas.

3. How do you decide when to compare numbers using ratios, rates, or percents rather than by finding the difference of the two numbers?

4. Suppose you are given information that the ratio of two quantities is 3 to 5. How can you express that relationship in other written forms?

5. Suppose that the ratio of two quantities is 24 to 18.

   a. State five other equivalent ratios in the form "p to q."

   b. Use whole numbers to write an equivalent ratio that cannot be scaled down without using fractions or decimals.

6. What strategies can you use to solve proportions such as $\frac{5}{8} = \frac{12}{x}$ and $\frac{5}{8} = \frac{x}{24}$?

7. How does proportional reasoning enter into the solution of each problem?

   a. You want to prepare enough of a recipe to serve a large crowd.

   b. You want to use the scale of a map to find the actual distance between two points in a park from their locations on the map.

   c. You want to find which package of raisins is the better value.

   d. You want to use a design drawn on a coordinate grid to make several larger copies and several smaller copies of that design.

Look Ahead

Proportional reasoning is an important way to compare measured quantities. It includes comparing numerical information by ratios, rates, and percents. It is used in geometry to enlarge and reduce figures while retaining their shapes. You will apply proportional reasoning in future *Connected Mathematics* units such as *Filling and Wrapping*, *Moving Straight Ahead*, and *What Do You Expect?*

English/Spanish Glossary

P

proportion An equation stating that two ratios are equal. For example:

$$\frac{\text{hours spent on homework}}{\text{hours spent in school}} = \frac{2}{7}$$

Note that this does not necessarily imply that hours spent on homework = 2 or that hours spent in school = 7. During a week, 10 hours may have been spent on homework while 35 hours were spent in school. The proportion is still true because $\frac{10}{35} = \frac{2}{7}$.

proporción Una ecuación que indica que dos razones son iguales. Por ejemplo:

$$\frac{\text{horas dedicadas a la tarea}}{\text{horas en la escuela}} = \frac{2}{7}$$

Fíjate que esto no implica necesariamente que las horas dedicadas a la tarea = 2, ó que las horas en la escuela = 7. Durante una semana, puedes haber pasado 10 horas haciendo tarea y 35 horas en la escuela. La proporción sigue siendo verdadera porque $\frac{10}{35} = \frac{2}{7}$.

R

rate A comparison of quantities measured in two different units is called a rate. A rate can be thought of as a direct comparison of two sets (20 cookies for 5 children) or as an average amount (4 cookies per child). A rate such as 5.5 miles per hour can be written as $\frac{5.5 \text{ miles}}{1 \text{ hour}}$, or 5.5 miles : 1 hour.

tasa Una comparación de cantidades medidas en dos unidades diferentes se llama tasa. Una tasa se puede interpretar como una comparación directa entre dos grupos (20 galletas para 5 niños) o como una cantidad promedio (4 galletas por niño). Una tasa como 5.5 millas por hora se puede escribir como $\frac{5.5 \text{ millas}}{1 \text{ hora}}$, o como 5.5 millas a 1 hora.

rate table You can use a rate to find and organize equivalent rates in a rate table. For example, you can use the rate "five limes for $1.00" to make this rate table.

tabla de tasas Puedes usar una tasa para hallar y organizar tasas equivalentes en una tabla de tasas. Por ejemplo, puedes usar la tasa "cinco limas por $1.00" para hacer esta tabla de tasas, en la cual se indica el número de limas y el costo de las limas.

Cost of Limes

Number of Limes	1	2	3	4	5	10	15	20
Cost of Limes	$0.20	$0.40	$0.60	$0.80	$1.00	$2.00	$3.00	$4.00

ratio A ratio is a number, often expressed as a fraction, used to make comparisons between two quantities. Ratios may also be expressed as equivalent decimals or percents, or given in the form $a:b$. Here are some examples of uses of ratios:

- The ratio of females to males on the swim team is 2 to 3, or $\frac{2 \text{ females}}{3 \text{ males}}$.
- The train travels at a speed of 80 miles per hour, or $\frac{80 \text{ miles}}{1 \text{ hour}}$.
- If a small figure is enlarged by a scale factor of 2, the new figure will have an area four times its original size. The ratio of the small figure's area to the large figure's area will be $\frac{1}{4}$. The ratio of the large figure's area to the small figure's area will be $\frac{4}{1}$, or 4.
- In the example above, the ratio of the length of a side of the small figure to the length of the corresponding side of the large figure is $\frac{1}{2}$. The ratio of the length of a side of the large figure to the length of the corresponding side of the small figure is $\frac{2}{1}$, or 2.

razón Una razón es un número, a menudo expresado como fracción, que se usa para hacer comparaciones entre dos cantidades. Las razones también se pueden expresar como decimales equivalentes o porcentajes, o darse de la forma $a:b$. Estos son algunos ejemplos del uso de razones:

- La razón entre mujeres y hombres en el equipo de natación es 2 a 3, es decir, $\frac{2 \text{ mujeres}}{3 \text{ hombres}}$.
- El tren viaja a una velocidad de 80 millas por hora, o sea, $\frac{80 \text{ millas}}{1 \text{ hora}}$.
- Si se amplía una figura pequeña por un factor de escala 2, la nueva figura tendrá un área cuatro veces mayor que su tamaño original. La razón entre el área de la figura pequeña y el área de la figura grande será $\frac{1}{4}$. La razón entre el área de la figura grande y el área de la figura pequeña será $\frac{4}{1}$, o sea, 4.
- En el ejemplo anterior, la razón entre la longitud de un lado de la figura pequeña y la longitud del lado correspondiente de la figura grande es $\frac{1}{2}$. La razón entre la longitud de un lado de la figura grande y la longitud del lado correspondiente de la figura pequeña es $\frac{2}{1}$, o sea, 2.

S

scale, scaling The scale is the number used to multiply both parts of a ratio to produce an equal, but possibly more informative, ratio. A ratio can be scaled to produce a number of equivalent ratios. For example, multiplying the rate of 4.5 gallons per hour by a scale of 2 yields the rate of 9 gallons per 2 hours. Scales are also used on maps to give the relationship between a measurement on the map to the actual physical measurement.

escala, aplicar una escala La escala es el número que se usa para multiplicar las dos partes de una razón para producir una razón igual, pero posiblemente más informativa. Se puede aplicar una escala a una razón para producir un número de razones equivalentes. Por ejemplo, al multiplicar la razón de 4.5 galones por hora por una escala de 2, se obtiene una razón de 9 galones por 2 horas. Las escalas también se usan en los mapas para indicar la relación que existe entre una distancia en el mapa y una distancia real.

U

unit rate A unit rate is a rate in which the second number (usually written as the denominator) is 1, or 1 of a quantity. For example, 1.9 children per family, 32 miles per gallon, and $\frac{3 \text{ flavors of ice cream}}{1 \text{ banana split}}$ are unit rates. Unit rates are often found by scaling other rates.

tasa unitaria Una tasa unitaria es una tasa en la que el segundo número (normalmente escrito como el denominador) es 1 ó 1 de una cantidad. Por ejemplo, 1.9 niños por familia, 32 millas por galón, y $\frac{3 \text{ sabores de helado}}{1 \text{ banana split}}$ son tasas unitarias. Las tasas unitarias se calculan a menudo aplicando escalas a otras tasas.

Index

Acknowledgments

Team Credits

The people who made up the **Connected Mathematics 2** team—representing editorial, editorial services, design services, and production services—are listed below. Bold type denotes core team members.

Leora Adler, Judith Buice, Kerry Cashman, Patrick Culleton, Sheila DeFazio, Richard Heater, **Barbara Hollingdale, Jayne Holman,** Karen Holtzman, **Etta Jacobs,** Christine Lee, Carolyn Lock, Catherine Maglio, **Dotti Marshall,** Rich McMahon, Eve Melnechuk, Kristin Mingrone, Terri Mitchell, **Marsha Novak,** Irene Rubin, Donna Russo, Robin Samper, Siri Schwartzman, **Nancy Smith,** Emily Soltanoff, **Mark Tricca,** Paula Vergith, Roberta Warshaw, Helen Young

Additional Credits

Diana Bonfilio, Mairead Reddin, Michael Torocsik, nSight, Inc.

Illustration

Michelle Barbera: 41, 53, 67

Technical Illustration

WestWords, Inc.

Cover Design

tom white.images

Photos

2 t, Richard Hutchings/PhotoEdit; **2 m,** Alden Pellett/The Image Works; **2 b,** Kevin Schafer/Corbis; **3,** M. Barrett/Robertstock.com; **5,** Stockbyte; **8,** AP Photo/Easton Star Democrat, Chris Polk; **9,** Grant Heilman Photography; **11,** PhotoDisc/Getty Images, Inc.; **16,** Russ Lappa; **18,** Ron Kimball/Ron Kimball Stock; **20,** Richard Haynes; **23,** Martin Harvey/Peter Arnold, Inc.; **25,** Richard Hutchings/PhotoEdit; **29,** Art Wolfe/Getty Images, Inc.; **30,** Ariel Skelley/Corbis; **33,** Larry Kolvoord/The Image Works; **35,** Sam Kleinman/Corbis; **36,** Digital Vision/Getty Images, Inc.; **39,** Alden Pellett/The Image Works; **41,** Peter Johansky/Index Stock Imagery; **43,** Lester Lefkowitz/Getty Images, Inc.; **46,** Kevin Radford/SuperStock; **48,** Zoran Milich/Masterfile; **52,** Renee Stockdale/Animals Animals/Earth Scenes; **55,** Felix Stensson/Alamy; **59,** Kevin Schafer/Corbis; **61,** Sandy Schaeffer/Mai/Mai/Time Life Pictures/Getty Images, Inc.; **61 frame,** Karen Beard/Getty Images, Inc.; **64,** Richard Haynes

Data Sources

The car color data on page 18 are from "Most Popular Colors by Type of Vehicle, 2001 Model Year" from THE WORLD ALMANAC. Used by permission of DuPont Automotive Products/ DuPont Performance Coatings.

The radio station formats on page 18 is data from U.S. Commercial Radio Stations, by Format from THE WORLD ALMANAC. Copyright © 2002 Inside Radio/ M Street Publications. Used by permission.

Monthly sales of *Reader's Digest* and *National Geographic* on page 21 is from FAS-FAX Report-12/31/2004. Copyright © 12/31/2004 by Audit Bureau of Circulations. All rights reserved. Used by permission.

The fastest bicycle speed on page 35 is from Guinness World Records, Ltd.

The American doctor data on page 48 are from "Doctors and Nurses: A Demographic Profile," February, 1998, by Leon Bouvier. Used by permission of the Center for Immigration Studies Washington, D.C.

Connected Mathematics 2 ™

Accentuate the Negative

Integers and Rational Numbers

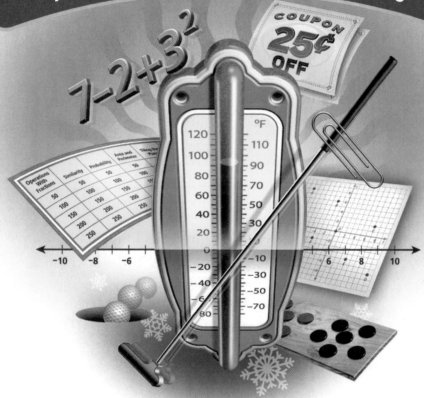

Glenda Lappan
James T. Fey
William M. Fitzgerald
Susan N. Friel
Elizabeth Difanis Phillips

PEARSON

Prentice
Hall

Boston, Massachusetts
Upper Saddle River, New Jersey

Accentuate the Negative

After the first five questions in a quiz show, player A has a score of −100 and player B has a score of −150. Which player has the lead and how great is the lead?

Hahn competes in a relay race. He goes from the 0 meter line to the 15 meter line in 5 seconds. At what rate (distance per second) does he run?

A new convenience store wants to attract customers. For a one-day special, they sell gasoline for $0.25 below their cost. They sell 5,750 gallons that day. How much money do they lose?

ost of the numbers you have worked with in math class this year have been greater than or equal to zero. However, numbers less than zero can provide important information. Winter temperatures in many places fall below 0°F. Businesses that lose money have profits less than $0. Scores in games or sports can be less than zero.

Numbers greater than zero are called *positive numbers*. Numbers less than zero are called *negative numbers*. In *Accentuate the Negative,* you will work with both positive and negative numbers. One subset of positive and negative numbers that you will study is called *integers*. You will explore models that help you think about adding, subtracting, multiplying, and dividing positive and negative numbers. You will also learn more about the properties of operations on positive and negative numbers.

In *Accentuate the Negative,* you will solve problems similar to those on the previous page that require understanding and skill in working with positive and negative numbers.

Mathematical Highlights

Integers and Rational Numbers

In *Accentuate the Negative*, you will extend your knowledge of negative numbers. You will explore ways to use negative numbers in solving problems.

You will learn how to

- Use appropriate notation to indicate positive and negative numbers
- Compare and order positive and negative rational numbers (fractions, decimals, and zero) and locate them on a number line
- Understand the relationship between a positive or negative number and its opposite (additive inverse)
- Develop algorithms for adding, subtracting, multiplying, and dividing positive and negative numbers
- Write mathematical sentences to show relationships
- Write and use related fact families for addition/subtraction and multiplication/division to solve simple equations
- Use parentheses and rules for the order of operations in computations
- Understand and use the Commutative Property for addition and multiplication
- Apply the Distributive Property to simplify expressions and solve problems
- Graph points in four quadrants
- Use positive and negative numbers to model and answer questions about problem situations

As you work on problems in this unit, ask yourself questions like these:

How do negative and positive numbers help in describing the situation?

What will addition, subtraction, multiplication, or division of positive and negative numbers tell about the problem?

What model(s) for positive and negative numbers would help in showing the relationships in the problem situation?

Extending the Number System

In your study of numbers, you have focused on operations (+, −, ×, and ÷) with whole numbers, fractions, and decimals. In this unit, you will learn about some important new numbers in the number system.

Suppose you start with a number line showing 0, 1, 2, 3, 4, and 5.

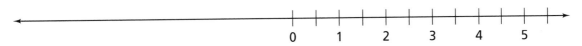

Take the number line and fold it around the zero point. Make marks on the left side of zero to match the marks on the right side.

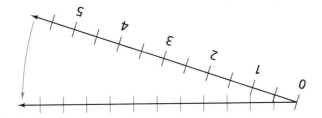

Label the new marks with numbers that have negative signs (⁻). These numbers (to the left of 0) are **negative numbers.**

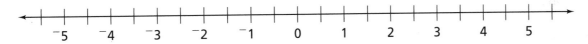

I owe my Dad 3 dollars, so I have ⁻3 dollars.

Each negative number is paired with a **positive number.** The numbers in the pair are the same distance from zero but in opposite directions on the number line. These number pairs are called **opposites.** You can label positive numbers with positive signs (⁺).

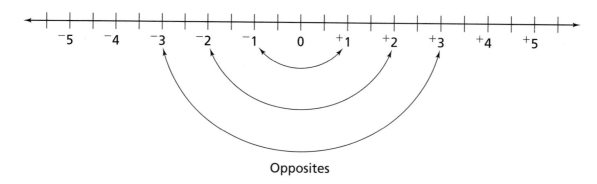

Opposites

Some subsets of the positive and negative numbers have special names. Whole numbers and their opposites are called **integers** (⁻4, ⁻3, ⁻2, ⁻1, 0, ⁺1, ⁺2, ⁺3, ⁺4).

Fractions also have opposites. For example, $^{+}\frac{1}{2}$ and $^{-}\frac{1}{2}$ are opposites. Positive and negative integers and fractions are called rational numbers. **Rational numbers** are numbers that can be expressed as one integer divided by another integer.

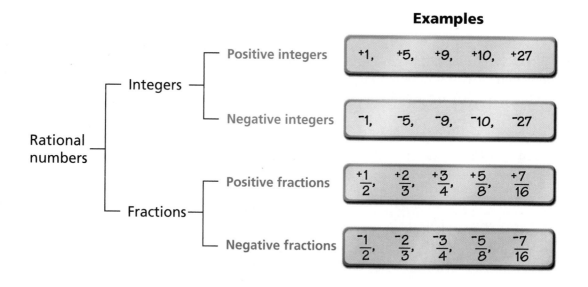

In mathematical notation, you can write a positive number with a raised plus sign ($^+150$) or without any sign (150). You can write a negative number with a raised minus sign ($^-150$). To avoid confusion with operation signs, it is common to use raised signs.

Many calculators have a special negative number key . When you press 5 ☐ (-) 2 , the calculator shows "5 − $^-$2."

Getting Ready for Problem 1.1

- Where would the following pairs of numbers be located on the number line?

  $^+7$ and $^-7$

  $^+2.7$ and $^-2.7$

  $^-3.8$ and $^+3.8$

  $-\frac{1}{2}$ and $^+\frac{1}{2}$

  $4\frac{3}{4}$ and $^-4\frac{3}{4}$

- If the same relationship holds true for all numbers, what would be the opposite of $^-1\frac{2}{3}$ and where would it be located?

1.1 Playing Math Fever

Ms. Bernoski's math classes often play Math Fever, a game similar to a popular television game show. The game board is shown. Below each category name are five cards. The front of each card shows a point value. The back of each card has a question related to the category. Cards with higher point values have more difficult questions.

Math Fever

Operations With Fractions	Similarity	Probability	Area and Perimeter	Tiling the Plane	Factors and Multiples
50	50	50	50	50	50
100	100	100	100	100	100
150	150	150	150	150	150
200	200	200	200	200	200
250	250	250	250	250	250

The game is played in teams. One team starts the game by choosing a card. The teacher asks the question on the back of the card. The first team to answer the question correctly gets the point value on the card. The card is then removed from the board. If a team answers the question incorrectly, the point value is subtracted from their score. The team that answers correctly chooses the next category and point value.

Problem 1.1 Using Positive and Negative Numbers

At one point in a game, the scores are as follows:

Super Brains	Rocket Scientists	Know-It-Alls
⁻300	150	⁻500

A. Which team has the highest score? Which team has the lowest score? Explain.

B. What is the difference in points for each pair of teams?

C. Use number sentences to describe two possible ways that each team reached its score.

D. The current scores are ⁻300 for Super Brains, 150 for Rocket Scientists, and ⁻500 for Know-It-Alls.

   1. Write number sentences to represent each sequence of points. Start with the current score for each team.

   a. Super Brains

Point Value	Answer
200	Correct
150	Incorrect
50	Correct
50	Correct

   b. Rocket Scientists

Point Value	Answer
50	Incorrect
200	Incorrect
100	Correct
150	Incorrect

   c. Know-It-Alls

Point Value	Answer
100	Incorrect
200	Correct
150	Incorrect
50	Incorrect

   2. Now which team has the highest score? Which team has the lowest score?

   3. What is the difference in points for each pair of teams?

E. The number sentences below describe what happens at a particular point during a game of Math Fever. Find each missing number. Explain what each sentence tells about a team's performance and overall score.

   1. BrainyActs: ⁻200 + 150 − 100 = ▦

   2. MathSperts: 450 − 200 = ▦

   3. ExCells: 200 − 250 = ▦

   4. SuperMs: ⁻350 + ▦ = ⁻150

ACE Homework starts on page 16.

The record high and low temperatures in the United States are 134°F in Death Valley, California and ⁻80°F in Prospect Creek, Alaska. Imagine going from 134°F to ⁻80°F in an instant!

In Finland, people think that such temperature shocks are fun and good for your health. This activity is called sauna-bathing.

In the winter, Finnish people sit for a certain amount of time in sauna houses. The houses are heated as high as 120°F. Then the people run outside, where the temperature might be as low as ⁻20°F.

Inside the Sauna

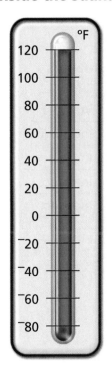

Outside in Snow

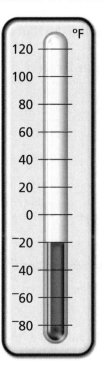

The two thermometers shown are similar to number lines. One horizontal number line can show the same information as the two thermometers.

On the number line, a move to the left is a move in a negative direction. The numbers decrease in value. A move to the right is a move in a positive direction. The numbers increase in value. On the thermometers, a move down means the number values decrease and the temperatures get colder. A move up means the number values increase and the temperatures get hotter.

Problem 1.2 Comparing and Ordering Positive and Negative Numbers

Sketch number lines to show your reasoning.

A. Order these temperatures from least to greatest.

0°F   115°F   ⁻15°F   ⁻32.5°F   ⁻40°F   113.2°F   ⁻32.7°F

B. For each pair of temperatures, identify which temperature is further from ⁻2°F.

1. 6°F or ⁻6°F?

2. ⁻7°F or 3°F?

3. 2°F or ⁻5°F?

4. ⁻10°F or 7°F?

C. Identify the temperature that is halfway between each pair of temperatures.

1. 0°F and 10°F

2. ⁻5°F and 15°F

3. 5°F and ⁻15°F

4. 0°F and ⁻20°F

5. ⁻8°F and 8°F

6. ⁻6°F and 6°F

7. During one week, the high temperature was 60°F. The halfway temperature was 15°F. What was the low temperature?

D. Name six temperatures between ⁻2°F and ⁺1°F. Order them from least to greatest.

E. 1. Estimate values for points A–E.

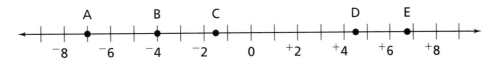

2. How does the number line help you find the smaller value of two numbers?

F. What are the opposites of these numbers?

1. 3

2. 7.5

3. ⁻2$\frac{2}{3}$

4. What is the sum of a number and its opposite?

ACE Homework starts on page 16.

In golf, scores can be negative. Each golf hole has a value called par. Par is the number of strokes a golfer usually needs to complete the hole. For example, a good golfer, like Vijay Singh, should be able to complete a par 4 hole in four strokes. If a golfer completes the hole in six strokes, then his or her score for that hole is "two over par" (⁺2). If a golfer completes the hole in two strokes, his or her score is "two under par" (⁻2). A player's score for a round of golf is the total of the number of strokes above or under par.

 **For:** Information about golf
PHSchool.com **Web Code:** ane-9031

1.3 What's the Change?

The National Weather Service keeps records of temperature changes.

The world record for fastest rise in outside air temperature occurred in Spearfish, South Dakota, on January 22, 1943. The temperature rose from ⁻4°F to 45°F in two minutes.

What was the change in temperature over that two minutes? How could you show this change, n, on the number line?

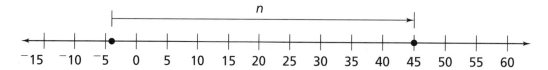

From ⁻4°F to 0°F is a change of ⁺4°F, and from 0°F to 45°F is a change of ⁺45°F. So the total change is ⁺49°F. The following number sentences show this.

$$^-4 + n = {}^+45$$
$$^-4 + {}^+49 = {}^+45$$

The sign of the change in temperature shows the direction of the change. In this case, ⁺49 means the temperature increased 49°F.

If the temperature had instead dropped 10° from ⁻4°F, you would write the change as ⁻10°F.

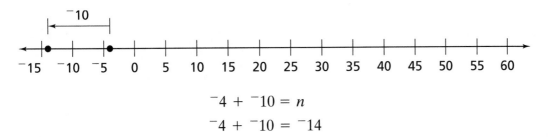

$$^-4 + {^-10} = n$$
$$^-4 + {^-10} = {^-14}$$

Problem 1.3 Using a Number Line Model

Sketch number lines and write number sentences for each question.

A. A person goes from a sauna at 120°F to an outside temperature of ⁻20°F. What is the change in temperature?

B. The temperature reading on a thermometer is 25°F. In the problems below, a positive number means the temperature is rising. A negative number means the temperature is falling. What is the new reading for each temperature change below?

1. ⁺10°F   **2.** ⁻2°F   **3.** ⁻30°F

C. The temperature reading on a thermometer is ⁻15°F. What is the new reading for each temperature change?

1. ⁺3°F   **2.** ⁻10°F   **3.** ⁺40°F

D. What is the change in temperature when the thermometer reading moves from the first temperature to the second temperature? Write an equation for each part.

1. 20°F to ⁻10°F   **2.** ⁻20°F to ⁻10°F

3. ⁻20°F to 10°F   **4.** ⁻10°F to ⁻20°F

5. 20°F to 10°F   **6.** 10°F to 20°F

E. The temperature was ⁻5°F when Sally went to school on Monday. The temperature rose 20°F during the day, but fell 25°F during the night. A heat wave the next day increased the temperature 40°F. But an arctic wind overnight decreased the temperature 70°F! What was the temperature after the 70° decrease?

ACE Homework starts on page 16.

1.4 In the Chips

When business records were kept by hand, accountants used red ink for expenses and black ink for income. If your income was greater than your expenses you were "in the black." If your expenses were greater than your income you were "in the red."

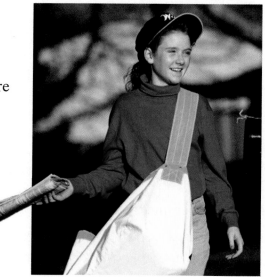

Julia has this problem to solve:

> Linda owes her sister $6 for helping her cut the lawn. She earns $4 delivering papers with her brother. Is she "in the red" or "in the black"?

Getting Ready for Problem 1.4

Julia uses red and black chips to model income and expenses. Each black chip represents $^+1$ dollar of income. Each red chip represents $^-1$ dollar of income (expenses).

Julia puts chips on the board to represent the situation. She decides Linda is "in the red" 2 dollars, or $^-2$ dollars.

Julia's Chip Board

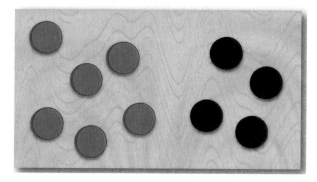

- Why do you think she concludes that $^-6 + {}^+4 = {}^-2$?
- What is another way to show $^-2$ on the board?

Find the missing part for each chip problem. What would be a number sentence for each problem?

	Start With	Rule	End With
1.	● ● ●	Add 5 ●	▪
2.	● ● ●	Subtract 3 ●	▪
3.	● ● ● ● ● ●	▪	● ●
4.	▪	Subtract 3 ●	● ● ● ●

Problem 1.4 Using a Chip Model

Use ideas about black and red chips to answer each question. Then write a number sentence.

A. Give three combinations of red and black chips (using at least one of each color) that will equal each value.

   1. 0   **2.** $^+12$ **3.** $^-7$ **4.** $^-125$

B. Use this chip board as the starting value for each part. Find the total value on each chip board.

   1. original chip board

   2. add 5 black chips

   3. remove 5 red chips

   4. remove 3 black chips

   5. add 3 red chips

C. Cybil owes her sister $7. Her aunt pays her $5 to walk her dog. How much money does she have after she pays her sister?

D. Tate earns $10 mowing a lawn. He needs to pay $15 to rent his equipment. How much more money does he need to pay his rent?

active math online

For: Interactive Chip Model
Visit: PHSchool.com
Web Code: and-4104

E. Describe chip board displays that would match these number sentences. Find the results in each case.

   1. $^+3 - {}^+2 = $ ▪   **2.** $^-4 - {}^+2 = $ ▪   **3.** $^-4 - {}^-2 = $ ▪

   4. $^+7 + $ ▪ $ = {}^+1$ **5.** $^-3 - {}^+5 = $ ▪   **6.** ▪ $ - {}^-2 = {}^+6$

ACE   Homework starts on page 16.

Applications

Describe a sequence of five correct or incorrect answers that would produce each Math Fever score.

1. Super Brains: 300

2. Rocket Scientists: ⁻200

3. Know-It-Alls: ⁻250

4. Teacher's Pets: 0

5. **Multiple Choice** Which order is from least to greatest?

   A. 300, 0, ⁻200, ⁻250

   B. ⁻250, ⁻200, 0, 300

   C. 0, ⁻200, ⁻250, 300

   D. ⁻200, ⁻250, 300, 0

Find each Math Fever team's score. Write number sentences for each team. Assume that each team starts with 0 points.

6. Protons

Point Value	Answer
250	Correct
100	Correct
200	Correct
150	Incorrect
200	Incorrect

7. Neutrons

Point Value	Answer
200	Incorrect
50	Correct
250	Correct
150	Incorrect
50	Incorrect

8. Electrons

Point Value	Answer
50	Incorrect
200	Incorrect
100	Correct
200	Correct
150	Incorrect

For each set of rational numbers in Exercises 9 and 10, draw a number line and locate the points. Remember to choose an appropriate scale.

9. $-\frac{2}{8}$, $\frac{1}{4}$, ⁻1.5, $1\frac{3}{4}$

10. ⁻1.25, $-\frac{1}{3}$, 1.5, $-\frac{1}{6}$

11. Order the numbers from least to greatest.

   23.6   ⁻45.2   50   ⁻0.5   0.3 $\frac{3}{5}$ $\frac{-4}{5}$

For: Help with Exercise 11
Web Code: ane-4111

Copy each pair of numbers in Exercises 12–19. Insert <, >, or = to make a true statement.

12. 3 ■ 0

13. ⁻23.4 ■ 23.4

14. 46 ■ ⁻79

15. ⁻75 ■ ⁻90

16. ⁻300 ■ 100

17. ⁻1,000 ■ ⁻999

18. ⁻1.73 ■ ⁻1.730

19. ⁻4.3 ■ ⁻4.03

 Go Online
PHSchool.com

For: Multiple-Choice Skills Practice
Web Code: ana-4154

For Exercises 20–29, follow the steps using the number line. What is the final position?

20. Start at 8. Add ⁻7.

21. Start at ⁻8. Add 10.

22. Start at ⁻3. Add ⁻5.

23. Start at 7. Add ⁻7.

24. Start at ⁻2. Add 12.

25. Start at 3. Subtract 5.

26. Start at ⁻2. Subtract 2.

27. Start at 4. Subtract 7.

28. Start at 0. Subtract 5.

29. Start at ⁻8. Subtract 3.

30. The greatest one-day temperature change in world records occurred at Browning, Montana (bordering Glacier National Park), from January 23–24 in 1916. The temperature fell from 44°F to ⁻56°F in less than 24 hours.

  a. What was the temperature change that day?

  b. Write a number sentence to represent the temperature change.

  c. Show the temperature change on a number line.

Investigation 1 Extending the Number System　**17**

31. Find the value for each labeled point on the number line. Then use the values to calculate each change.

a. A to B   **b.** A to C   **c.** B to C   **d.** C to A   **e.** B to A

Find the missing part for each situation.

	Start With	Rule	End With
32.	● ● ●	Add 5 ⚪	▪
33.	⚫ ⚫ ⚫	Subtract 3 ⚪	▪
34.	⚫ ⚫ ⚫ ⚫ ⚫	▪	⚫ ⚫
35.	▪	Subtract 3 ●	⚫ ⚫ ⚫ ⚫

36. Write a story problem for this situation. Find the value represented by the chips on the board.

For Exercises 37 and 38, use the chip board in Exercise 36.

37. Describe three different ways to change the numbers of black and red chips, but leave the value of the board unchanged.

38. Start with the original board. What is the new value of chips on the board when you

   a. remove 3 red chips?

   b. and then add 3 black chips?

   c. and then add 200 black chips and 195 red chips?

Connections

39. In a football game, one team makes seven plays in the first quarter. The results of those plays are (in order): gain of 7 yards, gain of 2 yards, loss of 5 yards, loss of 12 yards, gain of 16 yards, gain of 8 yards, loss of 8 yards.

   a. What is the overall gain (or loss) from all seven plays?

   b. What is the average gain (or loss) per play?

Find the number of strokes above or under par for each player. See the Did You Know? before the introduction to Problem 1.3 for the definition of par. Write number sentences with positive and negative numbers to show each result.

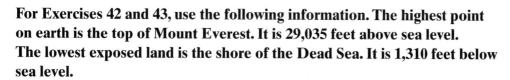

	Player	Round 1	Round 2	Round 3	Round 4
40.	**Tiger Woods**	4 over par	6 under par	3 under par	1 over par
41.	**Karrie Webb**	2 under par	1 under par	5 over par	5 under par

For Exercises 42 and 43, use the following information. The highest point on earth is the top of Mount Everest. It is 29,035 feet above sea level. The lowest exposed land is the shore of the Dead Sea. It is 1,310 feet below sea level.

42. Multiple Choice What is the change in elevation from the top of Everest to the shore of the Dead Sea?

   F. $^-$30,345 feet   **G.** $^-$27,725 feet

   H. 27,725 feet   **J.** 30,345 feet

43. Multiple Choice What is the change in elevation from the shore of the Dead Sea to the top of Everest?

   A. $^-$30,345 feet   **B.** $^-$27,725 feet

   C. 27,725 feet   **D.** 30,345 feet

Order the numbers from least to greatest.

44. $\frac{2}{5}$, $\frac{3}{10}$, $\frac{5}{9}$, $\frac{9}{25}$ **45.** 20.33,   2.505,   23.30,   23

46. 1.52, $1\frac{4}{7}$,   2, $\frac{9}{6}$ **47.** 3, $\frac{19}{6}$, $2\frac{8}{9}$,   2.95

Extensions

48. At the start of December, Kenji had a balance of $595.50 in his checking account. The following is a list of transactions he made during the month.

Date	Transaction	Balance
December 1		$595.50
December 5	Writes a check for $19.95	
December 12	Writes a check for $280.88	
December 15	Deposits $257.00	
December 17	Writes a check for $58.12	
December 21	Withdraws $50.00	
December 24	Writes checks for $17.50, $41.37, and $65.15	
December 26	Deposits $100.00	
December 31	Withdraws $50.00	

a. Copy and complete the table.

b. What was Kenji's balance at the end of December?

c. When was his balance the greatest?

d. When was his balance the least?

Find the missing temperature information in each situation.

49. The high temperature is 20°C. The low temperature is ⁻15°C. What temperature is halfway between the high and the low?

50. The low temperature is ⁻8°C. The temperature halfway between the high and the low is 5°C. What is the high temperature?

51. The high temperature is ⁻10°C. The low temperature is ⁻15°C. What is the temperature halfway between the high and the low?

Find values for A and B that make each mathematical sentence true.

52. $^{+}A + {}^{-}B = {}^{-}1$

53. $^{-}A + {}^{+}B = 0$

54. $^{-}A - {}^{-}B = {}^{-}2$

Mathematical Reflections 1

In this investigation, you learned ways to order and operate with positive and negative numbers. The following questions will help you summarize what you have learned.

Think about your answers to these questions. Discuss your ideas with other students and your teacher. Then write a summary of your findings in your notebook.

1. How do you decide which of two numbers is greater when
   a. both numbers are positive?
   b. both numbers are negative?
   c. one number is positive and one number is negative?

2. What does comparing locations of numbers on a number line tell you about the numbers?

Investigation ![2]

Adding and Subtracting Integers

In Investigation 1, you used number lines and chip boards to model operations with integers. Now, you will develop algorithms for adding and subtracting integers.

An **algorithm** is a plan, or series of steps, for doing a computation. In an effective algorithm, the steps lead to the correct answer, no matter what numbers you use. You may even develop more than one algorithm for each computation. Your goal should be to understand and skillfully use at least one algorithm for adding integers and at least one algorithm for subtracting integers.

2.1 Introducing Addition of Integers

There are two common ways that number problems lead to addition calculations like 8 + 5. The first involves combining two similar sets of objects, like in this example:

John has 8 video games and his friend has 5. Together they have 8 + 5 = 13 games.

You can represent this situation on a chip board.

8 + 5 = 13

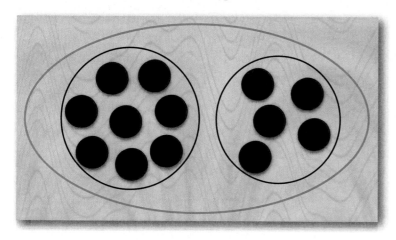

Number problems also lead to addition calculations when you add to a starting number. Take the following example:

> At a desert weather station, the temperature at sunrise was 10°C. It rose 25°C by noon. The temperature at noon was 10°C + 25°C = 35°C.

You can represent this situation on a number line. The starting point is $^+10$. The change in distance and direction is $^+25$. The sum ($^+35$) is the result of moving that distance and direction.

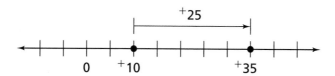

Suppose, instead of rising 25°C, the temperature fell 15°C. The next number line shows that $^+10°C + ^-15°C = ^-5°C$.

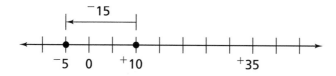

Use these ideas about addition as you develop an algorithm for addition of integers.

Problem 2.1 Introducing Addition of Integers

Use chip models or number line models.

A. 1. Find the sums in each group.

    2. Describe what the examples in each group have in common.

    3. Use your answer to part (2) to write two problems for each group.

    4. Describe an algorithm for adding integers in each group.

Group 1	Group 2
$^+2 + {}^+8$	$^+8 + {}^-12$
$^-3 + {}^-8$	$^-3 + {}^+2$
$^+20 + {}^+25$	$^+14 + {}^-23$
$^-24 + {}^-12$	$^-11 + {}^+13$

B. Write each number as a sum of integers in three different ways.

    1. $^-5$ **2.** $^+15$ **3.** 0

    4. Check to see whether your strategy for addition of integers works on these rational number problems.

        a. $^-1 + {}^+9$ **b.** $^-1\frac{1}{2} + {}^-\frac{3}{4}$ **c.** $^+1\frac{1}{2} + {}^-2\frac{3}{4}$

C. Write a story to match each number sentence. Find the solutions.

    1. $^+50 + {}^-65 = $ ▥   **2.** $^-15 + $ ▥ $ = {}^-25$ **3.** $^-300 + {}^-250 = $ ▥

D. Find both sums in parts (1) and (2). What do you notice?

    1. $^+12 + {}^-35$ $^-35 + {}^+12$ **2.** $^-7\frac{2}{3} + {}^-1\frac{1}{6}$ $^-1\frac{1}{6} + {}^-7\frac{2}{3}$

    3. The property of rational numbers that you have observed is called the **Commutative Property** of addition. What do you think the Commutative Property says about addition of rational numbers?

ACE **Homework starts on page 32.**

2.2 Introducing Subtraction of Integers

In some subtraction problems, you *take away* objects from a set, as in this first example:

    Example 1 Kim had 9 CDs. She sold 4 CDs at a yard sale. She now has only $9 - 4 = 5$ of those CDs left.

$$9 - 4 = 5$$

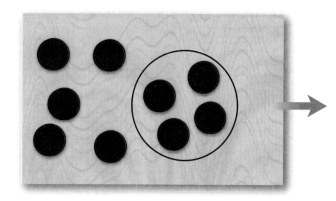

You can represent this situation on a chip board.

Here is another example.

Example 2 Otis earned $5 babysitting. He owes Latoya $7. He pays her the $5. Represent this integer subtraction on a chip board.

To subtract 7 from 5 ($^+5 - {}^+7$), start by showing $^+5$ as black chips.

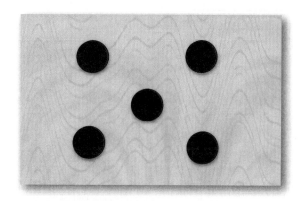

You can't take away $^+7$ because there aren't seven black chips to remove. Since adding both a red chip and a black chip does not change the value of the board, add two black chips and two red chips. The value of the board stays the same, but now there are 7 black chips to take away.

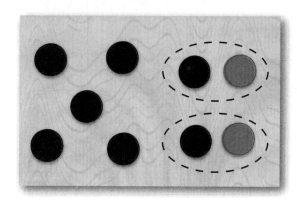

$$5 - 7 = {}^-2$$

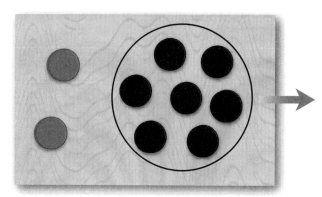

What is left on the board when you take away the 7 black chips?

The changes on the board can be represented by $(^-2 + 2) + 5 - 7 = {}^-2$. Otis now has $^-$\$2. He still owes Latoya $2.

In a third example of a subtraction problem, you find the *difference* between two numbers.

Example 3 The Arroyo family just passed mile 25 on the highway. They need to get to the exit at mile 80. How many more miles do they have to drive?

You can use a number line to show differences.

The arrow on the number line points in the direction of travel. The Arroyos are traveling in a positive direction from small values to greater values. They still have to travel $80 - 25 = 55$ miles.

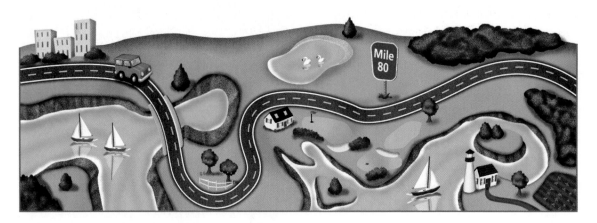

If the Arroyos drive back from mile 80 to mile 25, they still have to travel 55 miles. This time, however, they travel in the opposite direction. The number sentence $25 - 80 = {}^-55$ represents this situation.

Now, the arrow points to the left and has a label of $^-55$. The distance is 55, but the direction is negative.

Sometimes you only want the distance and not direction. You can show distance by putting vertical bars around the given number. This is called absolute value. The **absolute value** of a number is its distance from 0 on the number line.

$$|{}^-55| = 55 \qquad\qquad |{}^+55| = 55$$

You say "the absolute value of $^-55$ is 55" and "the absolute value of $^+55$ is 55."

When you write a number and a sign (or an implied sign for $+$) on an arrow above a number line, you are indicating both distance and direction.

In a problem that involves the amount of money you have and the amount that you owe, is the sign (direction) important?

Problem 2.2 Introducing Subtraction of Integers

Use chip models or number line models.

A. **1.** Find the differences in each group below.

Group 1
$^+12 - {^+8}$
$^-5 - {^-7}$
$^-4 - {^-2}$
$^+2 - {^+4}$

Group 2
$^+12 - {^-8}$
$^-5 - {^+7}$
$^-4 - {^+2}$
$^+2 - {^-4}$

   2. Describe what the examples in each group have in common.

   3. Use your answer to part (2) to write two problems for each group.

   4. Describe an algorithm for subtracting integers in each group.

   5. Check to see whether your strategy for subtraction of integers works on these rational number problems:

      a. $^-1 - {^+3}$ **b.** $^-1 - {^+\frac{3}{4}}$

      c. $^-1\frac{1}{2} - {^-2}$ **d.** $^-1\frac{1}{2} - {^-\frac{3}{4}}$

B. Write each number as a difference of integers in three different ways.

   1. $^-5$ **2.** $^+15$

   3. 0 **4.** $^-3.5$

C. For parts (1)–(4), decide whether the expressions are equal.

   1. $^-2 - {^+3} \stackrel{?}{=} {^+3} - {^-2}$ **2.** $^+12 - {^-4} \stackrel{?}{=} {^-4} - {^+12}$

   3. $^-15 - {^-20} \stackrel{?}{=} {^-20} - {^-15}$ **4.** $^+45 - {^+21} \stackrel{?}{=} {^+21} - {^+45}$

   5. Do you think there is a Commutative Property of subtraction?

ACE Homework starts on page 32.

2.3 The "+ / −" Connection

You have probably noticed that addition and subtraction are related to each other. You can write any addition sentence as an equivalent subtraction sentence. You can also write any subtraction sentence as an equivalent addition sentence.

Getting Ready for Problem 2.3

The chip board below shows a value of $^+5$.

- There are two possible moves, one addition and one subtraction, that would change the value on the board to $^+2$ in one step. How would you complete the number sentences to represent each move?

  $$^+5 + \blacksquare = {}^+2 \text{ and } {}^+5 - \blacksquare = {}^+2$$

- There are two possible moves, one addition and one subtraction, that would change the value on the board to $^+8$ in one step. How would you complete the number sentences to represent each move?

  $$^+5 + \blacksquare = {}^+8 \text{ and } {}^+5 - \blacksquare = {}^+8$$

- Can you describe a general relationship between addition and subtraction for integers?

Use your ideas about addition and subtraction of integers to explore the relationship between these two operations.

A. Complete each number sentence.

 1. $^+5 + ^-2 = ^+5 - \blacksquare$

 2. $^+5 + ^+4 = ^+5 - \blacksquare$

 3. $^-7 + ^-2 = ^-7 - \blacksquare$

 4. $^-7 + ^+2 = ^-7 - \blacksquare$

B. What patterns do you see in the results of Question A that suggest a way to restate any addition problem as an equivalent subtraction problem?

C. Complete each number sentence.

 1. $^+8 - ^+5 = 8 + \blacksquare$

 2. $^+8 - ^-5 = 8 + \blacksquare$

 3. $^-4 - ^+6 = ^-4 + \blacksquare$

 4. $^-4 - ^-6 = ^-4 + \blacksquare$

D. What patterns do you see in the results of Question C that suggest a way to restate any subtraction problem as an equivalent addition problem?

E. Write an equivalent problem for each. Then find the results.

 1. $^+396 - ^-400$

 2. $^-75.8 - ^-35.2$

 3. $^-25.6 + ^-4.4$

 4. $^+\frac{3}{2} - ^+\frac{1}{4}$

 5. $^+\frac{5}{8} + ^-\frac{3}{4}$

 6. $^-3\frac{1}{2} - ^+5$

ACE Homework starts on page 32.

2.4 Fact Families

$\mathbf{Y}$ou can rewrite $3 + 2 = 5$ to make a fact family that shows how the addition sentence is related to two subtraction sentences.

$$3 + 2 = 5$$
$$2 + 3 = 5$$
$$5 - 3 = 2$$
$$5 - 2 = 3$$

Problem 2.4 Fact Families

A. Write a related subtraction fact for each.

1. $^-3 + {}^-2 = {}^-5$ **2.** $^+25 + {}^-32 = {}^-7$

B. Write a related addition fact for each.

1. $^+8 - {}^-2 = {}^+10$ **2.** $^-14 - {}^-20 = 6$

C. 1. Write a related sentence for each.

   a. $n - {}^+5 = {}^+35$ **b.** $n - {}^-5 = {}^+35$ **c.** $n + {}^+5 = {}^+35$

  2. Do your related sentences make it easier to find the value for n? Why or why not?

D. 1. Write a related sentence for each.

   a. $^+4 + n = {}^+43$ **b.** $^-4 + n = {}^+43$ **c.** $^-4 + n = {}^-43$

  2. Do your related sentences make it easier to find the value for n? Why or why not?

ACE Homework starts on page 32.

2.5 Coordinate Graphing

$\mathbf{I}$n your study of similar figures, you used positive number coordinates and arithmetic operations to locate and move points and figures around a coordinate grid. You can use negative number coordinates to produce a grid that extends in all directions.

Coordinate Plane

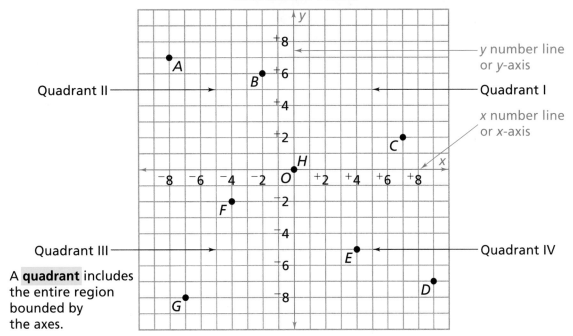

y number line
or y-axis

Quadrant II

Quadrant I

x number line
or x-axis

Quadrant III

Quadrant IV

A **quadrant** includes
the entire region
bounded by
the axes.

Problem 2.5 Coordinate Graphing

A. Write the coordinates for each point labeled with a letter.

B. What is the sign of the *x*-value and the *y*-value for any point in
Quadrant I? Quadrant II? Quadrant III? Quadrant IV?

C. The point "opposite" ($^-5$, $^+8$) has coordinates ($^+5$, $^-8$). Notice that
the sign of each coordinate in the pair changes. Write the coordinates
for the points "opposite" the labeled points. On a grid like the one
shown, graph and label each "opposite" point with a letter followed by
a tick mark. Point A′ is "opposite" point A.

D. Draw line segments connecting each pair of related points (A and A′,
B and B′, etc.). What do you notice about the line segments?

E. Plot the points in each part on a grid. Connect the points to form a
triangle. Draw each triangle in a different color, but on the same grid.

  1. ($^+1$, $^-1$)   ($^+2$, $^+3$)   ($^-4$, $^-2$)

  2. ($^-1$, $^-1$)   ($^-2$, $^+3$)   ($^+4$, $^-2$)

  3. ($^-1$, $^+1$)   ($^-2$, $^-3$)   ($^+4$, $^+2$)

  4. ($^+1$, $^+1$)   (2, $^-3$)   ($^-4$, $^+2$)

  5. How is triangle 1 related to triangle 2? How is triangle 1 related to
triangle 3? To triangle 4?

ACE Homework starts on page 32.

Applications

1. Use your algorithms to find each sum without using a calculator.

    a. $^+12 + {}^+4$ **b.** $^+12 + {}^-4$ **c.** $^-12 + {}^+4$

    d. $^-7 + {}^-8$ **e.** $^+4.5 + {}^-3.8$ **f.** $^-4.5 + {}^+3.8$

    g. $^-250 + {}^-750$ **h.** $^-6{,}200 + {}^+1{,}200$ **i.** $^+0.75 + {}^-0.25$

    j. $^+\frac{2}{3} + {}^-\frac{1}{6}$ **k.** $^-\frac{5}{12} + {}^+\frac{2}{3}$ **l.** $^-\frac{8}{5} + {}^-\frac{3}{5}$

2. Find each sum.

    a. $^+3.8 + {}^+2.7$ **b.** $^-3.8 + {}^-2.7$

    c. $^-3.8 + {}^+2.7$ **d.** $^+3.8 + {}^-2.7$

3. Write an addition number sentence that matches each diagram.

    a.

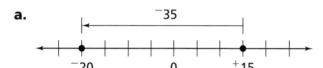

    b.

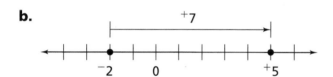

    c.

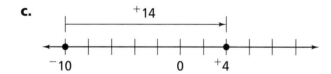

    d.

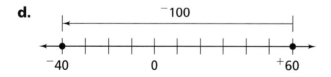

The chip board has 10 black and 13 red chips. Use the chip board for Exercises 4 and 5.

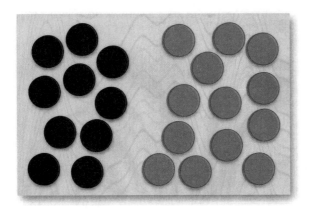

4. What is the value shown on the board?

5. Write a number sentence to represent each situation. Then find the new value of the chip board.

  a. Remove 5 red chips from the original board.

  b. Then add 5 black chips.

  c. Then add 4 black chips and 4 red chips.

6. Use your algorithms to find each difference without using a calculator. Show your work.

  a. $^+12 - {}^+4$ **b.** $^+4 - {}^+12$ **c.** $^-12 - {}^+4$

  d. $^-7 - {}^+8$ **e.** $^+45 - {}^-40$ **f.** $^+45 - {}^-50$

  g. $^-25 - {}^-75$ **h.** $^-62 - {}^-12$ **i.** $^+0.8 - {}^-0.5$

  j. $^+\frac{1}{2} - {}^+\frac{3}{4}$ **k.** $^-\frac{2}{5} - {}^+\frac{1}{5}$ **l.** $^-\frac{7}{10} - {}^+\frac{4}{5}$

Go Online
PHSchool.com
For: Multiple-Choice Skills Practice
Web Code: ana-4254

7. Find each value without using a calculator.

  a. $^+12 + {}^-12$ **b.** $^+12 - {}^+12$ **c.** $^-12 - {}^+12$

  d. $^-12 - {}^-12$ **e.** $^-12 + {}^-12$ **f.** $^-12 + {}^+12$

8. Find each value.

  a. $^+50 + {}^-35$ **b.** $^+50 - {}^-20$ **c.** $^-19 - {}^+11$

  d. $^-30 - {}^+50$ **e.** $^-35 + {}^-15$ **f.** $^+12 + {}^-18$

Investigation 2 Adding and Subtracting Integers   **33**

9. Write a story about temperature, money, or game scores to represent each number sentence.

   a. $^+7 - {}^-4 = {}^+11$ **b.** $^-20 + {}^+n = {}^+30$ **c.** $^-n + {}^-150 = {}^-350$

10. Without doing any calculations, decide which will give the greater result. Explain your reasoning.

   a. $^+5,280 + {}^-768$ OR $^+5,280 - {}^-768$

   b. $^+1,760 - {}^-880$ OR $^+1,760 - {}^+880$

   c. $^+1,500 + {}^+3,141$ OR $^+1,500 - {}^-3,141$

11. Without doing any calculations, determine whether each result is positive or negative. Explain.

   a. $^-23 + {}^+19$ **b.** $^+3.5 - {}^-2.7$

   c. $^-3.5 - {}^-2.04$ **d.** $^+3.1 + {}^-6.2$

12. Find each missing part.

	Start With	Rule	End With
a.	⬤ ⬤	▪	⬤ ⬤ ⬤ ⬤ ⬤ ⬤ ⬤
b.	⬤ ⬤ ⬤	▪	⬤ ⬤ ⬤
c.	? ?	Add 5 ⬤	⬤ ⬤ ⬤
d.	? ? ? ? ?	Subtract 5 ⬤	⬤ ⬤

13. Find each sum or difference. Show your work.

   a. $^+15 + {}^-10$ **b.** $^-20 - {}^+14$

   c. $^+200 - {}^-125$ **d.** $^-20 - {}^-14$

   e. $^-200 + {}^+125$ **f.** $^+7 - {}^+12$

14. Below is part of a time line with three years marked.

1986   1996   2006

  a. How does 1996 relate to 1986? How does 1996 relate to 2006?

  b. Write two number sentences. One must relate 1996 to 1986. The other must relate 1996 to 2006.

  c. How are these two number sentences alike and different?

15. Compute each value.

  a. $^+3 + {}^-3 + {}^-7$ **b.** $^+3 - {}^+3 - {}^+7$

  c. $^-10 + {}^-7 + {}^-28$ **d.** $^-10 - {}^+7 - {}^+28$

  e. $7 - {}^+8 + {}^-5$ **f.** $^+7 + {}^-8 - {}^+5$

  g. $^-97 + {}^-35 - {}^+10$ **h.** $^-97 - {}^+35 + {}^-10$

  i. What can you conclude about the relationship between subtracting a positive number $(- \; ^+)$ and adding a negative number $(+ \; ^-)$ with the same absolute value?

16. Compute each value.

  a. $^+3 - {}^-3 - {}^-7$ **b.** $^+3 + {}^+3 + {}^+7$

  c. $^-10 - {}^-7 - {}^-28$ **d.** $^-10 + {}^+7 + {}^+28$

  e. $^+7 + {}^+8 + {}^+5$ **f.** $^+7 - {}^-8 - {}^-5$

  g. $^-97 - {}^-35 - {}^+10$ **h.** $^-97 + {}^+35 + {}^-10$

  i. What can you conclude about the relationship between subtracting a negative number $(- \; ^-)$ and adding a positive number $(+ \; ^+)$ with the same absolute value?

Multiple Choice In each set of calculations, one result is different from the others. Find the different result without doing any calculations.

17. A. $54 + {}^-25$ **B.** $54 - 25$

    C. $25 - 54$ **D.** $^-25 + 54$

18. F. $^-6.28 - {}^-3.14$ **G.** $^-6.28 + 3.14$

    H. $3.14 + {}^-6.28$ **J.** $^-3.14 - {}^-6.28$

19. A. $534 - 275$ **B.** $275 - 534$

    C. $^-534 + 275$ **D.** $275 + {}^-534$

20. F. $175 + {}^-225$ **G.** $225 - 175$

    H. $175 - 225$ **J.** $^-225 + 175$

21. Fill in the missing information for each problem.

a. $^+5 + \dfrac{^-3}{4} = \blacksquare$ **b.** $\dfrac{^+4}{8} + {^-6} = \blacksquare$ **c.** $^-3\dfrac{3}{4} - \dfrac{^-3}{4} = \blacksquare$

d. $^+2\dfrac{2}{3} - \dfrac{^+1}{3} = \blacksquare$ **e.** $^-2 + \blacksquare = {^-2\dfrac{1}{2}}$ **f.** $^-4.5 + \blacksquare = {^-5}$

22. **Multiple Choice** Which is the correct addition and subtraction fact family for $^-2 + {^+3} = {^+1}$?

A. $^-2 + 3 = 1$
$^-2 + 1 = 3$
$3 - 1 = 2$

B. $^-2 + {^+3} = {^+1}$
$^-2 + 3 = 1$
$3 - 1 = 2$

C. $^-2 + 3 = 1$
$1 - 3 = {^-2}$
$1 - {^-2} = 3$

D. $1 - 3 = {^-2}$
$1 - {^-2} = 3$
$3 - 1 = 2$

23. Write a related fact for each number sentence to find n. What is the value of n?

a. $n - {^+7} = {^+10}$ **b.** $\dfrac{^-1}{2} + n = \dfrac{^-5}{8}$ **c.** $\dfrac{^+2}{3} - n = \dfrac{^-7}{9}$

24. Are $^+8 - {^+8}$ and $8 - 8$ equivalent? Explain.

25. Are $^+100 - {^+99}$ and $100 - 99$ equivalent? Explain.

26. Are the expressions in each group below equivalent? If so, which form makes the computation easiest?

a. $^+8 + {^-10}$
$8 - {^+10}$
$8 - 10$

b. $3 + {^-8}$
$3 - {^+8}$
$3 - 8$

27. Locate each pair of points on a coordinate grid. Describe the direction from the first point to the second point. Use these descriptions: to the left, to the right, downward, and upward.

a. $(^+3, {^+2}); (^-5, {^+2})$ **b.** $(^-7, {^+7}); (^+3, {^+7})$ **c.** $(^-8, {^-2}); (^+4, {^-2})$
d. $(^+4, {^+4}); (^+4, {^+20})$ **e.** $(^+18, {^+8}); (^+18, {^-8})$ **f.** $(^-20, {^-4}); (^-20, {^+9})$

g. Movement to the right or upward is in a positive direction. Movement to the left or downward is in a negative direction. Explain why this makes sense.

h. Now, describe the direction and the distance between the first point and the second point. For example, an answer of $^-15$ means you move in a negative direction a distance of 15. Whether the change is in the x-coordinate or the y-coordinate will tell whether $^-15$ means down 15 or to the left 15.

28. a. Locate three points on a coordinate grid that could be the vertices of a right triangle.

b. Find two different points that make a right triangle with coordinates ($^-$2, $^+$2) and ($^+$3, $^+$1).

Homework
Help ⏻nline
———PHSchool.com
For: Help with Exercise 28
Web Code: ane-4228

29. Find the opposite of each point in the graph. [Remember, the opposite of ($^+$2, $^-$1) is ($^-$2, $^+$1).]

a.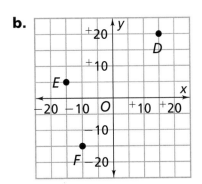

b.

Connections

30. The Spartan Bike Shop keeps a record of their business transactions. They start their account at zero dollars. Payments represent negative transactions. Sales represent positive transactions. Write a number sentence to represent each transaction. Then find the new balance.

a. rent payment for shop: $1,800

b. payment for 20 new bicycles: $2,150

c. payment on office equipment: $675

d. business insurance for 6 months: $2,300

e. sale of 3 bicycles: $665

f. sale of two helmets and one baby seat: $95

g. Web site advertising down payment: $250

h. sale of 6 bicycles: $1,150

i. refund to an unhappy customer: $225

j. sale of 2 bicycles, two helmets, and two air pumps: $750

k. check from manufacturer for 5 bicycles returned: $530

Investigation 2 Adding and Subtracting Integers **37**

Write a number sentence for each situation in Exercises 31 and 32.

31. The air temperature drops from 94° to 72° in 15 minutes. What is the change in temperature?

32. The Teacher's Pets team has 50 points in MathMania. They miss a 200-point question. What is their new score?

33. Find four different numbers, in order from least to greatest, that lie between the two given numbers.

   a. ⁻4.5 and ⁻3.5   **b.** ⁻0.5 and ⁺0.5

34. The diagram below shows Mug Wump drawn at the center of a coordinate grid and in four other positions.

   a. Find a sequence of coordinates to draw Mug's body at the center of the grid. Make a table to keep track of the points.

   b. You can write a coordinate rule to describe the movement of points from one location to another. For example, the coordinate rule $(x, y) \rightarrow (x - {}^{+}2, y + {}^{+}3)$ moves a point (x, y) to the left 2 units and up 3 units from its original location. The coordinate rule $(x, y) \rightarrow (x + {}^{+}6, y - {}^{+}7)$ moves points of the original Mug to produce which of the other drawings?

   c. Find coordinate rules for moving the original Mug to the other positions on the grid.

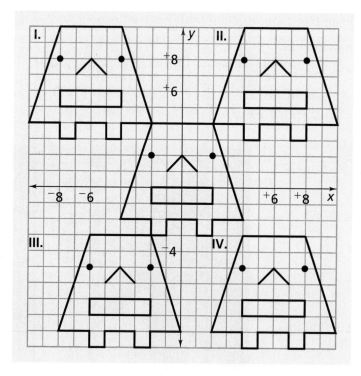

Use the points in each coordinate grid to determine what scale interval was used on each axis.

35.
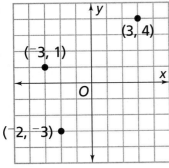
(3, 4)
(⁻3, 1)
O
x
(⁻2, ⁻3)

36.
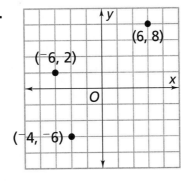
(6, 8)
(⁻6, 2)
O
x
(⁻4, ⁻6)

Extensions

37. Which numbers, when added to ⁻15, give a sum
  a. greater than 0   **b.** less than 0   **c.** equal to 0

38. Find the distance between each pair of numbers on a number line.
  a. ⁺8, ⁺4   **b.** ⁻8, ⁺4   **c.** ⁺8, ⁻4
  d. ⁻8, ⁻4   **e.** $⁻3\frac{1}{2}, ⁺\frac{3}{4}$ **f.** ⁺5.4, ⁻1.6

39. Find each absolute value.
  a. $|⁺8 - ⁺4|$ **b.** $|⁻8 - ⁺4|$ **c.** $|⁺8 - ⁻4|$
  d. $|⁻8 - ⁻4|$ **e.** $|⁻3\frac{1}{2} + ⁺\frac{3}{4}|$ **f.** $|⁺5.4 - ⁻1.6|$
  g. Compare the results of parts (a)–(f) with the distances found in Exercise 38. What do you notice? Why do you think this is so?

40. Replace *n* with a number to make each statement true.
  a. $n + ⁻18 = ⁺6$ **b.** $⁻24 - n = ⁺12$
  c. $⁺43 + n = ⁻12$ **d.** $⁻20 - n = ⁻50$

Connections   Extensions

41. The table shows the profits or losses (in millions of dollars) earned by three companies from 1997 to 2006. Find the range of the annual results and the overall profit (or loss) for each company over that time period.

	Company	'97	'98	'99	'00	'01	'02	'03	'04	'05	'06
a.	Sands Motor	⁻5.3	⁻4.8	⁻7.2	⁻2.1	1.4	6.5	3.2	⁻3.5	10.2	2.4
b.	Daily Trans	6.0	3.4	⁻5.8	⁻12.3	⁻20.3	⁻1.5	2.5	9.8	19.4	32.1
c.	Sell to You	120	98	⁻20	⁻40	⁻5	85	130	76	5	⁻30

42. Julia thinks a bit more about how to use red and black chips to model operations with integers. She draws the following chip board. She decides it represents $8 \times {}^-5 = {}^-40$ and ${}^-40 \div 8 = {}^-5$.

a. Explain why Julia's reasoning makes sense.

b. Use Julia's reasoning to find each value.

   i. $10 \times {}^-5$ **ii.** $4 \times {}^-15$ **iii.** $3 \times {}^-5$

   iv. ${}^-14 \div 2$ **v.** ${}^-14 \div 7$ **vi.** ${}^-35 \div 7$

43. Starting from 0, write an addition sentence for diagram below.

a.

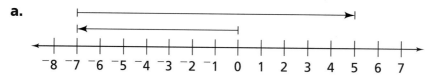

b.

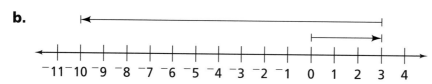

Mathematical Reflections 2

In this investigation, you applied your ideas about integers to develop algorithms for calculating any sums and differences.

Think about your answers to these questions. Discuss your ideas with other students and your teacher. Then write a summary of findings in your notebook.

1. **a.** How can you decide if the sum of two numbers is positive, negative, or zero without actually calculating the sum?

   b. How can you decide if the difference of two numbers is positive, negative, or zero without actually calculating the difference?

2. **a.** What procedure(s) will find the sum $a + b$ of two numbers where a and b represent any integer?

   b. What procedure(s) will find the difference $a - b$ of two numbers where a and b represent any integer?

3. How can any difference $a - b$ of two numbers be restated as an equivalent addition statement?

Multiplying and Dividing Integers

Some Notes on Notation

You have been writing integers with raised signs to avoid confusion with the symbols for addition and subtraction. However, most computer software and most writing in mathematics do not use raised signs.

Positive numbers are usually written without a sign.

$$^{+}3 = 3 \text{ and } ^{+}7.5 = 7.5$$

Negative numbers are usually written with a dash like a subtraction sign.

$$^{-}3 = -3 \text{ and } ^{-}7.5 = -7.5$$

From now on, we will use this notation to indicate a negative number.

This can be confusing if you don't read carefully. Parentheses can help.

$$^{-}5 - ^{-}8 = -5 - -8 = -5 - (-8)$$

The subtraction symbol also indicates the opposite of a number. For example, -8 represents the opposite of 8. The expression $-(-8)$ represents the opposite of -8.

$$-(-8) = 8$$

For multiplication, you can use a raised dot symbol.

$$3 \times 5 = 3 \cdot 5$$

In this investigation, you will use time, distance, speed, and direction to think about multiplication and division of integers. You will also look at number patterns and develop algorithms for multiplying and dividing these numbers.

Did You Know?

Michael Johnson set a world record by running 400 meters in 43.18 seconds at the world track championships in 1999. Florence Griffith Joyner set an Olympic record when she ran 100 meters in 10.62 seconds in 1988.

How long would it take each runner to run 1,000 meters at his or her record speed?

Go Online
PHSchool.com   **For:** Information about track
Web Code: ane-9031

The math department at Everett Middle School sponsors a contest called the Number Relay. A number line measured in meters is drawn on the school field. Each team has five runners. Runners 1, 3, and 5 stand at the −50 meter line. Runners 2 and 4 stand at the 50 meter line.

Team 1

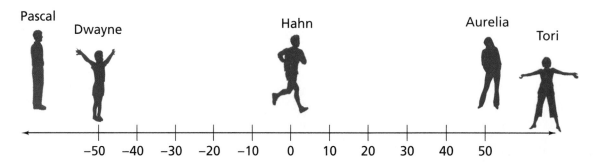

For Team 1:

- Hahn starts and runs from −50 to 50. He tags Aurelia.
- Aurelia runs back from 50 to −50. She tags Dwayne.
- Dwayne runs from −50 to 50. He tags Tori.
- Tori runs from 50 to −50. She tags Pascal.
- Pascal runs from −50 to the finish line at position 0.

The team whose final runner reaches the 0 point first wins.

A. Write number sentences that express your answers to these questions. Use positive numbers for running speeds to the right and negative numbers for running speeds to the left. Use positive numbers for time in the future and negative numbers for time in the past. Each runner runs at a constant speed.

1. Hahn passes the 0 point running 5 meters per second to the right. Where is he 10 seconds later?

2. Dwayne passes the 0 point running 4 meters per second to the right. Where is he 5 seconds later?

3. Aurelia passes the 0 point running to the left at 6 meters per second. Where is she 8 seconds later?

4. Pascal passes the 0 point running to the right at 3 meters per second. Where was he 6 seconds earlier?

5. Tori passes the 0 point running to the left at 5 meters per second. Where was she 7 seconds earlier?

B. 1. Find the products in each group below.

Group 1	Group 2	Group 3
4×3	$4 \times (-3)$	$-4 \times (-3)$
5.1×1	-1.5×2	$-7 \times (-4)$
3×4.5	$10 \times (-11)$	$-5.2 \times (-1)$

2. Describe what the examples in each group have in common.

3. Use your answer to part (2) to write two problems for each group.

4. Describe an algorithm for multiplying rational numbers.

5. Use your strategy to multiply these rational numbers.

   a. $-1\frac{1}{2} \times \frac{3}{4}$ **b.** $-\frac{1}{2} \times \left(-\frac{3}{4}\right)$ **c.** $2\frac{1}{2} \times \left(-\frac{3}{4}\right)$

6. Is multiplication commutative? Does the order of factors matter? For example, are these multiplication sentences correct?

$$2 \cdot 3 \stackrel{?}{=} 3 \cdot 2$$
$$-2 \times (-3) \stackrel{?}{=} -3 \times (-2)$$
$$-2 \times 3 \stackrel{?}{=} 3 \times (-2)$$

ACE **Homework starts on page 50.**

3.2 Multiplication Patterns

After studying the relay race problem, some students started playing with number patterns to see whether what they found in the relay race made sense. Study the equations below. Look for patterns.

$$5 \times 5 = 25$$
$$5 \times 4 = 20$$
$$5 \times 3 = 15$$
$$5 \times 2 = 10$$
$$5 \times 1 = 5$$
$$5 \times 0 = 0$$

Problem 3.2 Multiplication Patterns

A. 1. How do the products change as the numbers multiplied by 5 get smaller?

   2. Predict $5 \times (-1)$, $5 \times (-2)$, and $5 \times (-3)$. Explain your reasoning.

   3. Write the next four equations in the pattern.

B. 1. Complete the equations below.

$$(-4) \times 5 = \blacksquare$$
$$(-4) \times 4 = \blacksquare$$
$$(-4) \times 3 = \blacksquare$$
$$(-4) \times 2 = \blacksquare$$
$$(-4) \times 1 = \blacksquare$$
$$(-4) \times 0 = \blacksquare$$

   2. How do the products change as the numbers multiplied by -4 get smaller?

   3. Predict $-4 \times (-1)$. Explain.

   4. Write the next four equations in the pattern.

C. 1. Find each value.

   a. $7 \times (-8) \times (-3)$

   b. $-12 \times (-5) \times (-4)$

   c. $\frac{1}{2} \times \left(-\frac{2}{3}\right) \times 3$

   2. How do the patterns you found in this problem compare to the algorithm from Problem 3.1?

ACE Homework starts on page 50.

3.3 Introducing Division of Integers

You know there is a relationship between addition and subtraction facts. A similar relationship exists between multiplication and division. For any multiplication fact, we can write another multiplication fact and two different related division facts. Here are three examples.

$\left(\text{Remember that you can write } 15 \div 3 \text{ as a fraction, } \frac{15}{3}.\right)$

Example 1	Example 2	Example 3
$5 \times 3 = 15$	$6 \times (-3) = -18$	$4.5 \times (-2) = -9$
$3 \times 5 = 15$	$-3 \times 6 = -18$	$-2 \times 4.5 = -9$
$15 \div 3 = 5 \text{ or } \frac{15}{3} = 5$	$-18 \div (-3) = 6 \text{ or } \frac{-18}{-3} = 6$	$-9 \div (-2) = 4.5 \text{ or } \frac{-9}{-2} = 4.5$
$15 \div 5 = 3 \text{ or } \frac{15}{5} = 3$	$-18 \div 6 = -3 \text{ or } \frac{-18}{6} = -3$	$-9 \div 4.5 = -2 \text{ or } \frac{-9}{-4.5} = -2$

Getting Ready for Problem 3.3

- What patterns do you see in Examples 1–3?
- Write a fact family for $-2 \times 3 = -6$.
- How can you use what you know about the relationship between multiplication and division facts to help you solve these problems?

  1. $8 \times$ $= -48$

  2. ■ $\times (-9) = 108$

  3. $6 \times (-13) =$ ■

You can use this relationship and your ideas from the Number Relay questions to develop algorithms for dividing integers.

Problem 3.3 Introducing Division of Integers

A. Recall the Number Relay from Problem 3.1. Write division sentences that express your answers to the questions below.

    1. Dwayne goes from 0 to 15 in 5 seconds. At what rate (distance per second) does he run?

    2. Aurelia reaches −12 only 3 seconds after passing 0. At what rate does she run to the left?

    3. Pascal passes 0 running to the right at a rate of 5 meters per second. When did he leave the point −50? When did he leave the point −24?

    4. Tori wants to reach the point −40 running to the left at 8 meters per second. How long will it take her from the time she passes 0?

B. 1. Find the quotients in each group below.

Group 1	Group 2	Group 3
$12 \div 3$	$39 \div (-3)$	$-45 \div (-3)$
$51 \div 5$	$-15 \div 4$	$-4.8 \div (-4)$
$4.5 \div 9$	$10 \div (-5)$	$-72 \div (-12)$

    2. Describe what the examples in each group have in common.

    3. Use your answer to part (2) to write two problems for each group.

    4. Describe an algorithm for dividing rational numbers.

    5. Use your strategy to divide these rational numbers.

        a. $-1\frac{1}{2} \div \frac{3}{4}$ **b.** $-\frac{1}{2} \div \left(-\frac{3}{4}\right)$ **c.** $2\frac{1}{2} \div \left(-\frac{3}{4}\right)$

    6. Is division commutative? Does $-2 \div 3 = 3 \div (-2)$? Give two other examples to support your answer.

ACE Homework starts on page 50.

3.4 Playing the Integer Product Game

You have developed algorithms for multiplying and dividing integers. You will need them to play the Integer Product Game.

The game board consists of a list of factors and a grid of products. To play, you need a game board, two paper clips, and colored markers or chips.

Integer Product Game Rules

1. Player A puts a paper clip on a number in the factor list.
2. Player B puts the other paper clip on any number in the factor list, including the number chosen by Player A. Player B then marks the product of the two factors on the product grid.
3. Player A moves *either one* of the paper clips to another number. He or she then marks the new product with a different color than Player B.
4. Each player takes turns moving a paper clip and marking a product. A product can only be marked by one player.
5. The winner is the first player to mark four squares in a row (up and down, across, or diagonally).

Integer Product Game Board

−36	−30	−25	−24	−20	−18
−16	−15	−12	−10	−9	−8
−6	−5	−4	−3	−2	−1
1	2	3	4	5	6
8	9	10	12	15	16
18	20	24	25	30	36

Factors:

−6 −5 −4 −3 −2 −1 1 2 3 4 5 6

Problem 3.4 Multiplying Integers

Play the Integer Product Game with positive and negative factors. Look for strategies for picking the factors and products.

A. What strategies did you find useful in playing the game? Explain.

B. What pair(s) of numbers from the factor list will give each product?

1. 5   **2.** −12   **3.** 12   **4.** −25

C. Your opponent puts a paper clip on −4. List five products that you can form. Tell where you need to put your paper clip in each case.

D. Describe the moves to make in each case.

  1. The paper clips are on −5 and −2. You want a product of −15.
  2. The paper clips are on −3 and −2. You want a product of −6.
  3. Your opponent will win with 24. What numbers should you avoid with your paper clip moves?

For: Integer Product Game Activity
Visit: PHSchool.com
Web Code: and-4304

ACE Homework starts on page 50.

Applications

1. At some international airports, trains carry passengers between the separate terminal buildings. Suppose that one such train system moves along a track like the one below.

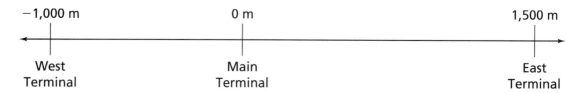

−1,000 m	0 m	1,500 m
West Terminal	Main Terminal	East Terminal

a. A train leaves the main terminal going east at 10 meters per second. Where will it be in 10 seconds? When will it reach the east terminal?

b. A train passes the main terminal going east at 10 meters per second. Where was that train 15 seconds ago? When was it at the west terminal?

c. A train leaves the main terminal going west at 10 meters per second. Where will it be in 20 seconds? When will it reach the west terminal?

d. A train passes the main terminal going west at 10 meters per second. When was it at the east terminal? Where was it 20 seconds ago?

The dot patterns illustrate commutative properties for operations on whole numbers. Write a number sentence for each case.

2.

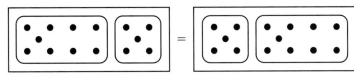

3.

4. Find each value.

a. $7 \cdot 2$ **b.** $-7 \times (-2)$ **c.** $7 \times (-2)$

d. -7×2 **e.** $8 \cdot 2.5$ **f.** $-9 \times (-4)$

g. $12 \times (-3)$ **h.** -1.5×4 **i.** 3.5×7

j. $-8.1 \cdot (-1)$ **k.** $1 \times (-6)$ **l.** $-2\frac{1}{2} \times 1$

5. Find the values for each pair.

a. $4 \times (-3)$ and -3×4 **b.** $2 \cdot (-4)$ and $-4 \cdot 2$

c. $-2 \times (-3)$ and $-3 \times (-2)$ **d.** $\frac{1}{5} \times \left(-\frac{4}{9}\right)$ and $-\frac{4}{9} \times \frac{1}{5}$

e. What can you conclude about multiplication with negative numbers?

6. Tell whether each product is greater than or less than zero.

a. $5 \times (-7)$ **b.** $-3.2 \cdot 1.5$

c. $10.5 \times (-4)$ **d.** $-2 \times (-3) \times (-1)$

e. $-\frac{2}{3} \cdot 2\frac{3}{4}$ **f.** $-\frac{3}{4} \times \left(-1\frac{5}{6}\right) \times \left(-\frac{7}{4}\right)$

g. $-\frac{3}{4} \times \left(-1\frac{5}{6}\right) \times \frac{7}{4}$ **h.** $-\frac{3}{4} \times \left(-1\frac{5}{6}\right) \times \left(-\frac{7}{4}\right) \times \left(-2\frac{3}{8}\right)$

i. $\frac{3}{4} \cdot \left(-1\frac{5}{6}\right) \cdot \frac{7}{4} \cdot \left(-2\frac{3}{8}\right)$ **j.** $\frac{3}{4} \times 1\frac{5}{6} \times \frac{7}{4} \times \left(-2\frac{3}{8}\right)$

7. You have located fractions such as $-\frac{5}{7}$ on a number line. You have also used fractions to show division: $\frac{-5}{7} = -5 \div 7$ and $\frac{5}{-7} = 5 \div (-7)$. Tell whether each statement is *true* or *false*. Explain.

a. $\frac{-1}{2} = \frac{1}{-2}$ **b.** $-\frac{1}{2} = \frac{-1}{-2}$

8. Find a value for n to make each sentence true.

   a. $24 \div 2 = n$ **b.** $-24 \div (-2) = n$

   c. $24 \div n = -12$ **d.** $n \div 2 = -12$

   e. $5 \div 2.5 = n$ **f.** $-12 \div n = 3$

   g. $n \div (-3) = -4$ **h.** $-16 \div \frac{1}{4} = n$

Write four related multiplication and division facts for each set of integers.

Sample $27, 9, 3$

$$9 \times 3 = 27$$
$$3 \times 9 = 27$$
$$27 \div 9 = 3$$
$$27 \div 3 = 9$$

9. $7, -3, -21$ **10.** $-4, -5, 20$ **11.** $1.5, -3, -4.5$

Without doing any calculations, determine whether each expression is greater than, less than, or equal to 0.

12. $-1{,}105.62 \div 24.3$ **13.** $0 \times (-67)$

14. $-27.5 \times (-63)$ **15.** $0 \div 89$

16. $-54.9 \div (-3)$ **17.** $-2{,}943 \times 1.06$

18. Use the algorithms you developed to find each value. Show your work.

For: Multiple-Choice Skills Practice
Web Code: ana-4354

   a. $12 \cdot 9$ **b.** $5 \times (-25)$ **c.** $-220 \div (-50)$

   d. $48 \div (-6)$ **e.** $-63 \div 9$ **f.** $\frac{2}{-3} \times \left(-\frac{4}{5}\right)$

   g. $\frac{-99}{33}$ **h.** $-2.7 \div (-0.3)$ **i.** -36×5

   j. $52.5 \div (-7)$ **k.** $-2\frac{1}{2} \times \left(-\frac{2}{3}\right)$ **l.** $9 \div 5$

   m. $-9 \times (-50)$ **n.** $-\frac{96}{24}$ **o.** $6 \times 1\frac{1}{2}$

   p. $-\frac{5}{8} \times \frac{8}{5}$ **q.** $4 \times \left(-1\frac{1}{4}\right)$ **r.** $-2.5 \times 2\frac{1}{5}$

Multiple Choice Find each value.

19. $-24 \div 4$

   A. -96 **B.** -6 **C.** 6 **D.** 96

20. $-10 \times (-5)$

   F. -50 **G.** -2 **H.** 2 **J.** 50

21. Chris and Elizabeth are making a version of the Integer Product Game in which players need three products in a row to win. What six factors do they need for their game?

Homework Help Online
PHSchool.com
For: Help with Exercise 21
Web Code: ane-4321

Chris and Elizabeth's Product Game

4	−4	6	−6
9	−9	10	−10
15	−15	25	−25

Factors:

Connections

22. Multiply or divide. Show your work.

a. 52×75

b. $52 \times (-75)$

c. $-2{,}262 \div (-58)$

d. $\frac{2}{3} \times \frac{4}{5}$

e. $-9{,}908 \div 89$

f. $-7.77 \div (-0.37)$

g. -34×15

h. $53.2 \div (-7)$

i. $-\frac{2}{3} \times \frac{6}{8}$

j. $90 \div 50$

k. $-90 \times (-50)$

l. $-108 \div 24$

m. $19.5 \div (-3)$

n. -8.4×6

o. $6 \times 2\frac{1}{2}$

p. $-3\frac{2}{3} \times (-9)$

q. $-4 \times \left(1\frac{1}{4}\right)$

r. $-2.5 \times -2\frac{1}{5}$

23. Find integers to make each sentence true.

a. $\blacksquare \times \blacksquare = 30$

b. $\blacksquare \times \blacksquare = -30$

c. $-24 \div \blacksquare = \blacksquare$

24. On Tuesday, the temperature changes $-2°F$ per hour from noon until 10:00 a.m. the next morning. The temperature at noon on Tuesday is 75°F.

a. What is the temperature at 4:00 p.m. on Tuesday?

b. What is the temperature at 9:00 a.m. on Wednesday?

c. Plot the (time, temperature) data on a coordinate graph using noon Tuesday as time 0.

d. Describe the pattern of points. How does the pattern relate to the rate of change in temperature?

Investigation 3 Multiplying and Dividing Integers **53**

25. The diagram below shows Mug Wump drawn on a coordinate grid.

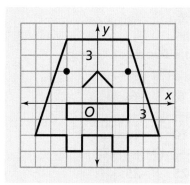

a. Complete the (x, y) column of a table like the one shown to record coordinates of key points needed to draw Mug, or copy your table from Exercise 34 of Investigation 2.

Coordinates for Mug and Variations

Rule	(x, y)	$(2x, 2y)$	$(-2x, -2y)$
Head Outline	(−4, −2)		
	(−2, −2)		
	(−2, −3)		
Nose	(−1, 1)		
Mouth	(−2, −1)		
Eyes	(−2, 2)		

b. Suppose you make scale drawings with rules $(x, y) \rightarrow (2x, 2y)$ and $(x, y) \rightarrow (-2x, -2y)$. Give coordinates for the images of Mug.

c. On graph paper, plot the images of Mug Wump produced by the new sets of coordinates in part (b).

d. Compare the length, width, and area of Mug's mouth to those of the figures drawn in part (c). Explain how you could have predicted those results by studying the coordinate rules for the drawings.

26. Write a number sentence to represent each situation.

   a. The Extraterrestrials have a score of −300. They answer four 50-point questions incorrectly. What is their new score?

   b. The Super Computers answer three 100-point questions incorrectly. They now have 200 points. What was their score before answering the three questions?

   c. The Bigtown Bears football team are at the 25-yard line. In the next three plays, they lose an average of 4 yards per play. Where are the Bears after the three plays?

   d. A new convenience store wants to attract customers. For a one-day special, they sell gasoline for $0.25 below their cost. They sell 5,750 gallons that day. How much money do they lose?

27. The list below gives average temperatures (in °C) for Fairbanks, Alaska, for each month of the year, from January through December.

−25, −20, −13, −2, 9, 15, 17, 14, 7, −4, −16, −23

   a. What is the median?

   b. What is the range?

   c. What is the mean?

   d. Number the months from 1 (for January) through 12 (for December). Plot a graph of the (month, temperature) data.

28. Find the sum, difference, product, or quotient without using a calculator.

   a. $-5 - 18$ **b.** $-23 + 48$ **c.** $\frac{3}{4} \times \left(\frac{-5}{9}\right)$

   d. $119 + (-19.3)$ **e.** $-1.5 - (-32.8)$ **f.** $12 \div 15$

   g. $-169 \div (-1.3)$ **h.** $0.47 - 1.56$ **i.** $6 \times (-3.5)$

   j. $\frac{2}{-3} \div \frac{5}{6}$ **k.** $\frac{7}{12} - \left(-\frac{2}{3}\right)$ **l.** $-\frac{4}{5} + \left(-\frac{1}{4}\right)$

29. Estimate the sum, difference, product, or quotient.

a. $-52 - 5$

b. $-43 + (-108)$

c. $2\frac{3}{4} \times \left(-\frac{5}{9}\right)$

d. $79 + (-25.3)$

e. $-12.5 - (-37.3)$

f. $89 \div 15$

g. $-169 \div (-13)$

h. $6.3 - 1.86$

i. $61 \times (-3.9)$

j. $-\frac{2}{3} \div 1\frac{5}{6}$

k. $5\frac{7}{12} - \left(-\frac{2}{3}\right)$

l. $-\frac{4}{5} \div \left(-\frac{1}{4}\right)$

Extensions

30. Many towns and small cities have water towers to store water. Water flows into and out of the towers all day long. Generally, flow out of the tower is greatest during the hours when most people are awake and active. The flow into the tower is greatest at night when most people are asleep.

The table below shows the water flow into and out of a water tower for a given time period. For each part, write a number sentence to find the change in water supply over the given time.

Water Tower Water Flow

	Water Flow In (gallons per hour)	Water Flow Out (gallons per hour)	Time (hours)
a.	5,000	0	4
b.	4,000	0	7
c.	0	7,500	3
d.	5,000	3,000	6.5

31. To add 5 + 3 + 2, you might think that it is easier to add the 3 + 2 and then add the answer to the 5. The mathematical property that allows you to change the grouping of addends (or factors) is called the *Associative Property*.

Test the Associative Property for addition and multiplication of integers by simplifying below. Find the values within the parentheses first. When you need a grouping symbol like parentheses inside another parentheses, you can use brackets to make it easier to read. For example, $(4 - (-6))$ can be written as $[4 - (-6)]$.

a. $[3 \times (-3)] \times 4$ and $3 \times (-3 \times 4)$

b. $(-5 \times 4) \times (-3)$ and $-5 \times [4 \times (-3)]$

c. $[-2 \times (-3)] \times (-5)$ and $-2 \times [-3 \times (-5)]$

d. $(3 \times 4) \times (-5)$ and $3 \times [4 \times (-5)]$

e. $[3 + (-3)] + 4$ and $3 + (-3 + 4)$

f. $(-5 + 4) + (-3)$ and $-5 + [4 + (-3)]$

g. $[-2 + (-3)] + (-5)$ and $-2 + [-3 + (-5)]$

h. $(3 + 4) + (-5)$ and $3 + [4 + (-5)]$

i. Does the Associative Property work for addition and multiplication of integers?

32. Explain how each rule changes the original shape, size, and location of Mug Wump.

a. $(x, y) \rightarrow (-x, y)$ **b.** $(x, y) \rightarrow (x, -y)$

c. $(x, y) \rightarrow (-0.5x, -0.5y)$ **d.** $(x, y) \rightarrow (-0.5x, y)$

e. $(x, y) \rightarrow (-3x, -3y)$ **f.** $(x, y) \rightarrow (-3x + 5, -3y - 4)$

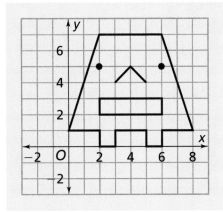

33. Tell whether each statement is *true* or *false*. Explain.

    a. $-1 = -1 + 0$ **b.** $-3\frac{3}{8} = -\frac{21}{8}$ **c.** $-6.75 = -6 + \left(-\frac{3}{4}\right)$

34. Find a set of numbers to make a Sum Game. Each sum on the board should be the sum of two numbers (possibly a single number added to itself). Each pair of numbers should add to a sum on the board.

    Hint: You need 11 numbers, all with different absolute values.

Sum Game Board

−24	−22	−20	−18	−16	−14
−12	−11	−10	−9	−8	−7
−6	−5	−4	−3	−2	−1
0	1	2	3	4	5
6	7	8	9	10	11
12	14	16	18	20	22

Numbers:

35. Write a story for a problem that is answered by finding the value of n.

    a. $-4n = -24$ **b.** $\frac{n}{2} = 16$

Mathematical Reflections 3

In the problems of this investigation you studied ways to use multiplication and division of integers to answer questions about speed, time, distance, and direction of motion. You used the results of those calculations to develop algorithms for multiplying and dividing any two integers. The questions that follow should help you to summarize your findings.

Think about your answers to these questions. Discuss your ideas with other students and your teacher. Then write a summary of your findings in your notebook.

1. How do you find the product of two numbers when
   a. both are positive?
   b. one is positive and one is negative?
   c. both are negative?
   d. one is 0?

2. How do you find the quotient of two numbers when
   a. both are positive?
   b. one is positive and the other is negative?
   c. both are negative?
   d. the numerator is 0?

3. Suppose three numbers are related by an equation in the form $a \times b = c$ where $a, b,$ and c are not equal to 0. Write two equivalent number sentences using division.

Properties of Operations

When you learn new types of numbers, you want to know what properties apply to them. You know that rational numbers are commutative for addition and multiplication.

$$-\frac{2}{3} + \frac{1}{6} = \frac{1}{6} + \left(-\frac{2}{3}\right) \text{ and } -\frac{2}{3} \times \frac{1}{6} = \frac{1}{6} \times \left(-\frac{2}{3}\right)$$

In this investigation, you will study another important property of rational numbers. You will also learn a mathematical rule that tells you the order in which to do arithmetic operations.

4.1 Order of Operations

Mathematicians have established rules called the **order of operations** in which to perform operations ($+, -, \times, \div$). Why do you need such rules?

Rules make this clear:
$6 + 20 \cdot 5$

The rugby club orders 20 new jerseys. The manufacturer charges a $100 setup fee and $15 per shirt. The total cost is represented by the equation, $C = 100 + 15n$, where C is the cost in dollars and n is the number of jerseys ordered. Pedro and David calculate the amount the club owes.

Pedro's calculation: $C = 100 + 15 \times 20$
$$= 100 + 300$$
$$= \$400$$

David's calculation: $C = 100 + 15 \times 20$
$$= 115 \times 20$$
$$= \$2,300$$

• Who did the calculations correctly?

Order of Operations

1. Compute any expressions within parentheses.

   Example 1

   $(-7 - 2) + 1 =$

   $-9 + 1 = -8$

   Example 2

   $(1 + 2) \times (-4) =$

   $3 \times (-4) = -12$

2. Compute any exponents.

   Example 1

   $-2 + 3^2 =$

   $-2 + 9 = 7$

   Example 2

   $6 - (-1 + 4)^2 =$

   $6 - (3)^2 = -3$

3. Multiply and divide in order from left to right.

   Example 1

   $1 + 2 \times 4 =$ Multiplication first

   $1 + 8 = 9$

   Example 2

   $200 \div 10 \times 2 =$ Division first

   $20 \times 2 = 40$ Multiplication second

4. Add and subtract in order from left to right.

   $1 + 2 - 3 \times 4 =$ Multiplication first

   $1 + 2 - 12 =$ Addition and subtraction

   $3 - 12 = -9$

Use the order of operations in Problem 4.1.

Problem 4.1 Order of Operations

A. In a game, the goal is to write a number sentence that gives the
greatest possible result using all the numbers on four cards. Jeremy
draws the following four cards.

1. Joshua writes $5 - (-6) \times 4 + (-3) = 41$. Sarah says the result
   should be 26. Who is correct and why?

2. Wendy starts by writing $-3 - (-6) + 5^4 =$. What is her result?

3. Insert parentheses into $-3 - (-6) + 5^4$ to give a greater result
   than in part (2).

B. Find each value.

1. $-7 \times 4 + 8 \div 2$

2. $(3 + 2)^2 \times 6 - 1$

3. $2\frac{2}{5} \times 4\frac{1}{2} - 5^3 + 3$

4. $8 \times (4 - 5)^3 + 3$

5. $-8 \times [4 - (-5 + 3)]$

6. $-16 \div 8 \times 2^3 + (-7)$

C. Use parentheses, if needed, to make the greatest and least possible
values.

1. $7 - 2 + 3^2$

2. $46 + 2.8 \times 7 - 2$

3. $25 \times (-3.12) + 21.3 \div 3$

4. $5.67 + 35.4 - 178 - 181$

D. Use the order of operations to solve this problem. Show your work.

$$3 + 4 \times 5 \div 2 \times 3 - 7^2 + 6 \div 3 = \blacksquare$$

ACE **Homework starts on page 69.**

Distributing Operations

In this problem, you will compute areas of rectangles using different expressions. Look for ways to rewrite an expression into an equivalent expression that is easier to compute.

Problem 4.2 Distributing Operations

A. Richard lives in a neighborhood with a rectangular field. Each part below shows a way to divide the field for different kinds of sports.

  1. Find the area.

50 yds

120 yds

  2. The field is divided into two parts.

30 yds

20 yds

120 yds

  a. Find the area of each part.

  b. Write a number sentence that shows that the sum of the smaller areas is equal to the area of the entire field.

  3. The field is divided into four parts.

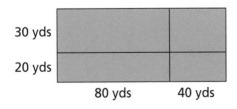

30 yds

20 yds

80 yds   40 yds

  a. Find the area of each part.

  b. Write a number sentence that shows that the sum of the smaller areas is equal to the area of the entire field.

B. Use what you learned in Question A. Write two different expressions to find the area of each rectangle. Tell which uses fewer operations.

1.
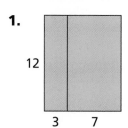
12
3   7

2.
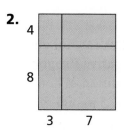
4
8
3   7

3.
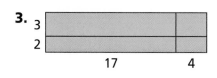
3
2
17   4

4.
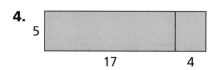
5
17   4

C. 1. Draw a rectangle whose area can be represented by $7 \times (11 + 9)$.

2. Write another expression for the area of the rectangle in part (1).

3. Draw a rectangle whose area can be represented by $(3 + 1) \times (3 + 4)$.

4. Write another expression for the area of the rectangle in part (3).

D. The unknown length in each rectangle is represented by a variable x.

1. Write an expression to represent the area of the rectangle.

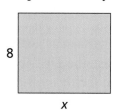
8

x

2. Write two different expressions to represent the area of each rectangle below.

a.
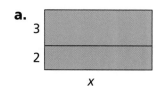
3
2
x

b.
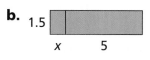
1.5
x 5

E. Find the missing part(s) to make each sentence true.

1. $12 \times (6 + 4) = (12 \times \blacksquare) + (12 \times 4)$

2. $2 \times (n + 4) = (2 \times \blacksquare) + (\blacksquare \times 4)$

3. $(n \times 5) + (n \times 3) = \blacksquare \cdot (5 + 3)$

4. $(-3 \times 5) + (\blacksquare \times 7) = -3 \cdot (\blacksquare + 7)$

5. $4n + 11n = n \cdot (\blacksquare + \blacksquare)$

ACE **Homework starts on page 69.**

4.3 The Distributive Property and Subtraction

The rectangles in Problem 4.2 illustrate an important property of numbers and operations called the **Distributive Property.** This property shows that multiplication *distributes* over addition. When you think about a multiplication problem like 512×5 as $500 \times 5 + 12 \times 5$, or $12 \times 5\frac{3}{4}$ as $12 \times 5 + 12 \times \frac{3}{4}$, you are using the Distributive Property.

Getting Ready for Problem 4.3

You can use the Distributive Property to rewrite an expression as one that is easier to calculate or gives new information. You can do this in two ways.

1. Suppose an expression is written as the product of two factors, one of which is a sum. You can use the Distributive Property to multiply one factor by each number in the second factor. This is called *expanding* the expression.

$$-3 \cdot (4 + 8) = -3 \cdot 4 + (-3) \cdot 8$$

With a variable: $-2 \cdot (x + 6) = -2x + (-2) \cdot 6$

2. Suppose an expression is written as a sum and the numbers have a common factor. You can use the Distributive Property to rewrite the expression as the common factor multiplied by the sum. This is called *factoring* the expression.

$$5 \cdot 4 + 5 \cdot 7 = 5 \cdot (4 + 7)$$

With a variable: $8 \cdot 2 + 8x = 8 \cdot (2 + x)$

- Do you think the Distributive Property can be used to expand or factor expressions with subtraction? Explain your reasoning.

A. Use the Distributive Property to expand each expression.

1. $5 \cdot (3 + 2)$

2. $5 \cdot [3 + (-2)]$

3. $5 \cdot (3 - 2)$

4. $5 \cdot [3 - (-2)]$

5. For parts (1)–(4), find the value of the expression.

6. Does the Distributive Property seem to hold for subtraction? Explain.

B. Use the Distributive Property to expand each expression.

1. $-5 \cdot (3 + 2)$

2. $-5 \cdot (3 - 2)$

3. $-5 \cdot [3 + (-2)]$

4. $-5 \cdot [3 - (-2)]$

5. For parts (1)–(4), find the value of the expression.

6. Explain how to distribute a negative number to expand an expression.

C. Write each expression in factored form.

1. $6 \cdot 2 + 6 \cdot 3$

2. $6 \cdot 2 - 6 \cdot 3$

3. $-6 \cdot 2 + (-6) \cdot 3$

4. $-6 \cdot 2 - (-6) \cdot 3$

5. $5x - 8x$

6. $-3x - 4x$

7. Explain how to factor an expression with subtraction.

D. Three friends are going hiking. Lisa buys 2 bottles of water and 3 packs of trail mix for each of them.

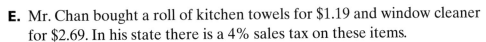

1. Can she go through the express checkout lane for customers with 15 or fewer items?

2. Write a number sentence to show how you found the total number of items.

3. Write another number sentence to find the total number of items.

E. Mr. Chan bought a roll of kitchen towels for $1.19 and window cleaner for $2.69. In his state there is a 4% sales tax on these items.

1. What is his total bill?

2. Write a number sentence to show how you found the total bill.

3. Suppose you add the prices of the two items and then compute the tax. Your friend finds the tax on each item and then adds the two together. Which method is better? Explain.

ACE Homework starts on page 69.

More on Notation

Now you can use the order of operations or the Distributive Property to find the value of an expression like $-8 \cdot [-2 + (-3)]$ that has parentheses.

Order of operations method:

$$-8 \cdot [-2 + (-3)] = -8 \cdot (-5) \qquad \text{Add } -2 \text{ and } -3 \text{ within the parentheses.}$$

$$= 40 \qquad \text{Multiply.}$$

Distributive Property method:

$$-8 \cdot [-2 + (-3)] = -8 \cdot (-2) + (-8) \cdot (-3) \qquad \text{Expand first.}$$

$$= 16 + 24 \qquad \text{Multiply.}$$

$$= 40$$

Either method is correct.

Applications

1. Find the values of each pair of expressions.

    a. $-12 + (-4 + 9)$ $[-12 + (-4)] + 9$

    b. $(14 - 20) - 2^3$ $14 - (20 - 2^3)$

    c. $[14 + (-20)] + -8$ $14 + [-20 + (-8)]$

    d. $-1 - [-1 + (-1)]$ $[-1 - (-1)] + (-1)$

    e. Which cases lead to expressions with different results? Explain.

2. Find the value of each expression.

    a. $(5 - 3) \div (-2) \times (-1)$ **b.** $2 + (-3) \times 4 - (-5)$

    c. $4 \times 2 \times (-3) + (-10) \div 5$ **d.** $-3 \times [2 + (-10)] - 2^2$

    e. $(4 - 20) \div 2^2 - 5 \times (-2)$ **f.** $10 - [50 \div (-2 \times 25) - 7] \times 2^2$

3. Draw and label the edges and areas of a rectangle to illustrate each pair of equivalent expressions.

    a. $(3 + 2) \cdot 12 = 3 \cdot 12 + 2 \cdot 12$

    b. $9 \cdot 3 + 9 \cdot 5 = 9 \cdot (3 + 5)$

    c. $x \cdot (5 + 9) = 5x + 9x$

    d. $2 \cdot (x + 8) = 2x + 16$

Homework
Help Online
PHSchool.com
For: Help with Exercise 3
Web Code: ane-4403

4. Write equivalent expressions to show two different ways to find the area of each rectangle. Use the ideas of the Distributive Property.

a.

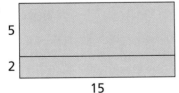

b.

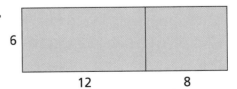

c.

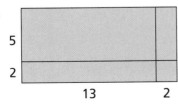

d.

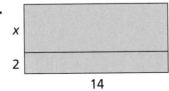

5. Rewrite each expression in an equivalent form to show a simpler way to do the arithmetic. Explain how you know the two results are equal without doing any calculations.

    a. $(-150 + 270) + 30$

    b. $(43 \times 120) + [43 \times (-20)]$

    c. $23 + (-75) + 14 + (-23) - (-75)$

    d. $(0.8 \times -23) + (0.8 \times -7)$

6. Without doing any calculations, determine whether each number sentence is true. Explain. Then check your answer.

    a. $50 \times 432 = (50 \times 400) + (50 \times 32)$

    b. $50 \times 368 = (50 \times 400) - (50 \times 32)$

    c. $-50 \times (-800) = (-50 \times (-1,000)) + (-50 \times 200)$

    d. $-50 + (400 \times 32) = (-50 + 400) \times (-50 + 32)$

    e. $(-70 \times 20) + (-50 \times 20) = (-120) \times 20$

    f. $6 \times 17 = 6 \times 20 - 6 \times 3$

7. For each part, use the Distributive Property to write an equivalent expression.

    a. $-2 \times [5 + (-8)]$ **b.** $(-3 \cdot 2) - [-3 \cdot (-12)]$

    c. $x \cdot (-3 + 5)$ **d.** $(-7x) + (4x)$

    e. $2x \cdot [2 - (-4)]$ **f.** $(x) - (3x)$

Connections

Find the sum, difference, product, or quotient.

8. $-10 \times (-11)$

9. -10×11

10. $10 - 11$

11. $-3 \div (-12)$

12. $3^2 \times 2^2$

13. $3^2 \times (-2)^2$

14. $-24 - (-12)$

15. $\dfrac{-24}{-12}$

16. $-48 \div 4^2$

17. 50×70

18. $50 \times (-70)$

19. $2,200 \div (-22)$

20. $-50 \times (-120)$

21. $-139 + 899$

22. $5,600 - 7,800$

23. $-4,400 - (-1,200)$

24. $\dfrac{-9,900}{-99}$

25. $-580 + (-320)$

26. When using negative numbers and exponents, parentheses are sometimes needed to make it clear what you are multiplying.

-5^4 can be thought of as "the opposite of 5^4" or
$-(5^4) = -(5 \cdot 5 \cdot 5 \cdot 5) = -625$

$(-5)^4$ can be thought of as "negative five to the fourth power" or
$-5 \cdot (-5) \cdot (-5) \cdot (-5) = 625$

Indicate whether each expression will be negative or positive.

a. -3^2 **b.** $(-6)^3$ **c.** $(-4)^4$ **d.** -1^6 **e.** $(-3)^4$

27. The following list shows the yards gained and lost on each play by the Mathville Mudhens in the fourth quarter of their last football game:

$$-8, 20, 3, 7, -15, 4, -12, 32, 5, 1$$

Write an expression that shows how to compute their average gain or loss per play. Then compute the average.

28. Complete each number sentence.

a. $-34 + (-15) = \blacksquare$ **b.** $-12 \times (-23) = \blacksquare$

c. $-532 \div (-7) = \blacksquare$ **d.** $-777 - (-37) = \blacksquare$

e. Write a fact family for part (a).   **f.** Write a fact family for part (b).

29. Write a related fact. Use it to find the value of n that makes the sentence true.

a. $n - (-5) = 35$ **b.** $4 + n = -43$

c. $-2n = -16$ **d.** $\frac{n}{4} = -32$

30. Multiple Choice Which set of numbers is in order from least to greatest?

A. 31.4, -14.2, $-55, 75$, -0.05, 0.5, 3.140

B. $\dfrac{2}{5}$, $\dfrac{-3}{5}$, $\dfrac{8}{7}$, $\dfrac{-9}{8}$, $\dfrac{-3}{2}$, $\dfrac{5}{3}$

C. -0.2, -0.5, 0.75, 0.6, -1, 1.5

D. None of these

31. Find the absolute values of the numbers for each set in Exercise 30. Write them in order from least to greatest.

32. A trucking company carries freight along a highway from New York City to San Francisco. Its home base is in Omaha, Nebraska, which is about halfway between the two cities. Truckers average about 50 miles per hour on this route.

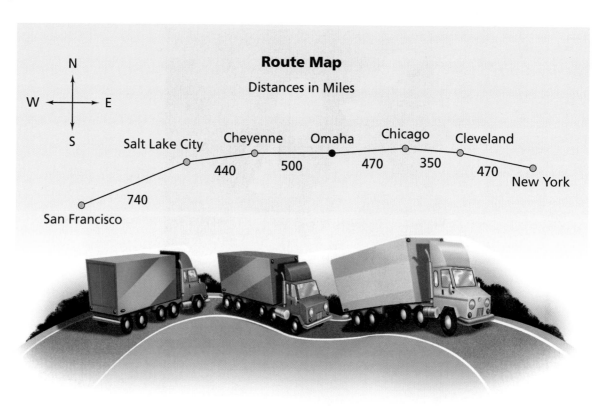

Make a number line to represent this truck route. Put Omaha at 0. Use positive numbers for cities east of Omaha and negative numbers for cities west of Omaha. Then write number sentences to answer each question.

a. A truck leaves Omaha heading east and travels for 7 hours. About how far does the truck go? Where on the number line does it stop?

b. A truck leaves Omaha heading west and travels for 4.5 hours. About how far does the truck go? Where on the number line does it stop?

c. A truck heading east arrives in Omaha. About where on the number line was the truck 12 hours earlier?

d. A truck heading west arrives in Omaha. About where on the number line was the truck 11 hours earlier?

33. Insert parentheses (or brackets) in each expression where needed to show how to get each result.

a. $1 + (-3) \times (-4) = 8$ **b.** $1 + (-3) \times (-4) = 13$

c. $-6 \div (-2) + (-4) = 1$ **d.** $-6 \div (-2) + (-4) = -1$

e. $-4 \times 2 - 10 = -18$ **f.** $-4 \times 2 - 10 = 32$

34. A grocery store receipt shows 5% state tax due on laundry detergent and a flower bouquet.

Laundry Detergent	$7.99	T
Flower Bouquet	$3.99	T

Does it matter whether the tax is calculated on each separate item or the total cost? Explain.

35. You can use dot patterns to illustrate distributive properties for operations on whole numbers. Write a number sentence to represent the pair of dot patterns.

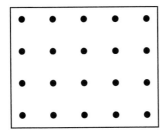 =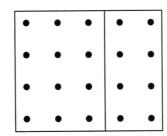

Extensions

Copy each pair of expressions in Exercises 36–40. Insert < or > to make a true statement.

36. -23 ■ -45

37. $-23 + 10$ ■ $-45 + 10$

38. $-23 - 10$ ■ $-45 - 10$

39. -23×10 ■ -45×10

40. $-23 \times (-10)$ ■ $-45 \times (-10)$

Based on your results in Exercises 36–40, complete each statement. Test your ideas with other numerical cases, or develop another kind of explanation, perhaps using chip board or number line ideas.

41. If $a > b$, then $a + c$ ■ $b + c$.

42. If $a > b$, then $a - c$ ■ $b - c$.

43. If $a > b$, then $a \times c$ ■ $b \times c$.

44. Find the value for n that makes the sentence true.

  a. $n - (-24) = 12$ **b.** $2.5n = -10$ **c.** $2.5n + (-3) = -13$

45. Complete each pair of calculations.

  a. $12 \div (-8 + 4) =$ ■ $[12 \div (-8)] + (12 \div 4) =$ ■

  b. $-12 \div [-5 - (-3)] =$ ■ $[-12 \div (-5)] - [-12 \div (-3)] =$ ■

  c. $4 \div (-2 - 6) =$ ■ $(4 \div -2) - (4 \div 6) =$ ■

  d. $3 \div (5 + 6) =$ ■ $(3 \div 5) + (3 \div 6) =$ ■

  e. What can you conclude from parts (a)–(d) about the Distributive Property?

46. When you find the mean (average) of two numbers, you add them together and divide by 2.

  a. Is the operation of finding the average of two numbers commutative? Give examples.

  b. Does multiplication distribute over the averaging operation? That is, will a number a times the average of two numbers, x and y, give the same thing as the average of ax and ay? Give examples.

Mathematical Reflections 4

In this investigation, you compared important properties of arithmetic with positive numbers to properties of arithmetic with negative numbers. The following questions will help you summarize what you have learned.

Think about your answers. Discuss your ideas with other students and your teacher. Then write a summary of your findings in your notebook.

1. **a.** What is the order of operations? Why is it important for you to understand?

   b. Give an example of an equation where the use of parentheses changes the result of the computation.

2. **a.** What does it mean to say that an operation is *commutative?*

   b. Which operations on integers are commutative? Give numerical examples.

3. What does it mean to say that *multiplication distributes over addition* and *subtraction*? Give numerical examples.

Unit Project

Dealing Down

Dealing Down is a mathematics card game that tests your creative skill at writing expressions. Play several rounds of the game. Then write a report on the strategies you found.

How to Play Dealing Down

- Work in small groups.
- Shuffle the 25 cards marked with the following numbers.
  $-10, -9, -8, -7, -6, -5, -4, -3, -2, -1, -\frac{1}{2}, -\frac{1}{3}, -\frac{1}{4}, 0,$
  $0.25, \frac{1}{3}, 0.5, 1, 2, 3, 4, 5, 7, 8, 10$
- Deal four cards to the center of the table.
- All players use the four numbers to write an expression with the least possible quantity.
- Players compare answers and discuss how they know their quantity is accurate and the least possible.
- Each player with an expression for the least quantity gets 1 point.
- Record the results of that round in a table like the one below and play more rounds.

Round 1

Cards Dealt	Expression With the Least Quantity	Who Scored a Point
Why That Expression Has the Least Quantity:		

- The player with the most points at the end of the game wins.

Write a Report

Write a report about strategies for writing the least possible quantity using four numbers.

Consider the following ideas as you look at the strategies in Dealing Down.

- Operating with negative and positive numbers
- Order of operations including the use of parentheses and exponents
- Commutative Property of Addition and Multiplication
- Distributive Property

Looking Back and Looking Ahead

Go Online
PHSchool.com

For: Vocabulary Review Puzzle
Web Code: anj-4051

In this unit, you investigated properties, operations, and applications of integers. You learned how to

- Add, subtract, multiply and divide with integers
- Represent integers and operations on a chip board and a number line
- Use integers in real-world problems

Use Your Understanding:
Integers and Rational Numbers

Test your understanding of integers by solving the following problems.

1. An absent-minded scorekeeper writes the number sentences below. Find the value of n that makes each sentence true. Explain what each sentence tells about the rounds of play.

   a. BrainyActs: $-250 + (-100) + 200 + n = 50$

   b. MathXperts: $450 + (-250) + n = 0$

   c. ExCells: $n + 50 + 200 + (-150) = -250$

   d. SuperM's: $350 + (-300) + n = -150$

2. Irving goes to college 127 miles away from home. When he drives home for vacation, he plans to drop off his friend, Whitney, along the way. Her exit is 93 miles before his exit,

   Irving and Whitney are so busy talking that they miss the exit to her house. They are now only 36 miles from Irving's exit! How far do they have to travel in all from college until they finally reach Whitney's exit? Model this problem on a number line.

3. **a.** Write a fact family for each sentence.

   i. $-2\frac{1}{2} + n = -3\frac{3}{4}$ **ii.** $\frac{2}{3}n = 10$

   b. Which member of each fact family would make it easy to solve for n? Explain.

   c. Find the value for n that makes each sentence true.

4. a. Locate point $(5, 2)$ on a coordinate grid.

b. Find a related point in each quadrant by changing the sign of one or both coordinates.

   i. Quadrant II   **ii.** Quadrant III   **iii.** Quadrant IV

c. Connect these points in order. Describe the figure formed.

d. Make a similar figure with an area four times as large and that has a vertex in each quadrant. Give the four vertices as ordered pairs.

Explain Your Reasoning

Answer the following questions to summarize what you know now.

5. Describe what a number line looks like now that the number system has been extended to include negative numbers.

6. Which number is greater? Explain.

   a. $-20, -35$ **b.** $-2\frac{3}{4}, -2\frac{1}{3}$ **c.** $-12.5, 10.5$

7. Use a number line or chip model to check each calculation. Show your work.

   a. $5 + (-7) = -2$ **b.** $-2 + (-9) = -11$

   c. $3 \times (-2) = -6$ **d.** $-3 \times (-2) = 6$

   e. Describe how a number line and chip model can be used to model an addition or multiplication problem.

8. Suppose you are given two integers. How do you find their

   a. sum?   **b.** difference?

   c. product?   **d.** quotient?

9. Which operations with integers have the following properties? Give numerical examples.

   a. commutative   **b.** distributive

Look Ahead

Positive and negative numbers are useful in solving a variety of problems that involve losses and gains. They also provide coordinates for points on an extended number line and coordinate plane. These ideas will be useful when you study graphs of functions and solve equations in future *Connected Mathematics* units such as *Moving Straight Ahead, Thinking With Mathematical Models, Say It With Symbols*, and *The Shapes of Algebra*.

English/Spanish Glossary

absolute value The absolute value of a number is its distance from 0 on a number line. It can be thought of as the value of a number when its sign is ignored. For example, −3 and 3 both have an absolute value of 3.

valor absoluto El valor absoluto de un número es su distancia de 0 sobre una recta numérica. Se puede interpretar como el valor de un número cuando no importa su signo. Por ejemplo, tanto −3 como 3 tienen un valor absoluto de 3.

algorithm A set of rules for performing a procedure. Mathematicians invent algorithms that are useful in many kinds of situations. Some examples of algorithms are the rules for long division or the rules for adding two fractions.

algoritmo Un conjunto de reglas para realizar un procedimiento. Los matemáticos inventan algoritmos que son útiles en muchos tipos de situaciones. Algunos ejemplos de algoritmos son las reglas para una división larga o las reglas para sumar dos fracciones.

Associative Property Allows addends or factors to be grouped and computed in different arrangements. For example, $2 + 3 + 5$ can be grouped as $(2 + 3) + 5$ or $2 + (3 + 5)$. So, $(2 + 3) + 5 = 5 + 5 = 10$ and $2 + (3 + 5) = 2 + 8 = 10$. This property does not work for subtraction or division. For example, $8 − (4 − 2) \neq (8 − 4) − 2$ and $8 \div (4 \div 2) \neq (8 \div 4) \div 2$.

propiedad asociativa Permite que sumandos o factores se agrupen y se calculen de diferentes maneras. Por ejemplo, $2 + 3 + 5$ se puede agrupar como $(2 + 3) + 5$ ó $2 + (3 + 5)$. Por lo tanto, $(2 + 3) + 5 = 5 + 5 = 10$ y $2 + (3 + 5) = 2 + 8 = 10$. Esta propiedad no funciona con la resta o la división. Por ejemplo, $8 − (4 − 2) \neq (8 − 4) − 2$ y $8 \div (4 \div 2) \neq (8 \div 4) \div 2$.

Commutative Property The order of the addition or multiplication of two numbers does not change the result. For two numbers a and b, $a + b = b + a$, and $a \cdot b = b \cdot a$.

propiedad conmutativa El orden en la suma o multiplicación de dos números no afecta el resultado. Para dos números a y b, $a + b = b + a$, y $a \cdot b = b \cdot a$.

Distributive Property The Distributive Property shows how multiplication combines with addition or subtraction. For three numbers a, b, and c, $a(b + c) = ab + ac$.

propiedad distributiva La propiedad distributiva muestra cómo la multiplicación se combina con la suma o la resta. Para tres números a, b y c, $a(b + c) = ab + ac$.

integers The whole numbers and their opposites. 0 is an integer, but is neither positive nor negative. The integers from −4 to 4 are shown on the number line below.

enteros Números enteros positivos y sus opuestos. 0 es un entero, pero no es ni positivo ni negativo. En la siguiente recta numérica figuran los enteros comprendidos entre −4 y 4.

$$-4 \quad -3 \quad -2 \quad -1 \quad 0 \quad 1 \quad 2 \quad 3 \quad 4$$

inverse operations Operations that "undo" each other. Addition and subtraction are inverse operations. For example, start with 7. Subtract 4. Then add 4. You are back to the original number 7. Thus, $7 - 4 + 4 = 7$. Multiplication and division are inverse operations. For example, start with 12. Multiply by 2. Then divide by 2. You are back at the original number 12. Thus, $(12 \times 2) \div 2 = 12$.

operaciones inversas Operaciones que se "anulan" mutuamente. La suma y la resta son operaciones inversas. Por ejemplo, empieza con 7. Resta 4. Luego, suma 4. Tienes otra vez el número 7. Por eso, $7 - 4 + 4 = 7$. La multiplicación y la división son operaciones inversas. Por ejemplo, empieza con 12. Multiplica por 2. Luego, divide por 2. Tienes otra vez el número 12. Por eso, $(12 \times 2) \div 2 = 12$.

N

negative number A number less than 0. On a number line, negative numbers are located to the left of 0 (on a vertical number line, negative numbers are located below 0).

número negativo Un número menor que 0. En una recta numérica, los números negativos están ubicados a la izquierda del 0 (en una recta numérica vertical, los números negativos están ubicados debajo del 0).

number sentence A mathematical statement that gives the relationship between two expressions that are composed of numbers and operation signs. For example, $3 + 2 = 5$ and $6 \times 2 > 10$ are number sentences; $3 + 2, 5, 6 \times 2$, and 10 are expressions.

oración numérica Un enunciado matemático que describe la relación entre dos expresiones compuestas por números y signos de operaciones. Por ejemplo, $3 + 2 = 5$ y $6 \times 2 > 10$ son oraciones numéricas. $3 + 2, 5, 6 \times 2$ y 10 son expresiones.

O

opposites Two numbers whose sum is 0. For example, -3 and 3 are opposites. On a number line, opposites are the same distance from 0 but in different directions from 0. The number 0 is its own opposite.

opuestos Dos números cuya suma da 0. Por ejemplo, -3 y 3 son opuestos. En una recta numérica, los opuestos se encuentran a la misma distancia de 0 pero en distintos sentidos. El número 0 es su propio opuesto.

order of operations Established order in which to perform mathematical operations.
1. Compute any expressions within parentheses.
2. Compute any exponents.
3. Multiply and divide in order from left to right.
4. Add and subtract in order from left to right.

orden de operaciones Orden establecido en el cual se deben realizar las operaciones matemáticas.
1. Calcular cualquier expresión dentro del paréntesis.
2. Calcular cualquier exponente.
3. Multiplicar y dividir de izquierda a derecha.
4. Sumar y restar de izquierda a derecha.

P

positive number A number greater than 0. (The number 0 is neither positive nor negative.) On a number line, positive numbers are located to the right of 0 (on a vertical number line, positive numbers are located above 0).

número positivo Un número mayor que 0. (El número 0 no es ni positivo ni negativo.) En una recta numérica, los números positivos se ubican a la derecha del 0 (en una recta numérica vertical, los números positivos están por encima del 0).

English/Spanish Glossary

quadrants The four sections into which the coordinate plane is divided by the *x*- and *y*-axes. The quadrants are labeled as follows:

cuadrantes Las cuatro secciones en las que un plano de coordenadas queda dividido por los ejes *x* e *y*. Los cuadrantes se identifican de la siguiente manera:

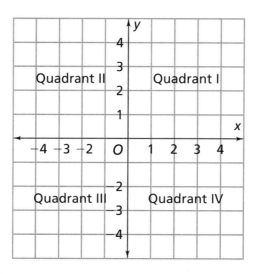

R

rational numbers Numbers that can be expressed as a quotient of two integers where the divisor is not zero. For example, $\frac{1}{2}$, $\frac{9}{11}$, and $-\frac{7}{5}$ are rational numbers. Also, 0.799 is a rational number, since $0.799 = \frac{799}{1,000}$.

números racionales Números que se pueden expresar como un cociente de dos números enteros donde el divisor no es cero. Por ejemplo, $\frac{1}{2}$, $\frac{9}{11}$ y $-\frac{7}{5}$ son números racionales. También 0.799 es un número racional, porque $0.799 = \frac{799}{1,000}$.

Index

Acknowledgments

Team Credits

The people who made up the **Connected Mathematics 2** team—representing editorial, editorial services, design services, and production services—are listed below. Bold type denotes core team members.

Leora Adler, Judith Buice, Kerry Cashman, Patrick Culleton, Sheila DeFazio, Katie Hallahan, Richard Heater, **Barbara Hollingdale, Jayne Holman,** Karen Holtzman, **Etta Jacobs,** Christine Lee, Carolyn Lock, Catherine Maglio, **Dotti Marshall,** Rich McMahon, Eve Melnechuk, Kristin Mingrone, Terri Mitchell, **Marsha Novak,** Irene Rubin, Donna Russo, Robin Samper, Siri Schwartzman, **Nancy Smith,** Emily Soltanoff, **Mark Tricca,** Paula Vergith, Roberta Warshaw, Helen Young

Additional Credits

Diana Bonfilio, Mairead Reddin, Michael Torocsik, nSight, Inc.

Technical Illustration

WestWords, Inc.

Cover Design

tom white.images

Photos

2, Richard Haynes; 3, AP Photo/Jonathan Hayward; 5, Richard Haynes; 8, Richard Haynes; 10, Stephanie Maze/Corbis; 12, AP Photo/Gregory Smith; 14, PhotoDisc/Getty Images, Inc.; 17, Josh Mitchell/Getty Images, Inc.; 22, Creatas/AGE Fotostock; 28, Richard Haynes; 37, Creatas/PictureQuest; 43, Paul J. Sutton/Corbis; 50, Dennis MacDonald/PhotoEdit; 53, Spencer Grant/PhotoEdit; 56, SuperStock, Inc./SuperStock; 60, Richard Haynes; 61, Syracuse Newspapers/The Image Works; 64, Tom Carter/PhotoEdit; 71, Dennis MacDonald/Index Stock Imagery, Inc.; 77, Richard Haynes

Connected Mathematics 2™

Moving Straight Ahead

Linear Relationships

Glenda Lappan

James T. Fey

William M. Fitzgerald

Susan N. Friel

Elizabeth Difanis Phillips

PEARSON

Prentice
Hall

Boston, Massachusetts
Upper Saddle River, New Jersey

Moving Straight Ahead

Linear Relationships

Henri challenges his older brother Emile to a walking race. Emile walks 2.5 meters per second, and Henri walks 1 meter per second. Emile gives Henri a 45-meter head start. What distance wll allow Henri to win in a close race?

You can estimate the temperature outside by counting cricket chirps. Suppose a cricket chirps n times in one minute. The temperature t in degrees Fahrenheit can be computed with the formula $t = \frac{1}{4}n + 40$. What is the temperature if a cricket chirps 150 times in a minute?

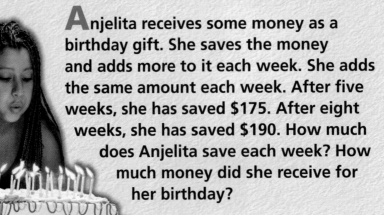

Anjelita receives some money as a birthday gift. She saves the money and adds more to it each week. She adds the same amount each week. After five weeks, she has saved $175. After eight weeks, she has saved $190. How much does Anjelita save each week? How much money did she receive for her birthday?

ll around you, things occur in patterns. Once you observe a pattern, you can use the pattern to predict information beyond and between the data observed. The ability to use patterns to make predictions makes it possible for a baseball player to run to the right position to catch a fly ball or for a pilot to estimate the flying time for a trip.

In *Variables and Patterns,* you investigated relationships between variables. The relationships were displayed as tables, graphs, and equations. Some of the graphs, such as the graph of distance and time for a van traveling at a steady rate, were straight lines. Relationships with graphs that are straight lines are called *linear relationships*.

In this unit, you will study linear relationships. You will learn about the characteristics of a linear relationship and how to determine whether a relationship is linear by looking at its equation or at a table of values. You will use what you learn about linear relationships to answer questions like those on the facing page.

Mathematical Highlights

Linear Relationships

In *Moving Straight Ahead*, you will explore properties of linearity.

You will learn how to

- Recognize problem situations in which two or more variables have a linear relationship to each other
- Construct tables, graphs, and symbolic equations that express linear relationships
- Translate information about linear relations given in a table, a graph, or an equation to one of the other forms
- Understand the connections between linear equations and the patterns in the tables and graphs of those equations: rate of change, slope, and *y*-intercept
- Solve linear equations
- Solve problems and make decisions about linear relationships using information given in tables, graphs, and symbolic expressions
- Use tables, graphs, and equations of linear relations to answer questions

As you work on the problems in this unit, ask yourself questions about problem situations that involve related quantities:

What are the variables in the problem?

Do the variables in this problem have a linear relationship to each other?

What patterns in the problem suggest that it is linear?

How can the linear relationship be represented in a problem, in a table, in a graph, or with an equation?

How do changes in one variable affect changes in a related variable?

How are these changes captured in a table, graph, or equation?

How can tables, graphs, and equations of linear relationships be used to answer questions?

Investigation 1

Walking Rates

In *Variables and Patterns*, you read about a bicycle touring business. You used tables, graphs, and equations to represent patterns relating variables such as cost, income, and profit. You looked at some linear relationships, like the relationship between cost and number of rental bikes represented in this graph:

Relationships that are represented by straight lines on a graph are called **linear relationships** or **linear functions.** From the graph, you see that the relationship between the number of bikes rented and the total rental cost is a linear function. In this investigation, you will consider the questions:

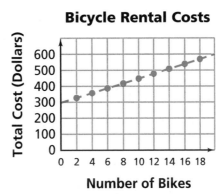

Bicycle Rental Costs

How can you determine whether a relationship is linear by examining a table of data or an equation?

How do changes in one variable affect changes in a related variable? How are these changes captured in a table, a graph, or an equation?

1.1 Walking Marathons

Ms. Chang's class decides to participate in a walkathon. Each participant must find sponsors to pledge a certain amount of money for each kilometer the participant walks. Leanne suggests that they determine their walking rates in meters per second so they can make predictions.

Do you know what your walking rate is?

To determine your walking rate:

- Line up ten meter sticks, end to end (or mark off 100 meters), in the hall of your school.

- Have a partner time your walk.

- Start at one end and walk the length of the ten meter sticks using your normal walking pace.

A. What is your walking rate in meters per second?

B. Assume you continue to walk at this constant rate.

    1. How long would it take you to walk 500 meters?

    2. How far could you walk in 30 seconds? In 10 minutes? In 1 hour?

    3. Describe in words the distance in meters you could walk in a given number of seconds.

    4. Write an equation that represents the distance d in meters that you could walk in t seconds if you maintain this pace.

    5. Use the equation to predict the distance you would walk in 45 seconds.

 Homework starts on page 12.

Walking Rates and Linear Relationships

Think about the effect a walking rate has on the relationship between time walked and distance walked. This will provide some important clues about how to identify linear relationships from tables, graphs, and equations.

 **Linear Relationships in Tables, Graphs, and Equations**

Here are the walking rates that Gilberto, Alana, and Leanne found in their experiment.

Name	Walking Rate
Alana	1 meter per second
Gilberto	2 meters per second
Leanne	2.5 meters per second

A. 1. Make a table showing the distance walked by each student for the first ten seconds. How does the walking rate affect the data?

2. Graph the time and distance on the same coordinate axes. Use a different color for each student's data. How does the walking rate affect the graph?

3. Write an equation that gives the relationship between the time t and the distance d walked for each student. How is the walking rate represented in the equations?

B. For each student:

1. If t increases by 1 second, by how much does the distance change? How is this change represented in a table? In a graph?

2. If t increases by 5 seconds, by how much does the distance change? How is this change represented in a table? In a graph?

3. What is the walking rate per minute? The walking rate per hour?

C. Four other friends who are part of the walkathon made the following representations of their data. Are any of these relationships linear relationships? Explain.

George's Walking Rate	
Time (seconds)	Distance (meters)
0	0
1	2
2	9
3	11
4	20
5	25

Elizabeth's Walking Rate	
Time (seconds)	Distance (meters)
0	0
2	3
4	6
6	9
8	12
10	15

Billie's Walking Rate
$$D = 2.25t$$

D represents distance
t represents time

Bob's Walking Rate
$$t = \frac{100}{r}$$

t represents time
r represents walking rate

ACE Homework starts on page 12.

1.3 Raising Money

In *Variables and Patterns*, you looked at situations that involved *dependent* and *independent variables*. Because the distance walked depends on the time, you know distance is the dependent variable and time is the independent variable. In this problem, you will look at relationships between two other variables in a walkathon.

Getting Ready for Problem 1.3

Each participant in the walkathon must find sponsors to pledge a certain amount of money for each kilometer the participant walks.

The students in Ms. Chang's class are trying to estimate how much money they might be able to raise. Several questions come up in their discussions:

- What variables can affect the amount of money that is collected?
- How can you use these variables to estimate the amount of money each student will collect?
- Will the amount of money collected be the same for each walker? Explain.

Each student found sponsors who are willing to pledge the following amounts.

- Leanne's sponsors will pay $10 regardless of how far she walks.
- Gilberto's sponsors will pay $2 per kilometer (km).
- Alana's sponsors will make a $5 donation plus 50¢ per kilometer.

The class refers to these as *pledge plans*.

Problem **1.3** Using Linear Relationships

A. 1. Make a table for each student's pledge plan, showing the amount of money each of his or her sponsors would owe if he or she walked distances from 0 to 6 kilometers. What are the dependent and independent variables?

2. Graph the three pledge plans on the same coordinate axes. Use a different color for each plan.

3. Write an equation for each pledge plan. Explain what information each number and variable in your equation represents.

4. a. What pattern of change for each pledge plan do you observe in the table?

b. How does this pattern appear in the graph? In the equation?

B. 1. Suppose each student walks 8 kilometers in the walkathon. How much money does each sponsor owe?

2. Suppose each student receives $10 from a sponsor. How many kilometers does each student walk?

3. On which graph does the point (12, 11) lie? What information does this point represent?

4. In Alana's plan, how is the fixed $5 donation represented in

a. the table? **b.** the graph? **c.** the equation?

C. Gilberto decides to give a T-shirt to each of his sponsors. Each shirt costs him $4.75. He plans to pay for each shirt with some of the money he collects from each sponsor.

1. Write an equation that represents the amount of money Gilberto makes from each sponsor after he has paid for the T-shirts. Explain what information each number and variable in the equation represents.

2. Graph the equation for distances from 0 to 5 kilometers.

3. Compare this graph to the graph of Gilberto's pledge plan in Question A, part (2).

ACE **Homework starts on page 12.**

active math
online

For: Climbing Monkeys
Activity
Visit: PHSchool.com
Web Code: and-5103

s. Chang's class decides to use their money from the walkathon to provide books for the children's ward at the hospital. They put the money in the school safe and withdraw a fixed amount each week to buy new books. To keep track of the money, Isabella makes a table of the amount of money in the account at the end of each week.

Week	Amount of Money at the End of Each Week
0	$144
1	$132
2	$120
3	$108
4	$96
5	$84

What do you think the graph would look like?

Is this a linear relationship?

Problem 1.4 Recognizing Linear Relationships

A. 1. How much money is in the account at the start of the project?

2. How much money is withdrawn from the account each week?

3. Is the relationship between the number of weeks and the amount of money left in the account a linear relationship? Explain.

4. Suppose the students continue withdrawing the same amount of money each week. Sketch a graph of this relationship.

5. Write an equation that represents the relationship. Explain what information each number and variable represents.

B. Mr. Mamer's class also raised money from the walkathon. They use their money to buy games and puzzles for the children's ward. Sade uses a graph to keep track of the amount of money in their account at the end of each week.

Money in Mr. Mamer's Class Account

1. What information does the graph represent about the money in Mr. Mamer's class account?

2. Make a table of data for the first 10 weeks. Explain why the table represents a linear relationship.

3. Write an equation that represents the linear relationship. Explain what information each number and variable represents.

C. How can you determine if a relationship is linear from a graph, table, or equation?

D. Compare the linear relationships in this problem with those in previous problems in this investigation.

ACE Homework starts on page 12.

Applications

1. Hoshi walks 10 meters in 3 seconds.

   a. What is her walking rate?

   b. At this rate, how long does it take her to walk 100 meters?

   c. Suppose she walks this same rate for 50 seconds. How far does she walk?

   d. Write an equation that represents the distance d that Hoshi walks in t seconds.

2. Milo walks 40 meters in 15 seconds and Mira walks 30 meters in 10 seconds. Whose walking rate is faster?

In Exercises 3–5, Jose, Mario, Melanie, Mike, and Alicia are on a weeklong cycling trip. Cycling times include only biking time, not time to eat, rest, and so on.

3. The table below gives the distance Jose, Mario, and Melanie travel for the first 3 hours. Assume that each person cycles at a constant rate.

Cycling Distance

Cycling Time (hours)	Distance (miles)		
	Jose	Mario	Melanie
0	0	0	0
1	5	7	9
2	10	14	18
3	15	21	27

   a. Find the average rate at which each person travels during the first 3 hours. Explain.

   b. Find the distance each person travels in 7 hours.

   c. Graph the time and distance data for all three riders on the same coordinate axes.

   d. Use the graphs to find the distance each person travels in $6\frac{1}{2}$ hours.

   e. Use the graphs to find the time it takes each person to travel 70 miles.

f. How does the rate at which each person rides affect each graph?

g. For each rider, write an equation that can be used to calculate the distance traveled after a given number of hours.

h. Use your equations from part (g) to calculate the distance each person travels in $6\frac{1}{2}$ hours.

i. How does a person's biking rate show up in his or her equation?

4. Mike makes the following table of the distances he travels during the first day of the trip.

a. Suppose Mike continues riding at this rate. Write an equation for the distance Mike travels after t hours.

b. Sketch a graph of the equation. How did you choose the range of values for the time axis? For the distance axis?

c. How can you find the distances Mike travels in 7 hours and in $9\frac{1}{2}$ hours, using the table? Using the graph? Using the equation?

d. How can you find the numbers of hours it takes Mike to travel 100 miles and 237 miles, using the table? Using the graph? Using the equation?

e. For parts (c) and (d), what are the advantages and disadvantages of using each form of representation—a table, a graph, and an equation—to find the answers?

f. Compare the rate at which Mike rides with the rates at which Jose, Mario, and Melanie ride. Who rides the fastest? How can you determine this from the tables? From the graphs? From the equations?

Cycling Distance

Time (hours)	Distance (miles)
0	0
1	6.5
2	13
3	19.5
4	26
5	32.5
6	39

5. The distance Alicia travels in t hours is represented by the equation $d = 7.5t$.

    a. At what rate does Alicia travel?

    b. Suppose the graph of Alicia's distance and time is put on the same set of axes as Mike's, Jose's, Mario's, and Melanie's graphs. Where would it be located in relationship to each of the graphs? Describe the location without actually making the graph.

6. The graph below represents the walkathon pledge plans from three sponsors.

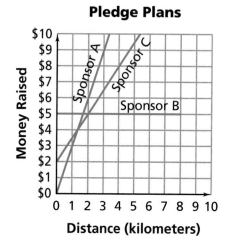

Pledge Plans

a. Describe each sponsor's pledge plan.

b. What is the number of dollars per kilometer each sponsor pledges?

c. What does the point where the line crosses the y-axis mean for each sponsor?

d. Write the coordinates of two points on each line. What information does each point represent for the sponsor's pledge plan?

7. The students in Ms. Chang's class decide to order water bottles that advertise the walkathon. Maliik obtains two different quotes for the costs of the bottles.

    Fill It Up charges $4 per bottle.

    Bottles by Bob charges $25 plus $3 per bottle.

    a. For each company, write an equation Maliik could use to calculate the cost for any number of bottles.

b. On the same set of axes, graph both equations from part (a). Which variable is the independent variable? Which is the dependent variable?

c. Which company do you think the class should buy water bottles from? What factors influenced your decision?

d. For what number of water bottles is the cost the same for both companies?

8. Multiple Choice The equation $C = 5n$ represents the cost C in dollars for n caps that advertise the walkathon. Which of the following pairs of numbers could represent a number of caps and the cost for that number of caps, (n, C)?

A. $(0, 5)$ **B.** $(3, 15)$ **C.** $(15, 60)$ **D.** $(5, 1)$

9. The equation $d = 3.5t + 50$ represents the distance d in meters that a cyclist is from his home after t seconds.

Homework
Help Online
PHSchool.com
For: Help with Exercise 9
Web Code: ane-5109

a. Which of the following pairs of numbers represent the coordinates of a point on the graph of this equation? Explain your answer.

    i. $(10, 85)$ **ii.** $(0, 0)$ **iii.** $(3, 60.5)$

b. What information do the coordinates represent about the cyclist?

10. Examine the patterns in each table.

Table 1

x	y
−2	3
−1	3
0	3
1	3
2	3

Table 2

x	y
−3	9
−2	4
−1	1
0	0
1	1

Table 3

x	y
0	10
3	19
5	25
10	40
12	46

Table 4

x	y
0	−3
2	−6
4	−9
6	−12
8	−15

a. Describe the similarities and differences in Tables 1–4.

b. Explain how you can use the tables to decide if the data represent a linear relationship.

c. Sketch a graph of the data in each table.

d. Write an equation for each linear relationship. Explain what information the numbers and variables represent in the relationship.

11. The temperature at the North Pole is 30°F and is expected to drop 5°F per hour for the next several hours. Write an equation that represents the relationship between temperature and time. Explain what information your numbers and variables mean. Is this a linear relationship?

12. Jamal's parents give him money to spend at camp. Jamal spends the same amount of money on snacks each day. The table below shows the amount of money, in dollars, he has left at the end of each day.

Snack Money

Days	Money Left
0	$20
1	$18
2	$16
3	$14
4	$12
5	$10
6	$8

a. How much money does Jamal have at the start of camp? Explain.

b. How much money is spent each day? Explain.

c. Assume that Jamal's spending pattern continues. Is the relationship between the number of days and the amount of money left in Jamal's wallet a linear relationship? Explain.

d. Check your answer to part (c) by sketching a graph of this relationship.

e. Write an equation that represents the relationship. Explain what information the numbers and variables represent.

13. Write an equation for each graph.

Go Online
PHSchool.com
For: Multiple-Choice Skills Practice
Web Code: ana-5154

Graph 1

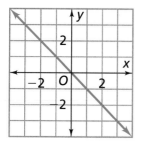

Graph 2

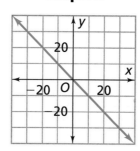

14. a. Give an example of a linear situation with a rate of change that is

     i. positive.   **ii.** zero (no change).   **iii.** negative.

  b. Write an equation that represents each situation in part (a).

Connections

15. Jelani is in a walking race at his school. In the first 20 seconds, he walks 60 meters. In the next 30 seconds, he walks 60 meters. In the next 10 seconds, he walks 35 meters. In the last 40 seconds, he walks 80 meters.

  a. Describe how Jelani's walking rate changes during the race.

  b. What would a graph of Jelani's walking race look like?

16. Insert parentheses where needed in each expression to show how to get each result.

  a. $2 + -3 \times 4 = -10$

  b. $4 + -3 \times -4 = -4$

  c. $-12 \div 2 + -4 = 6$

  d. $8 \div -2 + -2 = -6$

17. Which of the following number sentences are true? In each case, explain how you could answer without any calculation. Check your answers by doing the indicated calculations.

  a. $20 \times 410 = (20 \times 400) + (20 \times 10)$

  b. $20 \times 308 = (20 \times 340) - (20 \times 32)$

  c. $-20 \times -800 = (-20 \times -1{,}000) + (-20 \times 200)$

  d. $-20 + (300 \times 32) = (-20 + 300) \times (-20 + 32)$

18. Fill in the missing numbers to make each sentence true.

  a. $15 \times (6 + 4) = (15 \times \blacksquare) + (15 \times 4)$

  b. $2 \times (x + 6) = (2 \times \blacksquare) + (\blacksquare \times 6)$

  c. $(x \times 2) + (x \times 6) = \blacksquare \times (2 + 6)$

19. a. Draw a rectangle whose area can be represented by the expression $5 \times (12 + 6)$.

  b. Write another expression to represent the area of the rectangle in part (a).

20. Find the unit rate and use it to write an equation relating the two quantities.

   a. 50 dollars for 150 T-shirts

   b. 8 dollars to rent 14 video games

   c. 24 tablespoons of sugar in 3 glasses of Bolda Cola

21. The longest human-powered sporting event is the Tour de France cycling race. The record average speed for this race is 25.88 miles per hour, which was attained by Lance Armstrong in 2005.

   a. The race was 2,242 miles long. How long did it take Armstrong to complete the race in 2005?

   b. Suppose Lance had reduced his average cycling rate by 0.1 mile per hour. By how much would his time have changed?

22. a. In 2002, Gillian O'Sullivan set the record of the 5,000 m race-walking event. She finished the race in 20 minutes 2.60 seconds. What was O'Sullivan's average walking speed, in meters per second?

   b. In 1990, Nadezhda Ryashkina set the record for the 10,000 m race-walking event. She finished this race in 41 minutes 56.23 seconds. What was Ryashkina's average walking rate, in meters per second?

23. A recipe for orange juice calls for 2 cups of orange juice concentrate and 3 cups of water. The table below shows the amount of concentrate and water needed to make a given number of batches of juice.

Orange Juice Mixture Amounts

Batches of Juice (b)	Concentrate (c)	Water (w)	Juice (j)
1	2 cups	3 cups	5 cups
2	4 cups	6 cups	10 cups
3	6 cups	9 cups	15 cups
4	8 cups	12 cups	20 cups

The relationship between the number of batches b of juice and the number of cups c of concentrate is linear. The equation for this relationship is $c = 2b$. Are there other linear relationships in this table? Sketch graphs or write equations for the linear relationships you find.

24. The table below gives information about a pineapple punch recipe. The table shows the number of cups of orange juice, pineapple juice, and soda water needed for different quantities of punch.

Recipe

J (orange juice, cups)	P (pineapple juice, cups)	S (soda water, cups)
1	■	■
2	■	■
3	■	■
4	12	6
5	■	■
6	■	■
7	■	■
8	24	12

The relationship between cups of orange juice and cups of pineapple juice is linear, and the relationship between cups of orange juice and cups of soda water is linear.

a. Zahara makes the recipe using 6 cups of orange juice. How many cups of soda water does she use? Explain your reasoning.

b. Patrick makes the recipe using 6 cups of pineapple juice. How many cups of orange juice and how many cups of soda water does he use? Explain.

25. The graph below represents the distance John runs in a race. Use the graph to describe John's progress during the course of the race. Does he run at a constant rate during the trip? Explain.

Running Distance

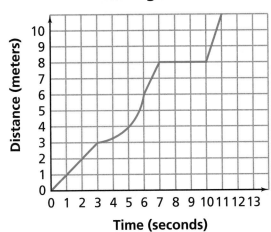

26. a. Does the graph represent a linear relationship? Explain.

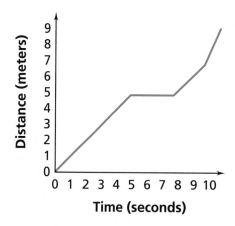

b. Could this graph represent a walking pattern? Explain.

In Exercises 27–29, students conduct an experiment to investigate the rate at which a leaking faucet loses water. They fill a paper cup with water, make a small hole in the bottom, and collect the dripping water in a measuring container, measuring the amount of water in the container at the end of each 10-second interval.

27. Students conducting the leaking-faucet experiment produce the table below. The measuring container they use holds only 100 milliliters.

a. Suppose the students continue their experiment. After how many seconds will the measuring container overflow?

Leaking Faucet

Time (seconds)	10	20	30	40	50	60	70
Water Loss (milliliters)	2	5	8.5	11.5	14	16.5	19.5

b. Is this relationship linear? Explain.

28. Denise and Takashi work together on the leaking-faucet experiment. Each of them makes a graph of the data they collect. What might have caused their graphs to look so different?

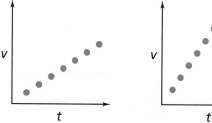

Denise's Graph   **Takashi's Graph**

29. What information might the graph below represent in the leaking-faucet experiment?

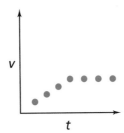

Extensions

30. a. The table below shows the population of four cities for the past eight years. Describe how the population of each city changed over the eight years.

Populations of Four Cities

Year	Population			
	Deep Valley	Nowhere	Swampville	Mount Silicon
0 (start)	1,000	1,000	1,000	1,000
1	1,500	900	1,500	2,000
2	2,000	800	2,500	4,000
3	2,500	750	3,000	8,000
4	3,000	700	5,000	16,000
5	3,500	725	3,000	32,000
6	4,000	900	2,500	64,000
7	4,500	1,500	1,500	128,000
8	5,000	1,700	1,000	256,000

b. Use the table to decide which relationships are linear.

c. Graph the data for each city. Describe how you selected ranges of values for the horizontal and vertical axes.

d. What are the advantages of using a table or a graph to represent the data?

31. In the walkathon, Jose decides to charge his patrons $10 for the first 5 kilometers he walks and $1 per kilometer after 5 kilometers.

    a. Sketch a graph that represents the relationship between money collected and kilometers walked.

    b. Compare this graph to the graphs of the other pledge plans in Problem 1.3.

32. The cost C to make T-shirts for the walkathon is represented by the equation $C = 20 + 5N$, where N is the number of T-shirts.

    a. Find the coordinates of a point that lies on the graph of this equation. Explain what the coordinates mean in this context.

    b. Find the coordinates of a point above the line. Explain what the coordinates mean in this context.

    c. Find the coordinates of a point below the line. Explain what the coordinates mean in this context.

33. Frankie is looking forward to walking in a walkathon. She writes some equations to use to answer some questions she has. For each part below, tell what you think the equation might represent and write one question she could use it to answer.

    a. $y = 3x + 20$

    b. $y = 0.25x$

    c. $y = 4x$

Mathematical Reflections 1

In this investigation, you began to explore linear relationships by examining the patterns of change between two variables. The following questions will help you summarize what you have learned.

Think about your answers to these questions. Discuss your ideas with other students and your teacher. Then, write a summary of your findings in your notebook.

1. Describe how the dependent variable changes as the independent variable changes in a linear relationship. Give examples.

2. How does the pattern of change for a linear relationship show up in a table, a graph, and an equation of the relationship?

Investigation 2

Exploring Linear Functions With Graphs and Tables

In the last investigation, you examined relationships that were linear functions. For example, the *distance* a person walks at a constant rate is a function of the amount of *time* a person walks. The *amount of money* a person collects from a walkathon sponsor who pays a fixed amount per *kilometer* is a function of the distance walked. You used tables, graphs, and equations to answer questions about these relationships.

In this investigation, you will continue to solve problems involving linear functions.

2.1 Walking to Win

In Ms. Chang's class, Emile found out that his walking rate is 2.5 meters per second. When he gets home from school, he times his little brother Henri as Henri walks 100 meters. He figured out that Henri's walking rate is 1 meter per second.

Problem 2.1 Finding the Point of Intersection

Henri challenges Emile to a walking race. Because Emile's walking rate is faster, Emile gives Henri a 45-meter head start. Emile knows his brother would enjoy winning the race, but he does not want to make the race so short that it is obvious his brother will win.

A. How long should the race be so that Henri will win in a close race?

B. Describe your strategy for finding your answer to Question A. Give evidence to support your answer.

ACE Homework starts on page 31.

2.2 Crossing the Line

Your class may have found some very interesting strategies for solving Problem 2.1, such as:

- Making a table showing time and distance data for both brothers
- Graphing time and distance data for both brothers on the same set of axes
- Writing an equation for each brother representing the relationship between time and distance

How can each of these strategies be used to solve the problem?

What other strategies were used in your class?

Problem 2.2 Using Tables, Graphs, and Equations

A. For each brother in Problem 2.1:

1. Make a table showing the *distance from the starting line* at several different times during the first 40 seconds.

2. Graph the time and the distance from the starting line on the same set of axes.

3. Write an equation representing the relationship. Explain what information each variable and number represents.

B. 1. How far does Emile walk in 20 seconds?

2. After 20 seconds, how far apart are the brothers? How is this distance represented in the table and on the graph?

3. Is the point (26, 70) on either graph? Explain.

4. When will Emile overtake Henri? Explain.

C. How can you determine which of two lines will be steeper

1. from a table of the data?

2. from an equation?

D. 1. At what points do Emile's and Henri's graphs cross the *y*-axis?

2. What information do these points represent in terms of the race?

3. How can these points be found in a table? In an equation?

ACE Homework starts on page 31.

Did You Know?

Have you ever seen a walking race? You may have thought the walking style of the racers seemed rather strange. Race walkers must follow two rules:

- The walker must always have one foot in contact with the ground.

- The walker's leg must be straight from the time it strikes the ground until it passes under the body.

A champion race walker can cover a mile in about 6.5 minutes. It takes most people 15 to 20 minutes to walk a mile.

Go Online
PHSchool.com
For: Information about race-walking
Web Code: ane-9031

In the last problem, you found the point at which Emile's and Henri's graphs cross the y-axis. These points are called the *y-intercepts*.

- The distance d_{Emile} that Emile walks after t seconds can be represented by the equation, $d_{\text{Emile}} = 2.5t$. The y-intercept is $(0, 0)$ and the *coefficient* of t is 2.5.

- The distance d_{Henri} that Henri is from where Emile started can be given by the equation, $d_{\text{Henri}} = 45 + t$, where t is the time in seconds. The y-intercept is $(0, 45)$ and the *coefficient* of t is 1.

All of the linear equations we have studied so far can be written in the form $y = mx + b$ or $y = b + mx$. In this equation, y depends on x.

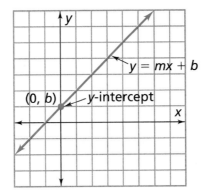

The **y-intercept** is the point where the line crosses the y-axis, or when $x = 0$. To save time, we sometimes refer to the number b, rather than the coordinates of the point $(0, b)$, as the y-intercept.

A **coefficient** is the number that multiplies a variable in an equation. The m in $y = mx + b$ is the coefficient of x, so mx means m times x.

Ms. Chang's class decides to give T-shirts to each person who participates in the Walkathon. They receive bids for the cost of the T-shirts from two different companies. Mighty Tee charges $49 plus $1 per T-shirt. No-Shrink Tee charges $4.50 per T-shirt. Ms. Chang writes the following equations to represent the relationship between cost and the number of T-shirts:

$$C_{Mighty} = 49 + n$$
$$C_{No\text{-}Shrink} = 4.5n$$

The number of T-shirts is n. C_{Mighty} is the cost in dollars for Mighty Tee and $C_{No\text{-}Shrink}$ is the cost in dollars for No-Shrink Tee.

A. 1. For each equation, explain what information the y-intercept and the coefficient of n represents.

   2. For each company, what is the cost for 20 T-shirts?

   3. Lani calculates that the school has about $120 to spend on T-shirts. From which company will $120 buy the most T-shirts?

   4. a. For what number of T-shirts is the cost of the two companies equal? What is that cost? Explain how you found the answers.

   b. How can this information be used to decide which plan to choose?

   5. Explain why the relationship between the cost and the number of T-shirts for each company is a linear relationship.

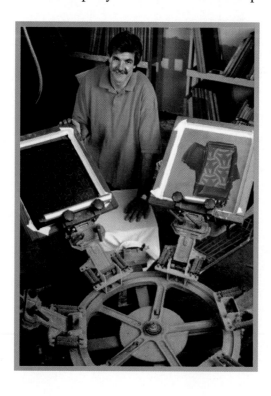

B. The table at the right represents the costs from another company, The Big T.

T-Shirt Costs

n	C
0	34
3	41.5
5	46.5
8	54
10	59

1. Compare the costs for this company with the costs for the two companies in Question A.

2. Does this plan represent a linear relationship? Explain.

3. **a.** Could the point (20, 84) lie on the graph of this cost plan? Explain.

   b. What information about the number of T-shirts and cost do the coordinates of the point (20, 84) represent?

ACE Homework starts on page 31.

2.4 Connecting Tables, Graphs, and Equations

Look again at Alana's pledge plan from Problem 1.3. Suppose *A* represents the dollars owed and *d* represents the number of kilometers walked. You can express this plan with the equation below:

Alana's pledge plan: $A = 5 + 0.5d$

Getting Ready for Problem 2.4

- Explain why the point (14, 12) is on the graph of Alana's pledge plan.

- Write a question you could answer by locating this point.

- How can you use the equation for Alana's pledge plan to check the answer to the question you made up?

- How can you use a graph to find the number of kilometers that Alana walks if a sponsor pays her $17? How could you use an equation to answer this question?

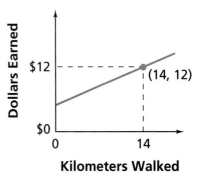

Alana's Pledge Plan

In the next problem, you will investigate similar questions relating to pledge plans for a walkathon.

Problem 2.4 Connecting Tables, Graphs, and Equations

Consider the following pledge plans. In each equation, y is the amount pledged in dollars, and x is the number of kilometers walked.

Plan 1 $y = 5x - 3$ Plan 2 $y = -x + 6$ Plan 3 $y = 2$

A. For each pledge plan:

  1. What information does the equation give about the pledge plan? Does the plan make sense?

  2. Make a table for values of x from -5 to 5.

  3. Sketch a graph.

  4. Do the y-values increase, decrease, or stay the same as the x-values increase?

B. Explain how you can use a graph, table, or equation to answer Question A, part (4).

C. 1. Which graph from Question A, part (3), can be traced to locate the point $(2, 4)$?

  2. How do the coordinates $(2, 4)$ relate to the equation of the line? To the corresponding table of data?

  3. Write a question you could answer by locating this point.

D. 1. Which equation has a graph you can trace to find the value of x that makes $8 = 5x - 3$ a true statement?

  2. How does finding the value of x in $8 = 5x - 3$ help you find the coordinates for a point on the line of the equation?

E. The following three points all lie on the graph of the same plan:

        $(-7, 13)$ $(1.2, \blacksquare)$ $(\blacksquare, -4)$

  1. Two of the points have a missing coordinate. Find the missing coordinate. Explain how you found it.

  2. Write a question you could answer by finding the missing coordinate.

ACE Homework starts on page 31.

Applications

1. Grace and Allie are going to meet at the fountain near their houses. They both leave their houses at the same time. Allie passes Grace's house on her way to the fountain.

   ● Allie's walking rate is 2 meters per second.

   ● Grace's walking rate is 1.5 meters per second.

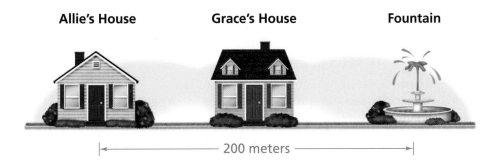

| Allie's House | Grace's House | Fountain |

← —————————— 200 meters —————————— →

   a. How many seconds will it take Allie to reach the fountain?

   b. Suppose Grace's house is 90 meters from the fountain. Who will reach the fountain first, Allie or Grace? Explain your reasoning.

2. In Problem 2.2, Emile's friend, Gilberto, joins the race. Gilberto has a head start of 20 meters and walks at 2 meters per second.

   a. Write an equation that gives the relationship between Gilberto's distance d from where Emile starts and the time, t.

   b. How would Gilberto's graph compare to Emile and Henri's graphs?

3. Ingrid stops at Tara's house on her way to school. Tara's mother says that Tara left 5 minutes ago. Ingrid leaves Tara's house, walking quickly to catch up with Tara. The graph below shows the distance each girl is from Tara's house, starting from the time Ingrid leaves Tara's house.

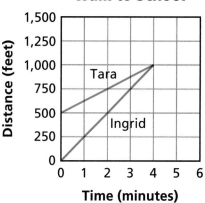

Tara's and Ingrid's Walk to School

a. In what way is this situation like the race between Henri and Emile? In what way is it different?

b. After how many minutes does Ingrid catch up with Tara?

c. How far from Tara's house does Ingrid catch up with Tara?

d. Each graph intersects the distance axis (the *y*-axis). What information do these points of intersection give about the problem?

e. Which line is steeper? How can you tell from the graph? How is the steepness of each line related to the rate at which the person travels?

f. What do you think the graphs would look like if we extended them to show distance and time after the girls meet?

4. A band decides to sell protein bars to raise money for an upcoming trip. The cost (the amount the band pays for the protein bars) and the income the band receives for the protein bars are represented on the graph below.

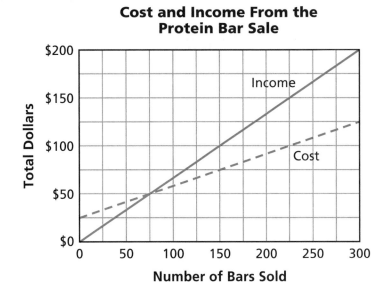

Cost and Income From the Protein Bar Sale

a. How many protein bars must be sold for the band's costs to equal the band's income?

b. What is the income from selling 50 protein bars? 125 bars?

c. Suppose the income is $200. How many protein bars were sold? How much of this income is profit?

Homework Help Online
PHSchool.com
For: Help with Exercise 4
Web Code: ane-5204

In Exercises 5 and 6, the student council asks for cost estimates for a skating party to celebrate the end of the school year.

5. The following tables represent the costs from two skating companies: Rollaway Skates and Wheelie's Skates and Stuff.

Rollaway Skates

Number of People	Cost
0	$0
1	$5
2	$10
3	$15
4	$20
5	$25
6	$30
7	$35
8	$40

Wheelie's Skates and Stuff

Number of People	Cost
0	$100
1	$103
2	$106
3	$109
4	$112
5	$115
6	$118
7	$121
8	$124

a. For each company, is the relationship between number of people and cost linear? Explain.

b. For each company, write an equation describing each cost plan.

c. Describe how you can use the table or graph to find when the costs of the two plans are equal. How can this information help the student council decide which company to choose?

6. A third company, Wheels to Go, gives their quote in the form of the equation $C_W = 35 + 4n$, where C_W is the cost in dollars for n students.

a. What information do the numbers 35 and 4 represent in this situation?

b. For 60 students, which of the three companies is the cheapest? Explain how you could determine the answer using tables, graphs, or equations.

c. Suppose the student council wants to keep the cost of the skating party to $500. How many people can they invite under each of the three plans?

d. The points below lie on one or more of the graphs of the three cost plans. Decide to which plan(s) each point belongs.

i. $(20, 115)$ **ii.** $(65, 295)$ **iii.** $(50, 250)$

e. Pick one of the points in part (d). Write a question that could be answered by locating this point.

7. Suppose each of the following patterns continues. Which are linear relationships? Explain your answer. For each pattern that is linear, write an equation that expresses the relationship.

a.

x	y
−10	−29
0	1
10	31
20	61
30	91

b.

x	y
1	9
5	17
7	21
20	47
21	49

c.

x	y
1	1
2	4
3	9
4	16
5	25

d.

x	y
1	9
5	22
7	25
20	56
21	60

8. The organizers of a walkathon get cost estimates from two printing companies to print brochures to advertise the event. The costs are given by the equations below, where C is the cost in dollars and n is the number of brochures.

$$\text{Company A: } C = 15 + 0.10n$$

$$\text{Company B: } C = 0.25n$$

a. For what number of brochures are the costs the same for both companies? What method did you use to get your answer?

b. The organizers have $65 to spend on brochures. How many brochures can they have printed if they use Company A? If they use Company B?

c. What information does the y-intercept represent for each equation?

d. What information does the coefficient of n represent for each equation?

9. A school committee is assigned the task of selecting a DJ for the end-of-school-year party. Susan obtains several quotes for the cost of three DJs.

Tom's Tunes charges $60 an hour.

Solidus' Sounds charges $100 plus $40 an hour.

Light Plastic charges $175 plus $30 an hour.

a. For each DJ, write an equation that shows how to calculate the total cost from the total number of hours.

b. What information does the coefficient of x represent for each DJ?

c. What information does the y-intercept represent for each DJ?

d. Suppose the DJ will need to work eight and one half hours. What is the cost of each DJ?

e. Suppose the committee has only $450 dollars to spend on a DJ. For how many hours could each DJ play?

10. A local department store offers two installment plans for buying a $270 skateboard.

> Plan 1: A fixed weekly payment of $10.80
>
> Plan 2: A $120 initial payment plus $6.00 per week

a. For each plan, how much money is owed after 12 weeks?

b. Which plan requires the least number of weeks to pay for the skateboard? Explain.

c. Write an equation to represent each plan. Explain what information the variables and numbers represent.

d. Suppose the skateboard costs $355. How would the answers to parts (a)–(c) change?

For each equation in Exercises 11–14, answer parts (a)–(d).

a. What is the rate of change between the variables?

b. State whether the *y*-values are increasing or decreasing, or neither, as *x* increases.

c. Give the *y*-intercept.

d. List the coordinates of two points that lie on a graph of the line of the equation.

Go Online
PHSchool.com
For: Multiple-Choice Skills Practice
Web Code: ana-5254

11. $y = 1.5x$

12. $y = -3x + 10$

13. $y = -2x + 6$

14. $y = 2x + 5$

15. Dani gets $7.50 per hour when she baby-sits.

a. Draw a graph that represents the number of hours she baby-sits and the total amount of money she earns.

b. Choose a point on the graph. Ask two questions that can be answered by finding the coordinates of this point.

16. Match each equation to a graph.

    a. $y = 3x + 5$ **b.** $y = x - 7$ **c.** $y = -x - 10$

Graph 1

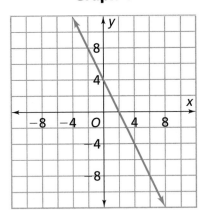

Graph 2

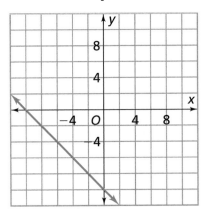

Graph 3

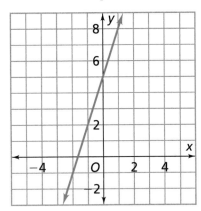

Graph 4

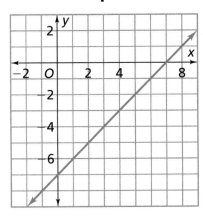

d. Write an equation for the graph that has no match.

17. Mary wants to use her calculator to find the value of x when $y = 22$ in the equation $y = 100 - 3x$. Explain how she can use each table or graph to find the value of x when $100 - 3x = 22$.

a.

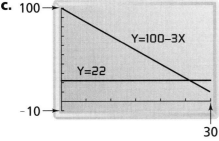

X	Y_1
21	37
22	34
23	31
24	28
25	25
26	22

$Y_1 = 100 - 3X$

b.

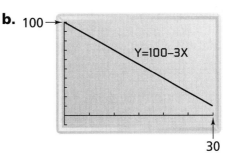

c.

For each equation in Exercises 18–21, give two values for x for which the value of y is negative.

18. $y = -2x - 5$

19. $y = -5$

20. $y = 2x - 5$

21. $y = \dfrac{3}{2}x - \dfrac{1}{4}$

For Exercises 22–28, consider the following equations:

i. $y = 2x$ **ii.** $y = -5x$ **iii.** $y = 2x - 6$

iv. $y = -2x + 1$ **v.** $y = 7$

22. Which equation has a graph you can trace to find the value of x that makes $8 = 2x - 6$ a true statement?

23. How does finding a solution to $8 = 2x - 6$ help you find the coordinates of a point on the line of the equation $y = 2x - 6$?

24. Which equation has a graph that contains the point $(7, -35)$?

25. The following two points lie on the graph that contains the point $(7, -35)$. Find the missing coordinate for each point.

$(-1.2, \blacksquare)$ $(\blacksquare, -15)$

26. Which equations have a positive rate of change?

27. Which equations have a negative rate of change?

28. Which equations have a rate of change equal to zero?

Connections

29. The Ferry family decides to buy a new DVD player that costs $215. The store has an installment plan that allows them to make a $35 down payment and then pay $15 a month. The graph below shows the relationship between the number of months the family has had a DVD player and the amount they still owe.

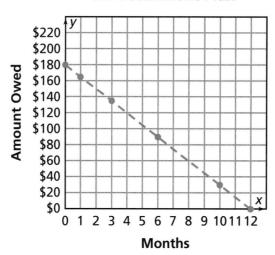

Paying for a DVD on an Installment Plan

a. Write an equation that represents the relationship between the amount the Ferry family still owes and the number of months after the purchase. Explain what information the numbers and variables represent.

b. The point where the graph of an equation intersects the x-axis is called the **x-intercept.** What are the x- and y-intercepts of the graph for this payment plan? Explain what information each intercept represents.

30. Use the Distributive Property to write two expressions that show two different ways to compute the area of each rectangle.

a.

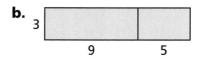

b.

c.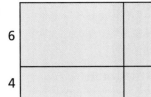

d.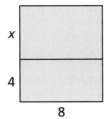

31. Use the distributive property to write an expression equal to each of the following:

    a. $x(-2 + 3)$ **b.** $(-4x) + (2x)$ **c.** $(x) - (4x)$

32. Decide whether each statement is true or false:

    a. $15 - 3x = 15 + -3x$

    b. $3.5x + 5 = 5(0.7x + 5)$

    c. $3(2x + 1) = (2x + 1) + (2x + 1) + (2x + 1)$

33. Shallah Middle School is planning a school trip. The cost is $5 per person. The organizers know that three adults are going on the trip, but they do not yet know the number of students who will go. Write an expression that represents the total cost for x students and three adults.

34. Harvest Foods has apples on sale at 12 for $3.

    a. What is the cost per apple?

    b. Complete the rate table to show the costs of different numbers of apples.

The Cost of Apples

Number of Apples	12	■	1	48	10	■
Cost	$3	$1.50	■	■	■	$4.50

    c. How many apples can you buy for $1?

    d. Is the relationship between number of apples and cost linear? Explain.

35. Ms. Peggy bought some bagels for her friends. She paid $15 for 20 bagels.

    a. How much did Ms. Peggy pay per bagel?

    b. Write an equation relating the number of bagels, n, to the total cost, c.

    c. Use your equation to find the cost of 150 bagels.

36. Ali says that $x = -1$ makes the equation $-8 = -3 + 5x$ true. Tamara checks this value for x in the equation. She says Ali is wrong because $-3 + 5 \times (-1)$ is -2, not -8. Why do you think these students disagree?

37. Determine whether the following mathematical sentences are true or false.

    a. $5 + 3 \times 2 = 16$ **b.** $3 \times 2 + 5 = 16$

    c. $5 + 3 \times 2 = 11$ **d.** $3 \times 2 + 5 = 11$

    e. $\dfrac{3}{2} \div \dfrac{4}{3} - \dfrac{1}{8} = 1$ **f.** $\dfrac{1}{2} + \dfrac{3}{2} \div \dfrac{1}{2} = 2$

38. Moesha feeds her dog the same amount of dog food each day from a very large bag. On the 3rd day, she has 44 cups left in the bag, and, on the 11th day, she has 28 cups left.

    a. How many cups of food does she feed her dog a day?

    b. How many cups of food were in the bag when she started?

    c. Write an equation for the total amount of dog food Moesha has left after feeding her dog for d days.

39. a. Match the following connecting paths for the last 5 minutes of Daren's race.

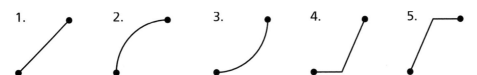

1.   2.   3.   4.   5.

    i.   Daren finishes running at a constant rate.

    ii.   Daren runs slowly at first and gradually increases his speed.

    iii. Daren runs fast and then gradually decreases his speed.

    iv. Daren runs very fast and reaches the finish line early.

    v.   After falling, Daren runs at a constant rate.

b. Which of the situations in part (a) was most likely to represent Daren's running for the race? Explain your answer.

40. In *Stretching and Shrinking*, you plotted the points $(8, 6), (8, 22)$, and $(24, 14)$ on grid paper to form a triangle.

a. Draw the triangle you get when you apply the rule $(0.5x, 0.5y)$ to the three points.

b. Draw the triangle you get when you apply the rule $(0.25x, 0.25y)$ to the three points.

c. How are the three triangles you have drawn related?

d. What are the areas of the three triangles?

e. Do you notice any linear relationships among the data of the three triangles, such as area, scale factor, lengths of sides, and so on?

41. In *Covering and Surrounding*, you looked at perimeters of rectangles.

a. Make a table of possible whole number values for the length and width of a rectangle with a perimeter of 20 meters.

b. What equation represents the data in this table? Make sure to define your variables.

c. Is the relationship between length and width linear in this case?

d. Find the area of each rectangle.

Extensions

42. Decide whether each equation represents a linear situation. Explain how you decided.

a. $y = 2x$ **b.** $y = \frac{2}{x}$ **c.** $y = x^2$

43. a. Write equations for three lines that intersect to form a triangle.

b. Sketch the graphs and label the coordinates of the vertices of the triangle.

c. Will any three lines intersect to form a triangle? Explain your reasoning.

44. a. Which one of the following points is on the line $y = 3x - 7$: $(3, 3)$, $(3, 2)$, $(3, 1)$, or $(3, 0)$? Describe where each of the other three points is in relation to the line.

b. Find another point on the line $y = 3x - 7$ and three more points above the line.

c. The points $(4, 5)$ and $(7, 14)$ lie on the graph of $y = 3x - 7$. Use this information to find two points that make the inequality $y < 3x - 7$ true and two points that make the inequality $y > 3x - 7$ true.

Mathematical Reflections 2

In this investigation, you continued to explore patterns of change in a linear relationship. You learned how to use tables and graphs to solve problems about linear relationships with equations of the form $y = mx + b$. The following questions will help you summarize what you have learned.

Think about your answers to these questions and discuss your ideas with other students and your teacher. Then write a summary of your findings in your notebook.

1. Summarize what you know about a linear relationship represented by an equation of the form $y = mx + b$.

2. a. Explain how a table or graph for a linear relationship can be used to solve a problem.

   b. Explain how you have used an equation to solve a problem.

Investigation 3

Solving Equations

In the last investigation, you examined the patterns in the table and graph for the relationship between Alana's distance d and money earned A in the walkathon.

The equation $A = 5 + 0.5d$ is another way to represent the relationship between the distance and the money earned. The graph of this equation is a line that contains infinitely many points. The coordinates of the points on the line can be substituted into the equation to make a true statement.

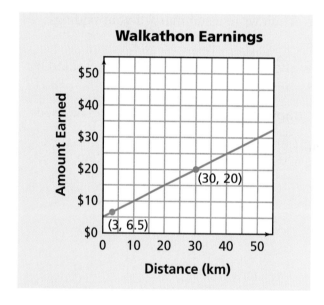

Walkathon Earnings

For example, the point $(3, 6.5)$ lies on the line. This means that $x = 3$ and $y = 6.5$. So, $6.5 = 5 + 0.5(3)$ is a true statement.

Similarly, the point $(30, 20)$ lies on the line which means that $x = 30$ and $y = 20$, and $20 = 5 + 0.5(30)$ is a true statement.

We say that $(3, 6.5)$ and $(30, 20)$ are *solutions* to the equation $A = 5 + 0.5d$ because when the values for d and A are substituted into the equation we get a true statement. There are infinitely many solutions to $A = 5 + 0.5d$.

Because the corresponding entries in a table are the coordinates of points on the line representing the equation, we can also find a solution to an equation by using a table.

d	A
0	5
1	5.5
2	6
3	**6.5**
4	7
20	15
25	17.5
30	**20**

3.1 Solving Equations Using Tables and Graphs

In an equation with two variables, if the value of one variable is known, you can use a table or graph to find the value of the other variable. For example, suppose Alana raises $10 from a sponsor. Then you can ask: How many kilometers does Alana walk?

In the equation $A = 5 + 0.5d$, this means that $A = 10$. The equation is now $10 = 5 + 0.5d$.

Which value of d *will make this a true statement?*

Finding the value of d that will make this a true statement is called *solving the equation* for d.

A. Use the equation $A = 5 + 0.5d$.

   1. Suppose Alana walks 23 kilometers. Show how you can use a table and a graph to find the amount of money Alana gets from each sponsor.

   2. Suppose Alana receives $60 from a sponsor. Show how you can use a table and a graph to find the number of kilometers she walks.

B. For each equation:

   - Tell what information Alana is looking for.
   - Describe how you can find the information.

   1. $A = 5 + 0.5(15)$

   2. $50 = 5 + 0.5d$

C. The following equations are related to situations that you have explored. Find the solution (the value of the variable) for each equation. Then, describe another way you can find the solution.

   1. $D = 25 + 2.5(7)$

   2. $70 = 25 + 2.5t$

ACE **Homework starts on page 57.**

3.2 Exploring Equality

An equation states that two quantities are equal. In the equation $A = 5 + 0.5d$, A and $5 + 0.5d$ are the two quantities. Both represent the amount of money that Alana collects from each sponsor. Since each quantity represents numbers, you can use the properties of numbers to solve equations with one unknown variable.

Before we begin to solve linear equations, we need to look more closely at equality.

What does it mean for two quantities to be equal?

Let's look first at numerical statements.

The equation $85 = 70 + 15$ states that the quantities 85 and $70 + 15$ are equal.

What do you have to do to maintain equality if you

- subtract 15 from the left-hand side of the equation?
- add 10 to the right-hand side of the original equation?
- divide the left-hand side of the original equation by 5?
- multiply the right-hand side of the original equation by 4?

Try your methods on another example of equality. Summarize what you know about maintaining equality between two quantities.

In the Kingdom of Montarek, the ambassadors carry diplomatic pouches. The contents of the pouches are unknown except by the ambassadors. Ambassador Milton wants to send one-dollar gold coins to another country.

$1 gold coin   **diplomatic pouch**

His daughter, Sarah, is a mathematician. She helps him devise a plan based on *equality* to keep track of the number of one-dollar gold coins in each pouch.

In each situation:

- Each pouch contains the same number of one-dollar gold coins.
- The number of gold coins on both sides of the equality sign is the same, but some coins are hidden in the pouches.

Try to find the number of gold coins in each pouch.

A. Sarah draws the following picture. Each pouch contains the same number of $1 gold coins.

How many gold coins are in each pouch? Explain your reasoning.

B. For each situation, find the number of gold coins in the pouch. Write down your steps so that someone else could follow your steps to find the same number of coins in a pouch.

1.

2.

3.

4.

5.

C. Describe how you can check your answer. That is, how do you know you found the correct number of gold coins in each pouch?

D. Describe how you maintained equality at each step of your solutions in Questions A and B.

ACE Homework starts on page 57.

3.3 From Pouches to Variables

Throughout this unit, you have been solving problems that involve two variables. Sometimes the value of one variable is known, and you want to find the value of the other variable. The next problem continues the search for finding a value for a variable without using a table or graph. In this investigation, you are learning to use *symbolic* methods to solve a linear equation.

Getting Ready for Problem 3.3

The picture below represents another diplomatic pouch situation.

Because the number of gold coins in each pouch is unknown, we can let x represent the number of coins in one pouch and 1 represent the value of one gold coin.

- Write an equation to represent this situation.
- Use your methods from Problem 3.2 to find the number of gold coins in each pouch.
- Next to your work, write down a similar method using the equation that represents this situation.

Problem 3.3 Writing Equations

A. For each situation:

- Represent the situation with an equation. Use an x to represent the number of gold coins in each pouch and a number to represent the number of coins on each side.
- Use the equation to find the number of gold coins in each pouch.

1.

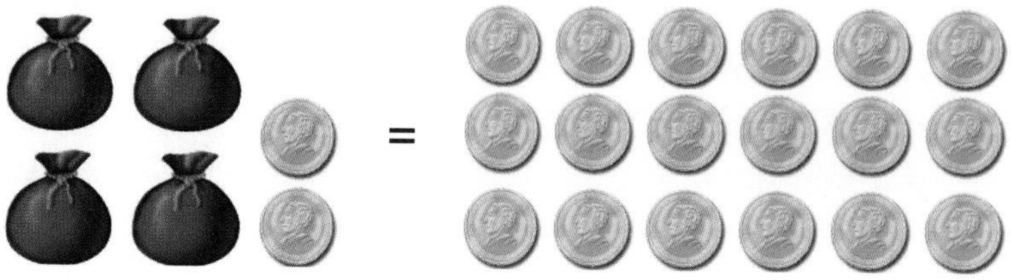

2.

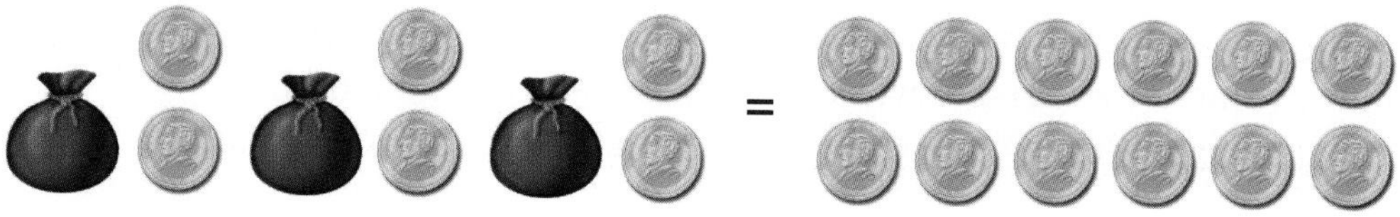

3.

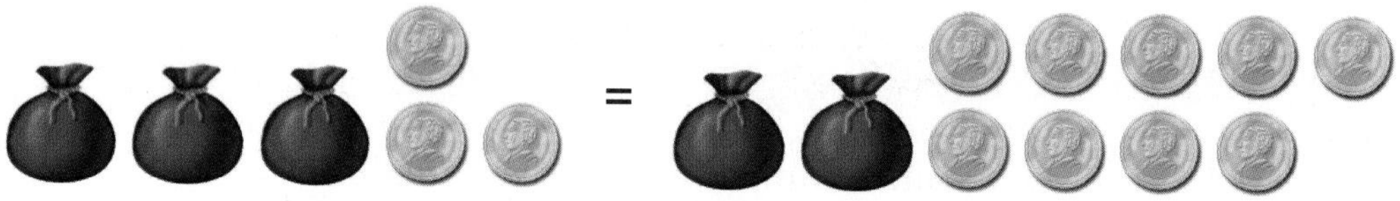

4.

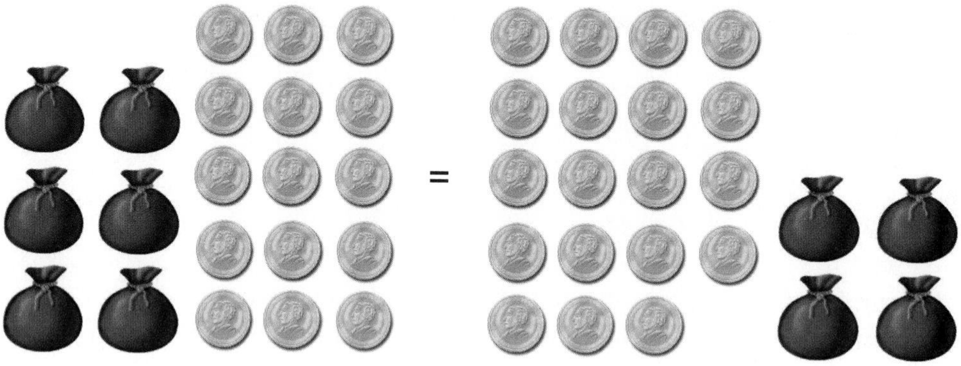

B. For each equation:
- Use your ideas from Question A to solve the equation.
- Check your answer.

  1. $30 = 6 + 4x$

  2. $7x = 5 + 5x$

  3. $7x + 2 = 12 + 5x$

  4. $2(x + 4) = 16$

C. Describe a general method for solving equations using what you know about equality.

ACE Homework starts on page 57.

3.4 Solving Linear Equations

You know that to maintain an equality, you can add, subtract, multiply, or divide both sides of the equality by the same number. These are called the **properties of equality.** In the last problem, you applied properties of equality and numbers to find a solution to an equation.

So far in this investigation, all of the situations have involved positive numbers.

Does it make sense to think about negative numbers in a coin situation?

Getting Ready for Problem 3.4

- How do these two equations compare?

  $2x + 10 = 16$ $\qquad\qquad$ $2x - 10 = 16$

  How would you solve each equation? That is, how would you find a value of x that makes each statement true?

- How do the equations below compare?

  $3x = 15$ $\qquad\qquad$ $-3x = 15$

  $3x = -15$ $\qquad\qquad$ $-3x = -15$

  Find a value of x that makes each statement true?

Use what you have learned in this investigation to solve each equation.

For Questions A–D, record each step you take to find your solution and check your answer.

A. 1. $5x + 10 = 20$

   2. $5x - 10 = 20$

   3. $5x + 10 = -20$

   4. $5x - 10 = -20$

B. 1. $10 - 5x = 20$

   2. $10 - 5x = -20$

C. 1. $4x + 9 = 7x$

   2. $4x + 9 = 7x + 3$

   3. $4x - 9 = 7x$

   4. $4x - 9 = -7x + 13$

D. 1. $3(x + 2) = 21$

   2. $-3(x - 5) = 2x$

   3. $5(x + 2) = 6x + 3$

E. In all of the equations in Questions A–D, the value of x was an integer, but the solution to an equation can be any real number. Solve the equations below, and check your answers.

   1. $5x + 10 = 19$

   2. $5x + 10 = 9x$

   3. $5x - 10 = -19$

   4. $5x - 10 = -7x + 1$

F. 1. Describe how you could use a graph or table to solve the equation $5x + 10 = -20$.

   2. Suppose you use a different letter or symbol to represent the value of the unknown variable. For example, $5n + 10 = 6n$ instead of $5x + 10 = 6x$.

   Does this make a difference in solving the equation? Explain.

ACE **Homework starts on page 57.**

3.5 Finding the Point of Intersection

In Problem 2.3, you used the graphs (or tables) to find when the costs of two different plans for buying T-shirts were equal. The **point of intersection** of the two lines represented by the two graphs gives us information about when the costs of the two T-shirt plans are equal. The graphs of the two cost plans are shown below.

Two T-Shirt Plans

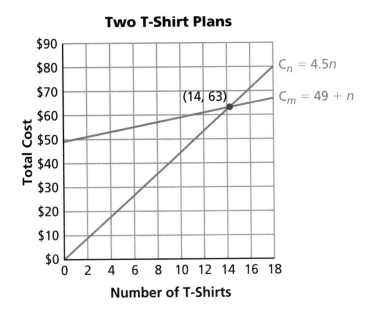

$C_n = 4.5n$

$C_m = 49 + n$

(14, 63)

C_m is the cost for Mighty Tee.

C_n is the cost for No-Shrink Tee.

Getting Ready for Problem 3.5

- What information do the coordinates of the point of intersection of the two graphs give you about this situation?
- For what number(s) of T-shirts is plan C_m less than plan C_n? ($C_m < C_n$)
- Show how you could use the two equations to find the coordinates of the point of intersection of the two lines ($C_m = C_n$).

At Fabulous Fabian's Bakery, the expenses E to make n cakes per month is given by the equation $E = 825 + 3.25n$.

The income I for selling n cakes is given by the equation $I = 8.20n$.

A. In the equations for I and E, what information do the y-intercepts represent? What about the coefficients of n?

B. Fabian sells 100 cakes in January.

   1. What are his expenses and his income?

   2. Does he make a profit? Describe how you found your answer.

C. In April, Fabian's expenses are $5,700.

   1. How many cakes does he sell?

   2. What is the income for producing this number of cakes?

   3. Does he make a profit? Explain.

D. The *break-even point* is when expenses equal income ($E = I$). Fabian thinks that this information is useful.

   1. Describe how you can find Fabian's break-even point symbolically. Find the break-even point.

   2. Describe another method for finding the break-even point.

ACE | **Homework starts on page 57.**

Applications

1. Ms. Chang's class decides to use the *Cool Tee's* company to make their T-shirts. The following equation represents the relationship between cost *C* and the number of T-shirts *n*.

$$C = 2n + 20$$

   a. The class wants to buy 25 T-shirts from *Cool Tee's*. Describe how you can use a table and a graph to find the cost for 25 T-shirts.

   b. Suppose the class has $80 to spend on T-shirts. Describe how you can use a table and a graph to find the number of T-shirts the class can buy.

   c. Sophia writes the following equation in her notebook:

$$C = 2(15) + 20$$

   What information is Sophia looking for?

   d. Elisa uses the coordinates (30, 80) to find information about the cost of the T-shirts. What information is she looking for?

2. The following equations represent some walkathon pledge plans.

   Plan 1: $14 = 2x$

   Plan 2: $y = 3.5(10) + 10$

   Plan 3: $100 = 1.5x + 55$

   In each equation, *y* is the amount owed in dollars, and *x* is the number of kilometers walked. For each equation:

   a. Tell what information is unknown.

   b. Describe how you could find the information.

3. Find the solution (the value of the variable for each equation).

   a. $y = 3(10) + 15$ **b.** $24 = x + 2$ **c.** $10 = 2x + 4$

Homework
Help Online
PHSchool.com

For: Help with Exercise 3
Web Code: ane-5303

4. Consider the equation: $y = 5x - 15$.

   a. Find *y* if $x = 1$.   **b.** Find *x* if $y = 50$.

   c. Describe how you can use a table or graph to answer parts (a) and (b).

For each situation in Exercises 5–8, find the number of coins in each pouch.

5.

6.

7.

8.

9. Rudo's grandfather gives Rudo $5 and then 50¢ for each math question he answers correctly on his math exams for the year.

   a. Write an equation that represents the amount of money that Rudo receives during a school year. Explain what the variables and numbers mean.

   b. Use the equation to find the number of correct answers Rudo needs to buy a new shirt that costs $25. Show your work.

   c. Rudo answered all 12 problems correctly on his first exam. How much money is he assured of receiving for the year? Show your work.

10. For each equation, sketch a picture using pouches and coins, and then determine how many coins are in a pouch.

   a. $3x = 12$ **b.** $2x + 5 = 19$

   c. $4x + 5 = 2x + 19$ **d.** $x + 12 = 2x + 6$

   e. $3(x + 4) = 18$

11. For parts (a) and (b), find the mystery number and explain your reasoning.

    a. If you add 15 to 3 times the mystery number, you get 78. What is the mystery number?

    b. If you subtract 27 from 5 times the mystery number, you get 83. What is the mystery number?

    c. Make up clues for a riddle whose mystery number is 9.

12. Use properties of equality and numbers to solve each equation for x. Check your answers.

    a. $7 + 3x = 5x + 13$ **b.** $3x - 7 = 5x + 13$

    c. $7 - 3x = 5x + 13$ **d.** $3x + 7 = 5x - 13$

13. **Multiple Choice** Which of the following is a solution to the equation $11 = -3x - 10$?

    A. 1.3   **B.** $-\dfrac{1}{3}$ **C.** -7 **D.** 24

14. Use properties of equality and numbers to solve each equation for x. Check your answers.

    a. $3x + 5 = 20$ **b.** $3x - 5 = 20$

    c. $3x + 5 = -20$ **d.** $-3x + 5 = 20$

    e. $-3x - 5 = -20$

For: Multiple-Choice Skills Practice
Web Code: ana-5354

15. Solve each equation. Check your answers.

    a. $3(x + 2) = 12$ **b.** $3(x + 2) = x - 18$

    c. $3(x + 2) = 2x$ **d.** $3(x + 2) = -15$

16. Two students' solutions to the equation $6(x + 4) = 3x - 2$ are shown. Both students made an error. Find the errors and give a correct solution.

Student 1	Student 2
$6(x + 4) = 3x - 2$	$6(x + 4) = 3x - 2$
$x + 4 = 3x - 2 - 6$	$6x + 4 = 3x - 2$
$x + 4 = 3x - 8$	$3x + 4 = -2$
$x + 4 + 8 = 3x - 8 + 8$	$3x + 4 - 4 = -2 - 4$
$x + 12 = 3x$	$3x = -6$
$12 = 2x$	$x = -2$ ✗
$x = 6$ ✗	

17. Two students' solutions to the equation $58.5 = 3.5x - 6$ are shown below. Both students made an error. Find the errors and give a correct solution.

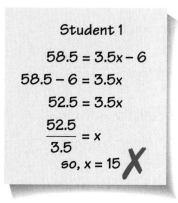

Student 1

$58.5 = 3.5x - 6$

$58.5 - 6 = 3.5x$

$52.5 = 3.5x$

$\dfrac{52.5}{3.5} = x$

so, $x = 15$ ✗

Student 2

$58.5 = 3.5x - 6$

$58.5 + 6 = 3.5x - 6 + 6$

$64.5 = 3.5x$

$\dfrac{64.5}{3.5} = \dfrac{3.5}{3.5}x$

so, $x \approx 1.84$ ✗

For Exercises 18 and 19, use the equation $y = 4 - 3x$.

18. Find y if

a. $x = 4$　　　　　　**b.** $x = -3$　　　　　　**c.** $x = 2$

d. $x = -\dfrac{4}{3}$　　　　**e.** $x = 0$

19. Find x when:

a. $y = 0$　　　　　　　　　**b.** $y = 21$

c. $y = -15$　　　　　　　　**d.** $y = 3.5$

20. Explain how the information you found for Exercises 18 and 19 relates to locating points on a line representing $y = 4 - 3x$.

21. Use the equation $P = 10 - 2.5c$.

a. Find P when $c = 3.2$.　　　　**b.** Find c when $P = 85$.

c. Describe how you can use a table or graph to answer parts (a) and (b).

22. Use the equation $m = 15.75 + 3.2d$.

a. Find m when:

i. $d = 20$　　　　　**ii.** $d = 0$　　　　　**iii.** $d = 3.2$

b. Find d when:

i. $m = 54.15$　　　**ii.** $m = 0$　　　　**iii.** $m = 100$

23. Forensic scientists can estimate a person's height by measuring the length of certain bones, including the femur, the tibia, the humerus, and the radius.

The table below gives equations for the relationships between the length of each bone and the estimated height of males and females. These relationships were found by scientists after much study and data collection.

In the table, F represents the length of the femur, T the length of the tibia, H the length of the humerus, R the length of the radius, and h the person's height. All measurements are in centimeters.

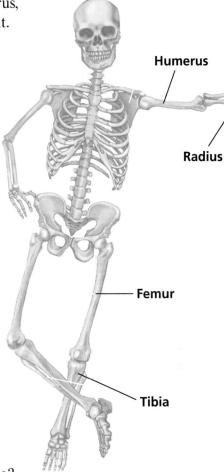

Humerus

Radius

Bone	Male	Female
Femur	$h = 69.089 + 2.238F$	$h = 61.412 + 2.317F$
Tibia	$h = 81.688 + 2.392T$	$h = 72.572 + 2.533T$
Humerus	$h = 73.570 + 2.970H$	$h = 64.977 + 3.144H$
Radius	$h = 80.405 + 3.650R$	$h = 73.502 + 3.876R$

a. About how tall is a female if her femur is 46.2 centimeters long?

b. About how tall is a male if his tibia is 50.1 centimeters long?

c. Suppose a woman is 152 centimeters tall. About how long is her femur? Her tibia? Her humerus? Her radius?

d. Suppose a man is 183 centimeters tall. About how long is his femur? His tibia? His humerus? His radius?

e. Describe what the graphs would look like for each equation. What do the x- and y-intercepts represent in this problem? Does this make sense? Why?

Femur

Tibia

24. The costs C and income I for making and selling T-shirts with a school logo are given by the equations $C = \$535 + 4.50n$ and $I = \$12n$, where n is the number of T-shirts.

    a. How many T-shirts must be bought and sold to break even? Explain.

    b. Suppose only 50 shirts are sold. Is there a profit or loss? Explain.

    c. Suppose the income is $1,200. Is there a profit or loss? Explain.

    d. i. For each equation, find the coordinates of a point that lies on the graph of the equation.

       ii. What information does this point give?

      iii. Describe how to use the equation to see that the point will be on the graph.

25. The International Links long-distance phone company charges no monthly fee but charges 18 cents per minute for long-distance calls. The World Connections long distance company charges $50 per month plus 10 cents per minute for long-distance calls. Compare the World Connections long-distance plan to that of International Links. Under what circumstances is it cheaper to use International Links? Explain your reasoning.

26. Students at Hammond Middle School are raising money for the end-of-year school party. They decide to sell roses for Valentine's Day. The students can buy the roses for 50 cents each from a wholesaler. They also need $60 to buy ribbon and paper to protect the roses as well as materials for advertising the sale. They sell each rose for $1.30.

    a. How many roses must they sell to break even? Explain.

    b. How much profit is there if they sell 50 roses? 100 roses? 200 roses?

27. Ruth considers two different cable television plans. Company A has a cost plan represented by the equation $C_A = 32N$, where N is the number of months she has the plan and C_A is the total cost. Company B has a cost plan represented by the equation $C_B = 36 + 26N$, where N is the number of months she is on the plan and C_B is the total cost.

   a. Graph both equations on the same axis.

   b. What is the point of intersection of the two graphs? What information does this give us?

Connections

28. Describe what operations are indicated in each expression, then write each expression as a single number.

   a. $-8(4)$
   b. $-2 \cdot 4$
   c. $6(-5) - 10$
   d. $2(-2) + 3(5)$

29. Decide whether each pair of quantities is equal. Explain.

   a. $6(5) + 2$ and $6(5 + 2)$
   b. $8 - 3x$ and $3x - 8$
   c. $4 + 5$ and $5 + 4$
   d. $-2(3)$ and $3(-2)$
   e. $3 - 5$ and $5 - 3$
   f. 2 quarters and 5 dimes
   g. 1.5 liters and 15 milliliters
   h. 2 out of 5 students prefer wearing sneakers to school and 50% of the students prefer wearing sneakers to school

30. a. Use your knowledge about fact families to write a related sentence for $n - (-3) = 30$. Does this related sentence make it easier to find the value for n? Why or why not?

   b. Write a related sentence for $5 + n = -36$. Does this related sentence make it easier to find the value for n? Why or why not?

31. Write two different expressions to represent the area of each rectangle.

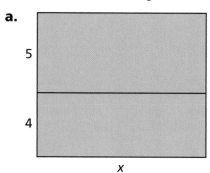

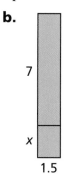

32. Find each quotient.

a. $\frac{12}{-3}$ **b.** $\frac{-12}{3}$ **c.** $\frac{-12}{-3}$ **d.** $\frac{0}{-10}$

e. $\frac{-5}{5}$ **f.** $\frac{5}{-5}$ **g.** $\frac{-5}{-5}$

33. Find the value of x that makes each equation true.

a. $3\frac{1}{2}x = \frac{3}{4}$ **b.** $3\frac{1}{2} = \frac{3}{4}x$

c. $\frac{7}{8}x = \frac{1}{8}$ **d.** $\frac{5}{6} = \frac{3}{4}x$

34. The sum S of the angles of a polygon with n sides is $S = 180(n - 2)$. Find the angle sum of each polygon.

a. triangle   **b.** quadrilateral   **c.** hexagon

d. decagon (10-sided polygon)

e. icosagon (20-sided polygon)

35. Suppose the polygons in Exercise 34 are regular polygons. Find the measure of an interior angle of each polygon.

36. How many sides does a polygon have if its angle sum is

a. 540 degrees   **b.** 1,080 degrees

37. The perimeter of each shape is 24 cm. Find the value of x.

a.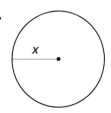

b.

c.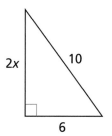

d. Find the area of each figure in parts (a)–(c).

38. World Connections long-distance phone company charges $50 per month plus 10¢ per minute for each call.

    a. Write an equation for the total monthly cost C for t minutes of long-distance calls.

    b. A customer makes $10\frac{1}{2}$ hours of long-distance calls in a month. How much is his bill for that month?

    c. A customer receives a $75 long-distance bill for last month's calls. How many minutes of long-distance calls did she make?

39. The number of times a cricket chirps in a minute is a function of the temperature. You can use the formula

$$n = 4t - 160$$

to determine the number of chirps n a cricket makes in a minute when the temperature is t degrees Fahrenheit. If you want to estimate the temperature by counting cricket chirps, you can use the following form of the equation:

$$t = \frac{1}{4}n + 40$$

    a. At 60°F, how many times does a cricket chirp in a minute?

    b. What is the temperature if a cricket chirps 150 times in a minute?

    c. At what temperature does a cricket stop chirping?

    d. Sketch a graph of the equation with number of chirps on the x-axis and temperature on the y-axis. What information do the y-intercept and the coefficient of n give you?

40. The higher the altitude, the colder the temperature. The formula $T = t - \frac{d}{150}$ is used to estimate the temperature T at different altitudes, where t is the ground temperature in degrees Celsius (Centigrade) and d is the altitude in meters.

    a. Suppose the ground temperature is 0 degrees Celsius. What is the temperature at an altitude of 1,500 meters?

    b. Suppose the temperature at 300 meters is 26 degrees Celsius. What is the ground temperature?

41. As a person ages beyond 30, his or her height can start to decrease by approximately 0.06 centimeter per year.

    a. Write an equation that represents a person's height h after the age of 30. Let t be the number of years beyond 30 and H be the height at age 30.

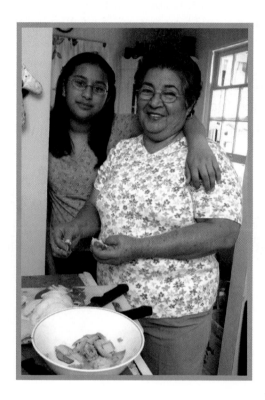

    b. Suppose a 60- to 70-year-old grandmother is 160 centimeters tall. About how tall was she at age 30? Explain how you found your answer.

    c. Suppose a basketball player is 6 feet, 6 inches tall on his thirtieth birthday. About how tall will he be at age 80? (Remember, 1 inch ≈ 2.54 centimeters.) Explain.

Extensions

42. The Small World long-distance phone company charges 55¢ for the first minute of a long-distance call and 23¢ for each additional minute.

   a. Write an equation for the total cost C of an m-minute long-distance call. Explain what your variables and numbers mean.

   b. How much does a 10-minute long-distance call cost?

   c. Suppose a call costs $4.55. How long does the call last?

43. The maximum weight allowed in an elevator is 1,500 pounds.

   a. The average weight per adult is 150 pounds, and the average weight per child is 40 pounds. Write an equation for the number of adults A and the number of children C the elevator can hold.

   b. Suppose ten children are in the elevator. How many adults can get in?

   c. Suppose six adults are in the elevator. How many children can get in?

44. Solve each equation for x. Check your answers.

   a. $5 - 2(x - 1) = 12$

   b. $5 + 2(x - 1) = 12$

   c. $5 - 2(x + 2) = 12$

   d. $5 - 2x + 2 = 12$

45. Solve each equation for x. Explain what your answers might mean.

   a. $2(x + 3) = 3x + 3$ **b.** $2(x + 3) = 2x + 6$

   c. $2(x + 3) = 2x + 3$

46. Wind can affect the speed of an airplane. Suppose a plane is flying round-trip from New York City to San Francisco. The plane has a cruising speed of 300 miles per hour. The wind is blowing from west to east at 30 miles per hour.

When the plane flies into (in the opposite direction of) the wind, its speed decreases by 30 miles per hour. When the plane flies with (in the same direction as) the wind, its speed increases by 30 miles per hour.

a. The distance between New York City and San Francisco is 3,000 miles. Make a table that shows the total time the plane has traveled after each 200-mile interval on its trip from New York City to San Francisco and back.

Airplane Flight Times

Distance (mi)	NYC to SF Time (h)	SF to NYC Time (h)
0	▦	▦
200	▦	▦
400	▦	▦
600	▦	▦
▦	▦	▦

b. For each direction, write an equation for the distance *d* traveled in *t* hours.

c. On the same set of axes, sketch graphs of the time and distance data for travel in both directions.

d. How long does it take a plane to fly 5,000 miles against a 30-mile-per-hour wind? With a 30-mile-per-hour wind? Explain how you found your answers.

Mathematical Reflections 3

In this investigation, you learned how to solve equations by operating on the symbols. These questions will help you summarize what you have learned.

Think about your answers to these questions. Discuss your ideas with other students and your teacher. Then, write a summary of your findings in your notebook.

1. Describe a symbolic method for solving a linear equation. Use an example to illustrate the method.

2. Compare the symbolic method for solving linear equations to the methods of using a table or graph.

Investigation 4

Exploring Slope

All of the patterns of change you have explored in this unit involved constant rates. For example, you worked with walking rates expressed as meters per second and pledge rates expressed as dollars per mile. In these situations, you found that the rate affects the following things:

- the steepness of the graph
- the coefficient, m, of x in the equation $y = mx + b$
- how the y-values in the table change for each unit change in the x-values

In this investigation, you will explore another way to express the constant rate.

4.1 Climbing Stairs

Climbing stairs is good exercise, so some athletes run up and down stairs as part of their training. The steepness of stairs determines how difficult they are to climb. By investigating the steepness of stairs you can find another important way to describe the steepness of a line.

Getting Ready for Problem 4.1

Consider these questions about the stairs you use at home, in your school, and in other buildings.

- How can you describe the steepness of the stairs?
- Is the steepness the same between any two consecutive steps?

Carpenters have developed the guidelines below to ensure that the stairs they build are relatively easy for a person to climb. Steps are measured in inches.

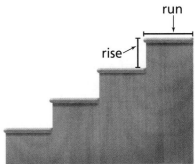

- The ratio of rise to run for each step should be between 0.45 and 0.60.

- The rise plus the run for each step should be between 17 and $17\frac{1}{2}$ inches.

The steepness of stairs is determined by the ratio of the rise to the run for each step. The rise and run are labeled in the diagram at the right.

<hr />

Problem 4.1 Using Rise and Run

A. 1. Determine the steepness of a set of stairs in your school or home. To calculate the steepness you will need to

- measure the rise and run of at least two steps in the set of stairs.

- make a sketch of the stairs, and label the sketch with the measurements you found.

- find the ratio of rise to run.

2. How do the stairs you measured compare to the carpenters' guidelines above?

B. A set of stairs is being built for the front of the new Arch Middle School. The ratio of rise to run is 3 to 5.

1. Is this ratio within the carpenters' guidelines?

2. Make a sketch of a set of stairs that meet this ratio. Label the lengths of the rise and run of a step.

3. Sketch the graph of a line that passes through the origin and whose y-values change by 3 units for each 5-unit change in the x-values.

4. Write an equation for the line in part (3).

   a. What is the coefficient of x in the equation?

   b. How is the coefficient related to the steepness of the line represented by the equation?

   c. How is the coefficient related to the steepness of a set of stairs with this ratio?

ACE Homework starts on page 78.

The method for finding the steepness of stairs suggests a way to find the steepness of a line. A line drawn from the bottom step of a set of stairs to the top step touches each step in one point. The rise and the run of a step are the vertical and the horizontal changes, respectively, between two points on the line.

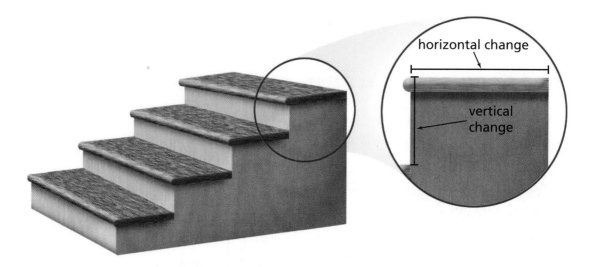

The steepness of the line is the ratio of rise to run, or vertical change to horizontal change, for this step. We call this ratio the **slope** of the line.

$$\text{slope} = \frac{\text{vertical change}}{\text{horizontal change}} \quad \text{or} \quad \frac{\text{rise}}{\text{run}}$$

Unlike the steepness of stairs, the slope of a line can be negative. To determine the slope of a line, you need to consider the direction, or sign, of the vertical and horizontal changes from one point to another. If vertical change is negative for positive horizontal change, the slope will be negative. Lines that slant *upward* from left to right have *positive slope*; lines that slant *downward* from left to right have *negative slope*.

- For each graph, describe how you can find the slope of the line.

**Line With
Positive Slope**

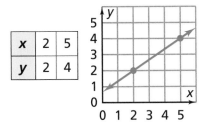

x	2	5
y	2	4

**Line With
Negative Slope**

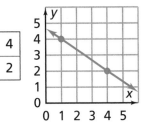

x	1	4
y	4	2

- The data in the table represent a linear relationship. Describe how you can find the slope of the line that represents the data.

x	−1	0	1	2	3	4
y	0	3	6	9	12	15

Information about a linear situation can be given in several different representations, such as a table, graph, equation, or verbal situation. These representations are useful in answering questions about linear situations.

How can we calculate the slope of a line from these representations?

A. The graphs, tables and equations all represent linear situations.

Graph 1	**Graph 2**
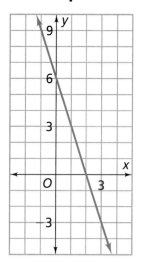	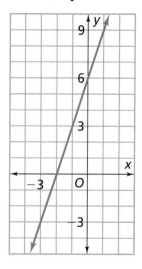

Table 1

x	−6	−4	−2	0	2	4
y	−10	−7	−4	−1	2	5

Table 2

x	1	2	3	4	5	6
y	4.5	4.0	3.5	3.0	2.5	2.0

Equation 1
$y = 2.5x + 5$

Equation 2
$y = 20 - 3x$

1. Find the slope and *y*-intercept of the line represented in each situation.

2. Write an equation for each graph and table.

B. The points $(3, 5)$ and $(-2, 10)$ lie on a line. Find two more points that lie on this line. Explain your method.

C. Compare your methods for finding the slope of a line from a graph, table, and equation.

ACE Homework starts on page 78.

4.3 Exploring Patterns With Lines

Your understanding of linear relationships can be used to explore some ideas about groups of lines.

Getting Ready for Problem

The slope of a line is 3.

- Sketch a line with this slope.
- Can you sketch a different line with this slope? Explain.

Problem 4.3 Exploring Patterns With Lines

A. Consider the two groups of lines shown below.

Group 1: $y = 3x$ $y = 5 + 3x$ $y = 10 + 3x$ $y = -5 + 3x$
Group 2: $y = -2x$ $y = 4 - 2x$ $y = 8 - 2x$ $y = -4 - 2x$

For each group:

1. What features do the equations have in common?

2. Graph each equation on the same coordinate axes. What patterns do you observe in the graphs?

3. Describe another group of lines that have the same pattern.

B. Consider the three pairs of lines shown below.

Pair 1: $y = 2x$ Pair 2: $y = 4x$ Pair 3: $y = -3x + 5$
$y = -\frac{1}{2}x$ $y = -0.25x$ $y = \frac{1}{3}x - 1$

For each pair:

1. What features do the equations have in common?

2. Graph each equation on the same coordinate axes. What patterns do you observe in the graphs?

3. Describe another pair of lines that have the same pattern.

C. Write equations for four lines that intersect to form the sides of a parallelogram. Explain what must be true about such lines.

D. Write equations for three lines that intersect to form a right triangle. Explain what must be true about such lines.

E. Describe how you can decide if two lines are parallel or perpendicular from the equations of the lines.

ACE Homework starts on page 78.

Pulling it All Together

Throughout this unit, you have learned several ways to represent linear relationships. You have also learned ways to move back and forth between these representations, tables, graphs, and equations to solve problems. The next problem pulls some of these ideas together.

Problem 4.4 Writing Equations With Two Variables

A. Anjelita's Birthday

Today is Anjelita's birthday. Her grandfather gave Anjelita some money as a birthday gift. Anjelita plans to put her birthday money in a safe place and add part of her allowance to it each week. Her sister, Maria, wants to know how much their grandfather gave her and how much of her allowance she is planning to save each week. As usual, Anjelita does not answer her sister directly. Instead, she wants her to figure out the answer for herself. She gives her these clues:

- After five weeks, I will have saved a total of $175.
- After eight weeks, I will have saved $190.

1. How much of her allowance is Anjelita planning to save each week?

2. How much birthday money did Anjelita's grandfather give her for her birthday?

3. Write an equation for the total amount of money A Anjelita will have saved after n weeks. What information do the y-intercept and coefficient of n represent in this context?

B. Converting Temperatures

Detroit, Michigan, is just across the Detroit River from the Canadian city of Windsor, Ontario. Because Canada uses the Celsius temperature scale, weather reports in Detroit often give temperatures in both degrees Fahrenheit and in degrees Celsius. The relationship between degrees Fahrenheit and degrees Celsius is linear.

Two important reference points for temperature are:

● Water freezes at 0°C, or 32°F.

● Water boils at 100°C, or 212°F.

1. Use this information to write an equation for the relationship between degrees Fahrenheit and degrees Celsius.

2. How did you find the *y*-intercept? What does the *y* -intercept tell you about this situation?

55° F	58° F	63° F	70° F	58° F
13° C	14° C	17° C	21° C	14° C
Mon	**Tues**	**Wed**	**Thurs**	**Fri**

ACE Homework starts on page 78.

Applications

1. Plans for a set of stairs for the front of a new community center use the ratio of rise to run of 2 units to 5 units.

   a. Are these stairs within carpenters' guidelines, which state that the ratio of rise to run should be between 0.45 and 0.60?

   b. Sketch a set of stairs that meets the rise-to-run ratio of 2 units to 5 units.

   c. Sketch the graph of a line where the y-values change by 2 units for each 5-unit change in the x-values.

   d. Write an equation for your line in part (c).

2. a. Find the horizontal distance and the vertical distance between the two points at the right.

   b. What is the slope of the line?

   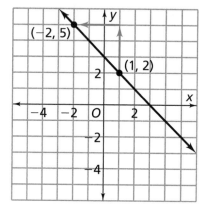

3. Seven possible descriptions of lines are listed below.

   i. positive slope   **ii.** negative slope

   iii. y-intercept equals 0   **iv.** passes through the point $(1, 2)$

   v. slope of zero   **vi.** positive y-intercept

   vii. negative y-intercept

For each equation, list *all* of the descriptions i–vii that describe the graph of that equation.

   a. $y = 2x$ **b.** $y = 3 - 3x$

   c. $y = 2x + 3$ **d.** $y = 5x - 3$

   e. $y = 2$

For Exercises 4–7, find the slope and the y-intercept of the line associated with the equation.

   4. $y = 10 + 3x$ **5.** $y = 0.5x$

   6. $y = -3x$ **7.** $y = -5x + 2$

In Exercises 8–12, the tables represent linear relationships. Give the slope and the y-intercept of the graph of each relationship. Then determine which of the five equations listed below fits each relationship.

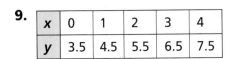

$y = 5 - 2x$ $y = 2x$ $y = -3x - 5$

$y = 2x - 1$ $y = x + 3.5$

8.

x	0	1	2	3	4
y	0	2	4	6	8

9.

x	0	1	2	3	4
y	3.5	4.5	5.5	6.5	7.5

10.

x	1	2	3	4	5
y	1	3	5	7	9

11.

x	0	1	2	3	4
y	5	3	1	−1	−3

12.

x	2	3	4	5	6
y	−11	−14	−17	−20	−23

13. **a.** Find the slope of the line represented by the equation
$y = x - 1$.

   b. Make a table of x- and y-values for the equation $y = x - 1$.
   How is the slope related to the table entries?

14. **a.** Find the slope of the line represented by the equation
$y = -2x + 3$.

   b. Make a table of x- and y-values for the equation $y = -2x + 3$.
   How is the slope related to the table entries?

15. In parts (a) and (b), the equations represent linear relationships.
Use the given information to find the value of b.

   a. The point $(1, 5)$ lies on the line representing $y = b - 3.5x$.

   b. The point $(0, -2)$ lies on the line representing $y = 5x - b$.

   c. What are the y-intercepts in the linear relationships in parts (a) and
   (b)? What are the patterns of change for the linear relationships in
   parts (a) and (b)?

   d. Find the x-intercepts for the linear relationships in parts (a) and (b).
   (The x-intercept is the point where the graph intersects the x-axis.)

For each pair of points in Exercises 16–19, do parts (a)–(e).

   a. Plot the points on a coordinate grid and draw a line through them.

   b. Find the slope of the line.

   c. Find the y-intercept from the graph. Explain how you found the
   y-intercept.

   d. Use your answers from parts (b) and (c) to write an equation for
   the line.

   e. Find one more point that lies on the line.

16. $(0, 0)$ and $(3, 3)$ 17. $(-1, 1)$ and $(3, -3)$

18. $(0, -5)$ and $(-2, -3)$ 19. $(3, 6)$ and $(5, 6)$

For Exercises 20–22, determine which of the linear relationships A–K fit each description.

A.
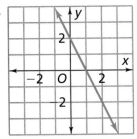

B.
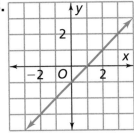

C.
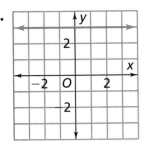

D.
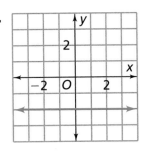

E.
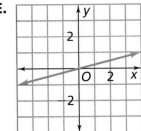

F.

x	−3	−2	−1	0
y	7	5	3	1

G.

x	−4	−2	−1	0
y	2	2	2	2

H. $y = 1.5$ **J.** $y = -5 + 3x$ **K.** $y = 4 + -2x$

20. The line representing this relationship has positive slope.

21. The line representing this relationship has a slope of −2.

22. The line representing this relationship has a slope of 0.

23. Decide which graph from Exercises 20–22 matches each equation.

   a. $y = x - 1$ **b.** $y = -2$ **c.** $y = \frac{1}{4}x$

Go Online
PHSchool.com

For: Multiple-Choice Skills Practice
Web Code: ana-5454

For each equation in Exercises 24–26, do parts (a)–(d).

24. $y = x$ **25.** $y = 2x - 2$ **26.** $y = -0.5x + 2$

   a. Make a table of x- and y-values for the equation.

   b. Sketch a graph of the equation.

   c. Find the slope of the line.

   d. Make up a problem that can be represented by each equation.

27. a. Graph a line with slope 3.

     i.   Find two points on your line.

     ii. Write an equation for the line.

   b. On the same set of axes, graph a line with slope $-\frac{1}{3}$.

     i.   Find two points on your line.

     ii. Write an equation for the line.

   c. Compare the two graphs you made in parts (a) and (b).

28. Use the line in the graph below to answer each question.

   a. Find the equation for a line that is parallel to this line.

   b. Find the equation of a line that is perpendicular to this line.

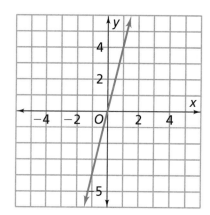

29. Descriptions of three possible lines are listed below.

   • a line that *does not* pass through the first quadrant

   • a line that passes through exactly two quadrants

   • a line that passes through only one quadrant

   a. For each, decide whether such a line exists. Explain.

   b. If a line exists, what must be true about the equation of the line that satisfies the conditions?

   c. Sketch a graph, then write the equation of the line next to the graph.

30. a. Find the slope of each line. Then, write an equation for the line.

i.

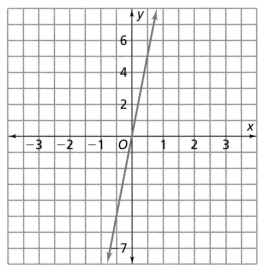

ii.

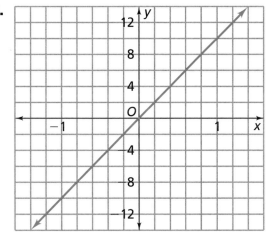

iii.

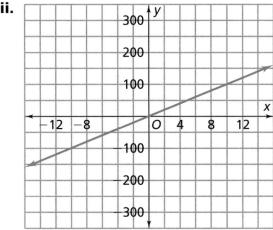

b. Compare the slopes of the three lines.

c. How are the three graphs similar? How are they different?

31. The slopes of two lines are the negative reciprocal of each other. For example:

$$y = 2x \qquad \text{and} \qquad y = -\frac{1}{2}x$$

What must be true about the two lines? Is your conjecture true if the y-intercept of either equation is not zero? Explain.

32. At noon, the temperature is 30°F. For the next several hours, the temperature falls by an average of 3°F an hour.

   a. Write an equation for the temperature T, n hours after noon.

   b. What is the y-intercept of the line the equation represents? What does the y-intercept tell us about this situation?

   c. What is the slope of the line the equation represents? What does the slope tell us about this situation?

33. Natasha never manages to make her allowance last for a whole week, so she borrows money from her sister. Suppose Natasha borrows 50 cents every week.

   a. Write an equation for the amount of money m Natasha owes her sister after n weeks.

   b. What is the slope of the graph of the equation from part (a)?

34. In 1990, the small town of Cactusville was destined for obscurity. However, due to hard work by its city officials, it began adding manufacturing jobs at a fast rate. As a result, the city's population grew 239% from 1990 to 2000. The population of Cactusville in 2000 was 37,000.

   a. What was the population of Cactusville in 1990?

   b. Suppose the same rate of population increase continues. What might the population be in the year 2010?

35. James and Shani share a veterinary practice. They each make farm visits two days a week. They take cellular phones on these trips to keep in touch with the office. James makes his farm visits on weekdays. His cellular phone rate is $14.95 a month plus $0.50 a minute. Shani makes her visits on Saturday and Sunday and is charged a weekend rate of $34 a month.

   a. Write an equation for each billing plan.

   b. Is it possible for James's cellular phone bill to be more than Shani's? Explain how you know this.

   c. Suppose James and Shani made the same number of calls in the month of May. Is it possible for James's and Shani's phone bills to be for the same amount? If so, how many minutes of phone calls would each person have to make for their bills to be equal?

   d. Shani finds another phone company that offers one rate for both weekday and weekend calls. The billing plan for this company can be expressed by the equation $A = 25 + 0.25m$, where A is the total monthly bill and m is the number of minutes of calls. Compare this billing plan with the other two plans.

Connections

36. In Europe, many hills have signs indicating their steepness, or slope. Two examples are shown at the right.

   On a coordinate grid, sketch hills with each of these slopes.

37. Solve each equation and check your answers.

   a. $2x + 3 = 9$

   b. $\frac{1}{2}x + 3 = 9$

   c. $x + 3 = \frac{9}{2}$

   d. $x + \frac{1}{2} = 9$

   e. $\frac{x + 3}{2} = 9$

38. Use properties of equality and numbers to solve each equation for x. Check your answers.

   a. $3 + 6x = 4x + 9$

   b. $6x + 3 = 4x + 9$

   c. $6x - 3 = 4x + 9$

   d. $3 - 6x = 4x + 9$

39. Use the graph to answer each question.

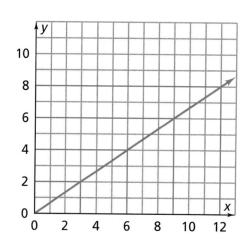

a. Are any of the rectangles in the picture above similar? If so, which rectangles, and explain why they are similar.

b. Find the slope of the diagonal line. How is it related to the similar rectangles?

c. Which of these rectangles belong to the set of rectangles in the graph? Explain.

40. The graph below shows the height of a rocket from 10 seconds before liftoff through 7 seconds after liftoff.

a. Describe the relationship between the height of the rocket and time.

b. What is the slope for the part of the graph that is a straight line? What does this slope represent in this situation?

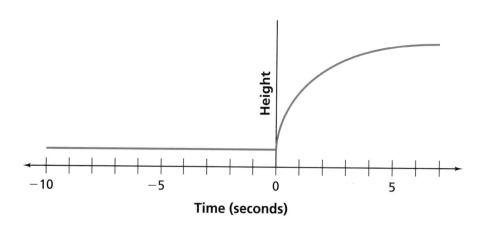

41. Solve each equation. Check your answers.

    a. $2(x + 5) = 18$ **b.** $2(x + 5) = x - 8$

    c. $2(x + 5) = x$ **d.** $2(x + 5) = -15$

42. Multiple Choice Which equation has a graph that contains the point $(-1, 6)$?

    A. $y = 4x + 1$ **B.** $y = -x + 5$ **C.** $y = 3x - 11$ **D.** $y = -3x + 11$

43. Each pair of figures is similar. Find the lengths of the sides marked x.

    a.

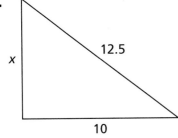

    b.

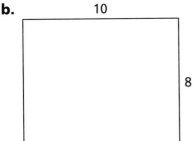

44. Find a value of n that will make each statement true.

    a. $\dfrac{n}{10} = \dfrac{3}{2}$ **b.** $\dfrac{5}{6} = \dfrac{n}{18}$ **c.** $-\dfrac{4}{6} = \dfrac{n}{3}$ **d.** $\dfrac{5}{18} = \dfrac{20}{n}$

    e. Write an equation for a line whose slope is $-\dfrac{4}{6}$.

45. Find a value of n that will make each statement true.

    a. $15\%(90) = n$ **b.** $20\%(n) = 80$ **c.** $n\%(50) = 5$

Extensions

46. On a March flight from Boston to Detroit, a monitor displayed the altitude and the outside air temperature. Two passengers that were on that flight tried to find a formula for temperature t in degrees Fahrenheit at an altitude of a feet above sea level. One passenger said the formula was $t = 46 - 0.003a$, and the other said it was $t = 46 + 0.003a$.

   a. Which formula makes more sense to you? Why?

   b. The Detroit Metropolitan Airport is 620 feet above sea level. Use the formula you chose in part (a) to find the temperature at the airport on that day.

   c. Does the temperature you found in part (b) seem reasonable? Why or why not?

47. Andy's track team decides to convert their running rates from miles per hour to kilometers per hour (1 mile $\approx$ 1.6 kilometers).

   a. Which method would you use to help the team do their converting: graph, table, or equation? Explain why you chose your method.

   b. One of Andy's teammates said that he could write an equation for his spreadsheet program that could convert any team member's running rate from miles per hour to kilometers per hour. Write an equation that each member could use for this conversion.

Mathematical Reflections 4

In this investigation, you learned about the slope, or steepness, of a line. You learned how slope is related to an equation of the line and to a table or a graph of the equation. These questions will help you summarize what you have learned.

Think about your answers to these questions. Discuss your ideas with other students and your teacher. Then, write a summary of your findings in your notebook.

1. Explain what the slope of a line is. How does finding slope compare to finding the rate of change between two variables in a linear relationship?

2. How can you find the slope of a line from
   a. an equation?
   b. a graph?
   c. a table of values of the line?
   d. the coordinates of two points on the line?

3. For parts (a) and (b), explain how you can write an equation of a line from the information. Use examples to illustrate your thinking.
   a. the slope and the *y*-intercept of the line
   b. two points on the line

Unit Project

Conducting an Experiment

In many situations, patterns become apparent only after sufficient data are collected, organized, and displayed. Your group will be carrying out one of these experiments.

- In Project 1, you will investigate the rate at which a leaking faucet loses water.

- In Project 2, you will investigate how the drop height of a ball is related to its bounce height.

You will examine and use the patterns in the data collected from these experiments to make predictions.

Project 1: Wasted Water Experiment

In this experiment, you will simulate a leaking faucet and collect data about the volume of water lost at 5-second intervals. You will then use the patterns in your results to predict how much water is wasted when a faucet leaks for one month. Read the directions carefully before you start. Be prepared to explain your findings to the rest of the class.

Materials:

a styrofoam or paper cup

water

a paper clip

a clear measuring container (such as a graduated cylinder)

a watch or clock with a second hand

Directions:

Divide the work among the members of your group.

1. Make a table with columns for recording time and the amount of water lost. Fill in the time column with values from 0 seconds to 60 seconds in 5-second intervals (that is, 5, 10, 15, and so on).

2. Use the paper clip to punch a hole in the bottom of the paper cup. Cover the hole with your finger.

3. Fill the cup with water.

4. Hold the paper cup over the measuring container.

5. When you are ready to begin timing, uncover the hole so that the water drips into the measuring container, simulating the leaky faucet.

6. Record the amount of water in the measuring container at 5-second intervals for a minute.

Use this experiment to write an article for your local paper, trying to convince the people in your town to conserve water and fix leaky faucets. In your article, include the following information:

- a coordinate graph of the data you collected

- a description of the variables you investigated in this experiment and a description of the relationship between the variables

- a list showing your predictions for:

  - the amount of water that would be wasted in 15 seconds, 2 minutes, in 2.5 minutes, and in 3 minutes if a faucet dripped at the same rate as your cup does

  - how long it would it take for the container to overflow if a faucet dripped into the measuring container at the same rate as your cup

  Explain how you made your predictions. Did you use the table, the graph, or some other method? What clues in the data helped you?

- a description of other variables, besides time, that affect the amount of water in the measuring container

- a description of how much water would be wasted in one month if a faucet leaked at the same rate as your paper cup. Explain how you made your predictions

- the cost of the water wasted by a leaking faucet in one month (To do this, you will need to find out how much water costs in your area. Then, use this information to figure out the cost of the wasted water.)

Project 2: Ball Bounce Experiment

In this experiment, you will investigate how the height from which a ball is dropped is related to the height it bounces. Read the directions carefully before you start. Be prepared to explain your findings to the rest of the class.

Materials:

a meter stick

a ball that bounces

Directions:

Divide the work among the members of your group.

1. Make a table with columns for recording drop height and bounce height.

2. Hold the meter stick perpendicular to a flat surface, such as an uncarpeted floor, a table, or a desk.

3. Choose and record a height on the meter stick as the height from which you will drop the ball. Hold the ball so that either the top of the ball or the bottom of the ball is at this height.

4. Drop the ball and record the height of the first bounce. If the *top* of the ball was at your starting height, look for the height of the *top* of the ball. If the *bottom* of the ball was at your starting height, look for the height of the *bottom* of the ball. (You may have to do this several times before you feel confident you have a good estimate of the bounce height.)

5. Repeat this for several different starting heights.

After you have done completed the experiment, write a report that includes the following:

- a coordinate graph of the data you collected

- a description of the variables you investigated in this experiment and a description of the relationship between the variables

- a list showing your predictions for

  (a) the bounce height for a drop height of 2 meters

  (b) the drop height needed for a bounce height of 2 meters

- a description of how you made your prediction, whether you used a table, a graph, or some other method, and the clues in the data that helped you make your predictions

- an explanation of the bounce height you would expect for a drop height of 0 centimeters and where you could find this on the graph

- a description of any other variables besides the drop height, which may affect the bounce height of the ball

Looking Back and Looking Ahead

In the problems of this unit, you explored many examples of *linear relationships* between variables. You learned how to recognize linear patterns in *graphs* and in *tables* of numerical data and how to express those patterns in words and in symbolic *equations* or *formulas*. Most importantly, you learned how to study tables, graphs, and equations to answer questions about linear relationships.

Go Online
PHSchool.com

For: Vocabulary Review Puzzle
Web Code: anj-5051

Use Your Understanding: Algebraic Reasoning

Test your understanding of linear relationships by solving the following problems about the operation of a movie theater.

1. Suppose that a theater charges a school group $4.50 per student to show a special film. Suppose that the theater's operating expenses include $130 for the staff and a film rental fee of $1.25 per student.

   a. What equation relates the number of students x to the theater's income I?

   b. What equation relates the theater's operating expenses E to x?

   c. Copy and complete the table below.

   Theater Income and Expenses

Number of Students, x	0	10	20	30	40	50	60	70
Income, I ($)	■	■	■	■	■	■	■	■
Expenses, E ($)	■	■	■	■	■	■	■	■

   d. On the same set of axes, graph the theater's income and operating expenses for any number of students from 0 to 100.

   e. Describe the patterns by which income and operating increase as the number of students increases.

   f. Write and solve an equation whose solution will answer the question "How many students need to attend the movie so that the theater's income will equal its operating expenses?"

2. At another theater, the income and expenses combine to give the equation $y = 3x - 115$ relating operating profit y to the number of students in a group x.

a. What do the numbers 3 and -115 tell about

   i. the relation between the number of students in a group and the theater's profit?

   ii. the pattern of entries that would appear in a table of sample (*students, profit*) pairs?

   iii. a graph of the relation between the number of students and the profit?

b. Use the equation to find the number of students necessary for the theater to

   i. break even (make 0 profit).

   ii. make a profit of $100.

c. Write and solve an equation that will find the number of students for which the theaters in Problem 1 and Problem 2 will make the same profit. Then find the amount of that profit.

Explain Your Reasoning

When you use mathematical calculations to solve a problem or make a decision, it is important to be able to justify each step in your reasoning. For Problems 1 and 2:

3. Consider the variables and relationships.

   a. What are the variables?

   b. Which pairs of variables are related to each other?

   c. In each pair of related variables, how does change in the value of one variable cause change in the value of the other?

4. Which relationships are linear and which are not? What patterns in the tables, graphs, and symbolic equations support your conclusions?

5. For those relationships that are linear, what do the slopes and intercepts of the graphs indicate about the relationships involved?

6. How do the slopes and intercepts relate to data patterns in the various tables of values?

7. Consider the strategies for solving linear equations such as those in Problem 1, part (f), and Problem 2, part (c).

  a. How can the equations be solved using tables of values?

  b. How can you solve those equations by using graphs?

  c. How can you solve the equations by reasoning about the equations alone?

8. Suppose you were asked to write a report describing the relationships among number of students, theater income, and operating costs. What value might be gained by including the table? Including the graph? Including the equation? What are the limitations of each type of display?

Look Ahead

Examples of linear relationships and equations arise in many situations, but there are also important nonlinear relationships such as inverse, exponential, and quadratic. The algebraic ideas and techniques you've used in this unit are useful in problems of science and business. They will be applied and extended to other relationships in future units of Connected Mathematics such as *Thinking With Mathematical Models* and *Say It With Symbols*.

C

coefficient A number that is multiplied by a variable in an equation or expression. In a linear equation of the form $y = mx + b$, the number m is the coefficient of x as well as the slope of the line. For example, in the equation $y = 3x + 5$, the coefficient of x is 3. This is also the slope of the line.

coeficiente Un número que se multiplica por una variable en una ecuación o expresión. En una ecuación de la forma $y = mx + b$, el número m es el coeficiente de x y la inclinación de la recta. Por ejemplo, en la ecuación $y = 3x + 5$, el coeficiente de x es 3. También representa la pendiente de la recta.

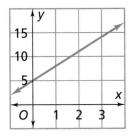

constant term A number in an equation that is not multiplied by a variable, or an amount added to or subtracted from the terms involving variables. In an equation of the form $y = mx + b$, the y-intercept, b, is a constant term. The effect of the constant term on a graph is to raise or lower the graph. The constant term in the equation $y = 3x + 5$ is 5. The graph of $y = 3x$ is raised vertically 5 units to give the graph of $y = 3x + 5$.

término constante Un número en una ecuación que no se multiplica por una variable, o una cantidad sumada o restada a los términos que contienen variables. En una ecuación de la forma $y = mx + b$, el punto de intersección de y, b, es un término constante. El término constante hace que la gráfica suba o baje. El término constante en la ecuación $y = 3x + 5$ es 5. Para obtener la gráfica de $y = 3x + 5$, la gráfica $y = 3x$ se sube 5 unidades sobre el eje vertical.

coordinate pair A pair of numbers of the form (x, y) that gives the location of a point in the coordinate plane. The x term gives the distance left or right from the origin $(0, 0)$, and the y term gives the distance up or down from the origin.

par de coordenadas Un par de números con la forma (x, y) que determina la ubicación de un punto en el plano de las coordenadas. El término x determina la distancia hacia la derecha o izquierda desde el punto de origen $(0, 0)$, y el término y determina la distancia hacia arriba o abajo desde el punto de origen.

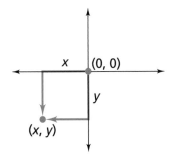

function A relationship between two variables in which the value of one variable depends on the value of the other variable. For example, the distance *d* in miles covered in *t* hours by a car traveling at 55 mph is given by the equation $d = 55t$. The relationship between distance and the time is a function, and we say that the distance is a *function* of the time. This function is a *linear function*, and its graph is a straight line whose slope is 55. In future units, you will learn about functions that are not linear.

función Una relación entre dos variables en la que el valor de una variable depende del valor de la otra. Por ejemplo, la distancia, *d*, recorrida en un número de *t* horas por un automóvil que viaja a 55 mph está representada por la ecuación $d = 55t$. La relación entre la distancia y el tiempo es una función, y decimos que la distancia es una *función* del tiempo. Esta función es una *función lineal* y se representa gráficamente como una línea recta con una pendiente de 55. En las próximas unidades vas a estudiar relaciones que no son lineales.

intersecting lines Lines that cross or *intersect*. The coordinates of the point where the lines intersect are solutions to the equations for both lines. The graphs of the equations $y = x$ and $y = 2x - 3$ intersect at the point (3, 3). This number pair is a solution to each equation.

rectas secantes Rectas que se cruzan o *intersectan*. Las coordenadas del punto del punto de intersección de las rectas son la solución de las ecuaciones de las dos rectas. Las gráficas de las ecuaciones $y = x$ e $y = 2x - 3$ se cortan en el punto (3, 3). Este par de números es la solución de las dos ecuaciones.

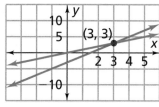

linear function See *function*.

función lineal Ver *función*.

linear relationship A relationship in which there is a constant rate of change between two variables; for each unit increase in one variable, there is a constant change in the other variable. For example, as *x* changes by a constant amount, *y* changes by a constant amount. A linear relationship between two variables can be represented by a straight-line graph and by an equation of the form $y = mx + b$. The rate of change is *m*, the coefficient of *x*. For example, if you save \$2 each month, the relationship between the amount you save and the number of months is a linear relationship that can be represented by the equation $y = 2x$. The constant rate of change is 2.

relación lineal Una relación en la que hay una tasa de variación constante entre dos variables; por cada unidad que aumenta una variable, hay una variación constante en la otra variable. Por ejemplo, a medida que *x* cambia una cantidad constante, *y* cambia en una cantidad constante. Una relación lineal entre dos variables puede representarse con una gráfica de línea recta y con una ecuación de la forma $y = mx + b$. La tasa de variación es *m*, el coeficiente de *x*. Por ejemplo, si ahorras \$2 por mes, la relación entre la cantidad que ahorras por mes y el número de meses es una relación lineal que puede representarse con la ecuación $y = 2x$. La tasa de variación constante es 2.

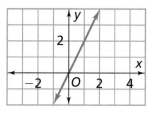

origin The point where the *x*- and *y*-axes intersect on a coordinate graph. With coordinates $(0, 0)$, the origin is the center of the coordinate plane.

origen El punto en que los ejes de las *x* y las *y* se cortan en una gráfica de coordenadas. Si las coordenadas son $(0, 0)$, el origen se halla en el centro del plano de las coordenadas.

point of intersection The point where two lines intersect. If the lines are represented on a coordinate grid, the coordinates for the point of intersection can be read from the graph.

punto de intersección El punto donde dos rectas se intersecan. Si las rectas están representadas en una cuadrícula de coordenadas, las coordenadas del punto de intersección se pueden leer de la gráfica.

properties of equality For all real numbers, *a*, *b*, and *c*:
Addition: If $a = b$, then $a + c = b + c$.
Subtraction: If $a = b$, then $a - c = b - c$.
Multiplication: If $a = b$, then $a \cdot c = b \cdot c$.
Division: If $a = b$, and $c \neq 0$, then $\frac{a}{c} = \frac{b}{c}$.

propiedades de una igualdad Para todos los números reales *a*, *b*, y *c*:
Suma: Si $a = b$, entonces $a + c = b + c$.
Resta: Si $a = b$, entonces $a - c = b - c$.
Multiplicación: Si $a = b$, entonces $a \cdot c = b \cdot c$.
División: Si $a = b$, y $c \neq 0$, entonces $\frac{a}{c} = \frac{b}{c}$.

rise The vertical change between two points on a graph. The slope of a line is the rise divided by the run.

alzada La variación vertical entre dos puntos en la gráfica. La inclinación de una recta es la alzada dividida por la huella.

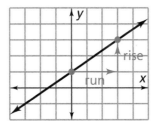

run The horizontal change between two points on a graph. The slope of a line is the rise divided by the run.

huella La variación horizontal entre dos puntos en la gráfica. La pendiente de una recta es la alzada dividida por la huella.

scale The distance between two consecutive tick marks on the *x*- and *y*-axes of a coordinate grid. When graphing, an appropriate scale must be selected so that the resulting graph will be clearly shown. For example, when graphing the equation $y = 60x$, a scale of 1 for the *x*-axis and a scale of 15 or 30 for the *y*-axis would be reasonable.

escala La distancia entre dos marcas consecutivas en los ejes *x* e *y* de una cuadrícula de coordenadas. Cuando se realiza una gráfica, se debe seleccionar una escala apropiada de manera que represente con claridad la gráfica resultante. Por ejemplo, para la representación gráfica de la ecuación $y = 60x$, una escala razonable resultaría 1 para el eje de *x* y una escala de 15 ó 30 para el eje de *y*.

slope The number that expresses the steepness of a line. The slope is the ratio of the vertical change to the horizontal change between any two points on the line. Sometimes this ratio is referred to as *the rise over the run*. The slope of a horizontal line is 0. Slopes are positive if the *y*-values increase from left to right on a coordinate grid and negative if the *y*-values decrease from left to right. The slope of a vertical line is undefined. The slope of a line is the same as the constant rate of change between the two variables. For example, the points $(0, 0)$ and $(3, 6)$ lie on the graph of $y = 2x$. Between these points, the vertical change is 6 and the horizontal change is 3, so the slope is $\frac{6}{3} = 2$, which is the coefficient of *x* in the equation.

pendiente El número que expresa la inclinación de una recta. La pendiente es la razón entre la variación vertical y la horizontal entre dos puntos cualesquiera de la recta. A veces a esta razón se *la denomina alzada sobre huella*. La pendiente de una recta horizontal es 0. Las pendientes son positivas si los valores de *y* aumentan de izquierda a derecha en una cuadrícula de coordenadas, y negativas si los valores de *y* decrecen de izquierda a derecha. La pendiente de una recta vertical es indefinida. La pendiente de una recta es igual a la tasa de variación constante entre dos variables. Por ejemplo, los puntos $(0, 0)$ y $(3, 6)$ están representados en la gráfica de $y = 2x$. Entre estos puntos, la variación vertical es 6 y la variación horizontal es 3, de manera que la pendiente es $\frac{6}{3} = 2$, que es el coeficiente de x en la ecuación.

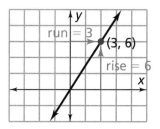

x-intercept The point where a graph crosses the *x*-axis. The *x*-intercept of the equation $y = 3x + 5$ is $\left(-\frac{5}{3}, 0\right)$ or $-\frac{5}{3}$.

punto de intersección de x El punto en el que la gráfica corta el eje de las *x*. El punto de intersección de x de la ecuación $y = 3x + 5$ es $\left(-\frac{5}{3}, 0\right)$ ó $-\frac{5}{3}$.

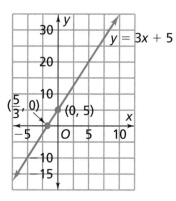

y-intercept The point where the graph crosses the *y*-axis. In a linear equation of the form $y = mx + b$, the *y*-intercept is the constant, *b*. In the graph above, the *y*-intercept is $(0, 5)$, or 5.

punto de intersección de y El punto en el que la gráfica corta el eje de las *y*. En una ecuación lineal de la forma $y = mx + b$, el punto de intersección de *y* es la constante, *b*. En la gráfica anterior, el punto de intersección de *y* es $(0, 5)$ ó 5.

Index

Acknowledgments

Team Credits

The people who made up the **Connected Mathematics 2** team—representing editorial, editorial services, design services, and production services—are listed below. Bold type denotes core team members.

Leora Adler, Judith Buice, Kerry Cashman, Patrick Culleton, Sheila DeFazio, Richard Heater, **Barbara Hollingdale, Jayne Holman,** Karen Holtzman, **Etta Jacobs,** Christine Lee, Carolyn Lock, Catherine Maglio, **Dotti Marshall,** Rich McMahon, Eve Melnechuk, Kristin Mingrone, Terri Mitchell, **Marsha Novak,** Irene Rubin, Donna Russo, Robin Samper, Siri Schwartzman, **Nancy Smith,** Emily Soltanoff, **Mark Tricca,** Paula Vergith, Roberta Warshaw, Helen Young

Additional Credits

Diana Bonfilio, Mairead Reddin, Michael Torocsik, nSight, Inc.

Technical Illustration

WestWords, Inc.

Cover Design

tom white.images

Photos

2 t, Joe Carini/The Image Works; **2 b,** David Young-Wolff/Alamy; **3,** Zoran Milich/Masterfile; **11,** Siri Schwartzman; **13,** David Stoecklein/Corbis; **18,** Martin Bureau/AFP/Getty Images, Inc.; **22,** Blasius Erlinger/Getty Images, Inc.; **24,** Mark Leibowitz/Masterfile; **25,** Joe Carini/The Image Works; **26,** Michael Steele/Getty Images, Inc.; **28,** Don Tremain/Getty Images, Inc.; **32,** David Young-Wolff/Photo Edit; **33,** Robert W. Ginn/PhotoEdit; **34,** AP Photo/The Paris News, Bill Ridder; **36,** Andrew Olney/Masterfile; **42,** Larry Williams/Corbis; **47,** Richard Haynes; **53,** Richard Haynes; **56,** AP Photo/The Plain Dealer, Chris Stephens; **62,** Royalty-Free/Corbis; **66,** Michael Newman/Photo Edit; **68,** Mike Dembeck/AFP/Getty Images, Inc.; **70,** Russ Schleipman/Index Stock Imagery, Inc.; **73,** Richard Haynes; **76,** David Young-Wolff/Alamy; **78,** OnRequest Images, Inc./Alamy; **85 l,** Powered by Light/Alan Spencer/Alamy; **85 r,** Ian Connellan/Lonely Planet Images; **88,** Bob Daemmrich/The Image Works; **93,** Royalty-Free/Corbis

Connected Mathematics 2™

Filling and Wrapping

Three-Dimensional Measurement

Glenda Lappan
James T. Fey
William M. Fitzgerald
Susan N. Friel
Elizabeth Difanis Phillips

PEARSON

Prentice
Hall

Boston, Massachusetts
Upper Saddle River, New Jersey

Filling and Wrapping

Three-Dimensional Measurement

Baseballs, basketballs, and soccer balls are spheres, but they often come in boxes shaped liked cubes. Why do you think balls are packaged in this way?

A popcorn vendor needs to order popcorn boxes. A rectangular box has a height of 20 centimeters and a square base with 12-centimeter sides. A cylindrical box has a height of 20 centimeters and a diameter of 12 centimeters. Which box will hold the most popcorn?

A rectangular compost box with dimensions 1 foot by 2 feet by 3 feet can decompose 0.5 pounds of garbage a day. Describe the dimensions of a box that will decompose 1 pound of garbage a day.

The way a product is packaged is important. Stores are filled with interesting three-dimensional shapes such as boxes, cans, bags, and bottles. A unique shape can attract shoppers to take a closer look at the product. When a company plans the packaging for a product, it must consider several questions, including how much of the product should be sold in each package; what and how much material is needed to make the package; and what package design is best for the product.

Thinking about how products are packaged can make you a smarter consumer. You can usually save money by comparing the cost of products in different-sized packages.

In this unit, you will look at two different measures involved in three-dimensional shapes. You will explore how much material it takes to *fill* a shape and how much material is needed to *wrap* a shape. As you work through the investigations, you will consider questions like those on the opposite page.

Mathematical Highlights

In *Filling and Wrapping*, **you will explore surface area and volume of objects, especially rectangular prisms, cylinders, cones, and spheres.**

You will learn how to

- Understand volume as a measure of *filling* an object and surface area as a measure of *wrapping* an object
- Develop strategies for finding the volume and surface area of objects including rectangular prisms and cylinders
- Develop strategies for finding the volume of square pyramids, cones, and spheres
- Explore patterns among the volumes of cylinders, cones, and spheres
- Design and use nets for rectangular prisms and cylinders to calculate surface areas of prisms and cylinders
- Understand that three-dimensional figures may have the same volume but different surface areas
- Investigate the effects of varying dimensions of rectangular prisms and cylinders on volume and surface area
- Recognize and solve problems involving volume and surface area

As you work on problems in this unit, ask yourself questions about volume and surface area.

What quantities are involved in the problem? Which measures of an object are involved—volume or surface area?

Is an exact answer required?

What method should I use to determine these measures?

What strategies or formulas might help?

Investigation 1

Building Boxes

The most common type of package is the rectangular box. Rectangular boxes contain everything from cereal to shoes and from pizza to paper clips. Most rectangular boxes begin as flat sheets of cardboard, which are cut and then folded into a box shape.

1.1 Making Cubic Boxes

Some boxes are shaped like cubes. A **cube** is a three-dimensional shape with six identical square faces.

What kinds of things might be packaged in cubic boxes?

The boxes you will work with in this problem are shaped like unit cubes. A **unit cube** is a cube with edges that are 1 unit long. For example, cubes that are 1 inch on each edge are called inch cubes. Cubes that are 1 centimeter on each edge are called centimeter cubes.

In this problem, you will make nets that can be folded to form boxes. A **net** is a two-dimensional pattern that can be folded to form a three-dimensional figure. The diagram below shows one possible net for a cubic box.

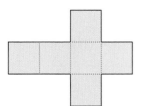
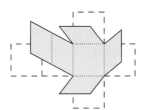

Problem 1.1 Making Cubic Boxes

On grid paper, draw nets that can be folded to make a unit cube.

A. How many different nets can you make that will fold into a box shaped like a unit cube?

B. What is the total area of each net, in square units?

ACE Homework starts on page 10.

1.2 Making Rectangular Boxes

Many boxes are not shaped like cubes. The rectangular box below has square ends, but the remaining faces are non-square rectangles.

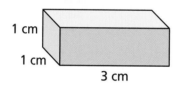

1 cm
1 cm
3 cm

Problem 1.2 Making Rectangular Boxes

A. On grid paper, draw two different nets for the rectangular box above. Cut each pattern out and fold it into a box.

B. Describe the faces of the box formed from each net you made. What are the dimensions of each face?

C. Find the total area of each net you made in Question A.

D. How many centimeter cubes will fit into the box formed from each net you made? Explain your reasoning.

E. Suppose you stand the rectangular 1 centimeter × 1 centimeter × 3 centimeters box on its end. Does the area of a net for the box or the number of cubes needed to fill the box change?

ACE Homework starts on page 10.

active math online

For: Virtual Box Activity
Visit: PHSchool.com
Web Code: and-6102

1.3 Testing Nets

All the boxes you have made so far are rectangular prisms. A **rectangular prism** is a three-dimensional shape with six rectangular faces. The size of a rectangular prism can be described by giving its *dimensions*. The dimensions are the length, the width, and the height.

The **base** of a rectangular prism is the face on the bottom (the face that rests on the table or floor). The length and width of a prism are the length and width of its rectangular base. The height is the distance from the base of the prism to its top.

Getting Ready for Problem

- Suppose you want to cut the box in the figure below to make a net for the box. Along which edges can you make the cut?

- Are there different choices of edges to cut that will work?

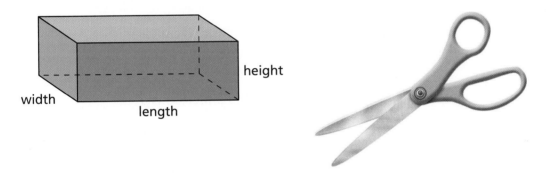

An engineer at the Save-a-Tree packaging company drew the nets below. He lost the notes that indicated the dimensions of the boxes. Use your thinking from the Getting Ready section to work backwards and determine the dimensions for him.

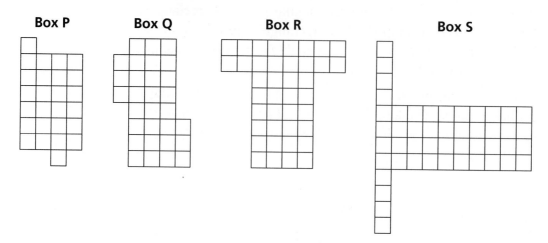

Box P   **Box Q**   **Box R**   **Box S**

Problem 1.3 Rectangular Prisms

A. Using a copy of the diagram above, draw in fold lines and cut each pattern and fold it to form a box. What are the dimensions of each box?

B. How are the dimensions of each box related to the dimensions of its faces?

C. What is the total area, in square units, of all the faces of each box?

D. Fill each box with unit cubes. How many unit cubes does it take to fill each box?

E. Design a net for a box that has a different shape than Box P but holds the same number of cubes as Box P.

ACE Homework starts on page 10.

1.4 Flattening a Box

Amy is a packaging engineer at the Save-a-Tree packaging company. Mr. Shu asks Amy to come to his class and explain her job to his students. She gives each student a box to do some exploring.

Problem 1.4 Surface Area of a Rectangular Prism

Your teacher will give you a box.

A. Find the dimensions of the box.

B. Use the dimensions of the box to make a net on centimeter grid paper. You may find it helpful to put the box on the paper, outline the base, and then roll the box over so a new face touches the paper.

C. Match each face of the box to your net in Question B. Label the net to show how the faces match.

D. Amy explained that one thing she considers when designing a box is the cost of the material. Suppose the material for the box costs $\frac{1}{10}$ of a cent per square centimeter. What is the total cost of the material for the box? Why might this information be useful?

E. What other information do you think is important to consider when designing a box?

ACE Homework starts on page 10.

Did You Know?

It is possible to receive a college degree in packaging. A packaging degree prepares a person to develop and produce packages for a variety of products. The designer must pay attention to cost, durability, transportability, safety and environmental regulations, and visual appeal. Many manufacturing companies want people with packaging degrees. However, there are only a few colleges or universities that offer a bachelor's degree in packaging.

Go Online
PHSchool.com **For:** Information about a degree in packaging
Web Code: ane-9031

Applications

For Exercises 1–4, decide if you can fold the net along the lines to form a closed cubic box. If you are unsure, draw the pattern on grid paper and cut it out to experiment.

1. 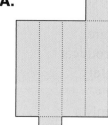   **2.** 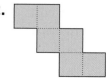   **3.**   **4.**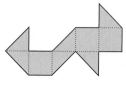

5. Which of these nets could be folded along the lines to form a closed rectangular box?

A.   **B.**   **C.**

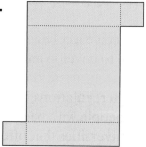

6. Do parts (a)–(c) for each pattern from Exercise 5 that forms a closed rectangular box.

   a. Use the unit square shown to help you find the dimensions of the box.

   b. Find the total area, in square units, of all the faces of the box.

   c. Find the number of unit cubes it would take to fill the box.

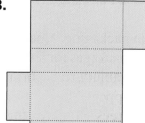

unit square

7. This closed rectangular box does not have square ends.

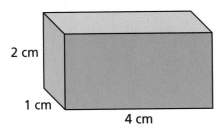

2 cm

1 cm

4 cm

  a. What are the dimensions of the box?

  b. On centimeter grid paper, sketch two nets for the box.

  c. Find the area, in square centimeters, of each net.

  d. Find the total area of all the faces of the box. How does your answer compare with the areas you found in part (c)?

8. Which of these patterns can be folded along the lines to form a closed rectangular box? Explain.

a.

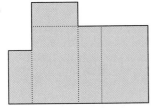

b.

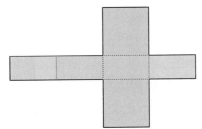

c.

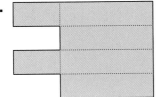

d.

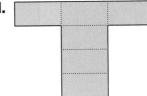

e.

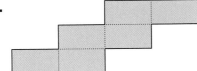

9. Can you fold this net along the lines to form an open cubic box? Explain your reasoning.

For each box described in Exercises 10–13:

- Make a sketch of the box and label the dimensions.
- Draw a net.
- Find the area of each face.
- Find the total area of all the faces.

10. a rectangular box with dimensions
2 centimeters × 3 centimeters × 5 centimeters

11. a rectangular box with dimensions
$2\frac{1}{2}$ centimeters × 2 centimeters × 1 centimeter

12. a cubic box with side lengths $3\frac{2}{3}$ centimeters

13. a cubic box that holds 125 unit cubes

14. An open box is a box without a top.

a. On grid paper, sketch nets for three different open cubic boxes.

b. On grid paper, sketch nets for three different open rectangular boxes (not cubic boxes) with square ends.

c. Find the area of each net you found in parts (a) and (b).

Homework
Help **⬤**nline
PHSchool.com

For: Help with Exercise 10
Web Code: ane-6110

Connections

For Exercises 15–18, use the following information: A *hexomino* is a shape made of six identical squares connected along their sides. The nets for a closed cubic box are examples of hexominos. Below are five different hexominos.

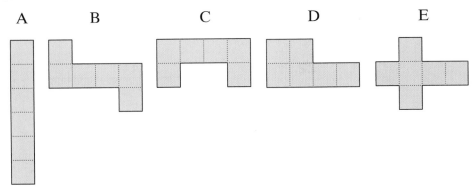

A   B   C   D   E

15. Find the perimeter of each hexomino shown above.

16. Which hexominos can you fold to form a closed cubic box?

17. From which hexominos can you remove one square to make a net for an open cubic box? For each hexomino you select, draw a diagram showing which square can be removed.

18. To which hexominos can you add the number of squares below without changing the perimeter? For each hexomino you select, draw a diagram. Explain why the perimeter does not change.

  a. one square　　　　　　　**b.** two squares

For Exercises 19–22, find the area and the perimeter of each figure. Figures are not drawn to scale.

Go Online
PHSchool.com

For: Multiple-Choice Skills Practice
Web Code: ana-6154

19.

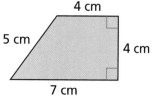

4 cm
5 cm
4 cm
7 cm

A = 23.5
P = 20

20.

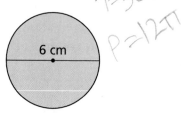

6 cm

A = 36π
P = 12π

21.

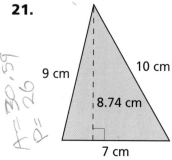

9 cm
10 cm
8.74 cm
7 cm

A = 30.59
P = 26

22.

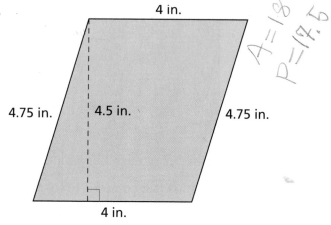

4 in.
4.75 in.   4.5 in.   4.75 in.
4 in.

A = 18
P = 17.5

23. Which pair of angles are complementary angles?

a.

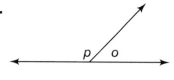

p   o

b.

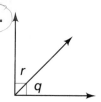

r
q

c.

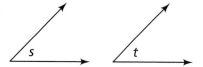

s   t

24. Angles *m* and *n* below are supplementary angles. Angle *m* has a measure of 78°. What is the measure of angle *n*?

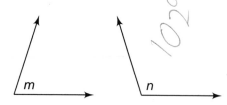

m   n

102°

25. Multiple Choice Which angle is supplementary to a 57° angle?

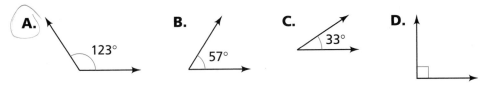

A. (circled) 123°

B. 57°

C. 33°

D.

26. What measurements do you need and how do you use those measurements to find the area and perimeter of each figure below?

a. rectangle

length & width

b. square

length

27. Mrs. Zhou is making wooden slats for doll beds from a strip of thin board.

She cuts $\frac{1}{12}$ of the strip for another project. Bed slats for one doll bed take $\frac{1}{8}$ of a strip.

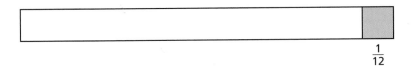

$\frac{1}{12}$

a. Suppose Mrs. Zhou uses the remainder of this strip for bed slats. How many doll beds can she make?

b. Draw diagrams to confirm your answer.

28. a. Four friends shared $\frac{3}{5}$ of a pizza. What fraction of the pizza did each receive?

b. Draw a picture to confirm your answer.

29. Mr. Bouck is making snack bars. The recipe calls for $\frac{3}{8}$ stick of butter. He has $3\frac{1}{2}$ sticks on hand.

a. How many recipes can he make?

b. Draw a picture to show your reasoning.

30. Tom plans to plant an herb garden in a glass tank. A scoop of dirt fills 0.15 of the volume of the tank. He needs to put in dirt equal to 65% of the volume. How many scoops of dirt does he need?

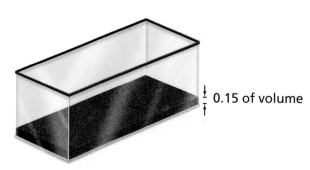

0.15 of volume

31. A glass container is 0.5 full of water. After 400 milliliters are poured out, the container is 0.34 full. How much does the container hold?

Extensions

32. A number cube is designed so that numbers on opposite sides add to 7. Write the integers from 1 to 6 on one of the nets you found in Problem 1.1 so that it can be folded to form this number cube. You may want to test your pattern by cutting it out and folding it.

33. Examine the nets you made for cubic boxes in Problem 1.1. Suppose you want to make boxes by tracing several copies of the same pattern onto a large sheet of cardboard and cutting them out.

Which pattern allows you to make the greatest number of boxes from a square sheet of cardboard with a side length of 10 units? Test your ideas on grid paper.

Mathematical Reflections 1

In this investigation, you explored rectangular boxes, and you made nets for boxes. You found the dimensions of a box, the total area of all its faces, and the number of unit cubes required to fill it. These questions will help you summarize what you have learned.

Think about your answers to these questions. Discuss your ideas with other students and your teacher. Then write a summary of your findings in your notebook.

1. Explain how to find the total area of all the faces of a rectangular box.

2. Explain how to find the number of identical cubes it will take to fill a rectangular box.

3. Suppose several different nets are made for a given box. What do all of the nets have in common? What might be different?

Investigation 2

Designing Rectangular Boxes

Finding the right box for a product requires thought and planning. A company must consider how much the box can hold as well as the amount and the cost of the material needed to make the box.

The amount that a box can hold depends on its volume. The **volume** of a box is the number of unit cubes that it would take to fill the box. The amount of material needed to make or to cover a box depends on its surface area. The **surface area** of a box is the total area of all of its faces.

The box shown below has dimensions of 1 centimeter by 3 centimeters by 1 centimeter. It would take three 1-centimeter cubes to fill this box, so the box has a volume of 3 cubic centimeters. Because the net for the box takes fourteen 1-centimeter grid squares to make the box, the box has a surface area of 14 square centimeters.

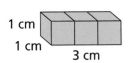

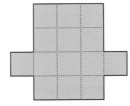

volume = 3 cubic centimeters

surface area = 14 square centimeters

In this investigation, you will explore the possible surface areas for a rectangular box that holds a given volume.

Packaging Blocks

ATC Toy Company is planning to market a set of children's alphabet blocks. Each block is a cube with 1-inch edges, so each block has a volume of 1 cubic inch.

Problem **2.1** Finding Surface Area

The company wants to arrange 24 blocks in the shape of a rectangular prism and then package them in a box that exactly fits the prism.

A. Find all the ways 24 cubes can be arranged into a rectangular prism. Make a sketch of each arrangement. Record the dimensions and surface area. It may help to organize your findings into a table like the one below:

Possible Arrangements of 24 Cubes

Length	Width	Height	Volume	Surface Area	Sketch
■	■	■	■	■	■
■	■	■	■	■	■
■	■	■	■	■	■

B. Which of your arrangements requires the box made with the least material? Which requires the box made with the most material?

C. Which arrangement would you recommend to ATC Toy Company? Explain why.

D. Why do you think the company makes 24 alphabet blocks rather than 26?

ACE Homework starts on page 24.

Saving Trees

You discovered that 24 blocks can be packaged in different ways that use varying amounts of packaging material. By using less material, a company can save money, reduce waste, and conserve natural resources.

Which rectangular arrangement of cubes uses the least amount of packaging material?

Problem 2.2 Finding the Least Surface Area

A. Explore the possible arrangements of each of the following numbers of cubes. Find the arrangement that requires the least amount of packaging material.

1. 8 cubes   **2.** 27 cubes   **3.** 12 cubes

B. 1. Make a conjecture about the rectangular arrangement of cubes that requires the least packaging material.

2. Does your conjecture work for 30 cubes? Does it work for 64 cubes? If not, change your conjecture so it works for any number of cubes. When you have a conjecture that you think is correct, give reasons why you think your conjecture is valid.

C. Describe a strategy for finding the total surface area of a closed box.

ACE **Homework starts on page 24.**

Area is expressed in square units, such as square inches or square centimeters. You can abbreviate square units by writing the abbreviation for the unit followed by a raised 2. For example, an abbreviation for square inches is in.^{2}.

Volume is expressed in cubic units. You can abbreviate cubic units by writing the abbreviation for the unit followed by a raised 3. For example, an abbreviation for cubic centimeters is cm^3.

Getting Ready for Problem 2.3

One seventh-grade student, Bernie, wonders if he can compare volumes without having to calculate them exactly. He figures that volume measures the contents of a container. He fills the prism on the left with rice and then pours the rice into the one on the right.

- How can you decide if there is enough rice or too much rice to fill the prism on the right?

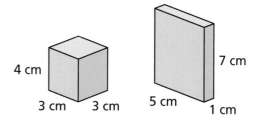

2.3 Filling Rectangular Boxes

A company may have boxes custom-made to package its products. However, a company may also buy ready-made boxes. The Save-a-Tree packaging company sells ready-made boxes in several sizes.

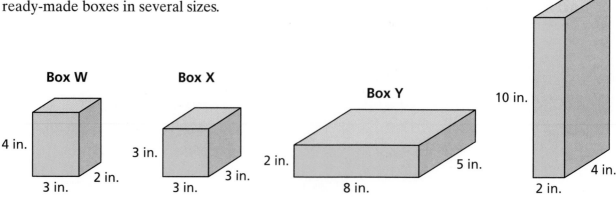

ATC Toy Company is considering using Save-a-Tree's Box Z to ship alphabet blocks. Each block is a 1-inch cube. ATC needs to know how many blocks will fit into Box Z and the surface area of the box.

A. The number of unit cubes that fit in a box is the volume of the box.

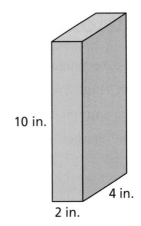

10 in.

4 in.

2 in.

1. How many cubes will fit in a single layer at the bottom of this box?

2. How many identical layers can be stacked in this box?

3. What is the total number of cubes that can be packed in this box?

4. Consider the number of cubes in each layer, the number of layers, the volume, and the dimensions of the box. What connections do you see among these measurements?

B. Find the surface area of Box Z.

C. Suppose Box Z is put down on its side so its base is 4 inches by 10 inches and its height is 2 inches. Does this affect the volume of the box? Does this affect the surface area? Explain your reasoning.

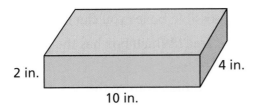

2 in.

4 in.

10 in.

D. Apply your strategies for finding volume and surface area to Boxes W, X, and Y.

ACE Homework starts on page 24.

Applications

In Exercises 1–3, rectangular prisms are made using 1-inch cubes.

   a. Find the length, width, and height of each prism.

   b. Find the amount of material needed to make a box for each prism.

   c. Find the number of cubes in each prism.

1.
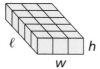

2.

3.
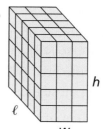

4. Suppose you plan to make a box that will hold exactly 40 one-inch cubes.

   a. Give the dimensions of all the possible boxes you can make.

   b. Which box has the least surface area? Which box has the greatest surface area?

   c. Why might you want to know the dimensions of the box with the least surface area?

5. Each of these boxes holds 36 ping-pong balls.

16 cm

12 cm

12 cm

8 cm

24 cm

12 cm

24 cm

8 cm

12 cm

48 cm

12 cm

4 cm

   a. Without figuring, which box has the least surface area? Why?

   b. Check your guess by finding the surface area of each box.

6. a. The box at the right is a $6 \times 2 \times 1$ arrangement of drink cans. Suppose the dimensions of the box are, in centimeters, $39 \times 13 \times 12.25$. Compare the surface area of the box with the more traditional $4 \times 3 \times 1$ arrangement, which measures, in centimeters, $26 \times 19.5 \times 12.25$.

b. The box at the right is a $4 \times 3 \times 2$ arrangement of drink cans. Suppose the dimensions of the box are, in centimeters, $26 \times 19.5 \times 24.5$. Compare the surface area of the box with the more traditional $6 \times 4 \times 1$ arrangement, which measures, in centimeters, $39 \times 26 \times 12.25$.

7. a. Sketch a rectangular box with dimensions 2 centimeters by 7 centimeters by 3 centimeters.

b. What is the surface area of the box?

c. Draw a net for the box on grid paper. What is the relationship between the area of the net and the surface area of the box?

In Exercises 8–10, rectangular prisms are drawn using inch cubes.

    a. Find the length, width, and height of each prism.

    b. Find the volume of each prism. Describe how you found the volume.

    c. Find the surface area of each prism. Describe how you found the surface area.

8.

9.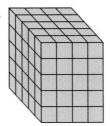

10.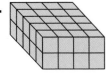

11. a. What is the total number of cubes, including the cubes already shown, needed to fill the closed box below?

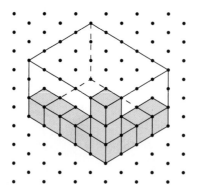

b. What is the surface area of the box?

For Exercises 12–14, find the volume and surface area of the closed box.

12.

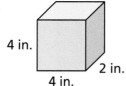

4 in.
4 in.
2 in.

13.

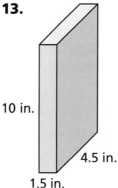

10 in.
1.5 in.
4.5 in.

14.

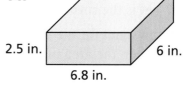

2.5 in.
6.8 in.
6 in.

15. a. Make a sketch of a closed box with dimensions 2 centimeters by 3 centimeters by 5 centimeters.

b. How many centimeter cubes will fit in one layer at the bottom of the box?

c. How many layers are needed to fill the box?

d. Find the volume of the box.

e. Find the surface area of the box.

16. Mr. Turner's classroom is 20 feet wide, 30 feet long, and 10 feet high.

a. Sketch a scale model of the classroom. Label the dimensions of the classroom on your sketch.

Go Online
PHSchool.com

For: Multiple-Choice Skills Practice
Web Code: ana-6254

b. Find the volume of the classroom. Why might this information be useful?

c. Find the total area of the walls, the floor, and the ceiling. Why might this information be useful?

17. Each expression below will help you to find the volume or surface area of one of the boxes pictured. Simplify each expression. Decide whether you have found a volume or a surface area, and for which box.

Homework Help nline
PHSchool.com
For: Help with Exercise 17
Web Code: ane-6217

a. $2 \times (3.5 \times 5.7) + 2 \times (5.7 \times 12) + 2 \times (3.5 \times 12)$

b. $6\frac{1}{4} \times 6$ **c.** $6 \times 6\frac{1}{2}$ **d.** $2\frac{1}{3} \times 2\frac{2}{5} \times 5$

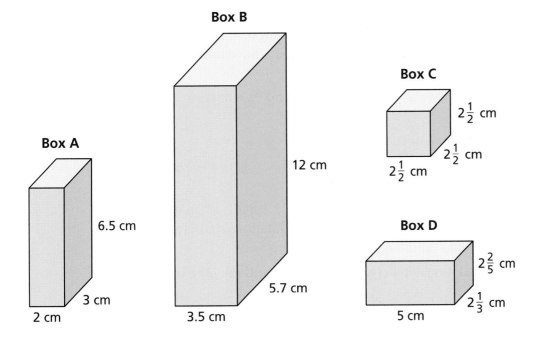

Box B

Box C

$2\frac{1}{2}$ cm

$2\frac{1}{2}$ cm

$2\frac{1}{2}$ cm

12 cm

Box A

6.5 cm

3 cm

2 cm

5.7 cm

3.5 cm

Box D

$2\frac{2}{5}$ cm

$2\frac{1}{3}$ cm

5 cm

Investigation 2 Designing Rectangular Boxes   **27**

18. The city of Centerville plans to dig a rectangular landfill. The landfill will have a base with dimensions 700 ft by 200 ft and a depth of 85 ft.

a. How many cubic feet of garbage will the landfill hold?

b. What information do you need to determine how long the landfill can be used until it is full?

c. Centerville hires an excavator to dig the hole for the landfill. How many cubic yards of dirt will he have to haul away?

19. Describe the dimensions of a rectangular prism with a volume of 80 cubic inches but a surface area of less than 132 square inches.

Connections

20. a. There is only one way to arrange five identical cubes into the shape of a rectangular prism. Sketch the rectangular prism made from five identical cubes.

b. Find more numbers of cubes that can be arranged into a rectangular prism in only one way. What do these numbers have in common?

21. a. Sketch every rectangular prism that can be made from ten identical cubes.

b. Find the surface area of each prism you sketched.

c. Give the dimensions of the prism that has the least surface area.

22. a. Each of the boxes you designed in Problem 2.1 had a rectangular base and a height. Use a graph to show the relationship between the area of the base and the height of each box.

b. Describe the relationship between the height and the area of the base.

c. How might your graph be useful to a packaging engineer at ATC Toy Company?

23. The dimensions of the recreation center floor are 150 ft by 45 ft, and the walls are 10 ft high. A gallon of paint will cover 400 ft^2. About how much paint is needed to paint the walls of the recreation center?

24. If a small can of paint will cover 1,400 square inches, about how many small cans are needed to paint the walls of the recreation center described in Exercise 23?

For Exercises 25–27, use the three given views of a three-dimensional building to sketch the building. Then, find its volume.

25.

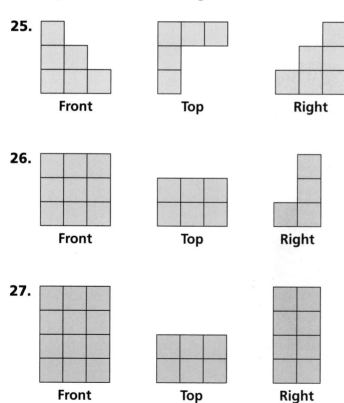

Front   Top   Right

26.

Front   Top   Right

27.

Front   Top   Right

Extensions

28. Many drinks are packaged in rectangular boxes of 24 cans.

    a. During the spring of 1993, a company announced that it was going to package 24 twelve-ounce cans into a more cube-like shape. Why might the company have decided to change their packaging?

    b. List all the ways 24 twelve-ounce cans of soda can be arranged and packaged in a rectangular box. Which arrangement do you recommend that a drink company use? Why?

29. Slam Dunk Sporting Goods packages its basketballs in cubic boxes with 1-foot edges. For shipping, the company packs 12 basketballs (in its boxes) into a large rectangular shipping box.

    a. Find the dimensions of every possible shipping box into which the boxes of basketballs would exactly fit.

    b. Find the surface area of each shipping box in part (a).

    c. Slam Dunk uses the shipping box that requires the least material. Which shipping box does it use?

    d. Slam Dunk decides to ship basketballs in boxes of 24. It wants to use the shipping box that requires the least material. Find the dimensions of the box it should use. How much more packaging material is needed to ship 24 basketballs than to ship 12 basketballs?

Mathematical Reflections 2

In this investigation, you arranged cubes in the shape of rectangular prisms, and you also found the arrangements with the least and greatest surface area. You developed methods for finding surface area and volume. These questions will help you summarize what you have learned.

Think about your answers to these questions. Discuss your ideas with other students and your teacher. Then write a summary of your findings in your notebook.

1. For a given number of cubes, what arrangement will give a rectangular prism with the least surface area? What arrangement will give a rectangular prism with the greatest surface area? Use specific examples to illustrate your ideas.

2. Describe how you can find the surface area of a rectangular prism. Give a rule for finding the surface area.

3. Describe how you can find the volume of any prism. Give a rule for finding the volume.

Investigation 3

Prisms and Cylinders

In Investigation 2, you found the volume of rectangular prisms by filling the prism with cubes. The number of cubes in the bottom layer is the same as the area of the rectangular base and the number of layers is the height. To find the volume, you multiply the area of the base ($\ell \times w$) times its height h, so that $V = \ell wh$.

A **prism** is a three-dimensional shape with a top and a base that are congruent polygons, and *lateral* (side) faces that are parallelograms. Each prism is named for the shape of its base. The boxes we have seen so far in this unit are rectangular prisms. A triangular prism has a triangular base.

A **cylinder** is a three-dimensional shape with a top and base that are congruent circles.

The prisms and cylinder below all have the same height.

Suppose you filled the triangular prism with rice and poured the rice into each of the other cylinders. How do you think the volumes would compare? What about the surface areas?

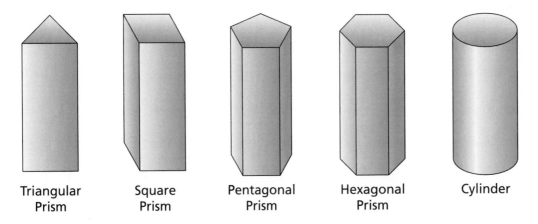

| Triangular Prism | Square Prism | Pentagonal Prism | Hexagonal Prism | Cylinder |

3.1 Filling Fancy Boxes

In this problem you will explore prisms with bases that are not rectangles. You will start by making models of prisms.

Directions for Making Paper Prisms (These paper models are open at the top and bottom.)

- Start with four identical sheets of paper.
- Use the shorter dimension as the height for each prism.
- Make a *triangular* prism by marking and folding one of the sheets of paper into three congruent rectangles. Tape the paper into the shape of a triangular prism.

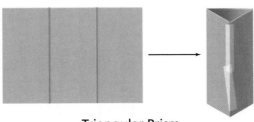

Triangular Prism

- Make a *square* prism by marking, folding, and taping a sheet of paper into four congruent rectangles.
- Make a *pentagonal* prism by marking, folding, and taping a sheet of paper into five congruent rectangles.
- Make a *hexagonal* prism by marking, folding, and taping a sheet of paper into six congruent rectangles.

Problem 3.1 Finding the Volumes of Other Prisms

A. In your group, follow the directions above. (Keep your models for Problem 3.2.)

B. How do the volumes of the prisms compare as the number of faces in the prisms increases? Does the volume remain the same? Explain.

C. Consider the number of cubes you need to cover the base as one layer. Next, think about the total number of layers of cubes needed to fill the prism. Does this seem like a reasonable method for computing the volume of each prism?

D. Suppose that each of your paper prisms has a top and a bottom. As the number of faces of a prism (with the same height) increases, what happens to the surface area of the prisms? Are the surface areas of the prisms the same? Explain your reasoning.

ACE **Homework starts on page 38.**

The last problem revealed some interesting connections among volume and surface area of prisms. A cylinder resembles a many-sided prism. In this problem you will explore cylinders and use what you have already learned about prisms to find the volume and surface area of a cylinder.

Directions for Making Paper Cylinders

- Start with two identical sheets of paper.
- Use the longer dimension of one sheet of paper as the height of the first cylinder. Tape the paper into the shape of a cylinder.
- Use the shorter dimension of the other sheet of paper as the height of the second cylinder. Tape the paper into the shape of a cylinder.

How do the volumes of the two cylinders compare?

You need an efficient way to compute the volume of a cylinder. In Problem 3.1 you found the volume of a prism by counting the number of cubes that fit in a single layer at the base and then counting the number of layers it would take to fill the prism. Let's see if a similar approach will work for cylinders.

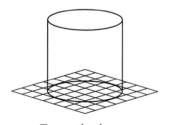

Trace the base.

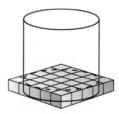

How many cubes would fit in one layer?

How many layers would it take to fill the cylinder?

As with rectangular prisms, the bottom of any prism or cylinder is called the base.

Problem 3.2 Finding the Volumes of Cylinders

A. Copy the circles at the right onto inch graph paper. With two identical sheets of paper, make two models of cylinders with open tops and bases that match the bases drawn on the grid paper.

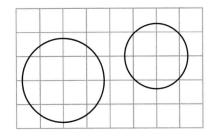

active math online

For: Virtual Cylinder Activity
Visit: PHSchool.com
Web Code: and-6302

B. Predict which of the two cylinders has the greater volume.

C. 1. How many inch cubes fit on the bottom layer of each cylinder?

    2. How many layers of inch cubes are needed to fill each cylinder?

    3. What is the total number of inch cubes needed to fill each cylinder?

    4. How can the dimensions help you calculate the volume of each cylinder?

D. Suppose Cylinder 1 has a height of 10 centimeters and a radius of 4 centimeters and Cylinder 2 has a height of 4 centimeters and a radius of 10 centimeters. Are the volumes equal? Explain.

E. Suppose that each of your paper cylinders had a top and a bottom. Describe how you could find the surface area of each cylinder.

ACE **Homework starts on page 38.**

3.3 Making Cylinders and Prisms from Nets

The distance from the base of a cylinder to the top is called the height. You can describe a cylinder by giving its dimensions.

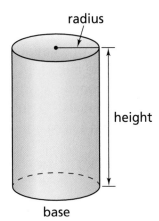

radius

height

base

Draw nets like the following on centimeter grid paper.

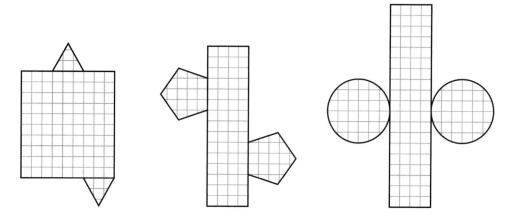

A. What is the surface area of each shape? Explain your reasoning.

B. Cut out your nets. Tape the pieces of the nets together to form a cylinder or a prism.

    1. Describe how to find the surface area of any prism or cylinder.

    2. Describe how the dimensions of a cylinder help you to find its surface area.

C. 1. Find the volume of each prism and cylinder.

    2. Compare the methods for finding the volume of a prism and finding the volume of a cylinder.

ACE | Homework starts on page 38.

The volume, or capacity, of a liquid container is often given in units like quarts, gallons, liters, and milliliters. These volumes do not tell you how many unit cubes each container will hold, but are based on cubic measures. For example, a gallon equals 231 cubic inches, a milliliter equals a cubic centimeter, and a liter is 1,000 cubic centimeters.

Go Online
PHSchool.com
For: Information about capacities
Web Code: ane-9031

3.4 Making a New Juice Container

online

For: Pouring and Filling Activity

Visit: PHSchool.com

Web Code: and-6304

Fruit Tree Juice Company packages its most popular drink, apple-prune juice, in cylindrical cans. Each can is 8 centimeters high and has a radius of 2 centimeters.

Recent reports indicate a decline in the sales of Fruit Tree juice. At the same time, sales of juice sold by a competitor, the Wrinkled Prune Company, are on the rise. Market researchers at Fruit Tree determine that Wrinkled Prune's success is due to its new rectangular juice boxes. Fruit Tree decides to package its juice in rectangular boxes.

Problem 3.4 Comparing Volumes

Fruit Tree wants the new rectangular box to have the same volume as the current cylindrical can.

A. 1. On centimeter grid paper, make a net for a box that will hold the same amount of juice as the cylindrical can. Cut out your net. When you are finished, fold and tape your pattern to form a rectangular box.

    2. Give the dimensions of your juice box. Are there other possibilities for the dimensions? Explain.

    3. Compare your juice box with the boxes made by your classmates. Which rectangular box shape do you think would make the best juice container? Why?

B. Compare the surface area of the cylindrical can with the surface area of your juice box. Which container has greater surface area?

ACE Homework starts on page 38.

Applications

1. Cut a sheet of paper in half so you have two identical half-sheets of paper. Tape the long sides of one sheet together to form a cylinder. Tape the short sides from the second sheet together to form another cylinder. Suppose that each cylinder has a top and a bottom.

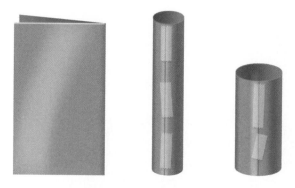

    a. Which cylinder has the greater volume? Explain.

    b. Which cylinder has the greater surface area? Explain.

2. A cylinder has a radius of 3 centimeters. Sand is poured into the cylinder to form a layer 1 centimeter deep.

    a. What is the volume of sand in the cylinder?

    b. Suppose the height of the cylinder is 20 centimeters. How many 1-centimeter deep layers of sand are needed to fill the cylinder?

    c. What is the volume of the cylinder?

3. Find a cylindrical object in your home or school. Record the dimensions and find the volume of the cylinder.

For Exercises 4–6, decide whether you have found an area, a surface area, or a volume. Then, identify whether the computation relates to Figure 1, 2, or 3.

4. $\left(\frac{1}{2} \times \frac{1}{2} \times \pi \times 2\right) + \left(2 \times \frac{1}{2} \times \pi \times 5\right)$

5. $3 \times 3 \times \pi$

6. $1 \times 1 \times \pi \times 3$

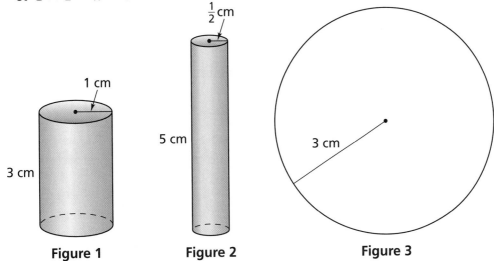

1 cm

3 cm

Figure 1

$\frac{1}{2}$ cm

5 cm

Figure 2

3 cm

Figure 3

7. A pipeline carrying oil is 5,000 kilometers long and has an inside diameter of 20 centimeters.

   a. How many cubic centimeters of oil will it take to fill 1 kilometer of the pipeline? (1 km = 100,000 cm)

   b. How many cubic centimeters of oil will it take to fill the entire pipeline?

Homework
Help 🌐**nline**
PHSchool.com
For: Help with Exercise 7
Web Code: ane-6307

8. What feature of a cylinder uses the given units?

   a. centimeters

   b. square centimeters

   c. cubic centimeters

For Exercises 9–11, find the volume of each cylinder.

For: Multiple-Choice Skills Practice

Web Code: ana-6354

   9. height = 10 centimeters, radius = 6.5 centimeters

   10. height = 6.5 centimeters, radius = 10 centimeters

   11. height = 12 inches, area of the base = 200 square inches

12. Find the surface area of each closed cylinder in Exercises 9 and 10.

13. a. Will all rectangular prisms with the same height and base area have the same shape? Explain.

   b. Will all cylinders with the same height and base area have the same shape? Explain.

14. A cylindrical storage tank has a radius of 15 feet and a height of 30 feet.

   a. Make a sketch of the tank and label its dimensions.

   b. Find the volume of the tank.

   c. Find the surface area of the tank.

15. a. Sketch two different prisms, each with a base of area 40 square centimeters and a height of 5 centimeters.

   b. Find the volumes of your prisms.

   c. Do you think everyone in your class drew the same prisms? Explain.

   d. Do you think all the prisms have the same volumes as your prisms? Explain.

16. Below are side and top views of a triangular prism with bases that are equilateral triangles.

    a. What is the volume of this prism? How did you find the volume?

    b. What is the surface area? How did you find the surface area?

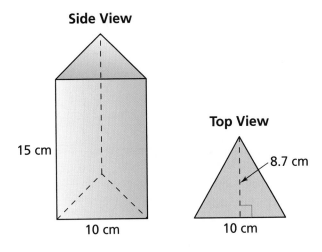

Side View

15 cm

10 cm

Top View

8.7 cm

10 cm

17. Below is a scale model of a net for a cylinder.

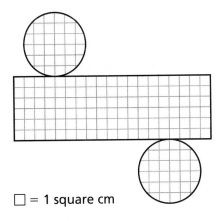

☐ = 1 square cm

    a. Suppose the net is assembled. Find the volume of the cylinder.

    b. Find the surface area of the cylinder.

18. Which container below has the greater volume? Greater surface area?

A *closed rectangular prism* whose height is 12 centimeters, width is 3 centimeters, and length is 4 centimeters.

A *closed cylinder* whose height is 12 centimeters and diameter is 3 centimeters.

19. The bases of the prisms you made in Problem 3.1 are shown at the right. Each prism has a height of 8.5 inches.

  a. Compute the volume of each prism.

  b. Compare these volumes with those you found in Problem 3.1.

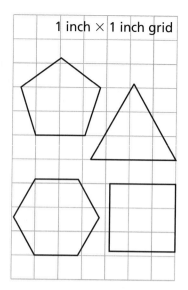

1 inch × 1 inch grid

20. Carlos wants to build a circular hot tub with a volume of 1,000 cubic feet. What is a good approximation for the radius of the tub?

21. Carlos decides he would rather build a rectangular hot tub that is 4 feet high and holds 400 cubic feet of water. What could the dimensions of the base of Carlos's hot tub be?

22. A popcorn vendor needs to order popcorn boxes. The vendor must decide between a cylindrical box and a rectangular box.

- The cylindrical box has a height of 20 centimeters and a radius of 7 centimeters.

- The rectangular box has a height of 20 centimeters and a square base with 12-centimeter sides.

- The price of each box is based on the amount of material needed to make the box.

- The vendor plans to charge $2.75 for popcorn, regardless of the shape of the box.

  a. Make a sketch of each box. Label the dimensions.

  b. Find the volume and surface area of each box.

  c. Which box would you choose? Give the reasons for your choice. What additional information might help you make a better decision?

Connections

23. Serge and Jorge were talking about the number π. Serge said that any problem involving π had to be about circles. Jorge disagreed and showed him the example below. What do you think?

1 inch ⎡
      ⎢
      ⎣

π inches

24. The Buy-and-Go Mart sells drinks in three sizes. Which size gives the most ounces of drink per dollar? Explain.

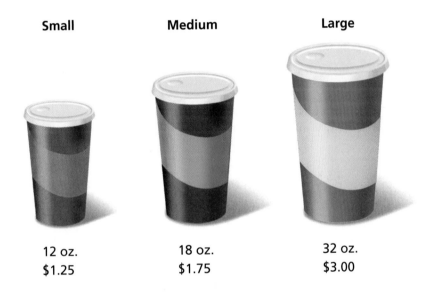

Small	Medium	Large
12 oz.	18 oz.	32 oz.
$1.25	$1.75	$3.00

25. a. Identify objects at school that are shaped like prisms, one rectangular and one or two non-rectangular prisms.

b. Without measuring, estimate the volume of each object.

c. How can you check the volumes you found in part (b)?

26. A drink can is a cylinder with radius 3 centimeters and height 12 centimeters. Ms. Doyle's classroom is 6 meters wide, 8 meters long, and 3 meters high. Estimate the number of drink cans that would fit inside Ms. Doyle's classroom. Explain your estimate.

27. a. Make a table showing the relationship between the diameter and the circumference of a circle. Include data for diameters 1, 2, 3, . . . 10 centimeters. Use this table for parts (b)–(d).

   b. Graph the data in your table.

   c. Suppose that each of the circles represented in your table is the base of a cylinder with height of 2 centimeters. Some of these cylinders are sketched below. Make a table to show the relationship between the diameter of the base and the volume of the cylinder.

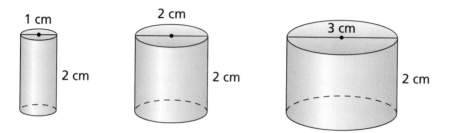

   d. Make a graph of the volume data.

   e. Compare the graphs of parts (b) and (d). How are they alike? How are they different?

28. Some take-out drink containers have a circular top and bottom that are not congruent. How can you estimate the volume of the container below?

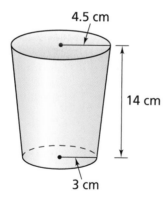

29. Leo has two prism-shaped containers. One has a volume of $3\frac{3}{4}$ cubic feet and the other has a volume of $\frac{1}{3}$ cubic feet.

   a. How many of the smaller prisms would it take to fill the larger prism?

   b. What operation did you use to find the answer? Explain.

30. Emily has two prism-shaped containers. One has a volume of $2\frac{2}{5}$ cubic feet, and the other has a volume of $\frac{2}{3}$ cubic feet.

   a. How many of the smaller prisms would it take to fill the larger prism?

   b. What operation did you use to find the answer? Explain.

31. The diagram shows a fish tank after a container of water is poured into the tank.

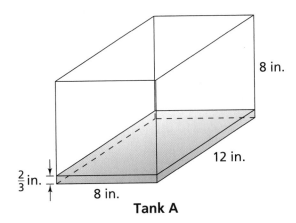

Tank A

a. How many containers of water are needed to fill the tank?

b. What fraction of the tank does the container fill?

c. A different container holds $12\frac{3}{4}$ cubic inches of water. How many of these containers are needed to fill the tank?

32. The diagram shows a fish tank after a container of water is poured into the tank.

Tank B

a. How many containers of water are needed to fill the tank?

b. What fraction of the tank does the container fill?

c. A different container holds $4\frac{4}{9}$ cubic inches of water. How many of these containers are needed to fill the tank?

Extensions

33. A cylindrical can is packed securely in a box as shown at the right.

   a. Find the radius and height of the can.

   b. What is the volume of the empty space between the can and the box?

   c. Find the ratio of the volume of the can to the volume of the box.

   d. Make up a similar example with a can and a box of different sizes. What is the ratio of the volume of your can to the volume of your box? How does the ratio compare with the ratio you found in part (c)?

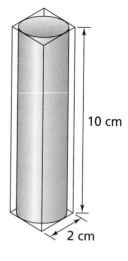

10 cm

2 cm

34. a. The drawing at the right shows a prism with an odd-shaped top and bottom and rectangular sides. The top and bottom each have an area of 10 square centimeters, and the height is 4 centimeters. What is the volume of the prism? Explain your reasoning.

   b. Is your estimate for the volume more than, less than, or equal to the exact volume? Explain.

35. Suppose you know the height and volume of a cylinder. Can you make a net for the cylinder?

Mathematical Reflections 3

In this investigation, you developed methods for finding the volume and surface area of prisms and cylinders. These questions will help you summarize what you have learned.

Think about your answers to these questions. Discuss your ideas with other students and your teacher. Then write a summary of your findings in your notebook.

1. Describe how to find the volume of a rectangular prism.

2. **a.** Describe how you can find the volume of a cylinder using its dimensions. Write a rule that represents your strategy.

   b. Describe how you can find the surface area of a cylinder using its dimensions. Write a rule that represents your strategy.

3. Discuss the similarities and differences in the methods for finding the volume of a cylinder, a rectangular prism, and a non-rectangular prism.

4. Discuss the similarities and differences in the methods for finding the surface area of a cylinder, a rectangular prism, and a non-rectangular prism.

Investigation 4

Cones, Spheres, and Pyramids

Many common and important three-dimensional objects are not shaped like prisms or cylinders. For example, ice cream is often served in **cones.** The planet we live on is nearly a **sphere.** Many monuments here and in other countries are shaped like **pyramids.**

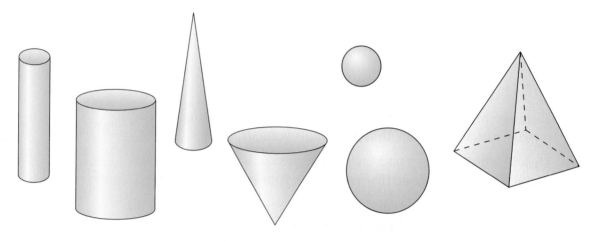

As with a cylinder and a prism, you can describe a cone or a square pyramid by giving its dimensions. The dimensions of a cone are the radius of its circular base and its height. The dimensions of a square pyramid are its length, width, and height.

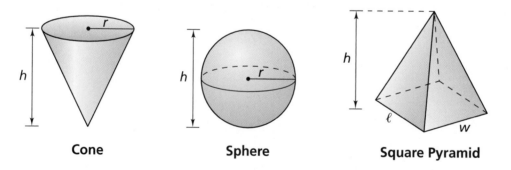

Cone   **Sphere**   **Square Pyramid**

Although spheres may differ in size, they are all the same shape. You can describe a sphere by giving its radius.

In this investigation, you will explore ways to determine the volumes of cones, pyramids, and spheres by looking for relationships between cones and pyramids and between cones and spheres.

Comparing Spheres and Cylinders

In this problem, you will make a sphere and a cylinder with the same diameter and the same height and then compare their volumes. (The height of a sphere is just its diameter.) You can use the relationship you observe to develop a method for finding the volume of a sphere.

Did You Know?

Earth is nearly a sphere. You may have heard that, until Christopher Columbus's voyage in 1492, most people believed Earth was flat. Actually, as early as the fourth century B.C., scientists had figured out that Earth was round.

The scientists observed the shadow of Earth as it passed across the moon during a lunar eclipse. The shadow was round. Combining this observation with evidence gathered from observing constellations, these scientists concluded that Earth was spherical. In the third century B.C., Eratosthenes, a Greek mathematician, was actually able to estimate the circumference of Earth.

 Go Online
PHSchool.com **For:** Information about historical views of Earth's shape
Web Code: ane-9031

Problem 4.1 Comparing Spheres and Cylinders

- Make a sphere from modeling clay. Measure its diameter.
- Make a cylinder with an open top and bottom from a sheet of stiff transparent plastic to fit snugly around your clay sphere. Trim the height of the cylinder to match the height of the sphere. This makes the diameter and the height of the cylinder equal to the diameter and the height of the sphere. Tape the cylinder together so that it remains rigid.

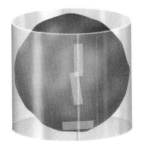

- Now, flatten the clay sphere so that it fits snugly in the bottom of the cylinder. Mark the height of the flattened sphere on the cylinder.

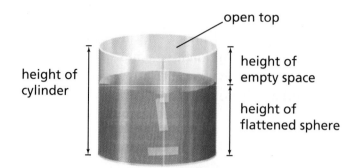

open top

height of cylinder

height of empty space

height of flattened sphere

A. Measure and record the height of the cylinder, the height of the empty space, and the height of the flattened sphere. Use this information to find the volume of the cylinder and the original sphere.

B. What is the relationship between the volume of the sphere and the volume of the cylinder?

C. A cylinder with a height equal to its diameter has a volume of 48 cubic inches. How can you use the relationship in Question B to find the volume of a sphere whose radius is the same as the cylinder?

Remove the clay from the cylinder and save the cylinder for Problem 4.2.

ACE Homework starts on page 54.

4.2 Cones and Cylinders, Pyramids and Cubes

In Problem 4.1, you discovered the relationship between the volume of a sphere and the volume of a cylinder. In this problem, you will look for the relationship between the volume of a cone and the volume of a cylinder, and between the volume of a pyramid and the volume of a square prism.

- Roll a piece of stiff paper into a cone shape so that the tip touches the bottom of the cylinder you made in Problem 4.1.

- Tape the cone shape along the seam. Trim the cone so that it is the same height as the cylinder.

- Fill the cone to the top with sand or rice, and empty the contents into the cylinder. Repeat this as many times as needed to fill the cylinder completely.

A. What is the relationship between the volume of the cone and the volume of the cylinder?

B. Suppose a cylinder, a cone, and a sphere have the same radius and the same height. What is the relationship between the volumes of the three shapes?

C. Suppose a cone, a cylinder, and a sphere all have the same height, and that the cylinder has a volume of 64 cubic inches. How do you use the relationship in Question B to find

   1. the volume of a sphere whose radius is the same as the cylinder?

   2. the volume of a cone whose radius is the same as the cylinder?

D. Suppose the radius of a cylinder, a cone, and a sphere is 5 centimeters and the height of the cylinder and cone is 8 centimeters. Find the volume of the cylinder, cone, and sphere.

E. 1. Use a square prism and a pyramid to conduct an experiment similar to the one on the previous page. The pyramid should have the same size base as the prism and the same height (shown at the right).

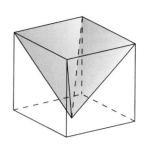

What is the relationship between the volume of the prism and the volume of the pyramid.

2. How are finding the volumes of the cones and pyramids alike?

ACE Homework starts on page 54.

4.3 Melting Ice Cream

Esther and Jasmine buy ice cream from Chilly's Ice Cream Parlor. They want to bring back an ice cream cone to Esther's little brother but decide the ice cream would melt before they got back home. Jasmine wonders, "If the ice cream all melts into the cone, will it fill the cone?"

Problem 4.3 Comparing Volumes of Spheres, Cylinders, and Cones

Esther gets a scoop of ice cream in a cone, and Jasmine gets a scoop in a cylindrical cup. Each container has a height of 8 centimeters and a radius of 4 centimeters. Each scoop of ice cream is a sphere with a radius of 4 centimeters.

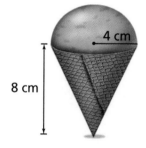

A. Suppose Jasmine allows her ice cream to melt. Will the melted ice cream fill her cup exactly? Explain.

B. Suppose Esther allows her ice cream to melt. Will the melted ice cream fill her cone exactly? Explain.

C. How many same-sized scoops of ice cream of the size shown on the previous page can be packed into each container?

ACE **Homework starts on page 54.**

Frank and Ernest

© 2002 Thaves. Reprinted with permission. Newspaper dist. by NEA, Inc.

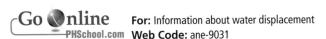

You have looked at prisms, cylinders, cones, and spheres. Many three-dimensional objects do not have such regular shapes.

According to legend, Archimedes (ahr kuh MEE deez) made an important discovery while taking a bath in the third century B.C. He noticed that the water level rose when he sat down in a tub. This was because his body had *displaced* some water. He determined that he could find the weight of any floating object by finding the weight of the water that the object displaced.

It is said that Archimedes was so excited about his discovery that he jumped from his bath and, without dressing, ran into the streets shouting "Eureka!"

Go **O**nline
PHSchool.com
For: Information about water displacement
Web Code: ane-9031

Applications

1. A playground ball has a diameter of 18 cm.

   a. Sketch a cylinder that fits the playground ball, and label its height and base.

   b. What is the volume of the cylinder?

   c. What is the volume of the ball?

2. Find the volume of an exercise ball with a diameter of 62 centimeters.

For Exercises 3–6, find the volume of the following spheres. In some spheres, the diameter is given. In others, the radius is given.

3.

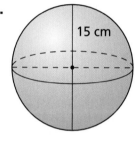

15 cm

4.

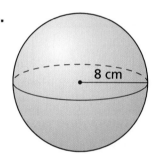

8 cm

5.

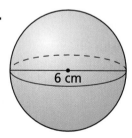

6 cm

6.

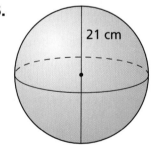

21 cm

For Exercises 7–9, each of the number sentences models the formula for the volume of a figure you have worked with in this unit. Name the figure, sketch and label the figure, and find the volume.

7. $2\frac{2}{3} \times 4\frac{4}{5} \times 3\frac{7}{8}$ 8. $\pi \times (2.2)^2 \times 6.5$ 9. $\frac{1}{3}\pi \times (4.25)^2 \times 10$

10. Watertown has three water storage tanks in different shapes: a cylinder, a cone, and a sphere. Each tank has a radius of 20 feet and a height of 40 feet.

   a. Sketch each tank, and label its dimensions.

   b. Estimate which tank will hold the most water. Explain.

   c. What is the volume of the cylindrical tank?

   d. What is the volume of the conical tank?

   e. What is the volume of the spherical tank?

11. Find the volume of each shape.

Homework
Help **O**nline
PHSchool.com
For: Help with Exercise 11
Web Code: ane-6411

a.

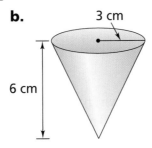

3 cm

6 cm

b.

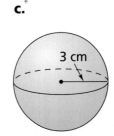

3 cm

6 cm

c.

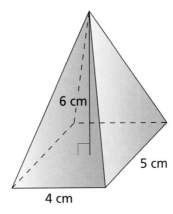

3 cm

   d. How do the volumes of the three shapes compare?

For Exercises 12 and 13, find the volume of each shape.

12.

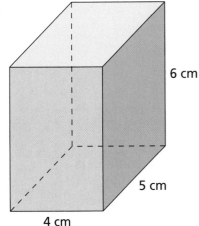

6 cm

5 cm

4 cm

13.

6 cm

6 cm

5 cm

4 cm

14. a. Sketch and label the dimensions of a pyramid with base dimensions 5 centimeters by 7 centimeters and height 8 centimeters.

   b. Find the volume of the pyramid in part (a).

15. The track-and-field club is planning a frozen yogurt sale to raise money. They need to buy containers to hold the yogurt. They must choose between the cup and the cone below. Each container costs the same. The club plans to charge customers $1.25 for a serving of yogurt. Which container should the club buy? Why?

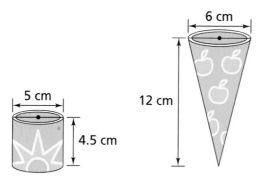

16. The Mathletes are planning their own frozen yogurt sale. They need to buy containers to hold the yogurt. They must choose between the prism and pyramid below. The other conditions that apply to the club in Exercise 15 also apply to the Mathletes. Which container should the club buy? Why?

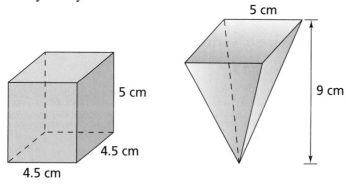

17. The prices and dimensions of several movie theater popcorn containers are shown below. Which container has the most popcorn per dollar? Explain. (Note: The diagrams below are not drawn to scale.)

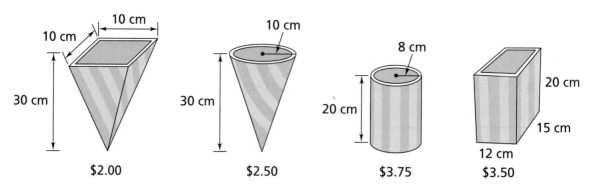

For Exercises 18–20, the volume of each shape is approximately 250 cubic inches.

18. Find the height of a cylinder with a radius of 3 inches.

19. Find the radius of a sphere.

20. Find the height of a cone with a radius of 3 inches.

For Exercises 21–22, suppose each shape has a square base, the side of the base is 3 inches, and the volume is 225 cubic inches. Find the height.

21. rectangular prism   **22.** pyramid

23. If a scoop of ice cream is a sphere with a radius of 1 inch, how many scoops can be packed into the cone at the right?

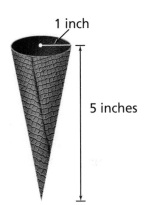

1 inch

5 inches

24. Chilly's Ice Cream Parlor purchases ice cream in $2\frac{1}{2}$-gallon cylindrical containers. Each container is $10\frac{5}{32}$ inches high and 9 inches in diameter. A jumbo scoop of ice cream comes in the shape of a sphere that is approximately 4 inches in diameter. How many jumbo scoops can Chilly's serve from one $2\frac{1}{2}$-gallon container of ice cream?

25. Chilly's Ice Cream Parlor is known for its root beer floats.

- The float is made by pouring root beer over 3 scoops of ice cream until the glass is filled $\frac{1}{2}$ inch from the top.
- A glass is in the shape of a cylinder with a radius of $1\frac{1}{4}$ inches and height of $8\frac{1}{2}$ inches.
- Each scoop of ice cream is a sphere with a radius of $1\frac{1}{4}$ inches.

Will there be more ice cream or more root beer in the float? Explain your reasoning.

Connections

26. A drink can is a cylinder with a radius of 3 centimeters and a height of 12 centimeters.

   a. Sketch the can, and label its dimensions.

   b. What is the circumference of the can?

   c. What is the volume?

   d. What is the surface area?

   e. How many cans will it take to fill a liter bottle? (A liter bottle contains 1,000 cubic centimeters.)

27. Three students measured the height of the same cylinder and their measurements are listed below. What is the average of the heights?

$2\frac{1}{2}$ feet $\qquad\qquad$ $2\frac{2}{3}$ feet $\qquad\qquad$ $2\frac{7}{12}$ feet

For: Multiple-Choice Skills Practice
Web Code: ana-6454

28. Five students measured the height of the same prism and their measurements are listed below. What is the average of the heights?

5.1 centimeters $\qquad\qquad$ 4.9 centimeters

5.25 centimeters $\qquad\qquad$ 5.15 centimeters

4.85 centimeters

Each number sentence in Exercises 29–31 is a model for the surface area of a three-dimensional figure. Identify which three-dimensional figure the number sentence describes. Find the surface area.

29. $2 \times (4) + 2 \times (8.5) + 2 \times (7.25)$

30. $2 \times (4 + 8.5 + 7.25)$

31. $2\pi \times (4)^2 + 2\pi \times (4)(8.5)$

32. Kaiya measures the circumference of a sphere and finds that it is 54 centimeters. What is the volume of the sphere?

Extensions

33. Ted made a scale model of a submarine for his science class.

  a. What is the volume of Ted's model?

  b. If 1 inch in the model represents 20 feet in the actual submarine, what is the volume of the actual submarine?

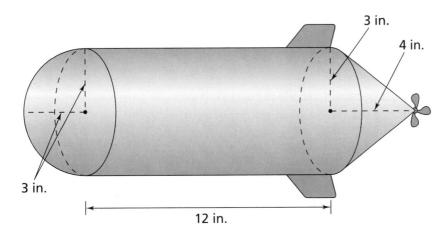

3 in.

4 in.

3 in.

12 in.

34. Some of the Inuit people build igloos shaped like hemispheres (halves of a sphere). Some of the Hopi people in Arizona build adobes shaped like rectangular boxes. Suppose an igloo has an inner diameter of 20 feet.

  a. Describe the shape of a Hopi dwelling that would provide the same amount of living space as the igloo described above.

  b. What dimensions of the floor would give the Hopi dwelling the same amount of floor space as the igloo?

35. A pyramid is named for the shape of its base. The left shape below is a triangular pyramid, the center shape is a square pyramid, and the right shape is a pentagonal pyramid.

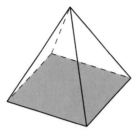

a. Suppose the bases of a pyramid are all regular polygons. What happens to the shape of the pyramid as the number of sides in the base increases?

b. Describe a method for finding the surface area of a pyramid.

36. For each shape below, find the dimensions that will most closely fit inside a cubic box with 5-centimeter edges.

a. sphere   **b.** cylinder   **c.** cone   **d.** pyramid

e. Does a sphere, a cylinder, or a cone fit best inside the cubic box? That is, for which shape is there the least space between the shape and the box?

37. The edges of a cube measure 10 centimeters. Describe the dimensions of a cylinder and a cone with the same volume as the cube. Explain.

Which shape should I start with?

Mathematical Reflections 4

In this investigation, you studied the relationships between the volumes of a cone, a sphere, and a cylinder with the same radius and height. You also studied the relationship between a square pyramid and a rectangular prism with the same base and height. These questions will help you summarize what you have learned.

Think about your answers to these questions. Discuss your ideas with other students and your teacher. Then write a summary of your findings in your notebook.

1. a. If a cone, a cylinder, and a sphere have the same radius and height, describe the relationships among their volumes. Use examples and sketches to illustrate your answer.

   b. If you know the radius of a sphere, how can you find the volume?

   c. If you know the radius and height of a cone, how can you find the volume?

2. a. Suppose a square pyramid and a rectangular prism have the same base and height. How do their volumes compare? Use examples and sketches to support your answer.

   b. Suppose you know the dimensions of the base and the height of a rectangular pyramid. How could you find the volume?

3. a. How are pyramids and cones alike and different?

   b. How are prisms and cylinders alike and different?

Scaling Boxes

The cost of packaging materials and finding enough landfill for garbage and waste materials is becoming a problem for many communities. Some communities are looking at composting as a way to recycle garbage into productive soil.

Composting is a method for turning organic waste into rich soil. Today, many people have compost boxes that break down kitchen waste quickly and with little odor. The secret is in the worms!

Recipe for a 1-2-3 Compost Box

- Start with an open rectangular wood box that is 1 foot high, 2 feet wide, and 3 feet long. This is a 1-2-3 box.

- Mix 10 pounds of shredded newspaper with 15 quarts of water. Put the mixture in the 1-2-3 box.

- Add a few handfuls of soil.

- Add about 1,000 redworms (about 1 pound).

Every day, mix collected kitchen waste with the soil in the box. The worms will do the rest of the work, turning the waste into new soil. A 1-2-3 box will decompose about 0.5 pound of garbage each day.

5.1 Building a Bigger Box

Deshondra chose composting as the topic of her science project. She plans to build a compost box at home and to keep records of the amount of soil produced over several weeks. She estimates that her family throws away 1 pound of garbage a day.

Problem 5.1 Doubling the Volume of a Rectangular Prism

Deshondra wants to build a box that will decompose twice the amount of the 1-2-3 box.

A. Using grid paper, make scale models of a 1-2-3 box that will decompose 0.5 pound of garbage per day and a box that will decompose 1 pound of garbage per day.

B. 1. What are the dimensions of the new box?

   2. How many of the original boxes will fit into the new box?

   3. How is the volume of the new box related to the volume of the original box?

C. How much plywood is needed to construct an open 1-pound box?

ACE Homework starts on page 67.

5.2 Scaling Up the Compost Box

In *Stretching and Shrinking,* you studied similar two-dimensional figures. The ideas you learned also apply to three-dimensional figures. For example, two rectangular prisms are similar if the ratios of the lengths of corresponding edges are equal. A 2-4-6 box is similar to the 1-2-3 box.

The *scale factor* is the number that each dimension of one rectangular prism must be multiplied by to get the dimensions of a similar prism. The scale factor from the 1-2-3 box to the 2-4-6 box is 2 because each edge length of the 1-2-3 box must be multiplied by 2 to get the corresponding edge length of the 2-4-6 box.

Problem 5.2 Applying Scale Factors to Rectangular Prisms

Ms. Fernandez's class decides that building and maintaining a compost is a fascinating project. One student suggests that they could earn money selling worms and soil to a local nursery.

They decide to build different-sized boxes that are similar to the 1-2-3 box. They need to know how much material is needed to build the boxes and how much garbage each box will decompose in a day.

A. Copy and complete the table.

Compost Box Project

Open Box (h-w-ℓ)	Scale Factor	Surface Area (ft²)	Volume (ft³)	Amount of Garbage Decomposed in a Day	Number of Worms Needed
1-2-3	▦	▦	▦	▦	▦
2-4-6	▦	▦	▦	▦	▦
3-6-9	▦	▦	▦	▦	▦
4-8-12	▦	▦	▦	▦	▦
▦	▦	▦	▦	▦	▦
▦	▦	1,024	▦	▦	▦
▦	▦	▦	▦	▦	▦
▦	▦	▦	6,000	▦	▦

B. How is the change in surface area from a 1-2-3 box to a similar box related to the scale factor from the 1-2-3 box to the similar box? Suppose the compost box has a top. Will your answer change? Explain.

C. How is the change in volume from a 1-2-3 box to a similar box related to the scale factor from the 1-2-3 box to the similar box? Explain.

D. How is the change in decomposed garbage related to the scale factor? Explain.

E. Suppose the scale factor between the 1-2-3 box and a similar box is N. Describe the dimensions, surface area, and volume of the similar box.

ACE Homework starts on page 67.

5.3 Building Model Ships

Builders and architects often make models of cars, ships, buildings, and parks. A model is useful in determining several aspects of the building process, including structural strength, expense, and appearance.

Problem 5.3 Similarity and Scale Factors

Natasha builds a model ship from a kit. She tries to picture what the actual ship looks like. The scale factor from the model to the actual ship is 200.

A. **1.** If the length of the model is 25 centimeters, what is the length of the actual ship?

2. If the length of the flagpole on the actual ship is 30 meters, what is the length of the flagpole on the model?

B. The area of a rectangular floor on the model is 20 square centimeters. What is the area of the floor on the actual ship?

C. The cylindrical smoke stack on the model has a height of 4 centimeters and a radius of 1.5 centimeters.

1. What are the dimensions of the smoke stack on the actual ship?

2. What is the volume of the smoke stack on the actual ship?

3. What is the surface area of the smoke stack on the actual ship?

ACE **Homework starts on page 67.**

Did You Know?

Most minerals occur naturally as crystals. Every crystal has an orderly, internal pattern of atoms, with a distinctive way of locking new atoms into that pattern. As the pattern repeats, larger similar-shaped crystals are formed. The shape of the resulting crystal, such as a cube (like salt) or a six-sided form (like a snowflake), is a similar crystal.

As crystals grow, differences in temperature and chemical composition cause fascinating variations. But you will rarely find in your backyard the perfectly shaped mineral crystals that you see in a museum. In order to readily show their geometric form and flat surfaces, crystals need ideal or controlled growing conditions as well as room to grow.

Go Online
PHSchool.com **For:** Information about growing crystals **Web Code:** ane-9031

Applications

1. a. Make a sketch of an open 1-3-5 box. Label the edges of the box.

   b. Sketch three boxes that have twice the volume of a 1-3-5 box. Label each box with its dimensions.

   c. Are any of the three boxes in part (b) similar to the 1-3-5 box? Explain.

For Exercises 2–4, find the volume and the surface area of each closed box.

2. 1-2-2　　　　　**3.** 1.5-1.5-3　　　　　**4.** 2-4-1

For Exercises 5–7, decide if each pair of cylinders are similar. For each pair of similar cylinders, describe how many times larger one is than the other.

5. Cylinder 1: height = 10 centimeters, radius = 5 centimeters
   Cylinder 2: height = 5 centimeters, radius = 2.5 centimeters

6. Cylinder 1: height = 10 centimeters, radius = 5 centimeters
   Cylinder 2: height = 30 centimeters, radius = 15 centimeters

7. Cylinder 1: height = 10 centimeters, radius = 5 centimeters
   Cylinder 2: height = 15 centimeters, radius = 10 centimeters

8. a. Make a sketch of an open 2-2-3 box and an open 2-2-6 box. Label the edges of the boxes.

   b. Find the volume of each box in part (a).

   c. Find the surface area of each box in part (a).

   d. Suppose you want to adapt the 1-2-3 compost box recipe for the boxes in part (a). How many worms and how much paper and water would you need for each box?

9. a. Give the dimensions of a rectangular box that will decompose 5 pounds of garbage per day. Explain your reasoning.

   b. Is your box similar to the 1-2-3 box? Explain.

10. One cube has edges measuring 1 foot. A second cube has edges measuring 2 feet. A third cube has edges measuring 3 feet.

    a. Make scale drawings of the three cubes. For each cube, tell what length in the drawing represents 1 foot.

    b. Find the surface area of each cube.

    c. Describe what happens to the surface area of a cube when the edge lengths are doubled, tripled, quadrupled, and so on.

11. a. Find the volume of each cube in Exercise 10.

    b. Describe what happens to the volume of a cube when the edge lengths are doubled, tripled, quadrupled, and so on.

For Exercises 12–14, decide if each pair of rectangular boxes is similar. For each pair of similar boxes, describe how many times larger one box is than the other box.

For: Help with Exercises 12–14
Web Code: ane-6512

12. 1-2-5 and 3-6-15

13. 2-3-2 and 5-6-5

14. 2-1-4 and 3-1.5-6

15. In the United States, an average of 2.7 pounds of garbage per person is delivered to landfills each day. A cubic foot of compressed garbage weighs about 50 pounds.

    a. Estimate the amount of garbage produced by a family of four in one year.

    b. Estimate the amount of garbage produced by the families of a class of 20 students in one year. Assume each family has four people.

16. Each year the United States generates 450 million cubic yards of solid waste. Mr. Costello's classroom is 42 feet long, 30 feet wide, and 12 feet high. How many rooms of this size would be needed to hold all this garbage?

17. For every ton of paper that is recycled, about 17 trees and 3.3 cubic yards of landfill space are saved. In the United States, the equivalent of 500,000 trees are used each week to produce the Sunday papers. Suppose all the Sunday papers this week are made from recycled paper. How much landfill is saved?

In Exercises 18 and 19, a company that specializes in creating models of buildings is hired to develop models of pools for the upcoming summer Olympics. The pools are rectangular prisms. The scale factor from the model to the actual pool is 120.

18. a. The dimensions of the actual diving pool are 20 meters by 20 meters by 4.9 meters. What are the dimensions of the model diving pool?

b. What is the capacity (volume) of the actual diving pool. What is the capacity of the model diving pool?

c. What is the surface area of the actual diving pool? What is the surface area of the model diving pool? (Do not include the surface of the water.)

19. a. The planned water capacity of the pool used for water polo and swimming is 1,650 cubic meters. What is the capacity of the model pool?

b. A sunken corridor with viewing windows is planned for the diving pool. The area of a window in the actual setting is 160 square feet. What is the area of the window on the model?

Connections

20. For parts (a)–(e), find the measure that makes a true statement.

a. 1 square foot = ■ square inches

b. 1 square yard = ■ square inches

c. 1 cubic yard = ■ cubic feet

d. 2 square yards = ■ square inches

e. 3 square yards = ■ square inches

f. For parts (a), (b), and (e) above, draw a diagram to justify your answer.

Go Online
PHSchool.com

For: Multiple-Choice Skills
Practice
Web Code: ana-6554

For Exercises 21–23, find the measure that makes a true statement.

21. 4 square meters = ■ square centimeters

22. 1 cubic meter = ■ cubic centimeters

23. 6 cubic centimeters = ■ cubic millimeters

24. For the compost boxes in Problem 5.2, find the ratios in parts (a)–(c).

a. the length of each side of the 1-2-3 box to the length of the corresponding side of the 2-4-6 box

b. the surface area of the 1-2-3 box to the surface area of the 2-4-6 box

c. the volume of the 1-2-3 box to the volume of the 2-4-6 box

d. How is each ratio in parts (a)–(c) related to the scale factor from the 1-2-3 box to the 2-4-6 box?

25. At the movie theater, a large cylindrical container of popcorn costs $5.00, and a small cylindrical container costs $2.50. Denzel thinks that the heights of the containers are about the same and that the radius of the large container is about twice the radius of the small container. To get the most popcorn for his $5.00, should Denzel buy one large popcorn or two small popcorns? Explain.

$2.50 $2.50 $5.00

26. A compost company builds and sells 1-2-3 compost boxes. They need to store a supply of the boxes in their warehouse to fill customers' orders. The sketches below show a 1-2-3 box on the right and the space in the warehouse allotted for the boxes on the left.

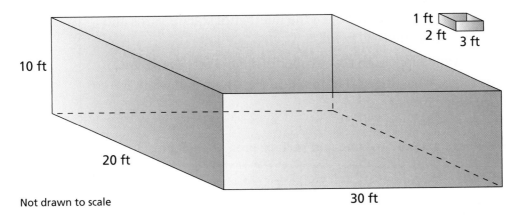

Not drawn to scale

a. How many 1-2-3 boxes can be stored in one layer on the floor of the storage space?

b. How many layers of boxes can be stacked in the storage space?

c. How many boxes can be stored in the storage space?

27. Mary's class decides to build a cylindrical compost box. Mary calculates that a cylindrical container with a height of 2 feet and a radius of 1 foot would decompose 0.5 pound of garbage each day. She calls this container a 1-2 cylinder.

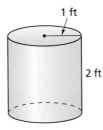

a. How does the volume of the 1-2 cylinder compare with the volume of the 1-2-3 box?

b. How does the surface area of the 1-2 cylinder compare with the surface area of the 1-2-3 box?

c. Mary's class estimates that they throw away about 1 pound of garbage at school each day. What size cylinder should they build to handle this much garbage?

28. The two legs of a right triangle are in the ratio 3 : 4.

a. Sketch and label the described triangle. Then sketch and label two other similar right triangles.

b. Suppose you create a similar right triangle by doubling the length of the legs. How will the area of the first triangle be related to the area of the second triangle?

29. A football field is 120 yards long, including the end zones, and $53\frac{1}{3}$ yards wide.

   a. How many square yards are in the football field?

   b. How many square feet are in the football field?

   c. What is the relationship between the number of square yards and square feet in the football field?

   d. Describe what happens to the number of square feet in the area of a rectangle when the unit of measure for length and width is $\frac{1}{3}$ the size of the original unit.

For Exercises 30–32, find the volume and surface area of each box shown.

30.
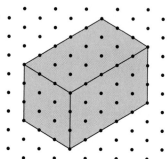

31.

32.
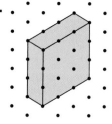

33. After a container of water is poured into a cylindrical tank, the tank is $\frac{2}{9}$ full. How many containers of water are needed to fill the tank to $\frac{3}{4}$ full?

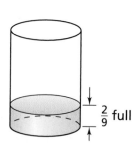

$\frac{2}{9}$ full

34. Anna uses exactly one small can of red paint to cover a strip around the top of an open chest. The red strip around the top is 0.15 of the total surface area (without the top and bottom of the chest).

   a. How many small cans of blue paint does she need to paint the rest?

   b. What is the surface area of the chest, not including the top and bottom?

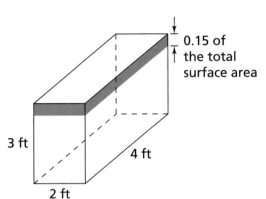

0.15 of the total surface area

3 ft

4 ft

2 ft

Extensions

35. The following sketches show the front, top, and right side views of a "tilted box" in which two of the six faces are non-rectangular parallelograms. The top and the bottom faces are identical rectangles, and the right and left faces are identical rectangles. (This is called an *oblique prism*.)

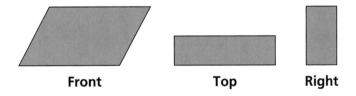

| Front | Top | Right |

   a. Make a sketch of the box.

   b. What measurements do you need to find the volume of the box? How can you use these measurements to find the volume?

   c. What measurements do you need to find the surface area of the box? How can you use these measurements to find the surface area?

36. Is the price of a box of cereal directly related to its volume? Collect some data to help you answer this question.

   a. Record the dimensions and prices of two or three different-sized boxes of the same cereal brand.

   b. Calculate the volume of each box.

   c. Calculate the cost per unit of volume for each box. Compare the results for the different boxes.

   d. Write a short report summarizing what you learned about the relationship between box size and cereal price.

37. A cake, a loaf of bread, or a brick of cheese could be called a "sliceable" rectangular prism.

   a. How many different ways can you slice such a prism into two pieces of equal volume?

   b. If the prism were a cube, how many ways could you slice it into two pieces of equal volume?

For each pair of cylinders in Exercises 38–40, find the ratio of each measurement of Cylinder A to the corresponding measurement of Cylinder B.

   a. the radius   **b.** the height

   c. the surface area   **d.** the volume

38. The dimensions of Cylinder A are twice the dimensions of Cylinder B.

39. The dimensions of Cylinder A are three times the dimensions of Cylinder B.

40. The dimensions of Cylinder A are four times the dimensions of Cylinder B.

Mathematical Reflections 5

In this investigation, you learned how changing the dimensions of a rectangular box affects its volume and surface area. These questions will help you summarize what you have learned.

Think about your answers to these questions. Discuss your ideas with other students and your teacher. Then write a summary of your findings in your notebook.

1. Suppose you want to build a rectangular box with eight times the volume of a given rectangular box. How can you determine the possible dimensions for the new box? Are the two boxes similar? Explain.

2. Describe how the volume and surface area of a rectangular prism change as each of its dimensions is doubled, tripled, quadrupled, and so on.

Unit Project

The Package Design Contest

The Worldwide Sporting Company (WSC) wants a new set of package designs for their table-tennis balls (Ping-Pong balls). The table-tennis balls are about 3.8 centimeters in diameter. WSC has decided to offer a scholarship to the students or groups of students who convince the company to use their design.

- The board of directors wants a small package, a medium package, and a large package of table-tennis balls.

- The president of the company wants the cost of the packages to be considered.

- The marketing division wants the packages to be appealing to customers, to stack easily, and to look good on store shelves.

Part 1: Design a Contest Entry

You are to prepare an entry for the package design contest. Your task is to design three different packages for table-tennis balls. Include the following things in your contest entry:

1. A description of the shape or shapes of the packages you have designed and an explanation for why you selected these shapes.

2. Nets for each of your packages that, when they are cut out, folded, and taped together, will make models of your packages. Use centimeter grid paper to make your patterns.

3. Calculations of how much each of your package designs will cost to construct. The packaging material costs $0.005 per square centimeter.

Part 2: Write a Report

You will submit your designs and a written proposal to WSC. Your written proposal should try to convince WSC that your designs are the ones they should use.

4. An explanation of how you have addressed WSC's three concerns (listed above).

Remember, you are trying to persuade WSC that your designs are the best and that they should select your work. Your report is to be written to the company officials. You need to think about the presentation of your written proposal. It should be neat (maybe even typed!), well organized, and easy to read so that the company officials can follow your work and ideas easily.

Looking Back and Looking Ahead

While working on the problems in this unit, you developed strategies for finding *surface area*, *volume*, and *nets* for rectangular prisms and cylinders. You used the relationships of other figures to cylinders to find the volumes of shapes such as *cones, spheres,* and *square pyramids*. Finally, you discovered the effects of enlargement and reduction on dimensions, surface area, and volume of prisms.

Go Online
PHSchool.com

For: Vocabulary Review Puzzle
Web Code: anj-6051

Use Your Understanding: Volume and Surface Area

To test your understanding of volume and surface area, consider the following problems.

1. Below is a net for a rectangular prism.

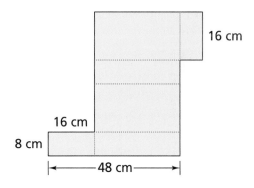

16 cm

16 cm

8 cm

|← 48 cm →|

a. What are the dimensions of the box that can be made from the net?

b. What is the surface area of the box?

c. What is the volume of the box?

d. Draw two other nets that will produce boxes of the same size and shape.

2. Sweet-Smile Chocolates is marketing a special assortment of caramels. The company wants to put the 40 individual caramels into a rectangular box. Each caramel is a 1-inch cube. The caramels should completely fill the box.

   a. Which arrangement of caramels requires the most cardboard for a box?

   b. Which arrangement of caramels requires the least cardboard?

   c. Make sketches of the boxes you described in parts (a) and (b). Label the dimensions.

   d. Suppose each dimension of the box in part (b) is doubled. How many more caramels can be packaged in the new box?

3. The Just-Add-Water Company has decided to change the packaging for a juuice drink. The drink used to come in cylindrical containers with a base diameter of 6 inches and a height of 10 inches. The new container is a square prism that fits inside the old cylinder, as shown in the sketch.

   a. What is the volume of the original cylindrical container?

   b. How much less juice can the rectangular prism hold than the cylindrical container?

   c. Suppose that the cost per cubic inch of juice is to be the same for both containers. The original container of juice cost $2.19. How much should a new box of juice cost if the amount of juice per dollar is the same?

   d. The company is also considering selling the juice in a cone with the same volume as the cylinder. Describe the possible dimensions for such a cone.

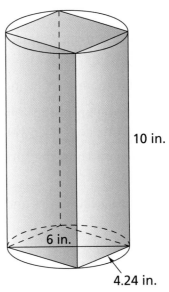

10 in.

6 in.

4.24 in.

Explain Your Reasoning

To answer problems about surface area and volume of solid figures, you have to know the meaning of those terms and some strategies for calculating the measurements from given dimensions of various figures.

4. What do *volume* and *surface area* measurements tell about a solid figure?

5. Which formulas will show how to find the surface area *A* and the volume *V* of each figure?

    a. a rectangular prism   **b.** a cylinder

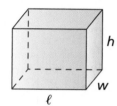 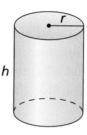

6. How can you convince someone that the formulas given in Exercise 5 are correct?

7. How are the volumes of cylinders, cones, and spheres related?

8. a. Suppose you know the volume of an object such as a box, a cylinder, or a cone. Can you determine its surface area?

    b. Suppose you know the surface area of an object. Can you find the volume?

9. How are the surface areas and volumes of square pyramids related to cubes?

Look Ahead

Measurement of surface area and volume for solid figures is used in many practical, scientific, and engineering problems. You will encounter the key ideas about area and volume in future *Connected Mathematics* units, in other mathematics subjects such as geometry, and in many situations of daily life such as packing, storing, and building tasks.

B

base The face of a three-dimensional shape chosen to be the "bottom" face.

base La cara de una figura tridimensional elegida para que sea la cara de la "base."

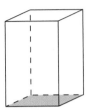 

C

cone A three-dimensional shape with a circular base and a vertex opposite the base.

cono Figura tridimensional con una base circular y un vértice opuesto a la base.

cube A three-dimensional shape with six identical square faces.

cubo Una figura tridimensional con seis caras cuadradas idénticas.

cylinder A three-dimensional shape with two opposite faces that are congruent circles. The side (lateral surface) is a rectangle that is "wrapped around" the circular faces at the ends.

cilindro Una figura tridimensional con dos caras opuestas que son círculos congruentes. El lado (la cara lateral) rectángulo es un está "envuelto alrededor de" que las dos caras circulares es los extremos.

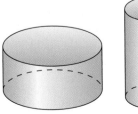 

edge A line segment formed where two faces of a three-dimensional shape meet.

arista El segmento de recta formado donde se encuentran dos caras de una figura tridimensional.

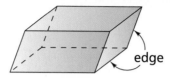

edge

edge

face A flat two-dimensional surface of a three-dimensional shape.

cara Superficie plana, bidimensional de una figura tridimensional.

height The vertical distance between the face chosen to be the base and

- the opposite face of a prism or cylinder, or
- the vertex of a cone or pyramid.

altura La distencia vertical entre la cara elegida para ser base y

- la cara opuesta de un prisma o cilindro, o
- el vértice de un cono o pirámide.

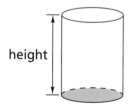

height

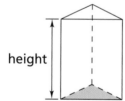

height

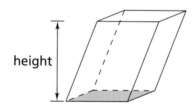

height

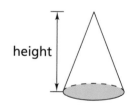

height

net A two-dimensional pattern that can be folded into a three-dimensional figure.

patrón plano Un patrón bidimensional que se puede plegar para formar una figura tridimensional.

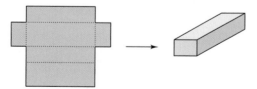

oblique prism A prism whose side faces are non-rectangular parallelograms.

prisma oblicuo Prisma cuyas caras laterales son paralelogramos no rectangulares.

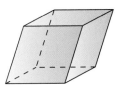

prism A three-dimensional shape with a top and bottom (base) that are congruent polygons and lateral faces that are parallelograms.

prisma Una figura tridimensional cuya parte superior y cuyo fondo (base) son polígonos congruentes y cuyas caras laterales son paralelogramos.

pyramid A three-dimensional shape with one polygonal base and lateral sides that are all triangles that meet at a vertex opposite the base.

pirámide Figura tridimensional cuya base es un polígono y cuyas caras laterales son tríangulos que se encuentran en un vértice opuesto a la base.

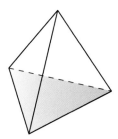 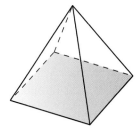 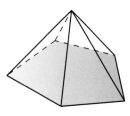

rectangular prism A prism with a top and bottom (base) that are congruent rectangles.

prisma rectangular Un prisma cuya parte superior e inferior (base) son rectángulos congruentes.

**Right
rectangular
prism**

**Oblique
rectangular
prism**

right prism A prism whose vertical faces are rectangles. The bases are congruent polygons.

prisma recto Un prisma cuyas caras verticales son rectángulos. Los bases son polígonos congruentes.

sphere A three-dimensional shape whose surface consists of all the points that are a given distance from the center of the shape.

esfera Una figura tridimensional cuya superficie consiste en todos los puntos ubicados a una distancia dada del centro de la figura.

surface area The area required to cover a three-dimensional shape.

área total El área requerida para cubrir una figura tridimensional.

unit cube A cube whose edges are 1 unit long. It is the basic unit of measurement for volume.

unidad cúbica Un cubo cuyas aristas miden 1 unidad de longitud. Es la unidad básica de medición para el volumen.

volume The amount of space occupied by, or the capacity of, a three-dimensional shape. The volume is the number of unit cubes that will fit into a three-dimensional shape.

volumen La cantidad de espacio que ocupa una figura tridimensional o la capacidad de dicha figura. Es el número de unidades cúbicas que cabrán en una figura tridimensional.

Index

Acknowledgments

Team Credits

The people who made up the **Connected Mathematics 2** team—representing editorial, editorial services, design services, and production services—are listed below. Bold type denotes core team members.

Leora Adler, Judith Buice, Kerry Cashman, Patrick Culleton, Sheila DeFazio, Richard Heater, **Barbara Hollingdale, Jayne Holman,** Karen Holtzman, **Etta Jacobs,** Christine Lee, Carolyn Lock, Catherine Maglio, **Dotti Marshall,** Rich McMahon, Eve Melnechuk, Kristin Mingrone, Terri Mitchell, **Marsha Novak,** Irene Rubin, Donna Russo, Robin Samper, Siri Schwartzman, **Nancy Smith,** Emily Soltanoff, **Mark Tricca,** Paula Vergith, Roberta Warshaw, Helen Young

Additional Credits

Diana Bonfilio, Mairead Reddin, Michael Torocsik, nSight, Inc.

Technical Illustration

WestWords, Inc.

Cover Design

tom white.images

Photos

2, Getty Images, Inc.; **3,** Geri Engberg; **5,** Jeff Greenberg/PhotoEdit; **9,** Jack Kurt/The Image Works; **15,** photolibrary.com pty. ltd./Index Stock Imagery, Inc.; **16,** Digital Vision/Getty Images, Inc.; **20,** Laura Dwight/PhotoEdit; **27,** BananaStock/Robertstock; **28,** IFA/PictureQuest; **29,** Andrew Olney/Masterfile; **30,** Bob Daemmrich/PhotoEdit; **37,** Lynn Stone/Getty Images, Inc.; **39,** Danita Delimont/Alamy; **40,** Richard Haynes; **42,** Getty Images, Inc.; **45,** Sam Yeh/AFP/Getty Images, Inc.; **52,** Francis Dean/The Image Works; **53,** ©2002 Thaves. Reprinted with permission. Newspaper dist. by NEA, Inc.; **59 l,** Bryan & Cherry Alexander/Photo Researchers, Inc.; **59 r,** A. Woolfitt/Robert Harding World Imagery; **60,** Richard Haynes; **62,** David Young-Wolff/PhotoEdit; **62 inset,** Wally Eberhart/Getty Images, Inc.; **65,** Clayton Sharrard/PhotoEdit; **66,** SuperStock, Inc./SuperStock; **68,** Jeff Mermelstein/Getty Images, Inc.; **69,** Masterfile (Royalty-Free Division); **73,** Richard Haynes; **77,** Brooke Slezak/Getty Images, Inc.

Connected Mathematics 2™

What Do You Expect?

Probability and Expected Value

Glenda Lappan

James T. Fey

William M. Fitzgerald

Susan N. Friel

Elizabeth Difanis Phillips

PEARSON

Prentice Hall

Boston, Massachusetts
Upper Saddle River, New Jersey

What Do You Expect?

Probability and Expected Value

In Raymundo's *Prime Number Multiplication Game*, a player rolls two number cubes. Player A gets 10 points if the product is prime. Player B gets 1 point if the product is not prime. Is Raymundo's game a fair game?

In the district finals, Nishi has just been fouled. She gets to try one free throw. If she makes it, she gets to try a second free throw. Nishi's free-throw average is 60%. Is Nishi most likely to score 0, 1, or 2 points?

Have you ever had to guess at the answers on a quiz? If you take a four-question true/false quiz and guess on every question, what are your chances of getting every question right?

Probabilities can help you make decisions. If there is a 75% chance of rain, you might decide to carry an umbrella. If a baseball player has a .245 batting average, you expect that he is more likely not to get a hit than to get a hit on a given at-bat.

Probabilities can also help you to predict what will happen over the long run. Suppose you and a friend toss a coin before each bus ride to decide who will sit by the window. You can predict that, over the long run, you will sit by the window about half of the time.

Many probability situations involve a payoff—points scored in a game, lives saved by promoting good health, or profit earned from a business venture. You can sometimes find the long-term average payoff called the expected value. For example, when deciding whether to make an investment, a company might figure out how much it can expect to earn over the long run.

In this unit, you will look at questions involving probability and expected value, including the three questions on the opposite page.

Mathematical Highlights

Probability and Expected Value

In *What Do You Expect?*, you will deepen your understanding of basic probability concepts. You will learn about the expected value of situations involving chance.

You will learn how to

- Interpret experimental and theoretical probabilities and the relationship between them
- Distinguish between equally likely and non-equally likely events
- Review strategies for identifying possible outcomes and analyzing probabilities, such as using lists or tree diagrams
- Determine if a game is fair or unfair
- Analyze situations that involve two stages (or actions)
- Use area models to analyze situations that involve two stages
- Determine the expected value of a probability situation
- Analyze situations that involve binomial outcomes
- Use probability and expected value to make decisions

As you work on problems in this unit, ask yourself questions about situations that involve analyzing probabilities:

What are the possible outcomes for the event(s) in this situation?

Are these outcomes equally likely?

Is this a fair or unfair situation?

Can I compute the theoretical probabilities or do I conduct an experiment?

How can I determine the probability of the outcome of one event followed by a second event?

How can I use expected value to help me make decisions?

Investigation 1

Evaluating Games of Chance

Many board games or computer games that you play involve chance. In some games, the square you land on depends on what numbers come up when you roll a pair of number cubes. Suppose you want to roll a sum of 10.

What is the probability that you will roll a sum of 10 on your turn?

In *How Likely Is It?*, you played the Roller Derby game, which involves finding the sum of two number cubes. You played the game several times and computed the **experimental probability** for each sum. To find the experimental probability of getting a sum of 10, you can use this formula:

$$P(\text{sum of } 10) = \frac{\text{number of times the sum of 10 occurred}}{\text{total number of trials}}$$

You also computed **theoretical probabilities** by listing all the possible outcomes. There are 36 outcomes, three of which result in a sum of 10.

What are the three ways in which you can get a sum of 10 when you roll a pair of number cubes?

The theoretical probability of getting a sum of 10 is

$$P(\text{sum of } 10) = \frac{\text{number of possible outcomes with a sum of 10}}{\text{total number of possible outcomes}} = \frac{3}{36} \text{ or } \frac{1}{12}$$

In this Investigation, you will explore several games involving chance. In each situation, you are asked to determine the chance, or probability, that certain outcomes will occur. In some situations, you will also be asked to determine whether a particular game is fair.

What do you think it means for a game to be fair?

1.1 Matching Colors

April and Tioko invented a two-player spinner game called Match/No-Match.

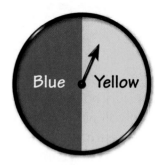

- Players take turns spinning a spinner like the one shown here.

- On each turn, a player spins the pointer of the spinner twice. If both spins land on the same color (a match), then Player A scores 1 point. If the two spins land on different colors (a no-match), then Player B scores 2 points.

- The player with the most points after 24 spins wins.

Do you think this is a fair or unfair game?

Are both players equally likely to win?

Problem 1.1 Experimental and Theoretical Probability

- Play the Match/No-Match game with a partner. Take a total of 24 turns (12 for each player).

- For each turn, record the color pair, for example, blue-yellow. Award points to the appropriate player.

For: Designer Dart Boards
Visit: PHSchool.com
Web Code: and-7101

A. Use the results you collect to find the experimental probabilities for a match and a no-match.

B. 1. List all of the possible outcomes of a turn (2 spins).

2. Use the possible outcomes to determine the theoretical probability of a match and a no-match.

3. Are the outcomes *equally likely*? That is, does each outcome have the same chance of occurring?

C. Compare the experimental and theoretical probabilities.

D. Is Match/No-Match a fair game? If it is fair, explain why. If it is not fair, explain how the rules can be changed to make the game fair.

ACE Homework starts on page 10.

Red and Blue Is a Winner!

In *How Likely Is It?*, you learned to find all the possible outcomes of a situation by making an organized list. April uses a tree diagram to show all the possible outcomes for the Match/No-Match game.

First, she lists the equally likely outcomes of the first spin.

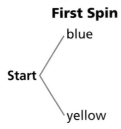

First Spin

Start
— blue
— yellow

From each result of the first spin, April draws and labels two branches to show the possible results of the second spin.

First Spin   Second Spin

Start
— blue
  — blue
  — yellow
— yellow
  — blue
  — yellow

April can read all the possible outcomes of a turn by following the paths from left to right. For example, she can follow the upper branch from start to blue, and then from there, she can follow the upper branch to blue. This path represents the outcome blue-blue. The right column below lists the possible outcomes. The outcomes are all equally likely.

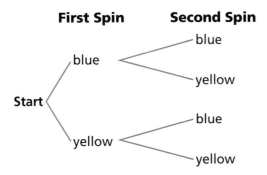

First Spin	Second Spin	Outcome
blue	blue	blue-blue
	yellow	blue-yellow
yellow	blue	yellow-blue
	yellow	yellow-yellow

A carnival committee is considering using the Red and Blue game. The game involves choosing one marble at random from each of two buckets. The first bucket contains one green, one blue, one red, and one yellow marble. The second bucket contains one green, one red, and one yellow marble.

Without looking, a player chooses one marble from each bucket in the Red and Blue game. If the player gets a red and a blue marble (the order makes no difference), the player wins. Each player pays $1 to play and receives $3 for each win.

Bucket 1   **Bucket 2**

A. Before playing the game, do you predict that the school will make money on this game? Explain.

B. Make a tree diagram to show the possible outcomes for this game. Explain how your tree shows all the possible outcomes.

C. What is the theoretical probability of choosing a red and blue marble on a turn?

D. Suppose the game is played 36 times.

  1. How much money can the school expect to collect?

  2. How much money can the school expect to pay out to the winners?

  3. Did the school make money? If so, how much?

E. Suppose one marble is chosen from each bucket. Find the probability of each situation.

  1. You choose a green marble from Bucket 1 and a yellow marble from Bucket 2.

  2. You do *not* choose a blue marble from either bucket.

  3. You choose two blue marbles.

  4. You choose at least one blue marble.

ACE Homework starts on page 10.

Playing the Multiplication Game

You have played games that use the sum of two number cubes. In the following game, scoring depends on the *product* of the numbers rolled.

Problem 1.3 Determining Whether a Game Is Fair

Multiplication Game Rules

- Player A and Player B take turns rolling two number cubes.
- If the product of the numbers rolled is odd, Player A wins a point. If the product of the numbers rolled is even, Player B wins a point.
- The player with the most points after 36 rolls wins.

A. 1. Play the Multiplication Game with a partner for a total of 36 turns. Keep track of your results.

   2. Based on your data, what is the experimental probability of rolling an odd product? What is the probability of an even product?

B. 1. List the possible products. In how many different ways can each product occur?

   2. Is each product equally likely? Explain.

   3. What is the theoretical probability of rolling an odd product? What is the theoretical probability of rolling an even product?

C. Suppose the game has 100 rolls instead of 36. How many points do you expect each player to have at the end of the game?

D. Do you think the Multiplication Game is fair? Explain. If the game is not fair, explain how the rules could be changed so that the game is fair.

ACE | Homework starts on page 10.

Applications

1. Decide whether the possible resulting events are equally likely.
Explain.

Action	**Possible resulting events**
a. You roll a number cube.	You roll an even number, or you roll an odd number.

b. A young child grows.   The child is left-handed, or the child is right-handed.

c. You toss a marshmallow.   The marshmallow lands on its end, or the marshmallow lands on its curved side.

d. You choose a card from a standard deck of 52 playing cards with no jokers.   The card is a heart, the card is a club, the card is a diamond, or the card is a spade.

e. You toss a coin three times.   You get three heads, two heads and a tail, a head and two tails, or three tails.

2. Lori's little sister Emily tore the labels from ten cans of vegetables.
Now all the cans look exactly the same. Three cans are corn, two
are spinach, four are beans, and one is tomatoes. Lori picks a can
at random. Find each probability.

For: Multiple-Choice Skills Practice
Web Code: ana-7154

a. *P*(corn)   **b.** *P*(beans)

c. *P*(not spinach)   **d.** *P*(beans or tomatoes)

e. Is each vegetable equally likely to be in the can? Explain.

3. Jacob has a probability party. He serves three items, each item selected at random from two options. Each guest gets a hamburger or a hot dog, cole slaw or potato salad, and an apple or an orange.

   a. Make a tree diagram to show all possibilities.

   b. What is the probability that Samantha gets a hot dog, cole slaw, and an orange?

   c. Rick does not like hot dogs. What is the probability that he will *not* be served a hot dog?

4. José is going to a party. He decides to wear his jeans and a sweater, but he hasn't decided what else to wear. The tree diagram shows the possible outfits he can make if he chooses sneakers or loafers; a pair of blue, red, or white socks; and a green, red, or plaid cap, at random.

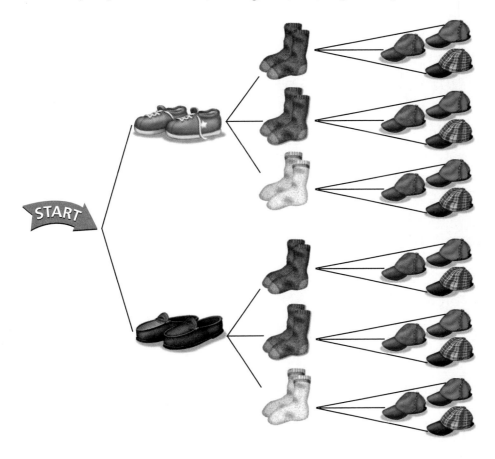

START

   a. What is the probability that José will wear loafers, blue socks, and a plaid cap?

   b. What is the probability that José will wear sneakers, either red or blue socks, and a green cap?

   c. What is the probability that José will wear neither red socks nor a red cap?

For Exercises 5–9, Monita and Kyan are analyzing a game involving two different spinners. A turn is one spin on each spinner. They make this tree diagram of equally likely outcomes to find theoretical probabilities.

5. Multiple Choice Choose the spinner that could be Spinner X.

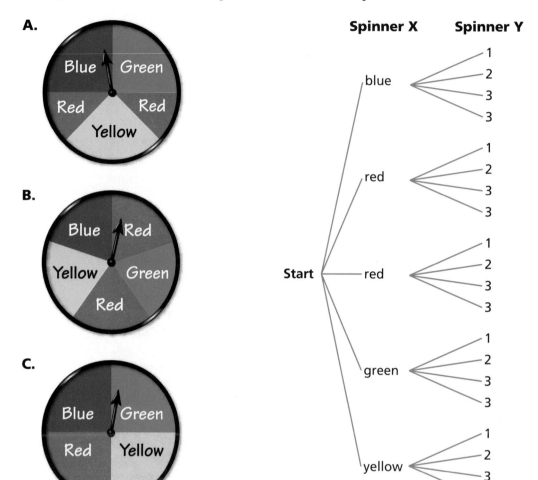

A.

B.

C.

D. None of these is correct.

6. List all possible outcomes of spinning each spinner, Spinner X and Spinner Y, once.

7. Which color and number combination has the greatest probability of occurring?

8. What is the probability of getting red on Spinner X and 3 on Spinner Y?

9. What is the probability of *not* getting a 3 on Spinner Y?

10. In the Gee Whiz Everyone Wins! game show, members of the audience choose a block at random from the bucket shown at the right. If a blue block is chosen, the contestant wins $5. If a red block is chosen, the contestant wins $10. If the yellow block is chosen, the contestant wins $50. The block is replaced after each turn.

    a. What is the probability of choosing each color? Explain your method.

    b. Suppose 24 contestants choose and replace a block. How much money can the game show expect to pay out?

11. In Raymundo's Prime Number Multiplication Game, a player rolls two number cubes. Player A gets 10 points if the product is prime. Player B gets 1 point if the product is not prime. Raymundo thinks this scoring system is reasonable because there are many more ways to roll a non-prime product than a prime product.

    a. If the cubes are rolled 100 times, how many points would you expect Player A to score? How many points would you expect Player B to score?

    b. Is Raymundo's game a fair game? Explain.

12. Rachel says that if she rolls two number cubes 36 times, she will get a product of 1 exactly once. Mariana said that she cannot be sure this will happen exactly once, but it will probably happen very few times. Who is right? Explain your reasoning.

13. Rachel told Mariana that if she rolls two number cubes 100 times, she will never get a product of 23. Mariana told her that she can't be sure. Who is right? Explain.

Connections

14. The probability of an event is a number between 0 (0%) and 1 (100%). The larger the probability, the greater the chances the event will occur. If an event is impossible, the probability that it will occur is 0 (or 0%). If an event is certain to happen, the probability that it will occur is 1, or 100%.

Copy the scale below. Place the letter of each event a–i on the scale at the spot that best describes its probability.

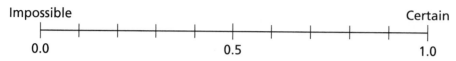

a. You get a head when you toss a coin.

b. You run 20 miles in one hour.

c. You roll a 6 on a number cube.

d. Your neighbor's cat has four legs.

e. The sun will rise tomorrow.

f. You toss a coin twice and get two heads.

g. You toss a coin twice and get at least one head.

h. You listen to a CD today.

i. You spin the spinner below, and it lands on red.

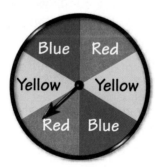

15. Multiple Choice What fraction of this diagram is shaded?

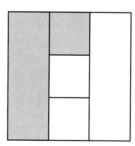

F. $\frac{1}{2}$ **G.** $\frac{2}{5}$ **H.** $\frac{1}{3}$ **J.** $\frac{4}{9}$

Homework Help Online
PHSchool.com

For: Help with Exercise 15
Web Code: ane-7115

16. Write three fractions equivalent to the fraction you chose in Exercise 15.

17. Multiple Choice What fraction of this diagram is shaded?

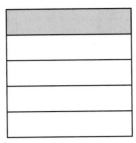

A. $\frac{20}{100}$ **B.** $\frac{4}{8}$ **C.** $\frac{1}{2}$ **D.** $\frac{1}{4}$

18. Write three fractions equivalent to the fraction you chose in Exercise 17.

19. Fala spins this spinner several times. The table shows the results.

 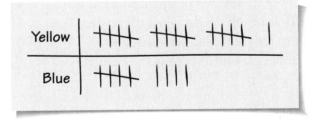

    a. How many times did Fala spin the spinner?

    b. What percent of the spins landed in the blue region? What percent landed in the yellow region?

    c. According to the theoretical probabilities, what is the percent of the spins expected to land in the blue region over the long run? In the yellow region?

    d. Compare the experimental probability of the spinner landing in each region with the theoretical probability. If the probabilities are different, explain why.

20. If you drop a tack on the floor, there are two possible outcomes: the tack lands on its side (point down), or the tack lands on its head (point up). Kalifa dropped a tack 100 times. The table shows the results.

point down   point up

Outcomes	Number of Times It Occurs
Tack lands point up	58
Tack lands point down	42

a. Suppose you drop Kalifa's tack 500 times. How many times do you expect it to land point up?

b. Is it equally likely that the tack will land point up or point down? Explain.

c. Is it possible to determine theoretical probabilities for this situation? Why or why not?

21. Juanita is deciding whether to play a game at an amusement park. It takes one ticket to play the game. A player tosses two plastic bottles. If both bottles land standing up, the player wins ten tickets to use for rides and games. Juanita watches people play and records the results.

Both land on side	One lands on side and one lands standing up	Both land standing up
~~||||~~ ~~||||~~ ~~||||~~ ~~||||~~ ||||	~~||||~~ ~~||||~~ ||||	||

a. Based on Juanita's results, what is the experimental probability of winning the game?

b. Suppose Juanita plays this game 20 times. How many times can she expect to win?

c. How many tickets can Juanita expect to be ahead or behind after playing the game 20 times? Explain your reasoning.

d. Is it possible to find the theoretical probability of winning this game? Why or why not?

22. A bucket contains 60 marbles. Some are red, some are blue, and some are white. The probability of drawing a red marble is 35%. The probability of drawing a blue marble is 25%. How many marbles of each color are in the bucket?

23. Hannah's teacher brought in a bucket containing 72 blocks. The blocks are red, yellow, or blue. Hannah wants to figure out the number of blue blocks without emptying the bucket.

Hannah chooses a block from the bucket, records its color, and then replaces it. Of her 14 draws, she records blue 5 times. Based on Hannah's experiment, how many of the blocks are blue? Explain.

24. Suppose you roll two number cubes. What is the probability that the product of the numbers will be a multiple of 5?

25. If you roll two number cubes 100 times, about how many times can you expect the product of the numbers to be a multiple of 5?

26. Suppose you roll two number cubes. What is the probability that the product of the numbers is a multiple of 7?

27. If you roll two number cubes a million times, about how many times can you expect the product of the numbers to be a multiple of 7?

28. Suppose you roll two number cubes and multiply the numbers. Find each probability.

  a. *P*(product is a multiple of 3 and 4)

  b. *P*(product is a multiple of 3 or 4)

  c. *P*(product has a factor of 5 and 3)

  d. *P*(product is a prime number)

  e. *P*(product is greater than 10)

  f. *P*(product is less than 18)

Extensions

29. Tricia wants to determine the probability of getting two 1's when two number cubes are rolled. She makes a tree diagram and uses it to list the possible outcomes.

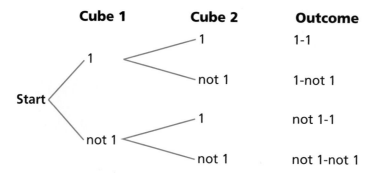

Cube 1	Cube 2	Outcome

She says that, because there are four possible outcomes, the probability of getting 1 on both number cubes is $\frac{1}{4}$. Is Tricia right? Explain.

30. Juan invented a two-person game in which players take turns rolling three number cubes. If the sum is even, Player A gets a point. If the sum is odd, Player B gets a point. Is Juan's game a fair game? Explain.

For Exercises 31–33, a computer places a dot at random on each dartboard below.

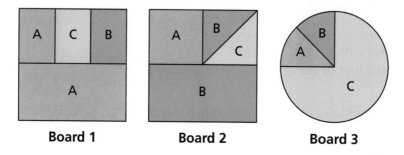

Board 1   Board 2   Board 3

31. For each dartboard, what is the probability that a dot will be in a region marked A? A region marked B? A region marked C?

32. For Board 1, what is the probability that a dot will be in a region marked A or B?

33. For Board 2, what is the probability that a dot will *not* be in region C?

Mathematical Reflections 1

In this investigation, you explored games of chance. Working on the problems gave you an opportunity to review ideas about experimental and theoretical probability. The following questions will help you summarize what you have learned.

Think about your answers to these questions. Discuss your ideas with other students and your teacher. Then write a summary of your findings in your notebook.

1. **a.** Compare experimental and theoretical probabilities.

   b. Describe some strategies you can use to find experimental probabilities.

   c. Describe some strategies you can use to find theoretical probabilities.

2. How do you use probabilities, either theoretical or experimental, to decide if a particular game of chance is fair?

3. In a game of chance, how can you predict the number of times out of 100 a given outcome will occur?

Investigation 2

Analyzing Situations Using an Area Model

Each turn in the games of chance in the last Investigation involved two actions. For example, in the spinner game, you spun the pointer twice and then determined the outcome. You determined the theoretical probabilities of these games using a variety of strategies.

In this Investigation, you will learn how to use an area model to analyze probability situations that involve more than one action on a turn. You can analyze games such as the Red and Blue game in Problem 1.2 using an **area model.**

Bucket 1 contains three marbles—one red and two greens. Bucket 2 contains four marbles—one red, one blue, one green, and one yellow.

Bucket 1   **Bucket 2**

- Draw a square on grid paper. Suppose the square has an area of 1 square unit. We use the square to represent a probability of 1.

Bucket 2

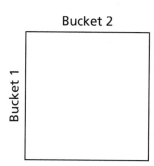

Bucket 1

- The first bucket has three equally likely choices: red, green, and the other green. Divide the square into three sections with equal areas. The areas of the sections represent the probabilities of the three choices. Label the sections.

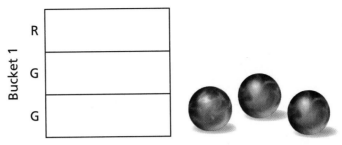

- For the second action of choosing a marble from Bucket 2, subdivide the diagram to represent the probabilities of the equally likely choices: red, blue, green, and yellow. Label these new Bucket 2 sections.

Bucket 2

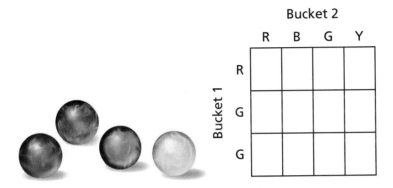

- Each subregion formed represents one of the outcomes: RR, RB, RG, RY, GR, GB, GG, and GY.

Bucket 2

	R	B	G	Y
R	RR	RB	RG	RY
G	GR	GB	GG	GY
G	GR	GB	GG	GY

Bucket 1

- The area of each subregion represents the probability for each outcome.

What is the probability of choosing an RR? RB? RG? RY? GR? GB? GG? GY? YY?

What is the probability of choosing a red from either bucket?

A popular game at a school carnival is a spinner game called
Making Purple. To play the game, a player spins the pointer of each spinner
below once. Suppose a player gets red on one spinner and blue on the other
spinner. The player wins, because red and blue together make purple.

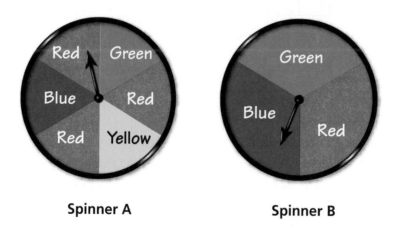

Spinner A   Spinner B

A. Play the Making Purple game several times. Record the results of each turn. Based on your results, what is the experimental probability that a player will "make purple" on a turn?

B. Use an area model to determine the theoretical probability that a player will make purple on a turn.

C. How does the experimental probability of making purple compare with the theoretical probability of making purple?

D. The cost to play the game is $2. The winner gets $6 for making purple. Suppose 36 people play the game.

  1. How much money will the school take in from this game?

  2. How much money do you expect the school to pay out in prizes?

  3. How much profit do you expect the school to make from this game?

ACE Homework starts on page 27.

Kenisha is designing a game involving paths through the woods that lead to caves. Before the game is played the player chooses either Cave A or Cave B. Next, the player starts at the beginning and chooses a path at random at each fork. If the player lands in the cave that was chosen in the beginning, he or she wins a prize.

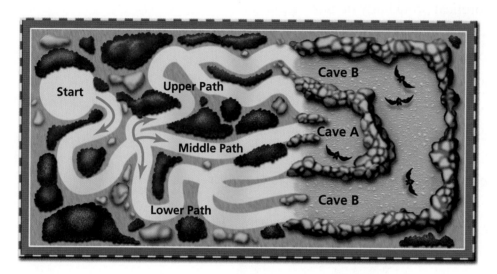

Getting Ready for Problem 2.2

- Are you more likely to end in Cave A or in Cave B? Why?

The 18 students in Sarah's class design an experiment to find the likelihood of ending in Cave A or in Cave B. For each trial, they trace the path beginning at Start, and use a number cube to make the choice of direction whenever there is a split in the path.

- Is this a good way to find the experimental probability of the game? Explain.

- Are there other ways to make choices at a split in the path? Explain.

A. Carry out the experiment to simulate the 18 students playing the game and note the cave where each student ends.

B. What is the experimental probability of landing in Cave A? Of landing in Cave B?

C. Miguel draws this diagram to help him find the theoretical probabilities of ending in Cave A or in Cave B.

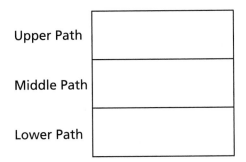

1. Explain what Miguel has done so far. Does this look reasonable?

2. Complete an area model to find the theoretical probabilities of ending in Cave A or Cave B. Show your work.

D. How are your experimental probabilities from Question A related to the theoretical probabilities?

E. Kenisha designs a new version of the game. It has a different arrangement of paths leading to Caves A and B. She makes the area model below to analyze the probabilities of ending in each cave.

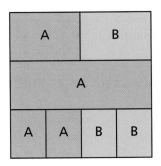

1. Create a path game that fits the model.

2. Find the probability for each outcome.

ACE **Homework starts on page 27.**

2.3 Finding the Best Arrangement

Brianna and Emmanuel are chosen from the studio audience of the Gee Whiz Everyone Wins! game show to play a game. While Emmanuel waits backstage, Brianna places two green marbles and two blue marbles in two identical containers in any arrangement she chooses.

After she places the marbles, Emmanuel returns. He chooses one of the containers at random. He then chooses a marble from that container without looking. If he chooses a green marble, the friends each win a prize. If he chooses a blue marble, or if the container he chooses is empty, the friends do not win anything.

Problem 2.3 Finding the Best Arrangement

A. List all the different ways Brianna can place the four marbles in the two containers.

B. For each arrangement, what is the probability that Emmanuel chooses a green marble?

C. Which arrangement will give Brianna and Emmanuel the greatest chance of winning? The least chance of winning? Explain.

ACE Homework starts on page 27.

Applications

1. Bonita and Deion are using the spinners from the Making Purple game in Problem 2.1. They take turns spinning. If the colors on the two spinners make purple, Deion scores. If they do not make purple, Bonita scores. For this to be a fair game, how many points should Deion score when the spinners make purple, and how many points should Bonita score when they do not make purple?

2. At the Flag Day Festival at Parker Middle School, there is a contest where a player chooses one block from each of two different bags. A player wins if he or she picks a red and a blue block. James makes the tree diagram below to find the probability of winning.

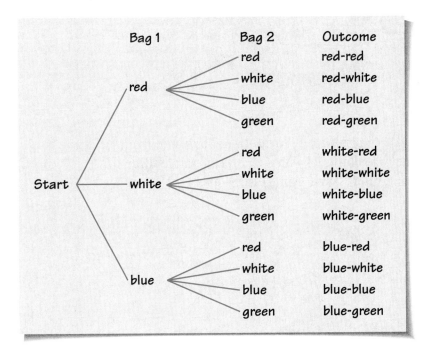

a. What blocks are in bag 1?

b. What blocks are in bag 2?

c. Draw an area model that represents this contest.

d. What is the probability of winning this contest?

For: Multiple-Choice Skills
Practice
Web Code: ana-7254

3. There are two No-Cavity prize bins at a dentist's office. One bin has two hot-pink toothbrushes and three neon-yellow toothbrushes. The other bin has four packs of sugar-free gum, three grape and one strawberry. Kira has no cavities. The dentist tells her to close her eyes and choose a prize from each bin.

a. What is the probability that Kira will choose a neon-yellow toothbrush and a pack of sugar-free grape gum? Draw an area model to support your solution.

b. The dental assistant refills the bins after every patient. Suppose the next 100 patients have no cavities. How many times do you expect the patients to get the same prizes that Kira chose?

4. Al is about to ski his last run on Morey Mountain. There are five trails to the base of the mountain. Al wants to take a trail leading to the lodge. He can't remember which trail(s) to take.

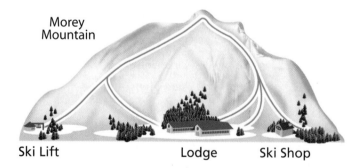

Morey Mountain

Ski Lift   Lodge   Ski Shop

a. Design an experiment using a number cube to find the experimental probability of Al ending at the lodge. Conduct the experiment 20 times. If you do not have a number cube, write the numbers 1–6 on pieces of paper. Then select one from a hat.

b. What is the experimental probability of Al ending at the lodge? At the lift? At the ski shop?

c. Find the theoretical probability of ending at the lodge, the lift, and the ski shop. Compare the experimental and theoretical probabilities. Do you have more confidence in the experimental or the theoretical probability? Why?

5. Kenisha changes the game in Problem 2.2 so it has the paths below.

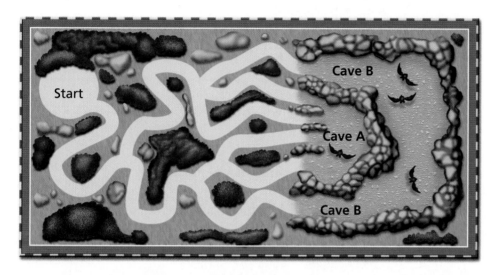

a. Suppose a player chooses a path at random at each fork. What is the theoretical probability that he or she will end in Cave A? In Cave B? Show your work.

b. If you play this game 100 times, how many times do you expect to end in Cave A? In Cave B?

6. Kenisha designs another version of the game in Problem 2.2. The new version has a different arrangement of paths leading into Caves A and B. She makes an area model to analyze the probabilities of landing in each cave.

For Kenisha's new version, what is the probability that a player will end in Cave A? In Cave B?

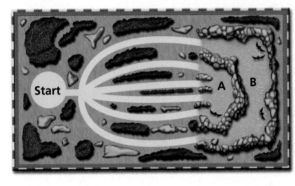

7. Multiple Choice Choose the map that the area model in Exercise 6 could represent.

A.

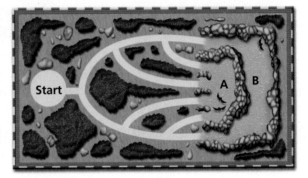

B.

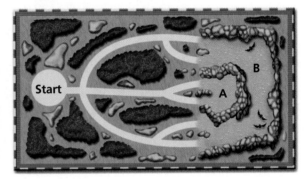

C.

D.

For Exercises 8–10, suppose a bag contains three orange marbles and two blue marbles. You are to choose a marble, return it to the bag, and then choose again.

8. Choose an appropriate method from those below for finding the possible outcomes. Describe how you would use your choice.

   a. make a tree diagram

   b. make a list

   c. use an area model

   d. make a table or chart

9. Suppose you do this experiment 50 times. Use the method you chose in Exercise 8 to predict the number of times you will choose two marbles of the same color.

10. Suppose this experiment is a two-person game in which one player scores if the marbles match, and the other player scores if they do not match. Suppose the two players play the game many times and total the points scored. Describe a scoring system that makes this a game in which each person has an equally likely chance of having the winning score.

Brianna (from Problem 2.3) is given each set of marbles to distribute between two containers. What arrangement gives Emmanuel the best chance of choosing a green marble?

11. three blue and two green marbles

12. two blue and three green marbles

Connections

13. In a survey, 100 seniors at a high school were asked these questions:

- Do you favor a rule that allows only seniors to drive to school?

- Do you drive to school?

Homework Help Online
PHSchool.com

For: Help with Exercise 13
Web Code: ane-7213

Driving Survey

	Drives to School	Does Not Drive to School	Row Totals
Favors Rule	40	30	70
Opposes Rule	20	10	30
Total	60	40	100

a. Based on this survey, what is the probability that a senior chosen at random favors the rule?

b. What is the probability that a senior chosen at random drives to school and favors the rule?

c. What is the probability that a senior chosen at random drives to school or opposes the rule?

d. Are the results of this survey a good indicator of how all the students at the high school feel about the driving rule? Explain.

14. Marni and Ira are playing a game with this square spinner. A game is 10 turns. Each turn is 2 spins. The numbers for the 2 spins are added. Marni scores 1 point for a sum that is negative, and Ira scores 1 point for a sum that is positive. After 10 turns, each player totals their points. The one with more points wins.

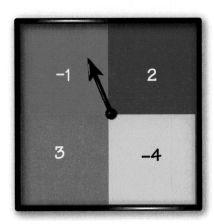

    a. List all of the possible outcomes.

    b. Are Marni and Ira equally likely to win?

Megan is designing a computer game called *Treasure Hunt*. The computer chooses a square at random on the grid at the right, and then hides a treasure in the room containing that square. For Exercises 15–19, use the grid to find the probability that the computer will hide the treasure in each room.

15. Library

16. Den

17. Dining hall

18. Great hall

19. Front hall

20. Multiple Choice Megan enlarges the floor plan in the game grid above by a scale factor of 2. How does this affect the probabilities that the treasure is in each room?

    F. They are unchanged.

    G. They are $\frac{1}{2}$ the original probability.

    H. They are twice the original.

    J. They are four times the original.

21. Carlos is also designing a *Treasure Hunt* game. He keeps track of the number of times the computer hides the treasure in each room. Here is a line plot of his results.

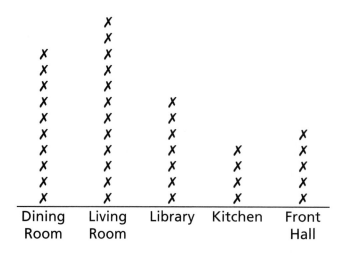

Design a floor plan that could give this data. State the area of each room on your floor plan.

22. Fergus designs a dartboard for a school carnival. His design is shown below. He must decide how much to charge a player and how much to pay out for a win. To do this, he needs to know the probabilities of landing in sections marked A and B. Assume the darts land at random on the dartboard.

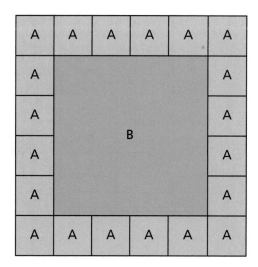

a. What is the probability of landing in a section marked A?

b. What is the probability of landing in a section marked B?

23. Fergus designs two more dartboards for the school carnival.

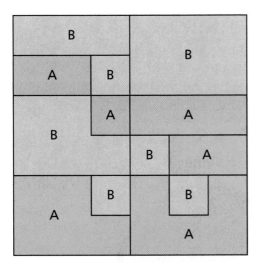

Dartboard 1

Dartboard 2

a. What is the probability of landing in sections marked A on Dartboard 1? On Dartboard 2? Explain.

b. A player pays $1 to play and wins $2 if the dart lands in sections marked B. If the dart lands in sections marked A, the player wins no money.

    i. How much money will the player expect to make (or lose) after 36 turns using Dartboard 1? Using Dartboard 2? Explain.

    ii. How much money will the carnival expect to make (or lose) after 36 turns using Dartboard 1? Using Dartboard 2?

c. Can the carnival expect to make a profit on this game with either board? Explain.

24. a. If you roll one number cube two times, what is the probability of getting a factor of 5 both times?

b. Suppose you roll two different number cubes. What is the probability of getting a factor of 5 on both cubes?

c. How do your answers to parts (a) and (b) compare? Explain why the answers have this relationship.

Extensions

25. Suppose you play a game using the two spinners below. You get two spins. You may spin each spinner once, or you may spin one of the spinners twice. If you get a red on one spin and a blue on the other spin (the order makes no difference), you win. To have the greatest chance of winning, should you spin Spinner A twice, spin Spinner B twice, or spin each spinner once? Explain.

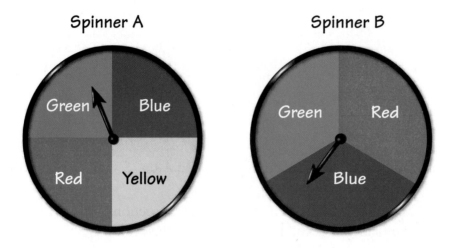

Spinner A

Spinner B

26. Suppose Brianna (from Problem 2.3) is given two green marbles, two blue marbles, and three buckets. How can she put the marbles in the three buckets to have the best chance of choosing a green marble?

27. Della is chosen as a contestant on a game show. The host gives her two red marbles, two green marbles, and two yellow marbles.

Della will put the marbles into two identical cans in any way she chooses. The host will then rearrange the cans, leaving the marbles as Della placed them. Della will then select a can and choose a marble. If she chooses a red marble, she wins a prize.

How should Della arrange the marbles so she has the best chance of choosing a red marble?

28. Make up your own marbles and buckets problem. Find the solution.

Mathematical Reflections 2

In this investigation, you analyzed probabilities of two-stage events by dividing the area of a square. The following questions will help you summarize what you have learned.

Think about your answers to these questions. Discuss your ideas with other students and your teacher. Then write a summary of your findings in your notebook.

1. Describe three or four probability situations that involve two actions. Describe the outcomes for these situations.

2. Describe how you can use an area model to determine the probability of a situation that involves two actions.

Expected Value

On April 14, 1993, during halftime of a basketball game between the Chicago Bulls and the Miami Heat, Don Calhoun won $1 million by making a basket from the free-throw line at the opposite end of the court. Don was chosen at random to attempt the basket as part of a promotional contest. A *Sports Illustrated* article explained:

> *The odds against one randomly chosen person given one shot from the opposite foul line and making it are considered astronomical. Scottie Pippen admitted that after practice one day he and Michael Jordan tried to hit the shot but couldn't.*
>
> (Source: Bessone, Lisa, "Sports People: Don Calhoun." *Sports Illustrated*, April 26, 1993, vol 48.)

Fortunately, not every basket is this difficult to make! In this Investigation, you will use a player's free-throw percent to figure out what is likely to happen in a given free-throw situation.

3.1 One-and-One Free-Throws

In the district finals, Nishi's basketball team is 1 point behind with 2 seconds left. Nishi has just been fouled, and she is in a one-and-one free-throw situation. This means that Nishi will try one free throw. If she makes it, she tries a second free throw. If she misses the first time, she does not get a second try. Nishi's free-throw average is 60%.

- What are the possible scores Nishi can make in a one-and-one free-throw situation?

- How can each score be made?

- How would you design an experiment to analyze this situation?

Problem 3.1 Simulating a Probability Situation

A. Is it most likely that Nishi will score 0 points, 1 point, or 2 points? Record what you think before you analyze the situation.

B. Use this spinner to simulate Nishi's one-and-one situation 20 times. Record the result of each trial.

C. Based on your results, what is the experimental probability that Nishi will score 0 points? That she will score 1 point? That she will score 2 points?

D. Make an area model for this situation using a 10 × 10 grid. What is the theoretical probability that Nishi will score 0 points? That she will score 1 point? That she will score 2 points? Compare the three theoretical probabilities with the three experimental probabilities.

E. Suppose Nishi's free-throw average is 70%. How does this affect the outcome? Explain.

F. How does the diagram in Question D help you predict how many times Nishi will score 2 points in 100 one-and-one situations? In 200 one-and-one situations?

ACE Homework starts on page 43.

3.2 Finding Expected Value

In Problem 3.1, you looked at the probabilities of different outcomes of Nishi's one-and-one free-throw situation. You might have been surprised about which outcome is most likely. In this Problem, you will look at the number of points Nishi can expect to make each time she is in a one-and-one free-throw situation.

Problem 3.2 Finding Expected Value

Suppose Nishi has a 60% free-throw percentage and is in a one-and-one free-throw situation 100 times during the season.

A. 1. How many times can she expect to score 0 points? What is the total number of points for these situations?

2. How many times can she expect to score 1 point? What is the total number of points for these situations?

3. How many times can she expect to score 2 points? What is the total number of points for these situations?

4. What total number of points do you expect Nishi to score in these 100 situations at the free-throw line?

5. What would Nishi's average number of points (expected value) per situation be?

B. 1. In a one-and-one situation, what score is most likely to happen for a player whose free-throw percentage is 20%? 40%? 60%? 80%?

2. Copy and complete the table at the right for the players in part (1) in 100 one-and-one situations. You will fill in the expected value column in part (3).

3. Calculate the average number of points for each situation. Record these values in the table in part (2). Describe any pattern you see.

Points Expected in 100 One-and-One Situations

Player's Free-Throw Percentage	Points			
	0	1	2	Expected Value, or Average
20%	■	■	■	■
40%	■	■	■	■
60%	■	■	■	■
80%	■	■	■	■

C. 1. Make a graph like the one started at the right for each of the players in your table. Use your graph to answer parts (2)–(4).

2. How does the average number of points compare for players with a 20% free-throw percentage, a 40% free-throw percentage, a 60% free-throw percentage, and an 80% free-throw percentage?

3. Nishi's dad noticed that he makes an average of about 1 point in one-and-one free-throw situations. What is his free-throw percentage?

4. Nishi's older sister has a 70% free-throw percentage. What is her average number of points in one-and-one situations? Check your answer by making an area model.

Points Expected in a One-and-One Situation

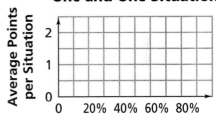

Free-Throw Percentage

ACE Homework starts on page 43.

3.3 Choosing Pay Plans

The average number of points in the one-and-one situation is the **expected value** for this situation. Expected value is used in a variety of other situations such as determining life-insurance premiums and lottery prizes, and for predicting gains and losses in businesses. The following problem shows another situation in which expected value is useful.

Julie and Brandon cut lawns for their neighbors to earn money to donate to a local charity. They thought that customers should pay $20. However, several customers offered a different pay plan and asked the students to choose. Julie and Brandon have to decide which of the pay plans would give them a fair deal over the long run.

In each case, calculate the expected value. Then, decide whether they should accept or reject the pay plan. Give reasons for your decision.

A. The customer spins each of these spinners once. If one spinner is red and the other is blue (the order makes no difference), Julie and Brandon get $24. Otherwise, they get $10.

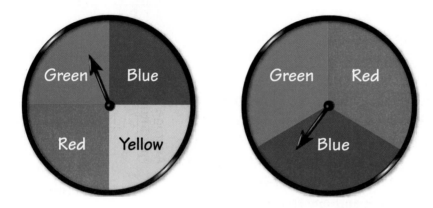

B. The customer rolls a pair of number cubes and adds the two numbers. If the sum is even, Julie and Brandon get $25. If it is odd, they get $18.

C. The customer rolls a pair of number cubes. If the product is 24, Julie and Brandon get $40. Otherwise, they get $10.

D. The customer places a twenty-dollar bill and three one-dollar bills in a bag. Julie and Brandon choose two bills. The money they choose is their payment.

E. The customer tosses three coins. If two or more land heads up, Julie and Brandon get $25. Otherwise, they get $15.

ACE Homework starts on page 43.

Applications

In a one-and-one free-throw situation, is the player with each free-throw average most likely to score 0 points, 1 point, or 2 points? Make an area model to support each answer.

1. an 80% average

2. a 40% average

For Exercises 3–5, use the information in the table. It shows statistics for some of the players on a basketball team.

Free-Throw Statistics

Name	Free Throws Attempted	Free Throws Made
Gerrit	54	27
David	49	39
Ken	73	45
Alex	60	42

3. a. Which player has the best chance of making his next free throw? Explain your reasoning.

 b. What is the free-throw probability for each player?

4. a. Alex has just been fouled and is in a one-and-one free-throw situation. What is the probability he will score 0 points? 1 point? 2 points?

 b. Suppose Alex is in a one-and-one situation 100 times. How many times do you expect each of the outcomes in part (a) to occur?

 c. What is the average number of points you expect Alex to make in a one-and-one situation?

 d. Repeat part (a) using Gerrit.

5. a. In a different type of free-throw situation, a player gets a second attempt, even if the first free-throw is missed. Suppose Gerrit is in this two-attempt free-throw situation. What is the probability he will score 0 points? 1 point? 2 points?

 b. Compare your answers to part (a) with Exercise 4(d). Explain why the answers are not exactly the same.

Homework
Help Online
PHSchool.com
For: Help with Exercise 6
Web Code: ane-7306

6. Nishi, who has a 60% free-throw average, is in a two-attempt free-throw situation. Remember, this means that she will attempt the second free-throw no matter what happens on the first.

    a. Is Nishi most likely to score 0 points, 1 point, or 2 points? Explain.

    b. Nishi plans to keep track of her score on two-attempt free-throw situations. What average number of points can she expect to score in two-attempt situations?

7. Repeat Exercise 6 for the player with each free-throw average.

    a. a 50% average   **b.** an 80% average

8. In each of the following situations, the customer should pay $10 per week for newspapers. Drew, the paper carrier, has to decide which customer suggestions give him a fair deal over the long run. In each case, decide if Drew should accept or reject his customer's suggestion.

    a. The customer puts a ten-dollar bill and two one-dollar bills in a bag. Drew chooses two bills.

    b. Drew tosses three coins. If they are all heads or all tails, Drew gets $30. Otherwise, he gets $2.

    c. Drew rolls a pair of number cubes. If the sum is 7, Drew gets $50. Otherwise, he gets $2.

Connections

A game show uses a large spinner with many sections. At least one section is labeled "bankrupt." If a player spins "bankrupt," he or she loses that turn and all his or her money. Carlota makes a version of the spinner at the right.

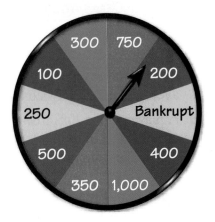

9. What is the probability that a player who spins the spinner one time will land on bankrupt?

10. What is the probability that a player who spins the spinner one time will get $500 or more?

11. Sam just spun the spinner and it landed on $350. What is the probability he will land on $350 on his next spin? Explain your reasoning.

Multiple Choice For Exercises 12–14, choose the answer that is the correct percent of the given number.

12. 30% of 90

   A. 60   **B.** 27   **C.** 30   **D.** 3

13. 25% of 80

   F. 20   **G.** 3.2   **H.** 0.3175   **J.** 200

14. 45% of 180

   A. 2.5   **B.** 40   **C.** 81   **D.** 4

Go Online
PHSchool.com

For: Multiple-Choice Skills Practice
Web Code: ana-7354

15. Wanda, the Channel 1 weather person, said there was a 30% chance of rain on Saturday and a 30% chance of rain on Sunday. It rained both days, and Wanda's station manager is wondering if she should fire Wanda.

   a. Suppose Wanda's calculations were correct and there was a 30% chance of rain each day. What was the probability that there would be rain on both days?

   b. Do you think Wanda should be fired? Why or why not?

   c. Wanda is working on her predictions for the next few days. She calculates that there is a 20% chance of rain on Monday and a 20% chance of rain on Tuesday. If she is correct, what is the probability that it will rain on at least one of these days?

16. A lake has 10,000 fish. When a fisherman scoops up his net, he catches 500 fish. Suppose 150 of the 500 fish in his net are salmon. How many salmon do you predict are in the lake?

17. a. Copy the table below. Use your answers from Problem 3.2, Question C to fill in your table.

Probability of One Basket	20%	40%	60%	80%	100%
Average Points per One-and-One Attempt	0.24	▨	0.96	▨	▨

b. Is the average for 80% twice that of 40%?

c. Use this table or your graph from Problem 3.2, Question C. Is the average for 100% twice the average of 50%?

d. A player with a 20% free-throw average makes 0.24 points, on average, in a one-and-one situation. Copy and complete this table. How are the relationships in this table different from the table in part (a)?

Number of One-and-One Situations by a Player With a 20% Average	1	10	20	100
Average Points Made	0.24	▨	▨	▨

For Exercises 18 and 19, spin each spinner once. Use the spinners below.

18. Suppose you add the results.

a. What is the probability of getting a positive number?

b. What is the average value?

19. Suppose you multiply the results.

a. What is the probability of getting a positive number?

b. What is the average value?

20. Fred and Joseph are experimenting with a new game. The probability Fred wins a round of this game is $\frac{1}{3}$ and the probability Joseph wins a round is $\frac{2}{3}$. They decide that to make the game fair, Fred scores 3 points when he wins a round, and Joseph scores 2 points when he wins a round.

a. They play 12 rounds of the game. How many points can Fred expect to win? How many points can Joseph expect to win?

b. How many points per round can each player expect to win? That is, what is the expected value for each player?

c. Is this a game in which Fred and Joseph have an equally-likely chance of making a winning total? Why or why not?

21. Ms. Rodriguez brought her dog to the vet for a distemper test. The test is correct 80% of the time. This means that 20% of the time the test of a dog with distemper indicates no distemper. The vet decides to test the dog twice.

a. If the dog has distemper, what is the probability that both tests will indicate no distemper? (It may help to make an area model of this situation.)

b. If the dog has distemper, what is the probability that at least one of the tests will indicate distemper?

22. A computer places a dot at random on a dartboard that is divided into four regions, A, B, C, and D. The dot has the same probability of being in region B, region C, or region D. The probability that the dot will be in region A is 40%.

a. What is the probability that the dot will *not* be in region A?

b. Make a square dartboard that meets the given conditions.

c. Make a circular dartboard that meets the given conditions.

Extensions

For Exercises 23 and 24, use the data about the basketball team from Exercises 3–5.

23. What is the probability that Alex will make all of his next three free throws? Explain your reasoning.

24. David is in a one-and-one free-throw situation. What is the probability that he will make both free-throws?

25. Emilio increases his free-throw average to 50%. His coach makes a deal with him. At tomorrow's practice, Emilio can attempt either to make three free throws in a row or to make at least four out of five free throws. If he is successful, he will start every game for the rest of the season. Which option should he choose? Explain.

26. a. Curt has made 60% of his free throws during recent practice sessions. The coach says that if Curt makes three free throws in a row, he can start Saturday's game. What is the probability that Curt will start Saturday's game?

b. Curt has a difficult time making three free throws in a row. The coach tells him to instead try making three out of four free throws. What is the probability that Curt will make at least three out of four free throws?

27. Natalie designs a carnival spinner game with 38 congruent sectors; 18 orange, 18 blue, and 2 white. A player pays $1 to play. The player picks either orange or blue. If the spinner stops on the chosen color, the player wins $2. If the spinner lands on any other color, the player does not get any money.

a. What is the probability that a player will lose on one spin of the wheel?

b. If a player plays the game many times, what is the average amount of money the player can expect to win or lose per spin of the wheel?

28. When a player is fouled while attempting a three-point basket, three free throws are awarded. Luis has an 80% free-throw average. He draws the diagrams below to analyze the probability of getting 1, 2, or 3 baskets.

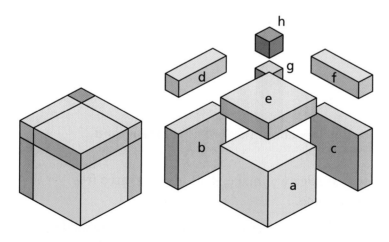

a. Which parts of the lettered diagram represent Luis making all three baskets? Exactly two baskets? Exactly one basket? Missing all three baskets?

b. What is the probability of Luis getting 1 point in a three free-throw situation? 2 points? 3 points? No points?

Mathematical Reflections 3

In this investigation, you learned how to find the average outcome for events, such as a basketball player attempting free throws in a one-and-one situation. The following questions will help you summarize what you have learned.

Think about your answers to these questions. Discuss your ideas with other students and your teacher. Then write a summary of your findings in your notebook.

1. Expected value is sometimes called the long-term average. Explain why this makes sense.

2. Describe how you would calculate the expected value for a probability situation.

3. Explain how expected value can be useful.

Investigation 4

Binomial Outcomes

4.1 Guessing Answers

Have you ever forgotten to study for a quiz and had to guess at the answers? If you take a true/false quiz and guess on every question, what are your chances of getting every question right?

Problem 4.1 Finding More Expected Values

A quiz has four true/false questions. Each question is worth 25 points.

- On a piece of paper, write the numbers 1 to 4 to represent the questions for the quiz.

- Toss a penny to determine the answer for each quiz item. Next to each number, write true (T) if a head shows and false (F) if a tail shows.

- After you have written your answers, your teacher will give you the correct answers.

- Mark your answers correct or incorrect. Record your score.

A. Compare answers with your classmates. How many papers had

1. exactly 4 correct (all correct)

2. exactly 3 correct (3 correct and 1 incorrect)

3. exactly 2 correct (2 correct and 2 incorrect)

4. exactly 1 correct (1 correct and 3 incorrect)

5. none correct (0 correct and 4 incorrect)

B. 1. If you guess on every question, how many different ways can you get exactly 1 incorrect answer? Exactly 2 incorrect answers? Exactly 3 incorrect answers? All 4 incorrect? All 4 correct?

2. What is the probability of getting

  a. a score of 100 (all correct)

  b. a score of 75 (exactly three correct)

  c. a score of 50 (exactly two correct)

  d. a score of 25 (exactly one correct)

  e. a score of 0 (all incorrect)

C. 1. Suppose you take the quiz 32 times. How many times do you expect to get the given number of correct answers?

  a. 4   **b.** 3   **c.** 2   **d.** 1   **e.** 0

2. What would your total score be in each case?

3. If you take the quiz 32 times, what is the expected average score? Will the expected value change if you take the quiz 100 times? Explain.

D. Suppose the true/false quiz has five questions and you guess each one. What is the probability that you will get them all correct?

ACE | Homework starts on page 54.

4.2 Ortonville

Situations like tossing a coin (or the true/false quiz) that have exactly two outcomes are binomial situations. The probability of getting one of two outcomes (like heads or tails) is called a **binomial probability.** In this problem, you will explore another binomial situation that has equally likely outcomes.

Problem 4.2 Binomial Probability

Ortonville is a very special town. Each family is named Orton and has exactly five children. The parents in Ortonville have agreed to call their children these names:

The Orton Children	Girl	Boy
First-Born Child	Gloria	Benson
Second-Born Child	Gilda	Berndt
Third-Born Child	Gail	Blair
Fourth-Born Child	Gerry	Blake
Fifth-Born Child	Gina	Brett

A. List all the possible outcomes for a family with five children.

B. What is the probability that a family has children named Gloria, Gilda, Blair, Blake, and Gina?

C. Find the probability that a family has

    1. exactly five girls or five boys

    2. two girls and three boys

    3. the first or last child a boy

    4. at least one boy

    5. at most one boy

ACE Homework starts on page 54.

4.3 A Baseball Series

Every fall the best baseball team in the American League plays the best team in the National League. The series has up to seven games. The first team to win four games wins the series.

Problem 4.3 Expanding Binomial Probability

Suppose the Bobcats are playing the Gazelles in your town's little league "world series." The teams enter the series evenly matched. That is, they each have an equally likely chance of winning each game.

The Gazelles win the first two games of the series. The owner of the concession stands must predict how much food to order for the rest of the series. He needs to know the probability that the series will end in 4, 5, 6, or 7 games. To find the answer, he must find all the possible outcomes.

Label the outcomes with a G for a Gazelles win or a B for a Bobcats win. For example, BBGG means that the Bobcats win the third and fourth games and the Gazelles win the fifth and sixth games. In this example, the series ends in six games, when the Gazelles have won four games. Write G-6 after BBGG.

A. Before you analyze the rest of the series, predict whether it is more probable that the series will end in 4, 5, 6, or 7 games.

B. Suppose all five remaining games are played. What are all of the possible outcomes for these five games?

C. 1. For each outcome, determine the length of the series.

2. What is the probability that the series ends in four games? Five games? Six games? Seven games?

D. Analyze the outcomes in Question C for wins. What is the probability that the Gazelles win the series? That the Bobcats win the series?

ACE Homework starts on page 54.

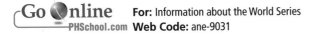

Did You Know?

The World Series started in 1903 as a best-of-nine-game series. From 1905 until 1919, the series changed to the best-of-seven games. After World War I ended, the series temporarily changed back to the best-of-nine games in 1919–1921. From 1922 until now, the series has remained a best-of-seven-game series. Between 1922 and 2003, the World Series ended in four games and five games both 15 times. It ended in six games 17 times and in seven games 34 times. There was no World Series in 1994.

Go Online
PHSchool.com **For:** Information about the World Series **Web Code:** ane-9031

Applications

1. It costs six tickets to play the Toss-a-Penny game at the school carnival. For each turn, a player tosses a penny three times. If the penny lands heads up two or more times in a turn, the player wins ten tickets to spend on food and games.

   a. Suppose Benito plays the game 80 times. How many tickets can he expect to win?

   b. What is the average number of tickets Benito can expect to win or lose per turn?

2. **a.** If you toss three coins at the same time, is the probability of getting three heads the same as or different from the probability of getting three heads when you toss one coin three times in a row? Explain your reasoning.

   b. If you toss three coins and get three tails, what is the probability you will get three tails when you toss the three coins again? Explain.

For Exercises 3–9, use this information: Scout, Ms. Rodriguez's dog, is about to have puppies. The vet thinks Scout will have four puppies. Assume that for each puppy, a male and female are equally likely.

3. **a.** List all the possible combinations of female and male puppies Scout might have.

   b. Is Scout more likely to have four male puppies or two male and two female puppies? Explain.

4. **Multiple Choice** What is the probability that Scout will have four female puppies?

   A. $\frac{1}{2}$ **B.** $\frac{1}{4}$ **C.** $\frac{1}{8}$ **D.** $\frac{1}{16}$

5. **Multiple Choice** What is the probability that Scout will have two male and two female puppies?

   F. $\frac{1}{2}$ **G.** $\frac{1}{4}$ **H.** $\frac{1}{8}$ **J.** $\frac{6}{16}$

6. **Multiple Choice** What is the probability that Scout will have at least one male puppy?

   A. $\frac{15}{16}$ **B.** $\frac{7}{8}$ **C.** $\frac{3}{4}$ **D.** $\frac{1}{2}$

7. Multiple Choice What is the probability that Scout will have at least one female puppy?

F. $\frac{15}{16}$ **G.** $\frac{7}{8}$ **H.** $\frac{3}{4}$ **J.** $\frac{1}{2}$

8. Ms. Rodriguez plans to sell her dog's female puppies for $250 each and her male puppies for $200 each. How much money can she expect to make from a litter of four puppies?

9. Suppose the vet thinks Scout will have a litter of five puppies. How much money can Ms. Rodriguez expect to make from selling the puppies?

10. Rajan's class is holding a world series. They divide the class into two teams, which are evenly matched. One team is the Champs and the other team is the Stars. The series is five games, and the first team to win three games wins the series. The Champs win the first game.

     a. What is the probability that the series will end in 3, 4, or 5 games?

     b. What is the probability that the Stars will win the series?

Connections

11. You might find that a tree diagram is a helpful model in this exercise.

     a. What are all the possible outcomes when you toss a coin three times?

     b. How many outcomes are there when you toss a coin four times? (You do not have to list them all.) Five times?

     c. How many ways can you get five heads in five tosses? How many ways can you get zero heads in five tosses? How many ways can you get four heads? One head? Three heads? Two heads?

     d. Explain why some symmetry in your answers in part (c) makes sense.

Go Online
PHSchool.com

For: Multiple-Choice Skills Practice
Web Code: ana-7454

12. The largest hamster litter on record consisted of 26 babies. Suppose a hamster has 26 babies. Assume that the birth of a female and the birth of a male are equally likely. What is the theoretical probability that all 26 babies will be male? Explain your reasoning.

13. In the unit *How Likely Is It?*, you learned about genetics. Every person has a combination of two tongue-curling alleles, TT, Tt, or tt, where T is the dominant tongue-curling allele, and t is the recessive non-tongue-curling allele. A person with at least one T allele will be able to curl his or her tongue.

Kent found out that his tongue-curling alleles are tt and his wife Diane's alleles are Tt. He makes this table to help him determine the possible outcomes for their children.

Kent

		t	t
Diane	T	Tt	Tt
	t	tt	tt

The possible combinations are Tt, Tt, tt, and tt. This means that a child of Kent and Diane has a 50% chance of being able to curl his or her tongue.

a. Suppose Kent and Diane have two children. What is the probability that both of the children will be able to curl their tongues? Make a tree diagram to help you answer this question.

b. Suppose Kent and Diane have four children. What is the probability that none of the children will be able to curl their tongues?

c. Suppose Kent and Diane have four children. What is the probability that only the oldest child will be able to curl his or her tongue?

14. King George's home, Castle Warwick, is under siege. King George must escape to his cousin's home, Castle Howard. The only escape route is through a series of canals, shown below.

There are five gates in the series of canals. Each gate opens and closes at random and is open half the time and closed the other half. The arrows show the way the water is flowing.

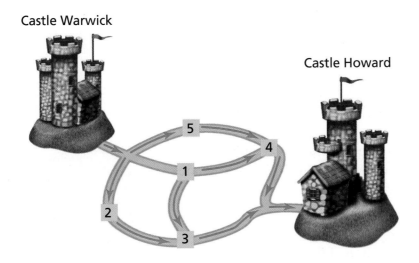

a. What is the probability that a water route from Castle Warwick to Castle Howard is open?

b. How is this exercise similar to Problem 4.3?

15. Drew, the paper carrier, collects $10 per week from each customer for the paper. One customer offers him these deals.

a. Toss five coins. If there are four or more heads, the customer pays $18. Otherwise, he pays $4. Find the expected value for this deal. Decide if it is a fair deal.

b. Toss five coins. If they are all the same, the customer pays $80. Otherwise, he pays $4. Find the expected value for this deal. Decide if it is a fair deal.

16. Ethan makes a game played on the number line. At the start of a turn, a player places a marker on 0. The player tosses a penny and moves the marker one unit to the right if the penny lands heads up and one unit to the left if it lands tails up. A turn is three tosses, and the score for that turn is the number naming the location of the marker at the end of that turn.

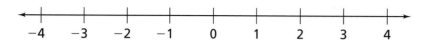

a. What scores are possible after one turn (three tosses)?

b. Suppose Ethan changes his game so that a turn consists of four tosses. What scores would be possible after one turn?

17. a. Spinning the pointer at the right once makes a binomial situation. What are the possible outcomes of a single spin? What is the probability of each outcome?

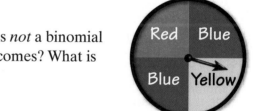

b. Spinning the spinner from part (a) three times is also a binomial situation. If the result of the first spin is Red, does this affect the possible outcomes of the second and third spins? What is the probability of RBB (in this order), assuming each spin is independent of the previous spin?

c. Using the spinner at the right once is *not* a binomial situation. What are the possible outcomes? What is the probability of each?

d. Does spinning the spinner at the right make a binomial situation? Explain.

e. Suppose you spin the spinner in part (d) three times. What is the probability of RBB (in this order)?

Extensions

Pascal's Triangle (on the left, below) can be used to summarize binomial probabilities and answer new questions in some binomial situations. The sum of each row is the same as the number of outcomes in a binomial probability. For example, some binomial situations are written across from their corresponding row.

Pascal's Triangle							Coin	True/False Test
			1					
		1		1			Tossing 1 coin	1 question
	1		2		1		Tossing 2 coins	2 questions
1		3		3		1	Tossing 3 coins	3 questions
1	4		6		4	1	Tossing 4 coins	4 questions
1	5	10		10	5	1	Tossing 5 coins	5 questions

18. Describe some patterns in Pascal's Triangle.

19. What is the sixth row (the next row in the diagram above) of Pascal's Triangle? Describe what probabilities each number represents in a situation that involves tossing 6 coins.

In your answers for Exercises 20–22, tell which row from Pascal's Triangle you used.

20. On a five-question true/false test, what is the probability that you will guess exactly two correct answers?

21. A coin is tossed six times. What is the probability that at least two heads occur?

22. On a nine-question true/false test, what is the probability that you will guess exactly three correct answers?

Mathematical Reflections 4

In this investigation, you looked at probabilities for situations involving a series of actions, each with two equally likely outcomes. The following questions will help you summarize what you have learned.

Think about your answers to these questions. Discuss your ideas with other students and your teacher. Then write a summary of your findings in your notebook.

1. Describe five different binomial situations. Explain why they are binomial situations.

2. Tossing a coin three times is an example of a situation involving a series of three actions, each with two equally likely outcomes.

   a. Pick one of the situations you described in Question 1. Describe a series of three actions, each with two equally likely outcomes. Make a list of all the possible outcomes.

   b. Write a question about your situation that can be answered by your list.

3. As you increase the number of actions for a binomial situation, what happens to the total number of possible outcomes? For example, if you increase the number of times a coin is tossed, what happens to the total number of outcomes?

Unit Project

The Carnival Game

This project requires you to use the mathematics you have studied in several units, including this one. You will make a game for a school carnival and test your game. Then, you will write a report about your game.

Part 1: Design a Carnival Game

You can design a new game or redesign one of the games you analyzed in this unit. Keep these guidelines in mind.

- The game should make a profit for the school.
- The game should be easy to set up and use at a school carnival. It should not require expensive equipment.
- The game should take a relatively short time to play.
- The rules should be easily understood by people your age.

Part 2: Test Your Game

After you have drafted a game design, play the game several times until you feel confident that you can predict what will happen in the long run. Keep track of your trials, and include that information in your report.

Part 3: Submit Your Design to the Carnival Committee

Once you are satisfied that your game is reasonable, prepare to submit your design. Your submission to the committee should include two things: a model or a scale model of the game and a written report.

Model or Scale Model

If you build a scale model instead of an actual model, give the scale factor from the scale model to the actual game.

You can either construct the model out of similar materials to those you would use for the actual game, or you can prepare scale drawings of the game. If you make drawings, be sure to include enough views of your game so that anyone could look at the drawings and construct the game.

Report

Include a set of rules that explains how the game is played, how much it costs to play, how a player wins, and how much a player wins.

Part 4: Write a Report

Write a report about your game to the carnival committee. Assume that the committee consists of teachers in the building (not just mathematics teachers), parents, and other students. Your report should include:

- The experimental probability of winning the game that you found from playing the game several times. If possible, give the theoretical probability as well. If you don't give the theoretical probability of winning your game, explain why you did not.

- The amount of money the school will collect and how much they should expect to pay out if the game is played many times. Explain how you determined these amounts.

- An explanation of why your game should be chosen. Explain why the game is worth having in the carnival and why you think people would want to play it.

Looking Back and Looking Ahead

Unit Review

In this unit, you studied some basic ideas of probability and some ways to use those ideas to solve problems about probability and expected value. In particular, you studied how to

Go Online
PHSchool.com

For: Vocabulary Review
Puzzle
Web Code: anj-7051

- find and interpret experimental and theoretical probabilities
- use simulations to gather experimental data
- use tree diagrams, and other listing techniques to find all of the possible outcomes
- use area models in which probabilities are shown as parts of a whole square or circle

Use Your Understanding: Probability Reasoning

To test your understanding and skill with probability ideas and strategies, consider the following problem situations.

1. Maria's homework problem is to design two dartboards that match these conditions:

- The probability of landing in region A is 30%.
- The probability of landing in region B is 25%.
- The probability of landing in region C is 20%.
- The remaining space on the dartboard is region D.

   a. Draw a square dartboard that meets the given conditions.

   b. Draw a circular dartboard that meets the given conditions.

   c. For each dartboard, find the probability that a dart will
   - **i.** land in region D
   - **ii.** land in a region other than D
   - **iii.** *not* land in region A

2. Gabrielle and Jim are playing the Match/No Match game. On each turn, the players spin the two spinners shown below. Gabrielle scores 1 point if the spins match, and Jim scores 1 point if they do not match.

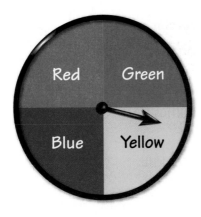 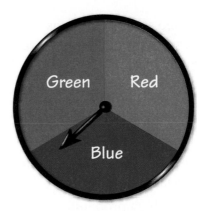

   a. Use a tree diagram to show all the possible outcomes for this game.

   b. What is the theoretical probability of getting a match?

   c. What is the theoretical probability of getting a non-match?

   d. Does each player have an equally-likely chance of winning?

   e. Is this a fair game? If so, explain why. If not, explain how you could change the rules to make it fair.

3. Kali and Antonio designed a new computer game. They programmed the game so the probability that a player will win is $\frac{1}{4}$ on each turn. If the player wins, the score increases by four points. If the player loses, two points are deducted from the score.

   a. Matthew plans to play 12 rounds of the game. How many points can he expect to score?

   b. How many points per round can Matthew expect to win or lose?

   c. Is this a fair game? If not, how would you change the points won or lost so that it is a fair game?

Explain Your Reasoning

When you use mathematical calculations or diagrams to solve a problem or make a decision, it is important to justify your reasoning. Answer these questions about your work.

4. What does it mean to say that the probability of an event is $\frac{1}{2}$ or $\frac{2}{3}$ or $\frac{5}{8}$?

5. How are experimental and theoretical probabilities of an event related to each other?

6. Explain and illustrate with specific examples how you could use each strategy to analyze probabilities.

    a. tree diagrams   **b.** area models

7. What does it mean to find the expected value of a chance activity with numerical outcomes? Give three examples of problems in this unit for which you had to find the expected value.

Look Ahead

You will almost certainly meet the ideas about probability of this unit in future study and problem solving in mathematics, science, and questions about games of chance. These are the basis of statistical reasoning that will be developed in the *Connected Mathematics* unit, *Samples and Populations,* and which you will see in areas as diverse as genetics, the payoffs in state lotteries, and local fundraisers.

English/Spanish Glossary

A

area model A diagram in which fractions of the area of the diagram correspond to probabilities in a situation. For example, suppose there are three blue blocks and two red blocks in a container. If two blocks are drawn out, one at a time, replacing the block drawn each time, the area model below shows that the probability of getting two red blocks is $\frac{4}{25}$.

Area models are particularly helpful when the outcomes being analyzed are not equally likely, because more likely outcomes take up larger areas. Area models are also helpful for outcomes involving more than one stage, such as rolling a number cube, then tossing a coin or choosing a bag, then drawing a block from it.

modelo por áreas Un diagrama en el que las fracciones del área del diagrama corresponden a las probabilidades en una situación. Por ejemplo, si hay tres bloques azules y dos bloques rojos en un recipiente y se saca un bloque cada vez sin reemplazarlo, el modelo por áreas de abajo muestra que la probabilidad de sacar dos bloques rojos es $\frac{4}{25}$.

Los modelos por áreas son especialmente útiles cuando los resultados que se analizan no son igualmente probables, porque los resultados más probables tienen áreas más grandes. Los modelos por áreas son también útiles para resultados que incluyen más de un paso, como tirar un cubo numérico y luego tirar una moneda, o elegir una bolsa y luego sacar un bloque de ella.

Second Choice

		B	B	B	R	R
	B	BB	BB	BB	BR	BR
	B	BB	BB	BB	BR	BR
First Choice	B	BB	BB	BB	BR	BR
	R	RB	RB	RB	RR	RR
	R	RB	RB	RB	RR	RR

B

binomial probability The probability of getting one of two outcomes (like heads or tails).

probabilidad binomial La probabilidad de obtener uno de dos resultados (como cara o cruz).

E

equally likely Two or more events that have the same probability of occurring. For example, when you toss a fair coin, heads and tails are equally likely; each has a 50% chance of happening. Rolling a six-sided number cube gives a $\frac{1}{6}$ probability for each number to come up. Each outcome is equally likely.

igualmente probables Dos o más sucesos que tienen la misma probabilidad de ocurrir. Por ejemplo, cuando se lanza una moneda "justa" la probabilidad de obtener cara es igual a la de obtener cruz; es decir, cada caso tiene una probabilidad del 50%. Tirar un cubo numérico de 6 lados supone $\frac{1}{6}$ de probabilidad de que salga cada número. Cada resultado es igualmente probable

expected value (or long-term average)
Intuitively, the average payoff over the long run. For example, suppose you are playing a game with two number cubes. You score 2 points when a sum of 6 is rolled, 1 point for a sum of 3, and 0 points for anything else. If you roll the cubes 36 times, you could expect to roll a sum of 6 about five times and a sum of 3 about twice. This means that you could expect to score $(5 \times 2) + (2 \times 1) = 12$ points for 36 rolls, an average of $\frac{12}{36} = \frac{1}{3}$ point per roll. Here, $\frac{1}{3}$ is the expected value (or average over the long run) of one roll.

valor esperado (o promedio a largo plazo) El promedio de puntos o la recompensa conseguidos tras realizar muchos intentos. Por ejemplo, imagínate un juego con dos cubos numéricos en el que obtienes 2 puntos por una suma de 6, 1 punto por una suma de 3 y 0 puntos por cualquier otra suma. Si lanzaras los cubos numéricos 36 veces, sería de esperar que obtuvieras una suma de 6 aproximadamente cinco veces y una de 3 aproximadamente dos veces. Es decir, cabría esperar conseguir $(5 \times 2) + (2 \times 1) = 12$ puntos en los 36 lanzamientos, o sea un promedio de $\frac{12}{36} = \frac{1}{3}$ punto por lanzamiento. Aquí $\frac{1}{3}$ es el valor esperado (o promedio a largo plazo) de un lanzamiento.

experimental probability A probability that is determined through experimentation. For example, you could find the experimental probability of getting a head when you toss a coin by tossing a coin many times and keeping track of the outcomes. The experimental probability would be the ratio of the number of heads to the total number of tosses, or trials. Experimental probability may not be the same as the theoretical probability. However, for a large number of trials, they are likely to be close. Experimental probabilities can be used to predict behavior over the long run.

probabilidad experimental La probabilidad determinada mediante la experimentación. Por ejemplo, para hallar la probabilidad experimental de obtener cara en el lanzamiento de una moneda, podrías efectuar numerosos lanzamientos y anotar los resultados. Dicha probabilidad sería la razón entre el número de caras y el número de lanzamientos, o intentos. La probabilidad experimental puede no ser igual a la probabilidad teórica. Sin embargo, es probable que estén muy cerca durante muchos lanzamientos. Las probabilidades experimentales sirven para predecir lo que ocurrirá a largo plazo.

F

fair game A game in which each player is equally likely to win. The probability of winning a two-person fair game is $\frac{1}{2}$. An unfair game can be made fair by adjusting the scoring system, or the payoffs. For example, suppose you play a game in which two fair coins are tossed. You score when both coins land heads up. Otherwise, your opponent scores. The probability that you will score is $\frac{1}{4}$, and the probability that your opponent will score is $\frac{3}{4}$. To make the game fair, you might adjust the scoring system so that you receive 3 points each time you score and your opponent receives 1 point when he or she scores. This would make the expected values for each player equal, which results in a fair game.

juego justo Un juego en el que cada jugador tiene igual probabilidad de ganar. La probabilidad de ganar en un juego justo entre dos personas es $\frac{1}{2}$. Para hacer justo un juego que no lo es, se puede ajustar el sistema de reparto de puntos o de recompensas. Por ejemplo, imagina un juego que consiste en lanzar dos monedas "justas". Si salen dos caras, tú obtienes puntos. Si no, los obtiene el otro jugador. La probabilidad de que tú consigas los puntos es $\frac{1}{4}$ y la probabilidad de que los consiga el otro jugador es $\frac{3}{4}$. Para hacer justo el juego, podrías ajustar el sistema de reparto de puntos de manera que, cada vez que salgan dos caras, tú recibas 3 puntos y en las demás ocasiones el otro jugador reciba 1 punto. Esto haría que los valores esperados para cada jugador fueran iguales, lo que resulta en un juego justo.

Law of Large Numbers This law states, in effect, that as more trials of an experiment are conducted, the experimental probability more closely approximates the theoretical probability. It is not at all unusual to have 100% heads after three tosses of a fair coin, but it would be extremely unusual to have even 60% heads after 1,000 tosses. This is expressed by the Law of Large Numbers.

Ley de números grandes Esta ley enuncia, en efecto, que cuantos más intentos de un experimento se realizan, más se aproximará la probabilidad experimental a la teórica. No es inusual tener 100% caras después de tres lanzamientos de una moneda justa, pero sería extremadamente inusual tener incluso 60% de caras después de 1,000 lanzamientos. Esto se expresa con la Ley de números grandes.

outcome A possible result. For example, when a number cube is rolled, the possible outcomes are 1, 2, 3, 4, 5, and 6. Other possible outcomes are even or odd. Others are three and not three. When determining probabilities, it is important to be clear about what the possible outcomes are.

resultado Consecuencia posible. Por ejemplo, cuando se lanza un cubo numérico, los resultados posibles son 1, 2, 3, 4, 5 y 6. Otros resultados posibles son pares o impares. Otros son es tres y no tres. Cuando se determinan las probabilidades, es importante definir cuáles son los resultados posibles.

payoff The number of points (or dollars or other objects of value) a player in a game receives for a particular outcome.

recompensa El número de puntos (o dólares u otros objetos de valor) que recibe un jugador por un resultado particular.

probability A number between 0 and 1 that describes the likelihood that an outcome will occur. For example, when a fair number cube is rolled, a 2 can be expected $\frac{1}{6}$ of the time, so the probability of rolling a 2 is $\frac{1}{6}$. The probability of a certain outcome is 1, while the probability of an impossible outcome is 0.

probabilidad Un número comprendido entre 0 y 1 que indica la probabilidad de que ocurra un suceso. Por ejemplo, cuando se lanza un cubo numérico justo, se puede esperar un 2 cada $\frac{1}{6}$ de las veces, por lo que la probabilidad de que salga un 2 es $\frac{1}{6}$. La probabilidad de un suceso seguro es 1, mientras que la probabilidad de un suceso imposible es 0.

random Outcomes that are uncertain when viewed individually, but which exhibit a predictable pattern over many trials, are random. For example, when you roll a fair number cube, you have no way of knowing what the next roll will be, but you do know that, over the long run, you will roll each number on the cube about the same number of times.

sucesos aleatorios Aquellos sucesos cuyos resultados, al considerarse separadamente, no son seguros, pero que podrían presentar un patrón previsible al observarse a lo largo de muchos intentos. Por ejemplo, en el caso de lanzar un cubo numérico perfecto es imposible saber cuál será el resultado del próximo lanzamiento; sin embargo, sí se sabe que a la larga saldrá cada uno de los números del cubo numérico aproximadamente la misma cantidad de veces.

sample space The set of all possible outcomes in a probability situation. When you toss two coins, the sample space consists of four outcomes: HH, HT, TH, and TT.

espacio muestral El conjunto de todos los resultados posibles en una probabilidad. Cuando lanzas dos monedas, el espacio muestral son cuatro resultados: CC, CX, XC y XX.

theoretical probability A probability obtained by analyzing a situation. If all of the outcomes are equally likely, you can find a theoretical probability of an event by listing all of the possible outcomes and then finding the ratio of the number of outcomes producing the desired event to the total number of outcomes. For example, there are 36 possible equally likely outcomes (number pairs) when two fair number cubes are rolled. Of these, six have a sum of 7, so the probability of rolling a sum of 7 is $\frac{6}{36}$, or $\frac{1}{6}$.

probabilidad teórica La probabilidad obtenida mediante el análisis de una situación. Si todos los resultados de un suceso son igualmente probables, entonces para hallar la probabilidad teórica del mismo se escribe una lista de todos los resultados posibles y luego se halla la razón entre el número de resultados que produce el suceso deseado para el número total de resultados. Por ejemplo, al lanzar dos cubos numéricos perfectos existen 36 resultados igualmente probables (pares de números). De ellos, seis tienen una suma de 7, por lo que la probabilidad de obtener una suma de 7 es $\frac{6}{36}$, o sea, $\frac{1}{6}$.

tree diagram A diagram used to determine the number of possible outcomes in a probability situation. The number of final branches is equal to the number of possible outcomes. The tree diagram below shows all the possible outcomes for randomly choosing a yellow or red rose and then a white or pink ribbon. The four possible outcomes are listed in the last column. Tree diagrams are handy to use when outcomes are equally likely.

diagrama de árbol Un diagrama que se utiliza para determinar el número de resultados posibles en una situación de probabilidad. El número de ramas finales es igual al número de resultados posibles. El siguiente diagrama de árbol muestra todos los resultados posibles al escoger al azar una rosa amarilla o roja, y luego una cinta blanca o rosada. Los cuatro resultados posibles aparecen en la última columna. Los diagramas de árbol son útiles cuando los resultados son igualmente probables..

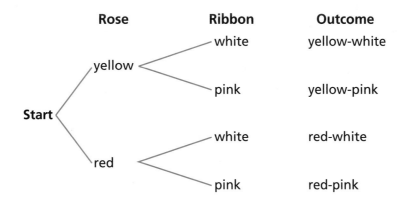

Index

Index

Acknowledgments

Team Credits

The people who made up the **Connected Mathematics 2** team—representing editorial, editorial services, design services, and production services—are listed below. Bold type denotes core team members.

Leora Adler, Judith Buice, Kerry Cashman, Patrick Culleton, Sheila DeFazio, Katie Hallahan, Richard Heater, **Barbara Hollingdale, Jayne Holman,** Karen Holtzman, **Etta Jacobs,** Christine Lee, Carolyn Lock, Catherine Maglio, **Dotti Marshall,** Rich McMahon, Eve Melnechuk, Kristin Mingrone, Terri Mitchell, **Marsha Novak,** Irene Rubin, Donna Russo, Robin Samper, Siri Schwartzman, **Nancy Smith,** Emily Soltanoff, **Mark Tricca,** Paula Vergith, Roberta Warshaw, Helen Young

Additional Credits

Diana Bonfilio, Mairead Reddin, Michael Torocsik, nSight, Inc.

Technical Illustration

WestWords, Inc.

Cover Design

tom white.images

Photos

2 t, David Young-Wolff/PhotoEdit; **2 b,** Comstock Images/Getty Images, Inc.; **3 foreground,** Russ Lappa; **3 background,** Bill Frymire/Masterfile; **5,** Lisette Le Bon/SuperStock; **9,** Richard Haynes; **14,** Jack Hollingsworth/Corbis; **17,** Russ Lappa; **28,** Peter Beck/Corbis; **32,** Stockbyte Royalty Free Photos; **40,** David Young-Wolff/PhotoEdit; **44,** Philip James Corwin/Corbis; **47,** Larry Williams/Corbis; **50,** Comstock Images/Getty Images, Inc.; **52,** Jed Jacobsohn/Getty Images, Inc.; **55,** Ron Kimball/Ron Kimball Studios; **56,** H. Reinhard/Masterfile ; **61,** Richard Haynes

Connected Mathematics 2™

Data Distributions

Describing Variability and Comparing Groups

Glenda Lappan
James T. Fey
William M. Fitzgerald
Susan N. Friel
Elizabeth Difanis Phillips

PEARSON
Prentice
Hall

Boston, Massachusetts
Upper Saddle River, New Jersey

Data Distributions

Describing Variability and Comparing Groups

Is the proportion of each of the colors of M&M's® in a bag of candies always the same?

In a graph displaying the kinds of pets that students have, there are several *repeated values*, such as "cat," "dog," "fish," and "rabbit." For other data, such as "pig," there are no repeated values. What do you think a repeated value means when we talk about data?

Willa, a video-game designer, needs an idea about how much time to give a player to react when an object appears on the screen. How can she use data from a reaction-time experiment to help her?

Statistics and data analysis are used to report health risks, to summarize consumer choices for CD players, to identify the most popular movies watched over a weekend, and to indicate favorite food choices. Think for a minute about some other ways statistics and graphs are used to report information.

There are important ideas about data analysis and statistics that can help you understand, analyze, critique, and respond to various reports that you encounter. Understanding data analysis and statistics can help you decide whether information is reliable or is distorted by the graphs used to display it. The investigations in *Data Distributions* will help you use ideas about statistics and data analysis to describe the variability in a data set, to compare groups, and to make decisions as you solve problems. Think about some interesting situations that involve statistical investigations, including the three on the previous page.

Mathematical Highlights

Describing Variability and Comparing Groups

In *Data Distributions*, **you will explore important ideas related to statistics and data analysis, especially those related to describing variability and center and to making comparisons.**

You will learn how to

- Apply the process of statistical investigation to pose questions, to identify ways data are collected, and to determine strategies for analyzing data in order to answer the questions posed

- Recognize that variability occurs whenever data are collected and describe the variability in the distribution of a given data set

- Identify sources of variability, including natural variability and variability that results from errors in measurement

- Determine whether to use the mean or median to describe a distribution

- Use the shape of a distribution to estimate the location of the mean and the median

- Use a variety of representations, including tables, bar graphs, and line plots, to display distributions

- Understand and use counts or percents to report frequencies of occurrence of data

- Compare the distributions of data sets using their related centers, variability, and shapes

- Decide if a difference among data values or summary measures matters

- Develop and use strategies to compare data sets to solve problems

As you work on problems in this unit, ask yourself questions about situations that involve analyzing distributions or comparing groups:

Is there anything surprising about the data and their distribution?

Where do the data cluster in the distribution?

How can I use the mean or median and range to help me understand and describe a data distribution?

What strategies can I use to compare two different data sets?

Making Sense of Variability

A statistical investigation begins with a question. Decisions about what data to collect are based on the question that is asked.

When data are collected to answer a question, the data may be similar to each other, such as the number of raisins found in each of 30 different half-ounce boxes of raisins. More often, however, the data are different from each other, such as pulse rates collected from 30 different people after each person rides a roller coaster.

Variability of a set of numerical data indicates how widely spread or closely clustered the data values are.

For each situation below, do you expect the data to be more similar to or different from each other? Why?

Each student records the number of each color of M&M's® candies found in his or her own bag of candies.

Each student measures the same student's head size in centimeters.

Each student collects his or her reaction times on five trials using a computer reaction-time game.

Each student records his or her grade level—sixth grade, seventh grade, or eighth grade—as part of the data collected on a school survey.

1.1 Variability in Categorical Data

Data that are specific labels or names for categories are called **categorical data.** Suppose you ask people in which months they were born or what their favorite rock groups are. Their answers are categorical data. When displaying categorical data using tables or graphs, you usually report the *frequency*, or "how many," of each category in the data set as a count or a percent.

Did You Know?

M&M's® candies have been around for a long time. They are named after Mars and Murrie, the people who started the candy company in the early 1940s. M&M's candies began as a high-energy field snack for American soldiers, because "The milk chocolate melts in your mouth -- not in your hand."® They were later introduced to the public.

For many years, M&M's candies came in six colors: brown, yellow, orange, green, tan, and red. Blue replaced tan in 1995, but in early 2004, M&M's candies were available only in black and white! The same six, but brighter, 1995 colors returned in March 2004.

Did the Mars Company plan a specific distribution of colors of M&M's candies before March 2004?

- What kinds of data would help answer the question?

- How might you collect such data?

- How would you analyze the data?

- How would you use your analysis to help answer the question?

One student uses a database that gives data for 200 bags of pre-2004 M&M's®. The database shows how many of each color candy were in each of the 200 bags. She uses the counts from the first bag to make a bar graph that shows the *percent* of each color of candies in the bag.

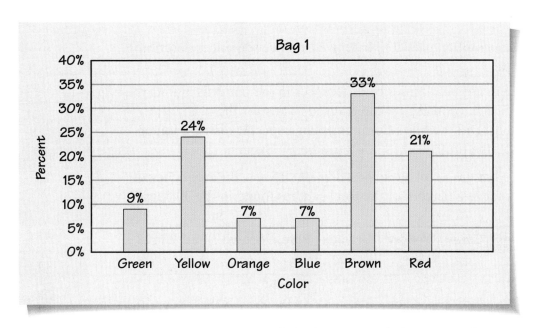

Bag Number	Green	Yellow	Orange	Blue	Brown	Red	Total
1	5	14	4	4	19	12	58

How did the student use the counts of the data to graph the percents?

The student noticed that the percent varied considerably from color to color.

There were more yellow, brown, and red candies than green, orange, and blue candies.

Brown candies took up the greatest percentage of the bag; $\frac{1}{3}$, or about 33%, of the bag of candies was brown.

The yellow and the red candies were close in quantity, with yellow a little less than $\frac{1}{4}$, or 25%, of the bag and red a little more than $\frac{1}{5}$, or 20%, of the bag.

The green, orange, and blue candies were each less than $\frac{1}{10}$, or 10%, of the bag.

A. 1. The table shows data from two other bags of candies. Make a bar graph for each set of data. Show the frequency of each color as a percent of the total candies in that bag.

Bag Number	Green	Yellow	Orange	Blue	Brown	Red	Total
2	5	15	2	7	15	10	54
3	3	13	5	5	19	10	55

2. For each graph in part (1), write two or more sentences describing the data.

3. Are there any similarities or differences in the patterns among the three bags of candies that can be used to answer the original question, "Did the Mars Company plan a specific distribution of colors of the pre-2004 M&M's® candies?" Explain.

B. 1. Make a bar graph for these pre-2004 data. Show the frequency of each color as a percent of the total candies found in the 30 bags.

Bag Number	Green	Yellow	Orange	Blue	Brown	Red	Total
1–30	92	449	109	90	576	415	1,731

2. Write two or more sentences describing the data in the bar graph.

3. How would you now answer the question, "Did the Mars Company plan a specific distribution of colors of the pre-2004 M&M's® candies?"

C. Look at the eight graphs on the next page. Did the company make a change in the distribution of colors in March 2004? If so, describe the change. Explain your reasoning.

ACE **Homework starts on page 17.**

1.2 **Variability in Numerical Counts**

Data that are counts or measures are called **numerical data.** We often count to gather numerical data. For example, we count people to find the population of each state in the United States in order to answer the question, "How much do state populations vary in size?"

Before March 2004

Bag A

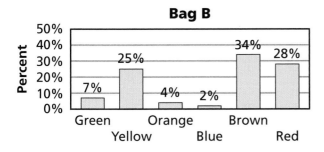

Bag B

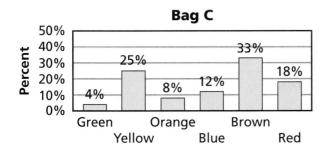

Bag C

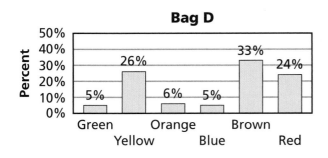

Bag D

Bag D chart: Green 5%, Yellow 26%, Orange 6%, Blue 5%, Brown 33%, Red 24%

After March 2004

Bag E

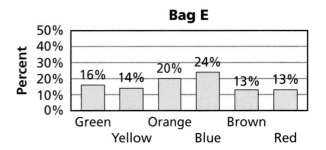

Bag F

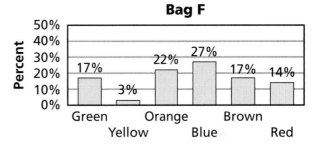

Bag G

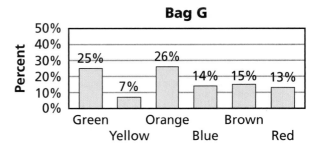

Bag H

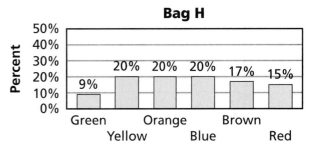

Use the table and related graphs to answer the questions in Problem 1.2.

Immigration to the United States

Decade	Immigrants From Europe (Graph 1)	Total Immigrants	Percent of Immigrants From Europe (Graph 2)
1820	7,650	8,385	82%
1821–1830	98,797	143,439	69%
1831–1840	495,681	599,125	83%
1831–1850	1,597,442	1,713,251	93%
1851–1860	2,452,577	2,598,214	94%
1861–1870	2,064,141	2,314,824	89%
1871–1880	2,271,925	2,812,191	81%
1881–1890	4,735,484	5,246,613	90%
1891–1900	3,555,352	3,687,564	96%
1901–1910	8,056,040	8,795,386	92%
1911–1920	4,321,887	5,735,811	75%
1921–1930	2,463,194	4,107,209	60%
1931–1940	347,566	528,431	66%
1941–1950	621,147	1,035,039	60%
1951–1960	1,325,727	2,515,479	53%
1961–1970	1,123,492	3,321,677	34%
1971–1980	800,368	4,493,314	18%
1981–1990	761,550	7,338,062	10%
1991–2000	1,359,737	9,095,417	15%

SOURCE: U.S. Citizenship and Immigration Services. Go to www.PHSchool.com for a data update.
Web Code: ang-9041

Graph 1: Immigration From Europe to the United States

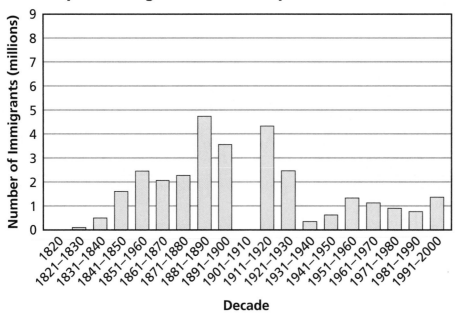

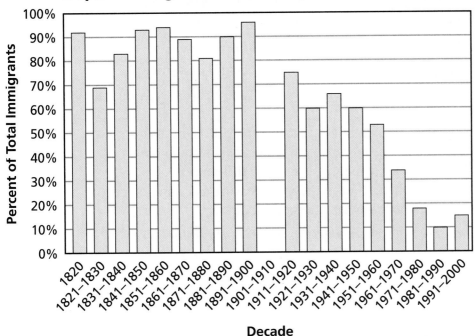

Graph 2: Immigration From Europe to the United States

How did immigration from Europe to the United States change from 1820 to 2000?

Problem 1.2 Variability in Numerical Counts

A. 1. a. In the decade from 1901 to 1910, how many immigrants came from Europe?

   b. Copy Graph 1 and add the bar for 1901–1910.

   c. Write two comparison statements about how the 1901–1910 data value is similar to or different from the values for other decades.

2. a. In the decade from 1901 to 1910, how many immigrants came from all countries?

   b. What percent of this number were immigrants from Europe?

   c. Copy Graph 2 and add the bar for 1901–1910.

   d. Write two comparison statements about how the percent in part (b) is similar to or different from the percents for other decades.

B. Describe any trends or patterns you notice in immigration to the United States from Europe from 1820 to 2000.

ACE Homework starts on page 17.

Investigation 1 Making Sense of Variability   **11**

1.3 Variability in Numerical Measurements

Measurements, such as the time to run a mile or the height of a student, are another kind of numerical data. You already know that any measurement is approximate.

The measurement tools we use to gather data affect the precision of the measures we obtain. For example, one scale measures mass to the nearest tenth of a gram while another scale measures mass to the nearest thousandth of a gram. Also, when different people measure the same object, the results may differ even when they use the same tool.

What tool(s) might you use to measure heads in order to determine sizes needed for fitted baseball caps?

Problem 1.3 Variability in Numerical Measurements

Suppose your class wants to order fitted baseball caps with the *Mugwump* as a logo.

- **A. 1.** Your teacher will choose one boy and one girl from the class to represent two different head sizes. Measure these two students' head sizes to the nearest tenth of a centimeter and record the data.

  2. Measure your own head size to the nearest tenth of a centimeter and record the data.

- **B.** Use the data gathered by your class for Question A. Make a line plot for each of the following:

  1. the head-size measurements for the girl chosen

  2. the head-size measurements for the boy chosen

  3. the head-size measurements of all the students in the class

- **C.** For each line plot in Question B:

  1. What are the minimum and maximum values of the distribution?

  2. What is the range of the distribution?

  3. Do you think the range of the measurements is great enough that recommending a single cap size would be difficult? Explain.

  4. Are there any unusually high or low data values, or *outliers*? If so, what are they?

  5. Do some or most of the data cluster in one or more locations? If so, where does this occur?

  6. Are there gaps in the data? If so, where do they occur?

7. What would you describe as a typical head size for these data? Explain.

8. Use these ideas to describe the variability in the data.

ACE Homework starts on page 17.

1.4 Two Kinds of Variability

Each of 13 students measured the circumference of Jasmine's head. The results are shown using a table and a graph called a **value bar graph.**

Head Measurements

Name	Measure (cm)
Santo	56.0
Sara	55.8
Pam	56.0
Melosa	55.9
Malik	55.5
Martin	56.0
Ming	55.2
Manny	56.5
Juanita	55.0
Jun	55.5
Tai	56.0
Kareem	55.5
Chip	55.8

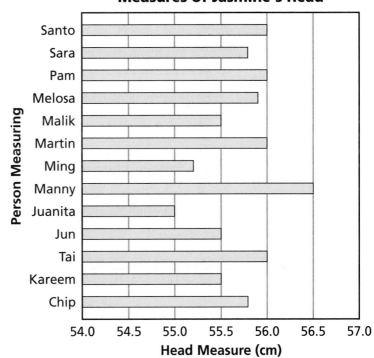

Measures of Jasmine's Head

How are the table and the value bar graph related?

What is a value bar graph?

The variability results from measurement errors as different students measured the circumference of Jasmine's head.

How do you think measurement errors occur?

Investigation 1 Making Sense of Variability **13**

The **ordered value bar graph** shows the data in order from minimum to maximum values.

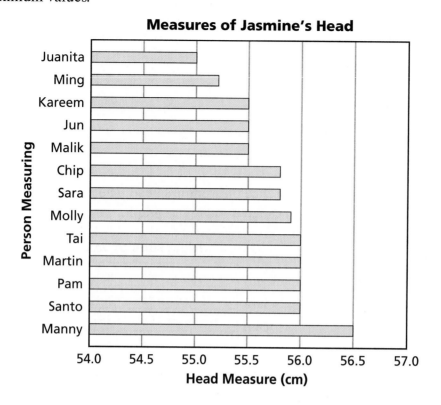

The **line plots** show the frequency of each measurement.

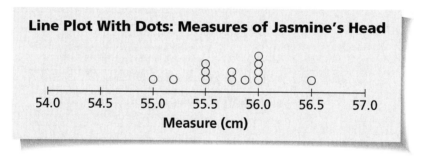

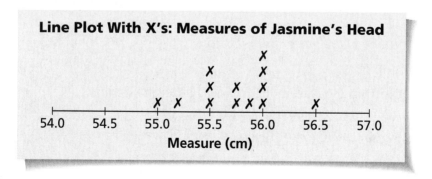

How are the ordered value bar graph and the line plots related?

What does each graph tell you about the distribution of these data?

Use the ordered value bar graph and the line plots on the facing page.

A. 1. Examine the distribution of the measurements. What are the minimum and maximum values?

2. What is the range?

3. Is the range of the measurements great enough that choosing a cap size for Jasmine would be difficult? Explain.

4. Are there any outliers? If so, what are they?

5. Do some or most of the data cluster in one or more locations? Explain.

6. Are there gaps in the data? If so, where do they occur?

7. What measurement would you recommend using to choose a cap size for Jasmine? Explain.

8. Use these ideas to describe the variability in the data set.

B. 1. Jasmine's classmates measured their own head sizes and recorded them in the table below. Make an ordered value bar graph and a line plot for these data.

Class Head Sizes

Initials	CK	KN	TB	JG	JW	MD	MG
Measure (cm)	55.8	58.0	56.5	58.0	55.5	58.0	55.2

Initials	MJ	MR	MS	PM	SF	SK
Measure (cm)	58.5	55.2	55.5	54.0	57.0	56.4

2. What are the minimum and maximum values?

3. What is the range?

4. Is the range of the measurements great enough that recommending one cap size for all the students would be difficult? Explain.

5. Are there any outliers? If so, what are they?

6. Do some or most of the data cluster in one or more locations? Explain.

7. Are there gaps in the data? If so, where do they occur?

8. What would you describe as the typical cap size for these students? Explain.

9. Use these ideas to describe the variability in the data set.

ACE Homework starts on page 17.

Applications

1. a. Use the M&M's® data for Bag 1, Bag 2, and Bag 3. For each bag, make a bar graph that shows the percent of each color found.

Candy Colors

Bag Number	Green	Yellow	Orange	Blue	Brown	Red	Total
1	3	10	9	5	10	18	55
2	5	12	4	6	19	11	57
3	7	10	9	4	16	12	58
4	4	14	2	1	14	19	54
5	12	7	8	7	14	13	61
6	10	9	6	5	15	8	53
7	11	11	6	6	12	12	58
8	8	15	5	3	16	10	57
9	2	11	4	4	24	12	57
10	5	7	4	1	26	13	56
11	6	13	4	4	15	18	60
12	5	8	4	2	23	16	58
13	9	13	4	4	14	11	55
14	9	10	5	5	14	14	57
15	5	19	5	2	13	14	58
Total	101	169	79	59	245	201	854

b. Write two or more comparison statements that describe the distribution of colors for the three bags.

c. Is there some plan to the distribution of colors in the bags? Explain.

2. a. Use the totals in the last row of the table for each color of candies. Make a bar graph for these data that shows the percent of each color found in the 15 bags.

b. Describe the data by writing two or more comparison statements.

c. Look back at the bar graph you made for Problem 1.1, Question B. Compare this graph with the graph you made in part (a). How would you now answer the question, "Did the Mars Company plan a specific distribution of colors of M&M's® candies?" Explain.

3. a. The line plot below shows the head measurements of several seventh-grade students. What are the minimum and maximum values?

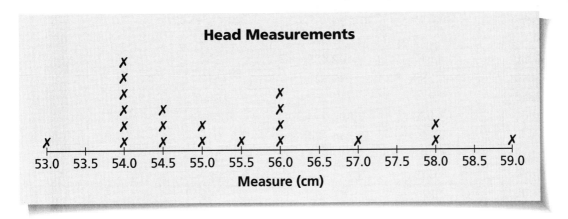

Head Measurements

Measure (cm)

b. What is the range?

c. Is the range of the measurements great enough that recommending one cap size for all the students would be difficult? Explain.

d. Are there any outliers? If so, what are they?

e. Do some or most of the data cluster in one or more locations? If so, where?

f. Are there gaps in the data? If so, where do they occur?

g. What would you describe as the typical cap size for these students?

h. How might you use these ideas to describe the variability in the data?

For each situation in Exercises 4–7, tell whether the data collected are categorical or numerical. Then, tell whether the data are widely spread out or closely clustered.

4. Each student records the number of people living in his or her household.

5. Each student measures the length of the same table in centimeters.

6. Each student randomly chooses a number from 1 to 10.

7. Each student records the time spent viewing television, videos, and DVD movies in the past week.

Homework
Help nline
PHSchool.com
For: Help with Exercises 4–7
Web Code: ane-8104

For Exercises 8–11, use the table below.

Immigration to the United States

Decade	Immigrants From Mexico	Total Immigrants	Percent of Immigrants From Mexico
1820	1	8,385	0%
1821–1830	4,817	143,439	3%
1831–1840	6,599	599,125	1%
1831–1850	3,271	1,713,251	0%
1851–1860	3,078	2,598,214	0%
1861–1870	2,191	2,314,824	0%
1871–1880	5,162	2,812,191	0%
1881–1890	1,913	5,246,613	0%
1891–1900	971	3,687,564	0%
1901–1910	49,642	8,795,386	1%
1911–1920	219,004	5,735,811	4%
1921–1930	459,287	4,107,209	11%
1931–1940	22,319	528,431	4%
1941–1950	60,589	1,035,039	6%
1951–1960	299,811	2,515,479	12%
1961–1970	453,937	3,321,677	14%
1971–1980	640,294	4,493,314	14%
1981–1990	1,655,843	7,338,062	23%
1991–2000	2,249,421	9,095,417	25%

SOURCE: U.S. Citizenship and Immigration Services. Go to www.PHSchool.com for a data update.
Web Code: ang-9041

8. a. In each of the decades 1961–1970 and 1971–1980, how many people were immigrants from Mexico?

   b. Copy the graph below. Add the bars for 1961–1970 and 1971–1980.

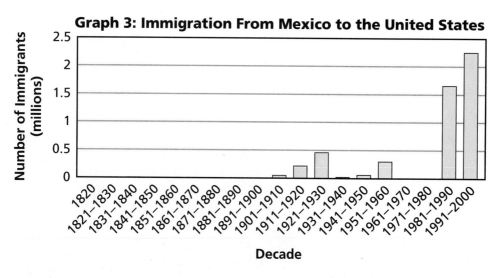

9. **Multiple Choice** Which statement is true?

   A. More immigrants came to the United States in the decade 1941–1950 than in the decade 1961–1970.

   B. About the same number of immigrants came to the United States in the decade 1921–1930 as in the decade 1961–1970.

   C. The number of immigrants in the decade 1991–2000 is about 50,000 more than the combined number of immigrants for the two decades 1971–1990.

   D. None of the above.

10. **a.** In each of the decades 1961–1970 and 1971–1980, how many people total were immigrants to the United States?

    b. What percent of each of the numbers in part (a) were immigrants from Mexico?

    c. Copy the graph below. Add the bars for 1961–1970 and 1971–1980.

Graph 4: Immigration From Mexico to the United States

(bar graph with vertical axis "Percent of Total Immigrants" ranging from 0 to 40% in 5% increments, horizontal axis "Decade" from 1820 to 1991–2000)

Decade

d. Write two comparison statements about how the data values in part (c) are similar to or different from the data values for other decades.

11. How has the pattern of immigration from Mexico to the United States changed from 1820 to 2000? Explain.

12. a. One of the line plots below shows several measures of Yukio's head. The other shows one measure of Yukio's head and one of each of his classmates' heads. Identify the line plot that shows Yukio's head measurements. Explain your reasoning.

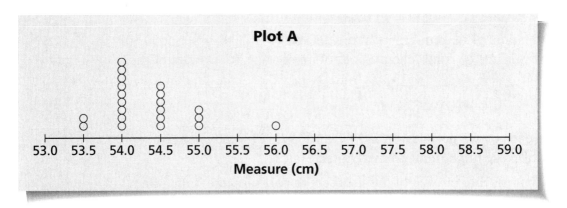

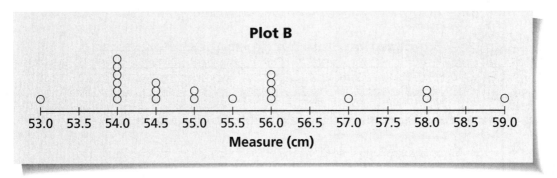

b. Identify the line plot that shows the head measurements of Yukio and his classmates.

13. a. The table below shows the data for the brown candies from Bags 4–9 of Exercise 1. Make an ordered value bar graph and a line plot for these data.

Brown M&M's®

Bag Number	4	5	6	7	8	9
Number of Brown Candies	14	14	15	12	16	24

b. What are the minimum and maximum values?

c. What is the range?

d. Are there gaps or clusters of data? Explain.

e. Would an ordered value bar graph or a line plot better represent the data? Explain.

Go Online
PHSchool.com
For: Multiple-Choice Skills Practice
Web Code: ana-8154

Connections

14. There are 100 candies in Bag A. Given the following statements, how many candies of each color are there?

- $\frac{3}{10}$ are brown
- 0.25 are yellow

- 0.1 are green

- $\frac{2}{10}$ are red
- the ratio of red candies to blue candies is 2 : 1

- 0.05 are orange

15. There are 80 candies in Bag B. Given the following statements, how many candies of each color are there?

- 30% are brown
- 0.25 are yellow
- the ratio of brown candies to blue candies is 3 : 1

- 20% are red
- 0.05 are green
- the ratio of orange candies to green candies is 2 : 1

16. Multiple Choice The stem-and-leaf plot shows the heights of a group of students. What percent of the students are more than 5 feet tall?

Student Heights

```
4 | 3 3 4 5 6 7 7 8 9
5 | 0 0 1 1 2 2 2 6 8 8 9
6 | 0 0 3 5 5
```

Key: 5 | 2 means 52 inches

F. 44%   **G.** 20%   **H.** 12%   **J.** 80%

17. a. Describe any trends or patterns in immigration to the United States from Asia from 1820 to 2000 using the graph below.

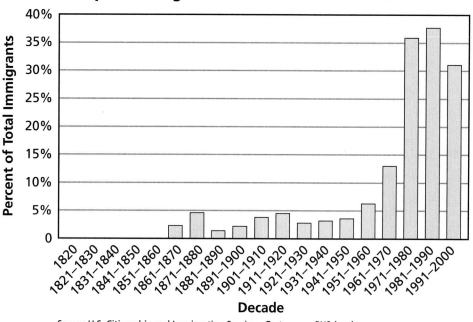

Graph 5: Immigration From Asia to the United States

SOURCE: U.S. Citizenship and Immigration Services. Go to www.PHSchool.com for a data update. Web Code: ang-9041

b. Write two comparison statements about the trends in immigration from Mexico to the United States (Exercises 8–11) and from Asia to the United States from 1820 to 2000.

c. Look back at Graph 2 in Problem 1.2. As the trend for immigration from Europe was decreasing from 1961 to 2000, what happened to the trends for immigration from Mexico and Asia?

18. Multiple Choice Ms. Turini's math class took a test on Monday. The scores for the exam were: 98, 79, 65, 84, 87, 92, 90, 61, 93, 76, 72, and 93. Which stem-and-leaf plot correctly displays these data?

A.

6	| |
7	| | |
8	| |
9	卌

B.

6	1 5
7	2 6 9
8	4 7
9	0 2 3 3 8

C.

6	5 1
7	9 6 2
8	4 7
9	8 2 0 3 3

D.

6	1 5
7	2 6 9
8	4 7
9	2 3 3 8

19. a. The tables below show prices for skateboards at four different sporting goods stores. For each store, make a stem-and-leaf plot that will show the distribution of prices for skateboards from that store.

Store A

$60	$50
$40	$50
$13	$60
$45	$50
$20	$25
$30	$15
$35	$70
$60	$120
$50	$90
$70	

Store B

$13	$70
$40	$50
$45	$70
$60	$50
$50	$10
$30	$120
$15	$90
$35	$120
$15	

Store C

$40	$50
$20	$60
$60	$70
$35	$70
$50	$50
$30	$90
$13	$120
$45	$120
$40	$200

Store D

$179	$145
$160	$149
$149	$149
$149	$149
$149	$149
$145	$145
$149	$150
$100	$149
$179	$149

b. How do the prices for skateboards compare across the four stores? Write statements that make your reasoning clear.

c. Look at the four stem-and-leaf plots. What is the typical price for skateboards? Explain your reasoning.

d. Describe the variability in the prices of skateboards.

20. Make a line plot to show the distribution of head-size measures that matches the criteria below.

● There are 10 data points.

● The measures vary from 54 cm to 57.5 cm.

● The mode is 55 cm; there are three data values at the mode.

● The median is 55.5 cm.

Extensions

For Exercise 21, use the data in the table below.

Presidential Fitness Test Standards

Tests	Time (seconds)			
	Age 11	Age 12	Age 13	Age 14
Boys—Shuttle Run	10.0	9.8	9.5	9.1
Girls—Shuttle Run	10.5	10.4	10.2	10.1
Boys—Mile Run	452	431	410	386
Girls—Mile Run	542	500	493	479

SOURCE: The President's Council on Physical Fitness and Sports

21. Each graph is marked with a reference line that shows the Presidential Fitness Standard Time for the age group.

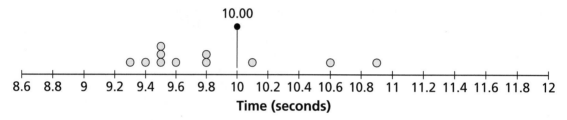

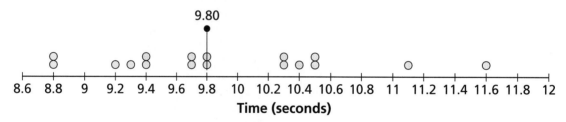

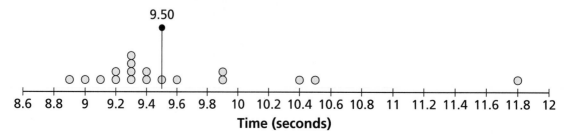

a. Estimate the minimum and maximum times in each distribution.

b. Estimate the range of each distribution.

c. Does the range seem "large" or "small" for each set of data? Explain your reasoning.

d. Are there any outliers? If so, what are they?

e. Do some or most of the data in each distribution cluster in one or more locations? If so, where?

f. Are there gaps in any set of data? If so, where do they occur?

g. How would you describe the typical shuttle run time for each age group of boys?

h. Describe the variability in each of the three distributions.

i. How do the fitness test results in each graph compare to the Presidential Standards for that age level? Explain.

22. a. Estimate the minimum and maximum shuttle run times shown in the scatter plot.

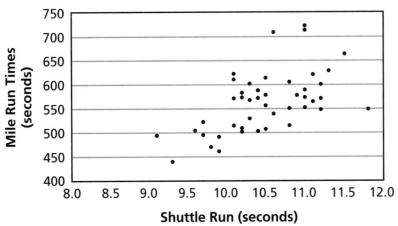

b. Estimate the minimum and maximum mile run times.

c. Copy the scatter plot. Sketch the line $y = 50x$ where y is the time for the mile run and x is the time for the shuttle run.

d. What can you say about the times that are on this line? Times that are above this line? Times that are below this line?

e. Is there a relationship between Times for Mile Run and Times for Shuttle Run? Explain.

23. Multiple Choice Janelle makes a scatter plot that shows the relationship between the number of music downloads she has made and the amount of unused disk space she has left. Which statement is true?

F. As the number of music downloads increases, the amount of unused disk space increases.

G. As the number of music downloads increases, the amount of unused disk space stays the same.

H. As the number of music downloads decreases, the amount of unused disk space increases.

J. As the number of music downloads decreases, the amount of disk space used decreases.

Mathematical Reflections 1

In this investigation, you explored how data in a distribution vary. These questions will help you summarize what you have learned.

Think over your answers to these questions. Discuss your ideas with other students and your teacher. Then write a summary of your findings in your notebook.

1. Use the situation below to help you answer parts (a)–(e).

   Students collected data from their classmates to answer each of these three questions:
   - *What is the typical bedtime for students?*
   - *What are students' favorite kinds of pets?*
   - *What is the typical number of pets students have?*

   a. What measures are used to describe variability?

   b. Define the range of a distribution of data so a sixth-grader would understand.

   c. How would you help a sixth-grade student understand the difference between categorical data and numerical data?

   d. What does it mean when we say categorical data vary?

   e. What does it mean when we say numerical data vary?

2. In which situations might you report frequencies of data using actual counts? In which might you use percents? How do you decide?

3. Describe how displaying data in tables or graphs can help you identify patterns or determine what is typical about a distribution.

Making Sense of Measures of Center

Statistics are numbers that are part of your everyday world. They are used in reporting on baseball, basketball, football, soccer, the Olympics, and other sports. Statistics are used to highlight the top hitters in baseball or top free-throw shooters in basketball. Identifying gold-medal skating champions depends on the statistics used to interpret scores from their performances during different events.

- What sports are these stats from? What do they mean?

RBI	free-throw percentage
ERA	yards per game

When you analyze data, the variability in a distribution is important. However, you also want to describe what is typical about a distribution. Three statistics that are often used to help describe what is typical about distributions are the *mean*, the *median*, and the *mode*.

Means, medians, and modes are called **measures of center.**

How is a measure of center influenced by the variability in a distribution of data?

There are other statistics you can use to describe variability. You can describe the distribution of data by its *range*. The **range** is the difference between the maximum and minimum values in a distribution. You can also give the minimum and maximum values to show how the data vary. You may notice unusual values and wonder if any of these data are **outliers.** Or you may notice that data with similar values form *clusters* in a distribution or that there are *gaps* with no data values.

2.1 The Mean as an Equal Share

The mean is one way to describe what is typical for a distribution. The **mean** is often called the "average" of the data. You can also think of the mean as the amount each person gets if everyone gets an equal share.

Getting Ready for Problem 2.1

Students are using beads for a class project. Marie has 5 beads, Sarah has 10 beads, Sri has 20 beads, and Jude has 25 beads. The students distribute their beads until everyone has the same number of beads. Each now has an equal share of the beads.

1. How many beads will each student have in the end?

2. How did you solve this problem?

When the redistributing is finished, each student has an equal share of the beads. This equal share of beads is the mean number of beads per person.

Marie's Beads

Sarah's Beads

Sri's Beads

Jude's Beads

Use the idea of mean as an equal share as you answer these questions.

A. Malaika has four 20-point projects in her science class.

1. The bar graph shows Malaika's scores on three of these projects. There is also a bar that shows Malaika's mean score for all four projects.

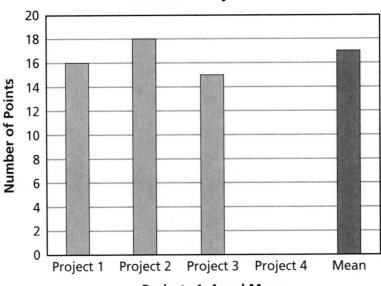

Malaika's Project Scores

a. Read the three project scores and the mean of the project scores. Use this information to find the number of points Malaika received on Project 4. Explain your reasoning.

b. What is the range of Malaika's scores on the four projects? What does this tell you about the variability of her scores?

2. a. When Malaika's total points for all four projects are distributed equally among the four projects, the result is 17 points per project, which is her mean score. Juan has a total of 60 points for the four projects. What is his mean score?

b. Give four possible project scores that would result in this mean score for Juan.

c. What is the range of Juan's scores on the four projects? Use the range to write a sentence about the variability of his scores.

d. Do Juan's scores vary more than Malaika's scores? Explain.

B. 1. a. On Monday, four servers receive the following amounts as tips while working at the Mugwump Diner. What is the range of the tips earned on Monday? What does this tell you about the variability of the tips?

Monday's Diner Tips

Server	Tip Amount
Maisha	$5.25
Brian	$4.75
Isabel	$6.50
Joe	$6.10

    b. The four servers decide to share the tips equally. How much money per server is this?

2. Imala was forgotten when tips were shared. She received $6.10, the same amount that Joe originally received. Suppose Imala's tips are included with the others' tips and shared equally among the five servers. Would the first four servers receive less than, the same as, or more than they did before Imala's tips were included? Explain your reasoning.

3. a. On Tuesday, the five servers share their tips equally. The result is a mean of $6.45 per server. Does this tell you that one of the servers originally received $6.45 in tips? Why or why not?

    b. What is a possible set of tips that would result in this mean?

4. a. On Wednesday, Isabel receives $3.40 in tips. When all of the tips are shared equally among the five servers, the result is $5.25 per server. Do you think this could happen? Explain.

    b. Based on the information in part (a), what can you say about the range of tips earned on Wednesday? Explain.

ACE Homework starts on page 44.

You can look at the mean as the balance point in a distribution. It acts like the fulcrum (FUL krum) for a seesaw. You can simulate this situation with a ruler, a cardboard tube (cut in half lengthwise), and some coins (all of the same type). The coins are placed along the board so that the board remains in balance on the cardboard tube. Look at the picture below for an example.

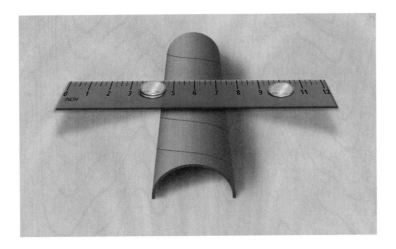

Notice that a coin placed far from the balance point can be balanced by a coin the same distance away on the other side of the balance point, by two coins half the distance away on the other side, or by three coins $\frac{1}{3}$ of the distance away on the other side.

The mean is a kind of fulcrum in a distribution of data. The data balance around the mean, much as the coins on the ruler balance around the fulcrum created by the tube.

The table below shows the number of calories and the amount of sugar per serving for nine cereals in the store.

Content Sugar of Cereals

Cereal	Calories	Sugar (g)
Cereal 1	90	5
Cereal 2	110	12
Cereal 3	220	8
Cereal 4	102	2
Cereal 5	120	6
Cereal 6	112	9
Cereal 7	107	12
Cereal 8	170	12
Cereal 9	121	6

SOURCE: Bowes & Church's Food Values of Portions Commonly Used

You can make a line plot to show the distribution. The mean is 8 grams of sugar, the data vary from 2 to 12 grams of sugar, and the range is 10 grams of sugar. The distribution balances at 8 grams of sugar.

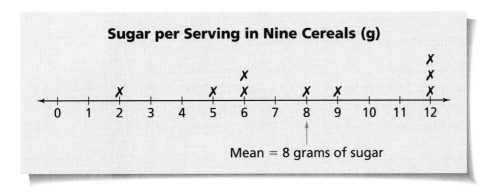

You can show this using a ruler and a cardboard tube. The ruler is marked with 13 main tick marks, one at 0 and one at each inch mark up to 12. Use nine coins of the same type. Place the ruler on the tube at the 8-inch mark, and place the coins along the ruler so they match the distribution shown above.

Use the idea of mean as a balance point as you answer these questions.

A. **1.** There are nine cereals in a data set. The mean amount of sugar in the cereals is 6 grams per serving. One of the cereals has 10 grams of sugar in one serving. Make a line plot that shows a distribution of the amount of sugar. Then make a different line plot that meets the criteria. Explain how you designed each distribution.

    2. **a.** What is the range of each distribution you made?

       b. How do the ranges compare? Are they the same, or is one range greater than the other?

B. **1.** Here is a set of data showing the amount of sugar in a serving for each of ten cereals, in grams:

1   3   6   6   6   6   6   6   10   10

    a. Make a line plot to show this new distribution.

    b. What is the mean for these data?

    2. Make one or more changes to the data set in part (1) so that the mean is 7 and the range is:

    a. the same as the range of the original data set

    b. greater than the range of the original data set

    c. less than the range of the original data set

C. **1.** Anica wonders if balancing the distribution has anything to do with how much the data values differ from the mean. She draws the diagram below. What is indicated by the arrows on each side of the line marking the mean?

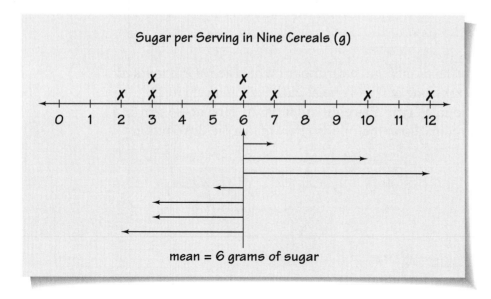

Sugar per Serving in Nine Cereals (g)

mean = 6 grams of sugar

2. Determine the length of each arrow. Find the sum of the lengths of the arrows on each side of the mean.

3. How do the two sums compare? Why do you think this is so?

4. Do you think this will always be true? Explain.

5. How might balancing the distribution relate to the distances of the data values from the mean? Explain.

D. Graph A and Graph B show two different distributions. Latoya guesses that each distribution has a mean of 5 grams of sugar per serving. For each distribution, answer parts (1)–(3).

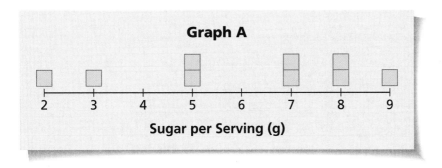

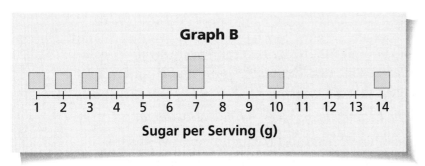

1. Find the difference from Latoya's guess of 5 for each data value that is greater than 5. What is their sum?

2. Find the difference from Latoya's guess of 5 for each data value that is less than the mean. What is their sum?

3. Is Latoya correct that the mean is 5? Does the distribution "balance?" If so, explain. If not, change one or more of the values to make it balance.

ACE **Homework starts on page 44.**

The graph below shows categorical data collected about the kinds of pets that 26 students have.

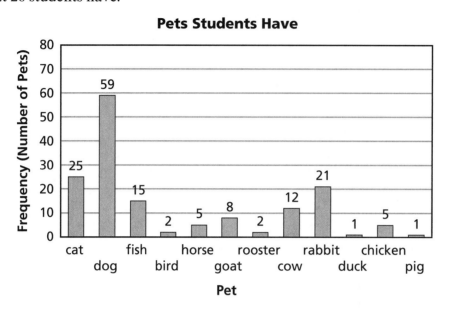

Pets Students Have

For "cat," "dog," "fish," and "rabbit," there are several *repeated values*. For other data, there are fewer repeated values. For both "duck" and "pig," there are no repeated values.

What do you think a repeated value means when we talk about data?

The **mode** is the data value that occurs most frequently in a set of data. For pets in this graph, the mode is "dog." When the data are categorical data, the mode is the only measure of center that can be used. It tells you the data value that is repeated the most often. For example, you can say that the mode kind of pet in the graph is a dog.

The **median** is the midpoint in an ordered distribution. In the graph of a distribution, data values are located below, above, or at this midpoint. The graph below shows numerical data about the numbers of pets each of the 26 students has.

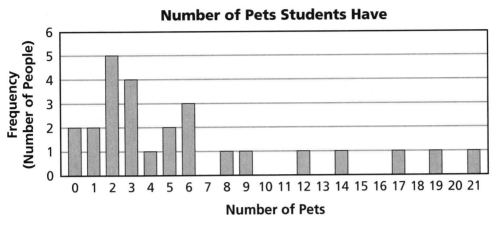

Number of Pets Students Have

Are there repeated values in this distribution?

Where would you mark the location of the median for these data?

Getting Ready for Problem

In Problem 2.2, you saw that the mean is like a fulcrum in a distribution. The data balance around the mean. Look at the graph above and consider these questions.

- What is the range of the data?
- What is the mean and where is it located?
- How does the location of the median compare to the location of the mean?
- Why do you think this is so?
- Do the data seem to cluster in some parts of the distribution?
- Does clustering of the data appear to be related to the locations of the median and the mean?

Problem 2.3 Repeated Values in a Distribution

A. Jorge is ordering pizza for a party. Tamika shows Jorge the graph at the right. She tells him to order only thin-crust pizzas because thin crust is the mode. Do you agree or disagree? Explain.

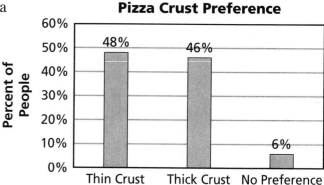

Pizza Crust Preference

B. The data from 70 cereals are shown below. Which option do you suggest using to find the typical amount of sugar in a serving of cereal? Explain.

Option 1 Use the mode, 3 grams. The typical amount of sugar in a serving of cereal is 3 grams.

Option 2 Use the median, 7.5 grams. The typical amount of sugar in a serving of cereal is 7.5 grams.

Option 3 Use clusters. There are several cereals that have either 3 or 6 grams of sugar per serving. 40% of the data seem to be evenly spread between 8 and 12 grams of sugar.

Option 4 Use something else. Write your own statement about what you consider to be the typical amount of sugar in a serving of cereal.

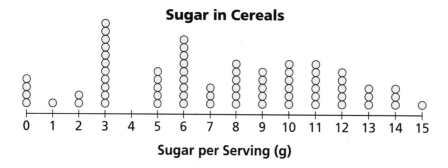

Sugar in Cereals

Sugar per Serving (g)

C. An advertiser wants more people to listen to a phone message. He uses the graph below.

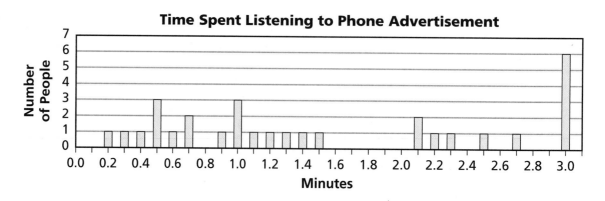

Time Spent Listening to Phone Advertisement

Minutes

Which of the options below should the advertiser use to decide how long the message should be? Explain.

Option 1 Use the mode. The most frequent amount of time spent listening to the phone advertisement was 3 minutes.

Option 2 Use the mean. Listening times lasted, on average, 1.51 minutes per person.

Option 3 Use clusters. One third of the people listened less than 1 minute and more than half listened less than 1.5 minutes. Only 20% of the people listened for 3 minutes.

Option 4 Use something else. Write your own response.

D. 1. In the plots below, the data for the 70 cereals in Question B are organized by the cereals' locations on the shelves in a supermarket. Use means, medians, clusters, or other strategies to compare the three distributions. Explain your reasoning.

   2. Use the information from part (1) to make a prediction about the sugar content per serving of a cereal based on its shelf location.

Sugar in Top Shelf Cereals

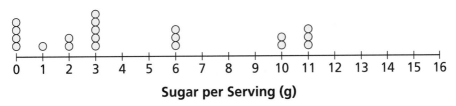

Sugar per Serving (g)

Sugar in Middle Shelf Cereals

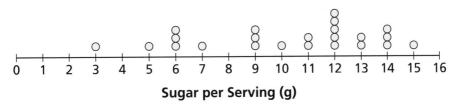

Sugar per Serving (g)

Sugar in Bottom Shelf Cereals

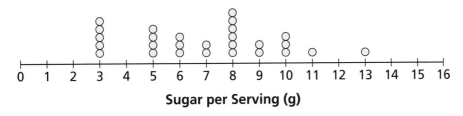

Sugar per Serving (g)

ACE **Homework starts on page 44.**

Unlike with categorical data, the mode is not always useful with numerical data. Sometimes there is no mode and sometimes there is more than one mode.

Sometimes the mean and median of a distribution are located close together. The graph below shows the distribution of the amount of sugar in cereals located on the bottom shelf in a supermarket. The mean and the median are marked. The median is 7 grams and the mean is 6.9 grams.

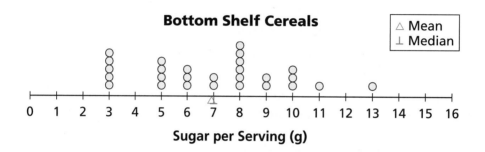

In some distributions the mean and median are located further apart. The graph below shows the distribution of the amount of sugar per serving in cereals on the top shelf in a supermarket. The mean and the median are marked. The median is 3 grams and the mean is 4.55 grams.

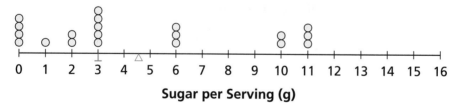

The overall shape of a distribution is determined by where the data cluster, where there are repeated values, and how spread out the data are. The shape of a distribution influences where the median and mean are located. In the next problem, you will experiment with making changes to distributions. Observe what these changes do to the locations of the mean and median in a distribution.

Measures of Center and Shapes of Distributions

For Questions A–C, predict what will happen. Then do the computation to see whether you are correct.

A. The graph below shows the distribution of the amount of sugar in 20 cereals found on the top shelf. The sum of the values in this distribution is 91 grams. Use stick-on notes to make a copy of the distribution. Note the location of the mean at 4.55 grams of sugar and the median at 3 grams of sugar.

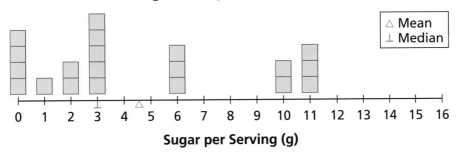

Sugar in Top Shelf Cereals

1. Suppose you remove the three cereals with 6 grams of sugar per serving and add three new cereals, each with 9 grams of sugar per serving. What happens to the mean and the median? Why do you think this happens?

2. **a.** Use the new distribution from part (1). Suppose you remove a cereal with 3 grams of sugar and add a cereal with 8 grams of sugar. How do the mean and the median change?

   b. Suppose you remove another cereal with 3 grams of sugar and add another cereal with 8 grams of sugar. How do the mean and the median change?

   c. Suppose you remove a third cereal with 3 grams of sugar and add a third cereal with 8 grams of sugar. How do the mean and the median change?

B. Use the new distribution from Question A, part (2). Experiment with removing data values and replacing them with new data values.

1. How does replacing smaller data values with larger data values affect the mean and the median?

2. How does replacing larger data values with smaller data values affect the mean and the median?

3. How does replacing larger and smaller data values with values that are closer to the middle of the distribution affect the mean and the median?

C. 1. Sort these eight distributions into two groups: one where the means and medians are the same or almost the same and one where they are not.

Sugar Distribution 1

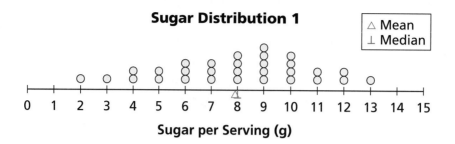

Sugar per Serving (g)

Sugar Distribution 2

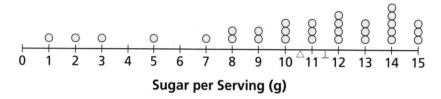

Sugar per Serving (g)

Sugar Distribution 3

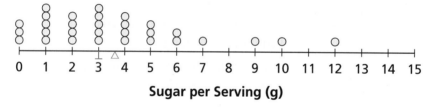

Sugar per Serving (g)

Sugar Distribution 4

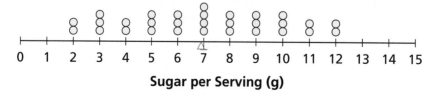

Sugar per Serving (g)

Sugar Distribution 5

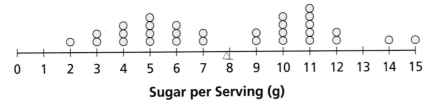

Sugar per Serving (g)

Sugar Distribution 6

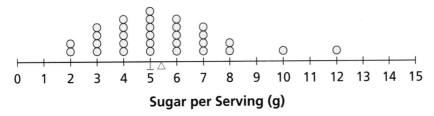

Sugar per Serving (g)

Sugar Distribution 7

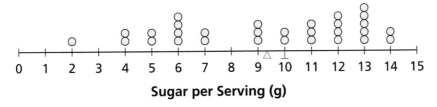

Sugar per Serving (g)

Sugar Distribution 8

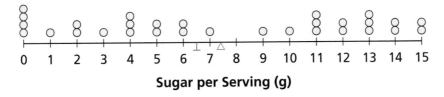

Sugar per Serving (g)

2. For each group of distributions, describe how the locations of the mean and median appear to be influenced by the shape of the distribution. Explain your reasoning.

ACE Homework starts on page 44.

Applications

1. a. Use the table at the right. What is the mean tip for each of the days?

b. Suppose Server 2 keeps her own tips. Does she get more for the week? Explain.

Tips

Day	Server 1	Server 2	Server 3	Server 4	Server 5
Monday	$3.55	$6.20	$4.70	$3.85	$4.95
Tuesday	$5.10	$5.20	$5.70	$3.15	$3.55
Wednesday	$7.25	$8.30	$4.00	$6.20	$5.85
Thursday	$4.05	$2.10	$7.60	$2.75	$8.40
Friday	$9.75	$8.50	$9.25	$6.20	$7.35

2. On Saturday, Server 4 forgets to count her tips. Server 3 gathers all of the tip money and distributes an equal share to each server.

Tips

Server 1	Server 2	Server 3	Server 4	Server 5	Mean
$5.65	$6.80	$4.45	▪	$7.55	$6.50

a. How much tip money did Server 4 receive originally? Explain.

b. Suppose the mean is $7.75. How much tip money did Server 4 receive originally?

Use the table on the next page for Exercises 3–6.

3. a. What is the mean amount of caffeine in the soda drinks?

b. Make a line plot for the soda drinks.

c. What is the mean amount of caffeine in the other drinks?

d. Make a line plot for the other drinks.

e. Write three statements comparing the amount of caffeine in soda and in other drinks.

4. Indicate whether each statement is true or false.

   a. Soda B has more caffeine than Soda F or Soda D.

   b. Energy Drink C has about three times as much caffeine as the same amount of Energy Drink A.

   c. Of the drinks in the table, 75% have 25 mg or less of caffeine in an 8-ounce serving.

Caffeine Content of Selected Beverages

Soda Drinks

Name	Caffeine in 8 Ounces (mg)
Soda A	38
Soda B	37
Soda C	27
Soda D	27
Soda E	26
Soda F	24
Soda G	21
Soda H	15
Soda J	23

Other Drinks

Name	Caffeine in 8 Ounces (mg)
Energy Drink A	77
Energy Drink B	70
Energy Drink C	25
Energy Drink D	21
Iced Tea A	19
Iced Tea B	10
Coffee Drink	83
Hot Cocoa	2
Juice Drink	33

5. Moderate caffeine intake for adults is 300 mg per day, but it is recommended that 10- to 12-year-olds have no more than 85 mg per day. Has a middle-school student who drinks three 12-ounce cans of Soda F consumed more of his or her recommended intake of caffeine than an adult who drinks two servings of Coffee Drink?

6. Predict whether or not the mean and the median for caffeine content in the graph below have almost the same values. Explain.

Caffeine in Drinks

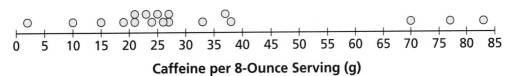

Caffeine per 8-Ounce Serving (g)

7. a. Compare the three sets of data. Which group of students has longer names? Explain your reasoning.

Name Length—30 Students From Japan

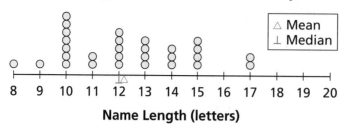

Name Length (letters)

Name Length—30 Students From Russia

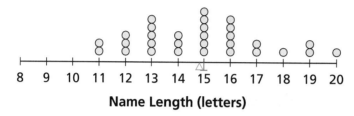

Name Length (letters)

Name Length—30 Students From the United States

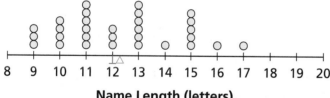

Name Length (letters)

b. Look at the distribution for the 30 students in the United States. Suppose the data for the six names with 13 letters were each changed to 16 letters.

   i. Draw a plot showing this change.

  ii. Will this change affect the median name length? Explain.

 iii. Will this change affect the mean name length? Explain.

Will this change affect the mean name length?

8. a. The next plots group the same 90 name lengths by gender. Compare the two plots. Which group of students has longer names? Explain.

Homework Help Online
PHSchool.com
For: Help with Exercise 8
Web Code: ane-8208

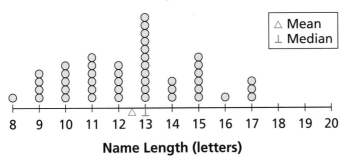

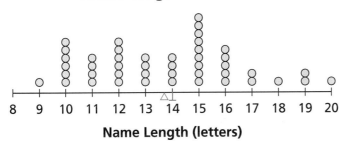

b. Look at the distribution for the females. Suppose that the data for four names with 18 or more letters were changed. These students now each have name lengths with 10 or fewer letters.

  i. Draw a plot showing this change.

  ii. Will this change affect the median name length for females?

  iii. Will this change affect the mean name length for females?

9. Multiple Choice Send It Quick Mail House mailed five packages with a mean weight of 6.7 pounds. Suppose the mean weight of four of these packages is 7.2 pounds. What is the weight, in pounds, of the fifth package?

  A. 3.35   **B.** 4.7   **C.** 6.95   **D.** 8.7

10. Multiple Choice In test trials for two new sneaker designs, performance was judged by measuring jump heights. The results are shown below.

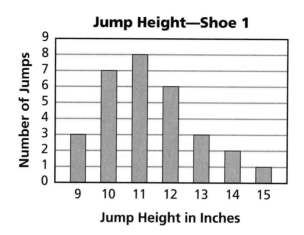

Jump Height—Shoe 1

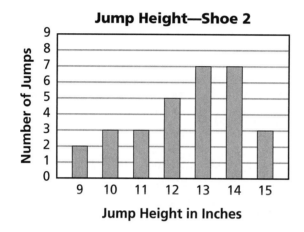

Jump Height—Shoe 2

Which response below helps the shoe designer decide which sneaker, Shoe 1 or Shoe 2, performs better?

F. Use the mode. The most frequent height jumped for Shoe 1 was 11 inches. The most frequent height jumped for Shoe 2 was 13 or 14 inches.

G. Use the mean. The average jump height for Shoe 1 was 11.3 feet. For Shoe 2, the average was 12.5 feet.

H. Use clusters. Overall, 70% of the students jumped 10 to 12 feet with Shoe 1 while the data varied from 9 to 15 feet. About 63% of the students jumped 12 to 14 feet with Shoe 2 while the data varied from 9 to 15 feet.

J. All of the above.

11. a. What aspect of the shape of a distribution tells you that the mean is greater than the median? Explain.

   b. What aspect of the shape of a distribution tells you that the mean is less than the median? Explain.

   c. What aspect of the shape of a distribution tells you that the mean and the median are about the same value? Explain.

12. Multiple Choice Del Kenya's test scores are 100, 83, 88, 96, and 100. His teacher tells the class that they can choose the measure of center she will use to determine final grades. Which measure should Del Kenya choose?

   A. Mean   **B.** Median   **C.** Mode   **D.** Range

Go Online
PHSchool.com
For: Multiple-Choice Skills Practice
Web Code: ana-8254

Connections

13. a. A gymnast receives these scores from five judges:

   7.6   8.2   8.5   8.2   8.9

   What happens to the mean of the scores when you multiply each data value by 2? By $\frac{2}{3}$? By 0.2?

   b. Why do you think the mean changes as it does in each situation?

14. Multiple Choice Suppose a number is selected at random from a set of data. The data set has an even number of data values, no two of which are alike. What is the probability that this number will be greater than the median?

F. $\frac{1}{4}$ **G.** $\frac{5}{8}$ **H.** $\frac{1}{2}$ **J.** 1

15. Brilliant Candle Company claims their candles have longer mean burning times than those of other companies. Jaime chooses the same size candles from Brilliant Candle, Firelight Candle, and Shimmering Candle. He burns 15 candles from each company and records the number of minutes that each candle burns.

Burning Time (min)

Candle Number	Brilliant Candle	Firelight Candle	Shimmering Candle
1	60	66	68
2	49	68	65
3	58	56	44
4	57	59	59
5	61	61	51
6	53	64	60
7	57	53	61
8	60	51	63
9	61	60	49
10	62	50	56
11	60	64	59
12	56	60	62
13	61	60	64
14	59	51	57
15	58	49	54

For each company:

a. Make a line plot or bar graph to display the distribution of the data.

b. Describe the variability within the set of data.

c. Estimate the mean and the median for each distribution.

d. Determine the mean and the median for each distribution. How do these values compare with your estimates in part (c)?

e. Do Brilliant Candle's products burn longer than the other two companies' products? Explain.

16. a. Make a circle graph that shows these results.

A survey about favorite colors reports that *exactly*:
12% of those surveyed prefer red
14% of those surveyed prefer orange
28% of those surveyed prefer purple
30% of those surveyed prefer blue
16% of those surveyed prefer green

b. What is the smallest number of people that could have taken the survey? Explain.

Extensions

17. A student gets 40 points out of 100 points on a test. Her teacher announces that this test and next week's test will be averaged together for her grade. The student wonders if she could still get a C if she gets a 100 on the next test. She reasons, "I think my average (mean) would be 70 because half of 40 is 20 and half of 100 is 50. That is a C because 20 plus 50 is 70." Does her method always work? Explain your thinking.

18. If you know the number of chirps made by a cricket in a specific amount of time, you can estimate the temperature in degrees Fahrenheit or degrees Celsius. There are different ways you might do this. For example, one formula involves counting the chirps (the number of wing vibrations per second) over a 13-second period and adding 40 to get the temperature in degrees Fahrenheit. This formula works for the snowy tree cricket.

a. It is possible to turn cricket-chirp recordings into sound intensity versus time graphs. Then you can see each individual chirp and the chirp rate. Look at the four graphs below. Describe how you can tell that the chirp rates vary with the changes in temperature.

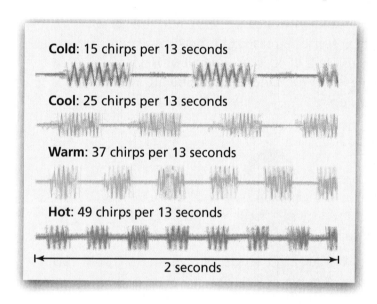

b. Another formula for estimating the temperature is more complicated. Count the chirps per minute, subtract 40, divide by 4, and add 50 to get the temperature in degrees Fahrenheit. Write this formula using x for the number of chirps per minute.

$$y = \text{Temperature in } °F = \underline{\ ?\ }$$

c. Use your formula from part (b). Draw a line on a coordinate graph that will allow you to relate the number of chirps per minute to temperatures from 0°F to 212°F. Use this line to predict the number of chirps expected for each temperature.

      0°F   50°F   100°F   212°F

19. a. The chirp frequency for a different kind of cricket lets you estimate temperatures in Celsius rather than in Fahrenheit. Make a coordinate graph of the data below.

Cricket Chirps per Minute

Frequency	Temperature (°C)
195	31.4
123	22
212	34.1
176	29.1
162	27
140	24
119	20.9
161	27.8
118	20.8
175	28.5
161	26.4
171	28.1
164	27
174	28.6
144	24.6

b. Determine a formula that lets you estimate the temperature in degrees Celsius for a given number of chirps.

c. Use the formula from part (b) to draw a line on the graph from part (a). Describe how well the line "matches" the data. Explain your thinking.

Mathematical Reflections 2

In this investigation, you explored three measures of center. These questions will help you summarize what you have learned.

Think about your answers to these questions. Discuss your ideas with other students and your teacher. Then write a summary of your findings in your notebook.

1. **a.** Explain how the mean can be interpreted as an equal share in a situation. Use examples.

   b. Explain how the mean can be interpreted as a balance point in a distribution. Use examples.

   c. In what kinds of situations can you use the mode, but not the mean or the median, to identify what is typical? Use examples.

2. Give an example of each method of summarizing data. Explain why you might choose to use this method with your example.

   a. clusters   **b.** mode

   c. median   **d.** mean

3. **a.** When the mean and the median are the same or very similar, what does this indicate about the shape of the distribution?

   b. When the mean and median are more different than similar, what does this indicate about the shape of the distribution?

   c. Medians and means are called measures of center. Why do you think this is so?

Investigation 3

Comparing Distributions: Equal Numbers of Data Values

Time is a measure that is used to answer many questions.

What was your time running a 50-yard dash or swimming 100 meters?

How fast is your reaction time to respond to events in a game?

Do wood roller coaster rides last longer than steel roller coaster rides?

You often compare times different people or groups take to complete a task. Think back to *Comparing and Scaling* and the ways you made comparisons between numbers using fractions, percents, and ratios. These ideas will help you make comparisons in data situations.

3.1 Measuring and Describing Reaction Times

When you hear, see, or touch something, a message is sent to the area of the brain that controls muscle activity. Then, a signal is sent out to muscles to respond. Sometimes it matters how quickly you react, for example:

- Swinging at a baseball with a bat or at a tennis ball with a racquet
- Swerving to miss a rock in the road while riding your bicycle
- Responding to actions in a video game

Computer programs can be used to test how quickly people react. For one such program, each trial begins with a colored circle appearing on the screen. When the circle appears, the person clicks on the circle as quickly as possible. When the trial is over, the person's time is reported.

Each student in a seventh-grade class completed five trials on a computer reaction-time game. In Problem 3.1, you will make comparisons among their reaction times.

Problem 3.1 Measuring and Describing Reaction Times

A. Write three different statements that describe the variability in Jasmine's times.

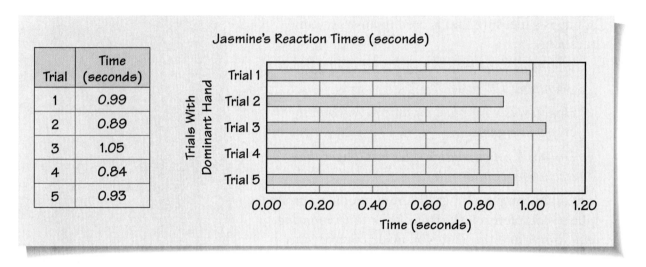

Trial	Time (seconds)
1	0.99
2	0.89
3	1.05
4	0.84
5	0.93

B. 1. Write three different statements that describe the variability in Nathaniel's times.

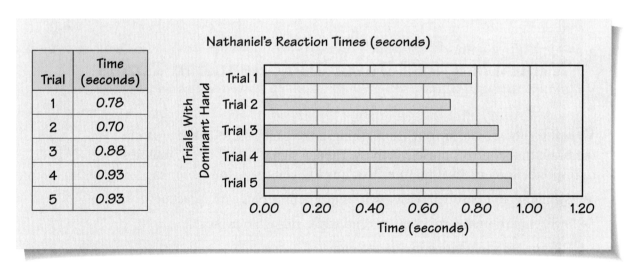

Trial	Time (seconds)
1	0.78
2	0.70
3	0.88
4	0.93
5	0.93

2. How do Nathaniel's and Jasmine's results compare? Remember, you can use fractions, percents, and ratios to make comparisons.

ACE Homework starts on page 62.

Comparing Reaction Times

The value bar graphs and data tables below show the computer game reaction times for Diana and Henry.

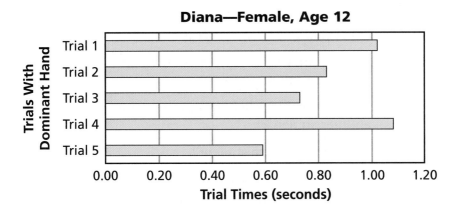

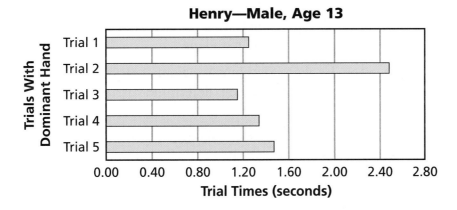

Diana's Reaction Times

Trial	1	2	3	4	5
Seconds	1.02	0.83	0.73	1.08	0.59

Henry's Reaction Times

Trial	1	2	3	4	5
Seconds	1.25	2.48	1.15	1.34	1.47

Who reacted faster, Diana or Henry?

When comparing performances, you can use variability, measures of center, and fraction, percent, or ratio statements.

Problem 3.2 Comparing Reaction Times

A. In the four bar graphs on the next page, each student's data are shown on the same scale. What is the advantage of having the same scale on each graph?

B. 1. What are the minimum and maximum reaction times for each of the four students?

   2. What is the range of reaction times for each of the students?

   3. Does comparing ranges of reaction times help you decide if one student is more consistent than another student?

   4. Does comparing ranges of reaction times help you decide if one student is quicker than another student?

C. 1. What is the median reaction time for each student?

   2. What is the mean reaction time for each student?

   3. Does comparing mean or median reaction times help you decide whether one student is more consistent than another student?

   4. Does comparing mean or median reaction times help you decide whether one student is quicker than another student?

D. Locate 1 second on each graph. Explain how comparing data below, at, or above the benchmark time of 1 second can help determine whether one student is quicker than another student.

E. Another class has challenged this class to choose one student to play the computer reaction-time game against their class champion. Would you recommend they choose Diana, Henry, Nathaniel, or Jasmine? Why?

ACE Homework starts on page 62.

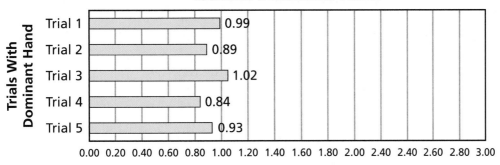

Jasmine's Reaction Times

Trial 1: 0.99
Trial 2: 0.89
Trial 3: 1.02
Trial 4: 0.84
Trial 5: 0.93

Trials With Dominant Hand / Trial Times (seconds)

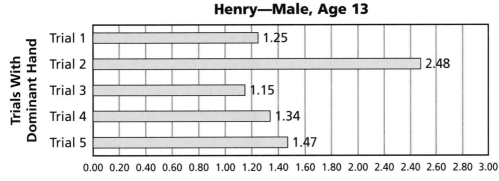

Nathaniel's Reaction Times

Trial 1: 0.78
Trial 2: 0.70
Trial 3: 0.88
Trial 4: 0.93
Trial 5: 0.93

Trials With Dominant Hand / Trial Times (seconds)

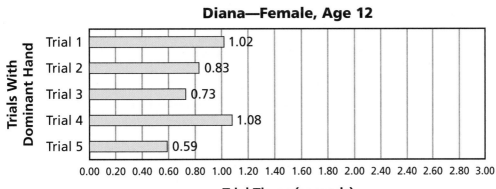

Diana—Female, Age 12

Trial 1: 1.02
Trial 2: 0.83
Trial 3: 0.73
Trial 4: 1.08
Trial 5: 0.59

Trials With Dominant Hand / Trial Times (seconds)

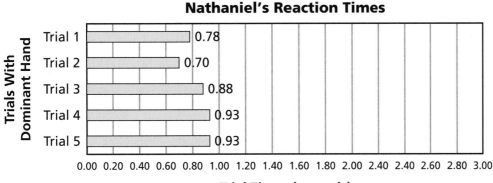

Henry—Male, Age 13

Trial 1: 1.25
Trial 2: 2.48
Trial 3: 1.15
Trial 4: 1.34
Trial 5: 1.47

Trials With Dominant Hand / Trial Times (seconds)

Comparing More Than a Few Students

For Problem 3.3, you will use a set of 40 case cards showing reaction times for a computer game. Copies of these cards can be found behind the Glossary.

Getting Ready for Problem **3.3**

How can you locate each piece of information about a student on a case card?

Name	Trial 1 reaction time
Gender	Trial 2 reaction time
Age	Trial 3 reaction time
Fastest Time for 5 trials	Trial 4 reaction time
Slowest Time for 5 trials	Trial 5 reaction time

- Which attributes are categorical data?
- Which attributes are numerical data?
- Which attributes have values that vary from one student to another? Why do you think this is so?
- Which attributes have constant (the same) values for several or all of the students? Why do you think this is so?

Problem 3.3 Comparing Many Data Values

Use the reaction-time data to help you answer these questions.

A. Compare the distributions of the girls' fastest times and the boys' fastest times.

  1. Is one group more consistent? Explain.

  2. Is one group quicker? Explain.

B. Compare the distributions of the girls' slowest times and the boys' slowest times.

  1. Is one group more consistent? Explain.

  2. Is one group quicker? Explain.

ACE Homework starts on page 62.

3.4 Comparing Fastest and Slowest Trials

Willa is a video-game designer. You will help her make some decisions about timing in her video game.

Problem 3.4 Comparing Larger Distributions

Use the reaction time data to help you answer these questions.

A. Compare the fastest reaction times of all the students to the slowest reaction times of all the students. What must be true about the scales of the two value bar graphs in order to make these comparisons easy to make?

B. 1. Describe how the means and the medians compare.

2. Describe how the ranges compare.

3. Where do the data cluster in each distribution? Describe how the locations of data clusters compare.

4. Is one distribution more variable than the other? Explain.

C. For each distribution, look at 0.5 second, 1 second, 1.5 seconds, and 2 seconds. Compare the numbers of students at, above, or below each of these benchmark times on each distribution. What do you notice?

D. Write a recommendation to Willa. Based on your work in Questions B and C, how much time should she give a player to react in a video game? Include recommendations for easy, medium, and hard levels. Justify your recommendations.

ACE Homework starts on page 62.

Applications

1. Write three different statements that describe the variability in Frank's reaction times.

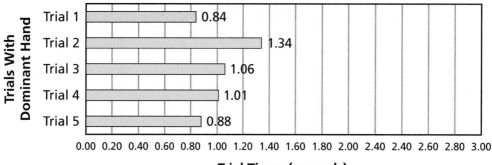

Frank's Reaction Times

2. Compare Matthew's reaction times to Frank's reaction times.

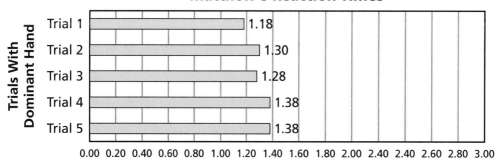

Matthew's Reaction Times

a. Determine the means, medians, minimum and maximum values, and ranges for each student.

b. Is one student quicker than the other student? Explain your reasoning.

c. Is one student more consistent than the other student? Explain.

Graph A and Graph B show the fastest reaction time on a computer reaction-time game with the non-dominant hand for each of the 40 students. Use these graphs for Exercises 3 and 4.

Graph A: Non-Dominant Hand Reaction Times

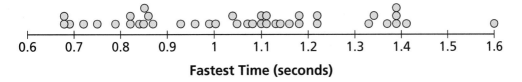

Fastest Time (seconds)

Graph B: Non-Dominant Hand Reaction Times

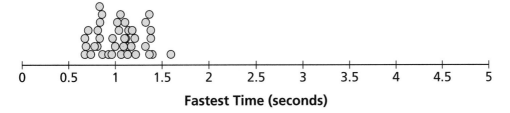

Fastest Time (seconds)

3. Tanisha says that Graph A and Graph B show the same data. Jeff says, "No way! These are not the same data." Do you agree with Jeff? Explain.

4. a. Use the statistics below and Graphs A and B above. Describe the distribution of fastest reaction times using the non-dominant hand.

Mean:	1.06 seconds
Median:	1.08 seconds
Minimum Value:	0.68 second
Maximum Value:	1.60 seconds
Range:	0.92 seconds

b. How would you answer the question, "What is the typical fastest reaction time for a student who uses his or her non-dominant hand?"

5. a. Describe the distribution of the data below.

Slowest Reaction Times With Non-Dominant Hand

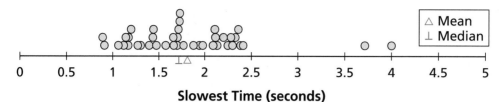

Slowest Time (seconds)

Mean:	1.82 seconds
Median:	1.73 seconds
Minimum Value:	0.90 second
Maximum Value:	4.01 seconds
Range:	3.11 seconds

b. How would you answer the question, "What is the typical slowest reaction time for a student who uses his or her non-dominant hand?" Explain.

6. Use the data in Exercise 5 and the data below to compare the fastest reaction times to the slowest reaction times for non-dominant hands. Explain your reasoning.

Fastest Reaction Times With Non-Dominant Hand

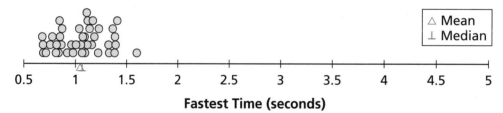

Fastest Time (seconds)

Mean:	1.06 seconds
Median:	1.08 seconds
Minimum Value:	0.68 second
Maximum Value:	1.60 seconds
Range:	0.92 second

7. Use the data from Exercises 5 and 6 and from the table on the facing page. Write statements to compare the values of each statistic for dominant and non-dominant hands.

a. means of the fastest reaction times

b. medians of the slowest reaction times

c. minimum and maximum values of the fastest reaction times

d. ranges of the fastest reaction times

Dominant Hand Reaction Times

Statistic	Fastest Reaction Times (seconds)	Slowest Reaction Times (seconds)
Mean	0.81	1.29
Median	0.79	1.22
Minimum Value	0.58	0.84
Maximum Value	1.18	2.48
Range	0.60	1.64

8. Use the line plots and table below. How much slower are the Trial 1 reaction times for non-dominant hands than the Trial 1 reaction times for dominant hands? Explain.

Homework Help Online
PHSchool.com

For: Help with Exercise 8
Web Code: ane-8308

Trial 1 Reaction Times With Dominant Hand

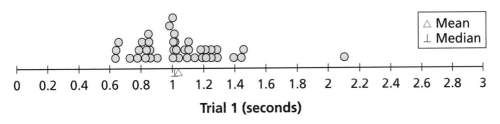

Trial 1 (seconds)

Trial 1 Reaction Times With Non-Dominant Hand

Trial 1 (seconds)

Trial 1 Reaction Times

Statistic	Dominant Hand (seconds)	Non-Dominant Hand (seconds)
Mean	1.048	1.324
Median	1.015	1.22
Minimum Value	0.64	0.83
Maximum Value	2.10	2.14
Range	1.50	1.31

Connections

9. **Multiple Choice** Suppose 27 is added as a data value to the set of data: 10, 29, 15, 29, 35, and 2. Which statement is true?

   A. The mean increases by 4.   **B.** The mode decreases by 10.

   C. The median decreases by 1.   **D.** Not here

10. **Multiple Choice** The mean of six numbers is 25. If one number is 15, what is the mean of the other five numbers?

   F. 15   **G.** 25   **H.** 27   **J.** 40

For Exercises 11–13, look at the mean and median for the data. Describe how the shape of each distribution is influencing the location of the mean and the median. Explain your reasoning.

11. Mean = 62 inches, Median = 62 inches,
Minimum and Maximum Values = 53 and 72 inches

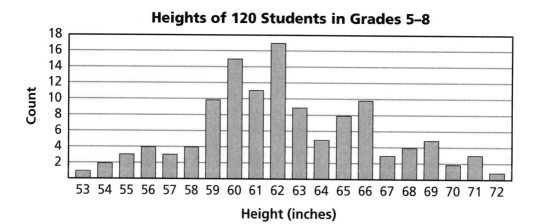

Heights of 120 Students in Grades 5–8

12. Mean = 24.7 grams, Median = 22.1 grams,
Minimum and Maximum Values = 21.3 and 37.1 grams

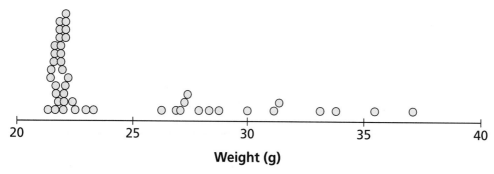

Weights of 45 Boxes of Cereal

13. Mean = 120.5 minutes, Median = 121 minutes,
Minimum and Maximum Values = 81 and 234 minutes

Runtimes for 100 of the Highest-Income Movies

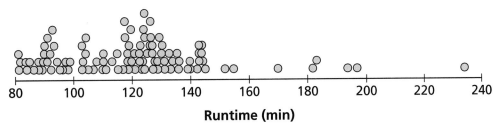

Runtime (min)

Source: www.worldwideboxoffice.com

Use this graph for Exercises 14–16.

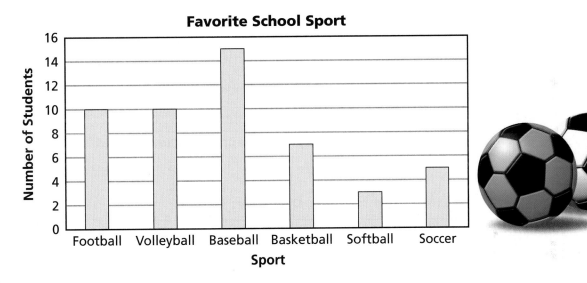

14. Multiple Choice Suppose a circle graph is used to display this data. What percent of the circle graph would represent baseball and softball?

A. 50%　　　**B.** 36%　　　**C.** 10%　　　**D.** 18%

15. Multiple Choice What fraction of a circle graph would include the students who choose soccer?

F. $\frac{2}{5}$　　　**G.** $\frac{3}{25}$　　　**H.** $\frac{30}{100}$　　　**J.** $\frac{10}{100}$

16. Multiple Choice What would be the measure of the central angle for the "volleyball" sector of a circle graph?

A. 20°　　　**B.** 36°　　　**C.** 72°　　　**D.** 18°

Go Online
PHSchool.com

For: Multiple-Choice Skills
Practice
Web Code: ana-8354

Investigation 3 Comparing Distributions: Equal Numbers of Data Values　　**67**

17. Elisa receives these four graphs showing her family's water usage.

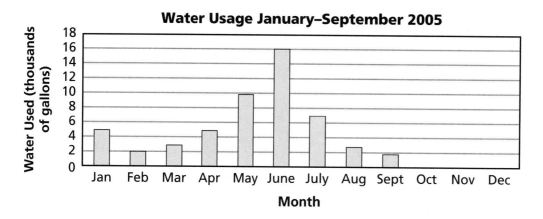

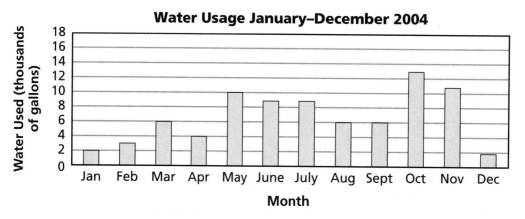

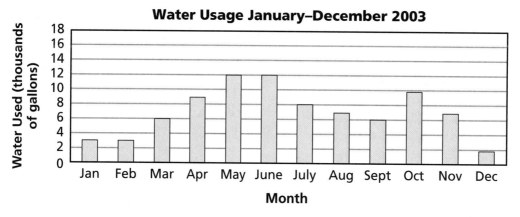

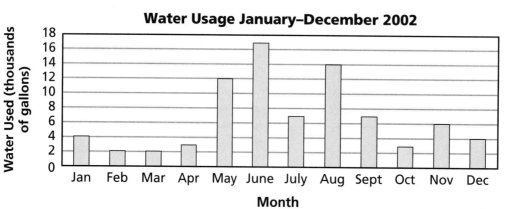

a. Describe any patterns in water usage that occur across years.

b. Use the graphs to find out how many gallons of water were used each month. Make a line plot for each of the years from 2003 to 2005 to show the distribution of the number of gallons used each month. For example, this line plot shows the data from 2002.

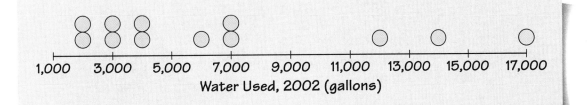

Water Used, 2002 (gallons)

c. Use the plots from part (b) to determine the mean monthly water usage for each year from 2002–2004. Mark these values on the plots. Using the mean monthly number of gallons used for each year, how does the water usage compare across the years? Explain.

d. Repeat part (c) for the median monthly water usage instead of the mean. Why should we not use the line plot for 2005 to estimate the mean or median?

e. Copy the data from your graphs in part (b) onto one line plot. You should have 45 data points. Determine the mean and the median for this new set of data. How do these two values compare? Why do you think this is so?

f. Is the median or the mean a better estimate of the typical monthly amount of water used during a year? Explain.

For Exercises 18–22, answer each question for each statement below.

Statement A
Garter snakes are the most typical snakes in North America. Fully grown, they can be 18 – 42 inches in length. They are generally about 3 feet long with a 1-inch girth. Although their coloring can be various shades of green, blue, brown, or red, they all have a pale but conspicuous stripe along the middle of the back and a less prominent stripe along each side.

Statement B
Each man, woman, and child in America eats an average of 46 slices (23 pounds) of pizza a year.

18. How do you think the process of data analysis was carried out?

19. What kinds of data—numerical or categorical—are used?

20. What kinds of variability might there be in the original data?

21. What kinds of patterns appear to have occurred in the data?

22. What is typical about the data and what might be outliers?

23. Multiple Choice A bag contains 36 chips. Each chip is either red or black. The probability of selecting a red chip from the bag is one fourth. What is the probability of drawing a black chip?

   F. $\frac{1}{4}$ **G.** $\frac{3}{5}$ **H.** $\frac{7}{8}$ **J.** $\frac{3}{4}$

24. Write a title that provides the viewer with a summary snapshot of the information provided in the graph. Be clever. Do not just restate the data.

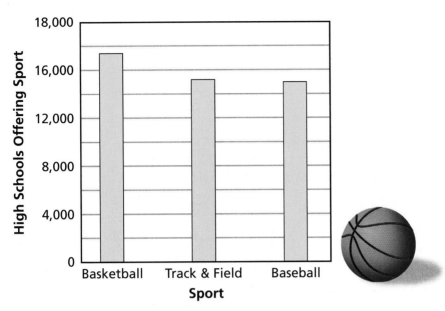

SOURCE: *National Federation of State High School Associations*

Extensions

25. The line plot below shows the median reaction times for the students in Problem 3.3. Describe the distribution of the median reaction times.

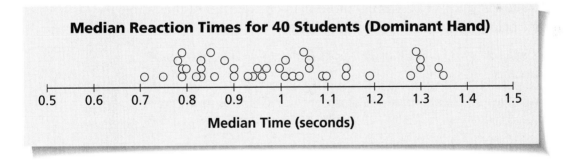

Median Reaction Times for 40 Students (Dominant Hand)

Median Time (seconds)

b. How do the median reaction times compare with the fastest reaction times, shown below?

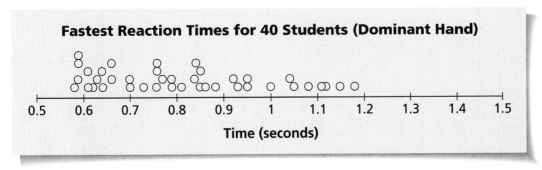

Fastest Reaction Times for 40 Students (Dominant Hand)

Time (seconds)

Use the circle graphs to determine whether each statement in Exercises 26–29 is true. For each statement that is not true, explain how you would change the statement to make it a true statement.

Daily Food Consumption

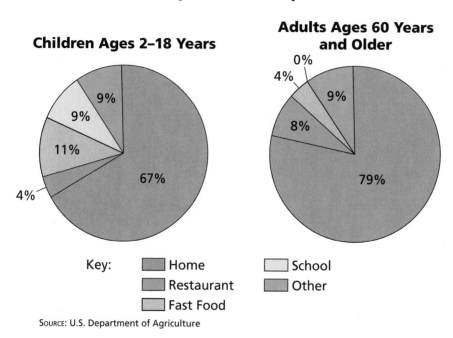

Children Ages 2–18 Years

9%
9%
11%
4%
67%

Adults Ages 60 Years and Older

0%
4%
9%
8%
79%

Key:
- Home
- Restaurant
- Fast Food
- School
- Other

Source: U.S. Department of Agriculture

26. Adults ages 60 years and older eat twice as many Calories at restaurants as do children ages 2–18.

27. Adults ages 60 years and older eat more than one quarter of their daily Calories at locations that are not their homes.

28. Adults ages 60 years and older eat more Calories at school than do children ages 2–18.

29. Children ages 2–18 eat about one third of their Calories at home.

Mathematical Reflections 3

In this investigation, you compared distributions of data with the same numbers of data values. These questions will help you summarize what you have learned.

Think about your answers to these questions. Discuss your ideas with other students and your teacher. Then write a summary of your findings in your notebook.

1. Sometimes you need to compare two or more distributions, each of which is shown on a different graph. Why is it helpful to make the scales of the axes the same on each graph?

2. Explain what a value bar graph and a line plot are. How are they related?

3. In several places you were asked to compare one or more students' reaction times. Use Henry's and Nathaniel's data from Problems 3.1 and 3.2. Describe how you can use fractions, percents, and ratios to make comparisons.

4. You also made comparisons among students' data to decide when one or more students were more consistent or quicker than other students.

   a. What does consistency mean when it refers to reaction times?

   b. What does quickness mean when it refers to reaction times?

   c. Identify a different situation in which you would compare consistency or quickness in performance. What does consistency or quickness mean in this situation?

Comparing Distributions: Unequal Numbers of Data Values

Many people love to ride roller coasters. There are different types of roller coasters, and people have preferences about the roller coasters they ride. In this investigation, you will look at data about roller coasters, and compare wood roller coasters with steel roller coasters.

4.1 Representing Survey Data

These two questions were asked in a survey.

1. Where do you like to sit on a roller coaster (choose one)?

   ___ Front ___ Middle ___ Back

2. Which of the following do you prefer to have on a roller coaster (may choose more than one)?

   ___ Airtime ___ Height ___ Inversions ___ Smooth Ride ___ Speed

The table below summarizes results from the survey and from three classes of seventh-grade students.

Roller Coaster Seating Preferences

Preference	Votes From Survey	Votes From Three Seventh-Grade Classes
Front	97	27
Middle	50	22
Back	18	14
Total Votes	165	63

Preferences for Roller Coaster Characteristics

Preference	Votes From Survey	Votes From Three Seventh-Grade Classes
Airtime	88	31
Height	36	24
Inversions	59	29
Smoothness	39	12
Speed	105	57
Total Votes	327	153

Problem 4.1 Representing Survey Data

A. Copy the tables above. Have the members of your class answer the two roller coaster questions. Add a column to each table for your class data.

B. Make bar graphs for each of the three data sets: the survey data, the data from the three classes, and the data from your class. Your bar graphs should allow you to compare the results from the three groups. You may use counts or percents to report frequencies.

C. Write three or more statements that make comparisons among the sets of data.

ACE Homework starts on page 78.

Are Steel Coasters Faster Than Wood Coasters?

Roller-coaster enthusiasts have preferences about the coasters they like to ride. There are Web sites devoted to wood roller coasters. Other people prefer to ride steel coasters.

Have you ever wondered how many roller coasters there are in the world? The table below shows roller coaster counts.

Roller Coaster Census (2005)

Continent	Total	Wood	Steel	Some of the Types of Steel Coasters			
				Inverted	Stand Up	Suspended	Sit Down
Africa	23	0	23	3	0	0	20
Asia	489	8	481	17	5	8	441
Australia	23	3	20	2	0	0	18
Europe	581	34	547	24	1	7	506
North America	748	131	617	50	11	10	531
South America	65	1	64	2	0	0	62
Total	**1,929**	**177**	**1,752**	**98**	**17**	**25**	**1,578**

SOURCE: Roller Coaster DataBase. Go to www.PHSchool.com for a data update. Web Code: ang-9041

How do you think these data were collected?

In Problem 4.2, you will use a roller coaster database that contains data on 50 wood coasters and 100 steel coasters.

Problem 4.2 Comparing Speed

Use the Roller Coaster Database to help you answer these questions.

A. Choose an attribute about roller coasters that interests you, such as Year Opened, Maximum Drop, or Top Speed. Explore this attribute in the database. Write a short paragraph about what you find.

B. 1. What do you consider to be a fast speed for a roller coaster? Discuss your idea with a partner.

  2. Suppose you have to choose which of two roller coasters to ride. Does knowing the top speed for each coaster help you make the decision? Explain.

C. 1. Are wood roller coasters faster than steel roller coasters? Scan the *top speed* data to predict an answer to the question. Explain your reasoning.

2. Now, look at the distributions of speeds of wood roller coasters and of steel roller coasters. Use strategies that make sense to you.

    a. Identify and compare minimum and maximum values, ranges, medians, and means for each type of roller coaster.

    b. Draw a reference line on each distribution at a particular speed. Look at the percents of each type of roller coaster at and above or below this speed.

3. Compare your prediction from part (1) with your analysis of the distributions from part (2). How would you now answer the question, "Are wood roller coasters faster than steel roller coasters?" Explain.

D. Why do some roller coasters go faster than other roller coasters? To help answer this question, look at the top speed in relation to other attributes. Do you think there is some relationship between *top speed and maximum drop*? Between *top speed and maximum height*? Between *top speed and year opened, duration, track length, or angle of descent*? Explore these questions. Be prepared to share your reasoning.

active math online
For: Stat Tools
Visit: PHSchool.com
Web Code: and–8402

ACE Homework starts on page 78.

Applications

1. This question was asked in a survey:

   What is your favorite kind of amusement-park ride?

   ___ Roller Coaster ___ Log Ride ___ Ferris Wheel ___ Other

   The table below summarizes results from this survey and from a survey of seventh-grade students at East Junior High and West Junior High.

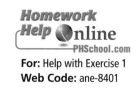
Favorite Amusement Park Rides

Favorite Ride	Votes From Survey	Votes From East Junior High	Votes From West Junior High
Roller Coaster	84	45	36
Log Ride	36	31	14
Ferris Wheel	17	3	6
Other	18	1	4
Total Votes	**155**	**80**	**60**

a. Make bar graphs for each of the three data sets: the survey data, the data from East Junior High, and the data from West Junior High. Your bar graphs should allow you to compare the results from the three groups. Use percents to report frequencies.

b. Write three or more statements that make comparisons among the sets of data.

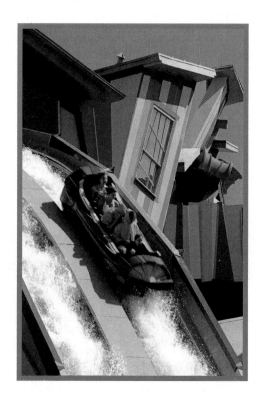

2. The three pairs of line plots below display data about 50 wood roller coasters. Means and medians are marked on each graph.

Graph A: Maximum Drop for Each Wood Coaster

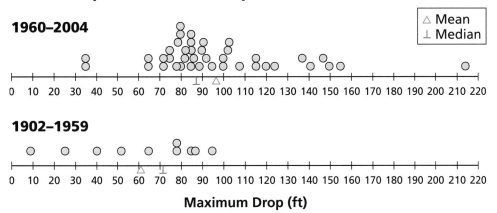

Graph B: Maximum Height for Each Wood Coaster

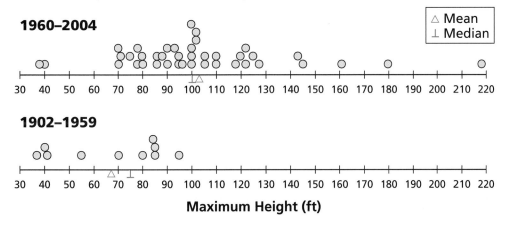

Graph C: Top Speed for Each Wood Coaster

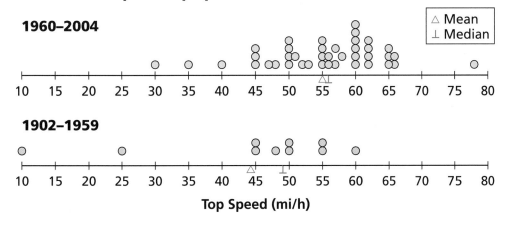

a. Write three statements comparing wood roller coasters built before 1960 with wood roller coasters built in 1960 or later.

b. Hector says there are too few roller coasters to make comparisons. Do you agree with Hector? Explain.

Use the Roller Coaster Census from Problem 4.2 for Exercises 3–7.

3. For every one wood roller coaster there are about ■ steel roller coasters.

4. North America has about ■ times as many roller coasters as South America.

5. Asia has about ■ as many roller coasters as North America.

6. North America has ■% of all the wood roller coasters in the world.

7. Write two of your own comparison statements.

Connections

8. The titles of the two circle graphs below have been separated from the graphs. Use the data from Exercises 3–7 to determine which title goes with which graph. Explain your reasoning.

   Title 1:   Wood Roller Coasters by Continent
   Title 2:   Steel Roller Coasters by Continent

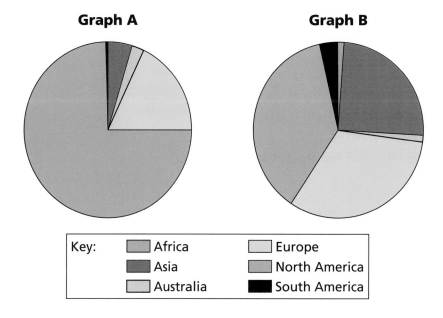

9. Multiple Choice Jasper's test scores for eight exams are shown.

    84   72   88   84   92   94   78 x

If the median for his scores is 86, what is a possible value for x?

A. 68   **B.** 84   **C.** 86   **D.** 95

10. Multiple Choice In Mr. Ramirez's math class, there are three times as many girls as boys. The girls' mean grade on a quiz is 90 and the boys' mean grade is 86. What is the mean grade for the class altogether?

F. 88   **G.** 44   **H.** 89   **J.** 95

11. People in the movie business track box-office profits and compare gains and losses each week. The graph below compares box-office income for consecutive weekends in the fall of 2005. Did box-office profits increase or decrease? Explain your reasoning.

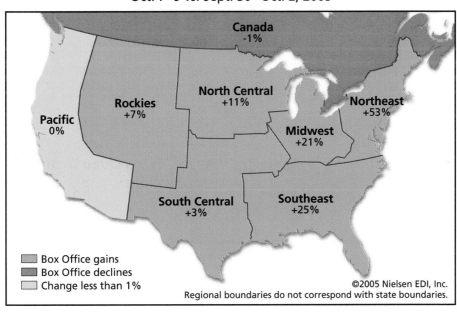

Regional Percentage Changes
Oct. 7–9 vs. Sept. 30–Oct. 2, 2005

12. In a large survey of nearly 15,000 children ages 5 to 15, 80% of the children were from the United States. Use the data below for parts (a)–(f).

Table 1: Years Lived in Current Home

Years	Children	Percent
<1	639	7.9%
1	776	9.6%
2	733	9.0%
3	735	▧
4	587	7.3%
5	612	7.5%
6	487	6.0%
7	431	5.3%
8	442	5.5%
9	412	5.1%
10	492	6.0%
11	520	6.5%
12	508	6.3%
13	339	4.1%
14	225	2.8%
15	176	2.2%
Total	**8,114**	**100.0%**

Source: National Geographic

Table 2: Apartments or Houses Lived in Since Birth

Number of Apartments or Houses	Children	Percent
1	1,645	20.7%
2	1,957	24.7%
3	1,331	16.8%
4	968	▧
5	661	8.3%
6	487	6.1%
7	291	3.7%
8	184	2.3%
9	80	1.0%
10	330	4.2%
Total	**7,934**	**100.0%**

Source: National Geographic

Table 3: Cities or Towns Lived in Since Birth

Number of Cities or Towns	Boys	Girls	Ages 5–12	Ages 13–15
1	▧	42.2%	42.1%	40.9%
>1	58.9%	57.8%	▧	59.1%
Total	**100%**	**100%**	**100%**	**100%**

Source: National Geographic

a. Find the missing percents in the tables above. Explain how you determined your answers.

b. Make a bar graph displaying the information in the third column of Table 2.

c. Write a summary paragraph about Table 2.

d. What percent of children have lived in the same home for 10 or more years? Justify your answer.

e. What percent of the children have lived in only one home since they were born? Justify your answer.

f. About what fraction of the boys have lived in the same city or town all their lives? Explain.

The graph below shows the amount of sugar per serving in the 47 cereals. Use the graph for Exercises 13 and 14.

Amount of Sugar per Serving

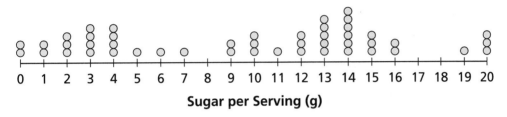

Sugar per Serving (g)

13. Describe the variability in the distribution of the amount of sugar per serving.

14. Estimate the locations of the mean and the median. How does the shape of the distribution influence your estimates?

The next graph shows the serving sizes of the 47 cereals in the graph above.

Serving Sizes of Cereals

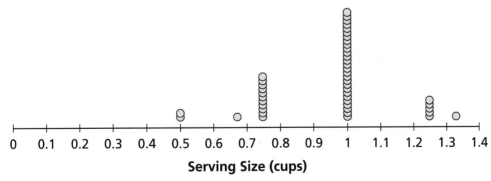

Serving Size (cups)

15. Describe the distribution of serving sizes.

16. Estimate the locations of the mean and the median. How does the shape of the distribution influence your estimates?

Extensions

17. a. Copy the scatter plot below. Locate the point $(443, 6)$ and circle it.

Track Length and Speed of 150 Wood and Steel Coasters

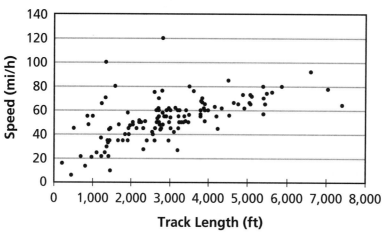

b. Locate the point $(6595, 92)$ and circle it.

c. Draw a line that connects these two points.

d. What is true about the points representing coasters that are on this line? That are above this line? That are below this line?

e. Using these two points, write an equation for the line in the form $y = mx$.

Mathematical Reflections 4

In this investigation, you developed strategies to compare two or more distributions with unequal amounts of data. These questions will help you summarize what you have learned.

Think about your answers to these questions. Discuss your ideas with other students and your teacher. Then write a summary of your findings in your notebook.

1. You can use different strategies to compare two or more data sets. Some strategies are listed below. Describe how each strategy helps you compare data sets. Add other strategies you would use to the list.

   a. Use the range for each distribution.

   b. Use the mean and median for each distribution.

   c. Use benchmarks to help you compare sections of distributions.

2. In Investigations 3 and 4, you compared groups by using counts to report actual frequencies or by using percents to report relative frequencies. How is your choice to use counts or percents affected by whether you are comparing distributions with equal numbers of data values or distributions with unequal numbers of data values? Explain.

Looking Back and Looking Ahead

While working on the problems in this unit, you explored distributions of data, measures of center, and comparing groups. You explored ways to describe and make sense of the variability that is in all data.

You often need to compare two or more groups of data. Sometimes you can compare actual counts. Other times you need to use percents. In this unit, you looked at ways to compare both kinds of distributions.

Go Online
PHSchool.com

For: Vocabulary Review
Puzzle
Web Code: anj-8051

Use Your Understanding: Statistical Reasoning

How do frozen pizzas compare with the real thing? The table on the next page displays some information about frozen pizza ratings.

1. Make a graph showing the number of Calories in one slice of each frozen pizza.

   a. What is the typical number of Calories per slice of pizza?

   b. Describe the variability in the number of Calories per slice of frozen pizza.

   c. Now, show separate distributions for cheese pizzas and for pepperoni pizzas. Compare the Calories in a slice of cheese pizza to those in a slice of pepperoni pizza. Do cheese pizzas have more Calories than pepperoni pizzas? Explain.

2. Make a graph showing the cost per slice of each frozen pizza.

   a. What is the typical cost per slice of pizza?

   b. Describe the variability in the cost per slice of frozen pizza.

   c. Now, show separate distributions for cheese pizzas and for pepperoni pizzas. Compare the cost of a slice of cheese pizza to that of a slice of pepperoni pizza. Do pepperoni pizzas cost more than cheese pizzas? Explain.

3. **a.** Make two scatter plots, one for (*fat grams, Calories*) data and one for (*cost, Calories*) data.

   b. What do you notice about the relationship between fat grams and Calories?

c. What do you notice about the relationship between cost and Calories?

d. Compare the relationships in parts (b) and (c). Which one seems "stronger"? Can you make predictions about the value of one variable if you know the value for another? Explain.

Frozen Pizza Ratings

Product	Overall Rating	Cost per Slice	Calories per Slice	Fat (g)
Cheese Pizza A	VG	$0.98	364	15
Cheese Pizza B	VG	$1.23	334	11
Cheese Pizza C	VG	$0.94	332	12
Cheese Pizza D	VG	$1.92	341	14
Cheese Pizza E	VG	$0.84	307	9
Cheese Pizza F	VG	$0.96	335	12
Cheese Pizza G	VG	$0.80	292	9
Cheese Pizza H	VG	$0.96	364	18
Cheese Pizza J	VG	$0.91	384	20
Cheese Pizza K	VG	$0.89	333	12
Cheese Pizza L	G	$0.94	328	14
Cheese Pizza M	G	$1.02	367	13
Cheese Pizza N	G	$0.92	325	13
Cheese Pizza P	G	$1.17	346	17
Cheese Pizza Q	F	$0.54	299	9
Cheese Pizza R	F	$1.28	394	19
Cheese Pizza S	F	$0.67	322	14
Pepperoni Pizza A	VG	$0.96	385	18
Pepperoni Pizza B	VG	$0.88	369	16
Pepperoni Pizza C	VG	$0.90	400	22
Pepperoni Pizza D	VG	$0.88	378	20
Pepperoni Pizza E	G	$0.89	400	23
Pepperoni Pizza F	G	$0.87	410	26
Pepperoni Pizza G	G	$1.28	412	25
Pepperoni Pizza H	F	$1.26	343	14
Pepperoni Pizza J	F	$1.51	283	6
Pepperoni Pizza K	F	$0.74	372	20
Pepperoni Pizza L	F	$0.64	367	20
Pepperoni Pizza M	F	$1.62	280	4

SOURCE: Consumer Reports

Explain Your Reasoning

When you describe a collection of data, you look for the shape of the distribution of the data. You can often visualize data patterns using graphs.

4. Explain how you would describe the variability in a distribution of data.

5. Describe how the location of the mean and the median are related to the shape of the distribution.

6. Describe strategies you can use to compare two groups of data that have equal numbers of data values.

7. Describe strategies you can use to compare two groups of data that have unequal numbers of data values.

8. What does it mean to say that the speed of a roller coaster *is related to* the maximum drop, or that the roller coaster rating *is related to* the speed of a roller coaster?

Look Ahead

You will use and extend ideas about data analysis in a variety of future *Connected Mathematics* units. In *Samples and Populations,* you will explore sampling, comparing samples, and comparing different variables in a sample. You will also find statistical plots and data summaries in everyday news reports as well as in the technical work of science, business, and government.

English / Spanish Glossary

A

attribute A property, quality, or characteristic of a person, place, or thing. For example, each person has attributes such as height, weight, name, gender, and eye color.

atributo Propiedad, cualidad o característica de una persona, lugar o cosa. Por ejemplo, cada persona tiene atributos, como altura, peso, nombre, género y color de ojos.

C

categorical data Data that can be placed into categories. For example, "gender" is a categorical data and the categories are "male" and "female." If you asked people in which month they were born or what their favorite class is, they would answer with names, which would be categorical data. However, if you asked them how many siblings they have, they would answer with numbers, not categories.

datos categóricos Datos que pueden ser colocados en categorías. Por ejemplo, "género" es un dato categórico y las categorías son "masculino" y "femenino." Si le preguntas a la gente en qué mes nacieron o cual es su clase favorita, responderían con nombres, lo cual es un dato categórico. Sin embargo, si le preguntas cuántos hermanos o hermanas tienen, responderán con números, no con categorías.

counts Data that give the number of occurrences (the frequency) of an attribute, for example, the number of occurrences of 3-child families.

cuentas Datos que dan el número de veces que ocurre (frecuencia) un evento, por ejemplo, el número de familias que tienen 3 niños.

D

distribution Data sets collected from observation or experiment. They can be described by measures of center and variability.

distribución Conjuntos de datos reunidos a partir de la observación o la experimentación. Pueden ser descritos con medidas de tendencia central y variabilidad.

G

graphs Any pictorial device, such as a scatter plot or bar graph, used to display categorical or numerical data.

gráficas Cualquier elemento pictórico, como una gráfica de dispersión o una gráfica de barras, usado para mostrar datos categóricos numéricos.

line plot Each data value is represented as a dot or an "x" positioned over a labeled number line. The line plot made with dots is sometimes referred to as a dot plot.

diagrama de puntos Cada valor de datos es representado como un punto o una "x" ubicada sobre una recta numérica rotulada. El diagrama de puntos hecho con puntos algunas veces se conoce como gráfica de puntos.

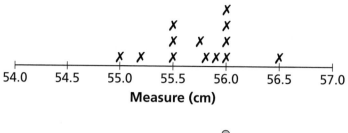

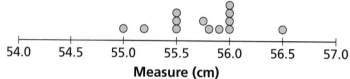

mean (1) The result if all of the data values are combined and then redistributed evenly among individuals so that each has the same amount. (2) The number that is the balance point in a distribution of numerical values. The mean is influenced by all of the values of the distribution, including outliers. It is often called the average, and is the sum of the numerical values divided by the number of values. For example, the mean of 1, 3, 7, 8, and 25 is 8.8 because the sum of the values, 44, is divided by the number of values, 5.

media (1) El resultado, si todos los valores de datos están combinados y luego redistribuidos uniformemente entre diferentes individuos, de modo que cada uno tenga la misma cantidad. (2) El número que es el punto de equilibrio en una distribución de valores numéricos. La media se ve afectada por todos los valores de la distribución, incluyendo los valores extremos. Por lo general se le llama promedio, es la suma de los valores numéricos dividida por el número de valores. Por ejemplo, la media de 1, 3, 7, 8 y 25 es 8.8 porque la suma de los valores, 44, se divide por el número de valores, 5.

measures Data obtained by making measurements. For example, we can measure the height of each person in a class.

medidas Datos obtenidos al hacer mediciones. Por ejemplo, podemos medir la altura de cada persona en una clase.

measures of center See *mean, median,* and *mode.*

medidas de tendencia central Ver *mean, median* y *mode.*

median The median is the number that is the midpoint of an ordered set of numerical data. This means that at least half of the data values lie at or above the median and at least half lie at or below it. For example, the median of 1, 3, 7, 8, and 25 is 7 because that number is third in the list of five data values. The median of 2, 3, 4, 4, 4, 5, 6, 12, and 13 is 4 because that number is fifth in the list of nine data values.

When a distribution contains an even number of data values, the median is computed by finding the average of the two middle data values in an ordered list of the data values. For example, the median of 1, 3, 7, 8, 25, and 30 is 7.5 because the data values 7 and 8 are third and fourth in the list of six data values.

mediana La mediana es el número que es el punto medio de un conjunto ordenado de datos numéricos. Esto significa que al menos la mitad de los valores de datos están en o sobre la mediana y al menos la mitad están en o bajo la mediana. Por ejemplo, la mediana de 1, 3, 7, 8 y 25 es 7, porque éste es tercer número en la lista de cinco valores de datos. La mediana de 2, 3, 4, 4, 4, 5, 6, 12 y 13 es 4, porque éste número es el quinto en la lista de nueve valores de datos.

Cuando una distribución contiene, un número par de valores de datos, la mediana se obtiene averiguando el promedio de los dos valores medios en una lista ordenada de valores de datos. Por ejemplo, la mediana de 1, 3, 7, 8, 25 y 30 es 7.5, porque los valores de datos 7 y 8 son tercero y cuarto en la lista de seis valores de datos.

---

mode The data value or category occurring with the greatest frequency. For example, the mode of 3, 4, 7, 11, 11, 11, 3, and 4 is 11.

moda El valor de dato o categoría que sucede con la mayor frecuencia. Por ejemplo, la moda de 3, 4, 7, 11, 11, 11, 3 y 4 es 11.

numerical data Data consisting of numbers, not categories, such as the heights of students.

dato numérico Dato que consiste en números, no categorías, tales como la altura de los estudiantes.

---

ordered value bar graph A value bar graph in which data values are arranged in increasing (or decreasing) order of length.

gráfica de barras con valores ordenados Gráfica de barras de valores en la cual los valores de los datos están ordenado en orden creciente (o decreciente).

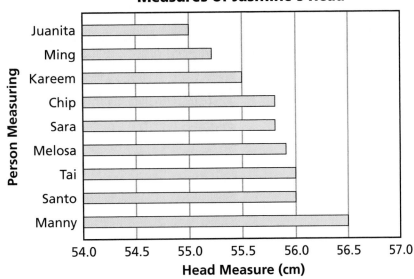

Measures of Jasmine's Head

Person Measuring: Juanita, Ming, Kareem, Chip, Sara, Melosa, Tai, Santo, Manny

Head Measure (cm): 54.0, 54.5, 55.0, 55.5, 56.0, 56.5, 57.0

outliers Unusually high or low data values in a distribution.

valores extremos o atípicos Valores de datos excepcionalmente altos o bajos en una distribución.

R

range A number found by subtracting the minimum value from the maximum value. If you know the range of the data is 12 grams of sugar per serving, you know that the difference between the minimum and maximum values is 12 grams.

rango Número que se halla al restar el valor mínimo del valor máximo. Si se sabe que el rango de los datos es 12 gramos de azúcar por porción, entonces se sabe que la diferencia entre el valor mínimo y el máximo es 12 gramos.

S

scatter plot A coordinate graph showing the relationship, if any, between two variables, for example, roller coaster track length and speed.

diagrama de dispersión Gráfica de coordenadas que muestra la relación, si la hay, entre dos variables, por ejemplo, largo de las vías de una montaña rusa y la velocidad.

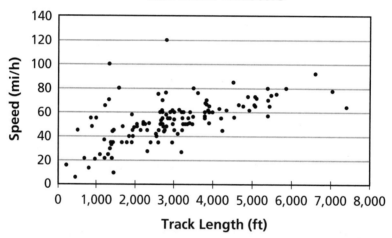

Track Length and Speed of 150 Wood and Steel Coasters

V

value of an attribute Values are the data that occur for each individual case of an attribute—that is, the number of red candies recorded for the attribute red from one bag of M&M™ candies or the time in seconds recorded for the attribute fastest time for one student who played the computer reaction-time game.

valor de un atributo Los valores son los datos que suceden para cada *caso* independiente de un atributo, o sea, el número de caramelos rojos registrados para el atributo *rojo* de una bolsa de caramelos M&M™ o el tiempo en segundos registrado para el atributo *tiempo más rápido* de un estudiante que jugó un juego de computadora de tiempo de reacción.

value bar graph Each data value is represented by a separate bar whose relative length corresponds to the magnitude of that data value.

gráfica de barras de valores Cada valor de dato se representa por una barra independiente, cuya longitud relativa corresponde con la magnitud de ese valor de dato. Por ejemplo, si hay 12 caramelos rojos en una bolsa de M&Ms, entonces la barra para los caramelos rojos llega hasta el 12.

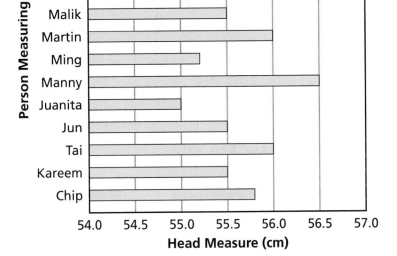

variability of a set of numerical data An indication of how widely spread or closely clustered the data values are. Range, minimum and maximum values, and clusters in the distribution give some indication of variability.

variabilidad de un conjunto de datos numéricos Indicación de cuán dispersos o conglomerados están los valores de datos. El rango, los valores mínimo y máximo, y las conglomeraciones en la distribución dan cierta indicación de variabilidad.

Reaction Time Cards

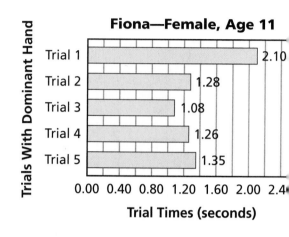

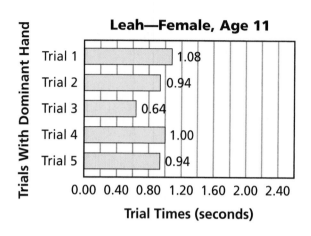

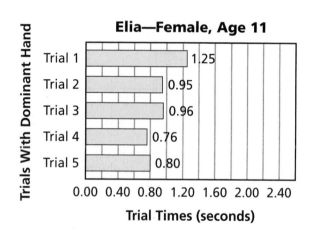

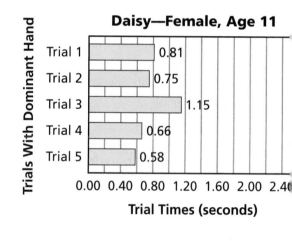

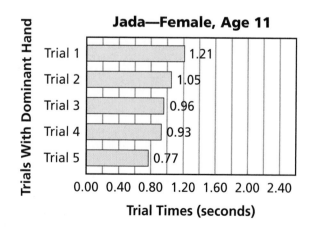

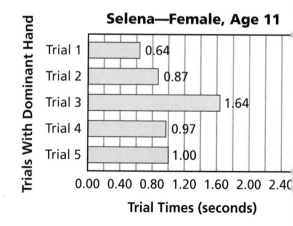

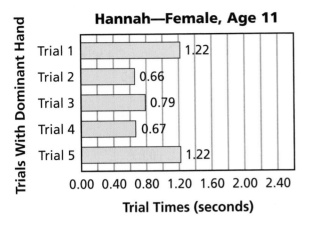

Hannah—Female, Age 11

Trials With Dominant Hand

Trial	Trial Times (seconds)
Trial 1	1.22
Trial 2	0.66
Trial 3	0.79
Trial 4	0.67
Trial 5	1.22

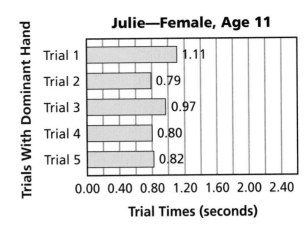

Julie—Female, Age 11

Trials With Dominant Hand

Trial	Trial Times (seconds)
Trial 1	1.11
Trial 2	0.79
Trial 3	0.97
Trial 4	0.80
Trial 5	0.82

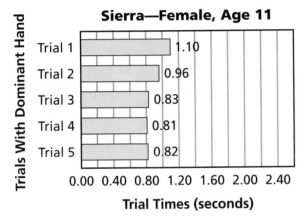

Sierra—Female, Age 11

Trials With Dominant Hand

Trial	Trial Times (seconds)
Trial 1	1.10
Trial 2	0.96
Trial 3	0.83
Trial 4	0.81
Trial 5	0.82

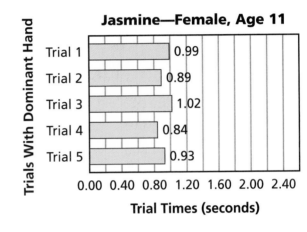

Jasmine—Female, Age 11

Trials With Dominant Hand

Trial	Trial Times (seconds)
Trial 1	0.99
Trial 2	0.89
Trial 3	1.02
Trial 4	0.84
Trial 5	0.93

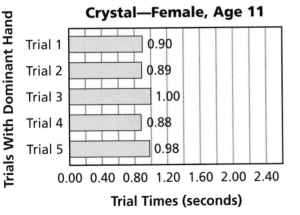

Crystal—Female, Age 11

Trials With Dominant Hand

Trial	Trial Times (seconds)
Trial 1	0.90
Trial 2	0.89
Trial 3	1.00
Trial 4	0.88
Trial 5	0.98

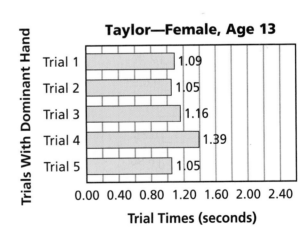

Taylor—Female, Age 13

Trials With Dominant Hand

Trial	Trial Times (seconds)
Trial 1	1.09
Trial 2	1.05
Trial 3	1.16
Trial 4	1.39
Trial 5	1.05

Reaction Time Cards

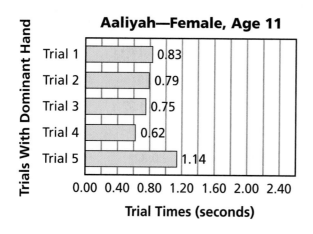

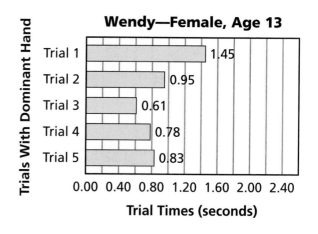

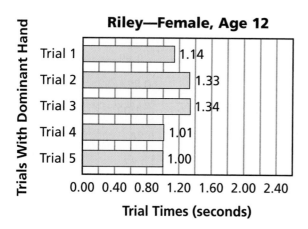

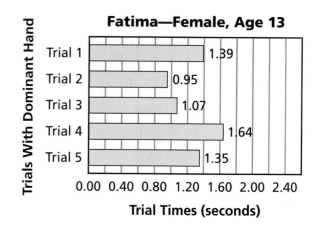

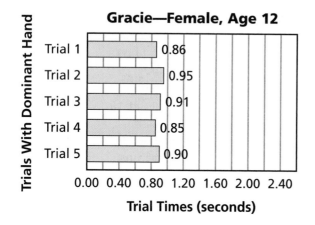

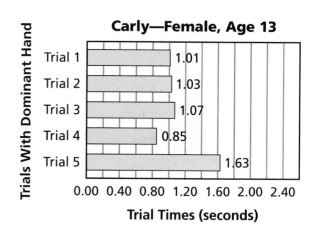

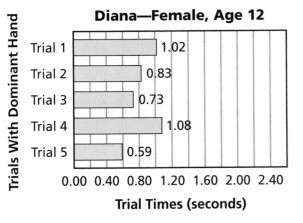

Diana—Female, Age 12

Trials With Dominant Hand

Trial	Trial Times (seconds)
Trial 1	1.02
Trial 2	0.83
Trial 3	0.73
Trial 4	1.08
Trial 5	0.59

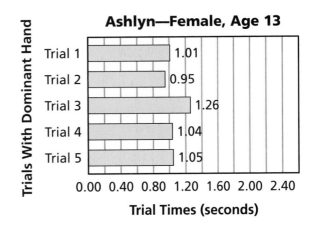

Ashlyn—Female, Age 13

Trials With Dominant Hand

Trial	Trial Times (seconds)
Trial 1	1.01
Trial 2	0.95
Trial 3	1.26
Trial 4	1.04
Trial 5	1.05

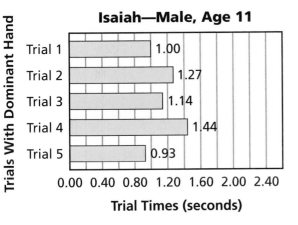

Isaiah—Male, Age 11

Trials With Dominant Hand

Trial	Trial Times (seconds)
Trial 1	1.00
Trial 2	1.27
Trial 3	1.14
Trial 4	1.44
Trial 5	0.93

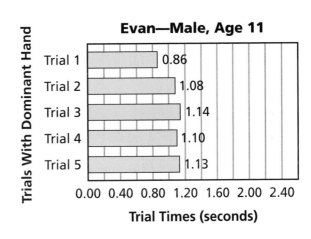

Evan—Male, Age 11

Trials With Dominant Hand

Trial	Trial Times (seconds)
Trial 1	0.86
Trial 2	1.08
Trial 3	1.14
Trial 4	1.10
Trial 5	1.13

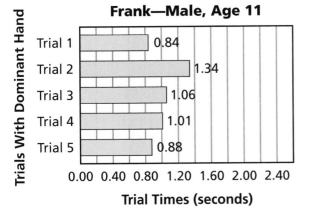

Frank—Male, Age 11

Trials With Dominant Hand

Trial	Trial Times (seconds)
Trial 1	0.84
Trial 2	1.34
Trial 3	1.06
Trial 4	1.01
Trial 5	0.88

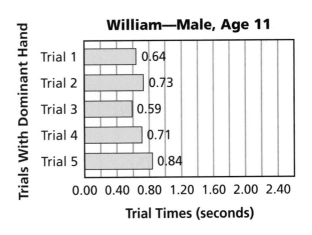

William—Male, Age 11

Trials With Dominant Hand

Trial	Trial Times (seconds)
Trial 1	0.64
Trial 2	0.73
Trial 3	0.59
Trial 4	0.71
Trial 5	0.84

Reaction Time Cards

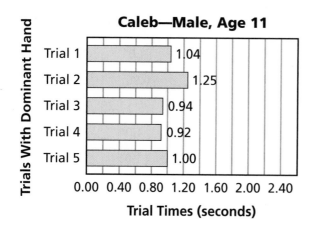

Caleb—Male, Age 11

Trials With Dominant Hand / Trial Times (seconds)

Trial 1: 1.04
Trial 2: 1.25
Trial 3: 0.94
Trial 4: 0.92
Trial 5: 1.00

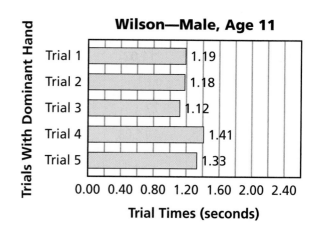

Wilson—Male, Age 11

Trials With Dominant Hand / Trial Times (seconds)

Trial 1: 1.19
Trial 2: 1.18
Trial 3: 1.12
Trial 4: 1.41
Trial 5: 1.33

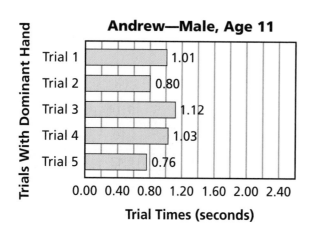

Andrew—Male, Age 11

Trials With Dominant Hand / Trial Times (seconds)

Trial 1: 1.01
Trial 2: 0.80
Trial 3: 1.12
Trial 4: 1.03
Trial 5: 0.76

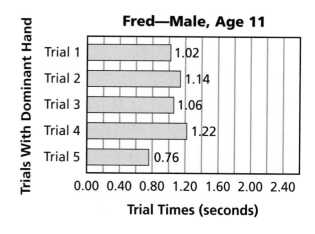

Fred—Male, Age 11

Trials With Dominant Hand / Trial Times (seconds)

Trial 1: 1.02
Trial 2: 1.14
Trial 3: 1.06
Trial 4: 1.22
Trial 5: 0.76

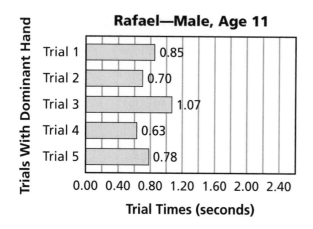

Rafael—Male, Age 11

Trials With Dominant Hand / Trial Times (seconds)

Trial 1: 0.85
Trial 2: 0.70
Trial 3: 1.07
Trial 4: 0.63
Trial 5: 0.78

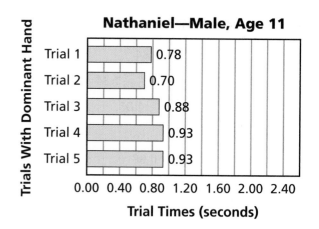

Nathaniel—Male, Age 11

Trials With Dominant Hand / Trial Times (seconds)

Trial 1: 0.78
Trial 2: 0.70
Trial 3: 0.88
Trial 4: 0.93
Trial 5: 0.93

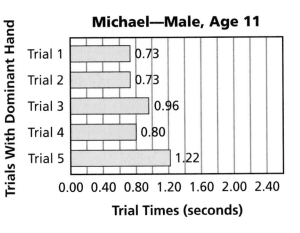

Michael—Male, Age 11

Trials With Dominant Hand

Trial	Time
Trial 1	0.73
Trial 2	0.73
Trial 3	0.96
Trial 4	0.80
Trial 5	1.22

Trial Times (seconds)

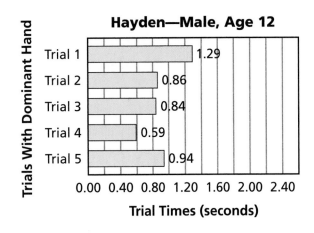

Hayden—Male, Age 12

Trials With Dominant Hand

Trial	Time
Trial 1	1.29
Trial 2	0.86
Trial 3	0.84
Trial 4	0.59
Trial 5	0.94

Trial Times (seconds)

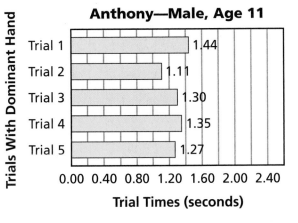

Anthony—Male, Age 11

Trials With Dominant Hand

Trial	Time
Trial 1	1.44
Trial 2	1.11
Trial 3	1.30
Trial 4	1.35
Trial 5	1.27

Trial Times (seconds)

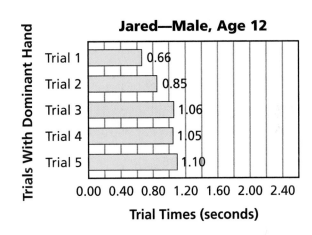

Jared—Male, Age 12

Trials With Dominant Hand

Trial	Time
Trial 1	0.66
Trial 2	0.85
Trial 3	1.06
Trial 4	1.05
Trial 5	1.10

Trial Times (seconds)

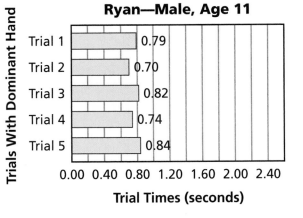

Ryan—Male, Age 11

Trials With Dominant Hand

Trial	Time
Trial 1	0.79
Trial 2	0.70
Trial 3	0.82
Trial 4	0.74
Trial 5	0.84

Trial Times (seconds)

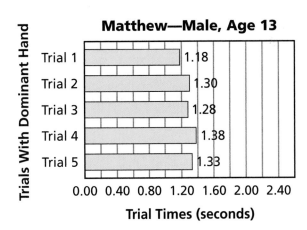

Matthew—Male, Age 13

Trials With Dominant Hand

Trial	Time
Trial 1	1.18
Trial 2	1.30
Trial 3	1.28
Trial 4	1.38
Trial 5	1.33

Trial Times (seconds)

Reaction Time Cards

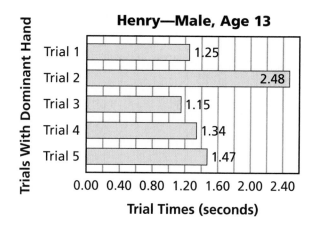

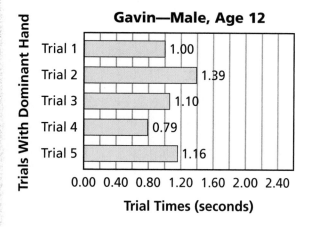

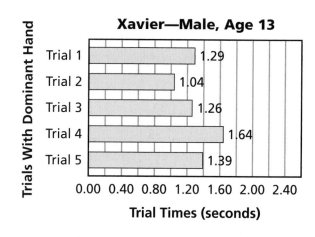

Index

Index

Acknowledgments

Team Credits

The people who made up the **Connected Mathematics 2** team—representing editorial, editorial services, design services, and production services—are listed below. Bold type denotes core team members.

Leora Adler, Judith Buice, Kerry Cashman, Patrick Culleton, Sheila DeFazio, Richard Heater, **Barbara Hollingdale, Jayne Holman,** Karen Holtzman, **Etta Jacobs,** Christine Lee, Carolyn Lock, Catherine Maglio, **Dotti Marshall,** Rich McMahon, Eve Melnechuk, Kristin Mingrone, Terri Mitchell, **Marsha Novak,** Irene Rubin, Donna Russo, Robin Samper, Siri Schwartzman, **Nancy Smith,** Emily Soltanoff, **Mark Tricca,** Paula Vergith, Roberta Warshaw, Helen Young

Additional Credits

Diana Bonfilio, Mairead Reddin, Michael Torocsik, nSight, Inc.

Technical Illustration

WestWords, Inc.

Cover Design

tom white.images

Photos

2 t, Rubberball/Getty Images, Inc.; **2 m,** Gail Mooney/Masterfile; **2 b,** AP Photo/Cheryl Hatch; **3,** RNT Productions/Corbis; **5,** Chad Slattery/Getty Images, Inc.; **6,** Rubberball/Getty Images, Inc.; **11,** Jonathan Nourok/PhotoEdit; **17,** Richard Haynes; **19,** Bob Daemmrich/The Image Works; **21,** Ryan McVay/Getty Images, Inc.; **23,** David Young-Wolff/PhotoEdit; **25,** John Walmsley/Education Photos; **28,** Matthew Stockman/Getty Images, Inc.; **36,** Chris Collins/Corbis; **37,** Gail Mooney/Masterfile; **46,** Richard Haynes; **49,** Dylan Martinez/Corbis; **51,** Richard Haynes; **52,** John R. MacGregor/Peter Arnold, Inc.; **55,** Spencer Grant/PhotoEdit; **58,** MedioImages/Getty Images, Inc.; **61,** AP Photo/Cheryl Hatch; **63,** Richard Hutchings/PhotoEdit; **69,** image100/Getty Images, Inc.; **74,** Jeff Greenberg/PhotoEdit; **78,** Gail Mooney/Masterfile; **84,** Lester Lefkowitz/Getty Images, Inc.

Data Sources

The "Did You Know" information on page 6 is from *The Story of M&M's ® Brand.* www.mms.com. M&M's and "The milk chocolate melts in your mouth--not in your hand" are registered trademarks of Mars, Incorporated. Copyright © 2006 Mars, Incorporated and its Affiliates. All Rights Reserved.

The nutritional content of ready-to-eat cereals on page 33 is from Bowes & Church's Food Values of Portions Commonly Used, 17th Edition by Jean A. T. Pennington. Copyright © 1998 by Lippencoti-Raven Publishers.

Pizza data on page 70 are from "Pizza Industry Facts," copyright © Packaged Facts, New York. Used by permission.

Roller coaster data used on pages 76 and 80 are from Roller Coaster Census Report, copyright © 1996–2005, Duane Marden. Used by permission.

The survey information on page 82 is from National Geographic Survey 2000. Copyright © 1999 National Geographic Society. All Rights Reserved.